CW01020062

Environmental policy-making
in Britain, Germany and the European Union

MANCHESTER
1824

Manchester University Press

Issues in Environmental Politics

series editors Mikael Skou Andersen and Duncan Liefferink

At the start of the twenty-first century, the environment has come to stay as a central concern of global politics. This series takes key problems for environmental policy and examines the politics behind their cause and possible resolution. Accessible and eloquent, the books make available for a non-specialist readership some of the best research and most provocative thinking on humanity's relationship with the planet.

already published in the series

Science and politics in international environmental regimes
Steinar Andresen, Tora Skodvin, Arild Underdal and Jørgen Wettestad

Animals, politics and morality (2nd edn)
Robert Garner

Implementing international environmental agreements in Russia
Geir Hønneland and Anne-Kristin Jørgensen

Implementing EU environmental policy
Christoph Knill and Andrea Lenschow (eds)

Sweden and ecological governance: straddling the fence
Lennart J. Lundqvist

Global warming policy in Japan and Britain: interactions between institutions and issue characteristics
Shizuka Oshitani

North Sea cooperation: linking international and domestic pollution control
Jon Birger Skjærseth

Climate change and the oil industry: common problem, varying strategies
Jon Birger Skjærseth and Tora Skodvin

Environmental policy-making in Britain, Germany and the European Union
Rüdiger K. W. Wurzel

Environmental policy-making in Britain, Germany and the European Union

The Europeanisation of air and water pollution control

Rüdiger K. W. Wurzel

Manchester University Press
Manchester and New York

distributed exclusively in the USA by Palgrave

Copyright © Rüdiger K. W. Wurzel 2002

The right of Rüdiger K. W. Wurzel to be identified as the author of this work has been asserted by him in accordance with the Copyright, Designs and Patents Act 1988

Published by Manchester University Press
Oxford Road, Manchester M13 9NR, UK
and Room 400, 175 Fifth Avenue, New York, NY 10010, USA
www.manchesteruniversitypress.co.uk

Distributed exclusively in the USA by
Palgrave, 175 Fifth Avenue, New York, NY 10010, USA

Distributed exclusively in Canada by
UBC Press, University of British Columbia, 2029 West Mall,
Vancouver, BC, Canada V6T 1Z2

British Library Cataloguing-in-Publication Data
A catalogue record for this book is available from the British Library

Library of Congress Cataloging-in-Publication Data applied for

ISBN   0 7190 5997 6 *hardback*
         0 7190 7334 0 *paperback*

First published in paperback in 2006

14 13 12 11 10 09 08 07 06   10 9 8 7 6 5 4 3 2 1

Typeset in Sabon by
Carnegie Publishing Ltd, Lancaster
Printed in Great Britain
by CPI, Bath

Contents

List of figures and tables   *page* vi
Acknowledgements   viii
List of abbreviations   x
List of interviewees   xiv

Part I   British and German environmental policy in Europe   1

1 Environmental pressures and regulatory styles   4
2 Theorising multilevel European Union policy-making   37
3 The European Union environmental governance system   58

Part II   Car emission regulation   83

4 The origins of car emission regulation   88
5 The catalytic converter versus the lean-burn engine controversy   115
6 The Auto-Oil Programmes   155

Part III   Bathing water protection   179

7 The origins of bathing water regulation   184
8 Implementation and sewage treatment policies   205
9 The revision process and bathing water science   238

Conclusion   256

Bibliography   277
Index   312

Tables and figures

Tables

1.1 Explanatory variables for domestic and
    EU environmental policy action   *page* 5

1.2 Environmental awareness in %, 1986–99   15

1.3 British and German standard-setting philosophies   20

3.1 Transposition of EU directives   69

3.2 Notifications of national environmental legislation,
    1973–77   77

II.1 EU car emission, fuel and ambient air quality directives   85

4.1 Health and environmental effects of car emission pollution   89

4.2 Total emissions from road transport in
    Britain and Germany, 1970–94   90

4.3 Relative contribution of traffic-related emissions in
    Britain and Germany, 1983–94   91

4.4 Numbers of cars registered in Britain and Germany,
    1950–99   92

4.5 ECE and US test cycles compared   98

4.6 Emission limits of ECE Regulation 15–04   100

5.1 German car exports and imports in 1983   121

5.2 Defoliation of trees in Britain and Germany, 1986–96   123

5.3 European car exports to America   132

5.4 EU car emission directives, 1987–91   135

5.5 Registration and production of cars in the main producer
    states in 1983   143

6.1 Euro II emission limits 156

6.2 Air quality targets for the Auto-Oil I Programme 163

6.3 Car emission limits for 2005 164

6.4 Controversial fuel standards for 2000 and 2005 165

6.5 Euro III and IV standards for petrol and diesel cars 169

6.6 Air quality targets for the Auto-Oil II Programme 173

III.1 Stages of the EU bathing water policy-making process 181

7.1 Textual changes to the Commission's proposal by the Council 192

7.2 Parameters of the Council directive and the Commission proposal 199

8.1 Number of EU bathing waters, 1979–99 208

8.2 Totals [and % pass rates] for bathing waters in England and Wales, 1991–99 217

8.3 Number of bathing waters in Germany according to *Länder*, 1979–99 220

8.4 Blue Flag awards for beaches, 1987–2000 224

8.5 Seaside Awards in Britain, 1992–2000 227

8.6 Percentage of population served by type of sewage treatment plant, 1970–95 232

9.1 Parameters of the Commission's 1994 proposal 240

C.1 EU policy networks 270

Figures

1.1 Emission limits and environmental quality objectives 21

3.1 Number of Council of Minister meetings, 1973–2000 60

3.2 EU environmental legislation adopted during 1972–99 65

4.1 Uptake of unleaded petrol in Britain and Germany, 1986–99 109

C.1 The policy–politics and polity–governance dimensions 274

Acknowledgements

This book grew out of my PhD thesis at the London School of Economics. I must therefore thank all those who commented on my draft thesis and provided financial and 'moral' support. I am grateful to the late Michael Hodges and Daphné Josselin who acted as my supervisors. Michael Burgess, Philip Cowley, Patrick Dunleavy and Edward Page commented on various draft chapters. Axel Friedrich and Jack Hayward read the entire draft of my thesis and made extremely valuable comments for which I am very grateful. I would like to express my gratitude to the German Academic Exchange Service and the University of London for awarding me scholarships and research travel grants which enabled me to undertake the fieldwork.

I am grateful to all interviewees for giving up precious time and/or granting access to unpublished documents. I would like to thank especially those interviewees who were willing to be interviewed again after the completion of my thesis in order to allow me to update the empirical findings for my book. Their names, which can be found in the List of interviewees, are simply too numerous to be stated in this Preface. Singling out a few individuals would not have been fair, although some individuals invested considerable time and effort to make available confidential documents and information for the completion of this book. Special thanks must also go to the staff of the British Library for Political Science at the London School of Economics, the Brynmor Jones Library at the University of Hull, Chatham House Library, the Commission's information office in London, the European Parliament's office in London, Brussels and Luxembourg, the Institute for European Environmental Policy (IEEP) in London, the Library of the German Bundestag, DG Environment's Information Centre in Brussels, the library of the German Federal Environmental

Agency, as well as to the staff responsible for a number of governmental archives in Britain and Germany. Updating the empirical
material was made easier by grants from the Anglo-German Foundation and the Nuffield Foundation which funded projects (numbers
9995/1258 and SOC/1000(1159) respectively) on related issues, the
main findings of which are published elsewhere.

Paul Taylor and Albert Weale, who acted as my examiners, put
forward many very perceptive and constructive criticisms which
helped me to sharpen my arguments for this book. Albert Weale went
well beyond his duties as an external examiner by providing me with
an extensive and extremely valuable report on my completed thesis.
The academic editors of the *Issues in Environmental Politics Series*,
Mikael Skou Andersen and Duncan Liefferink in particular, also
provided important feedback which greatly helped me to turn my
thesis into a book. Andrew Jordan suggested a number of changes to
the chapters on bathing water protection, and prevented me from
making several errors. Matthias Tappe made a number of valuable
comments on chapter 6. I am also indebted to Oliver Hug for making
such a professional job in compiling the illustrations for chapter 1
and the Conclusion on the basis of my (rather amateurish) pencil
drawings. I would like to thank my editors at Manchester University
Press, Richard Delahunty and Tony Mason, as well as the former
editors, Pippa Kenyon and Nicola Viinikka, for their excellent support
throughout. I remain solely responsible for the contents of this book
including any errors contained in it.

I am extremely grateful to my late father and my mother for their
unstinting support. My biggest thanks must go to Ita McGovern, my
wife, who suffered most from my efforts to write a PhD thesis and
turn it into a book. I would never have been able to complete this
book about Anglo-German relations within 'an ever closer Union'
without her great sense of humour, enduring patience, occasional
despair and numerous critical comments on various drafts. I therefore
dedicate this book to her.

Abbreviations

AA	Automobile Association
ACEA	Association of European Automobile Constructors
ADAC	General German Automobile Association (Allgemeiner Deutscher Automobilclub)
BAT	best available technology (*Stand der Technik*)
BATNEEC	best available technologies not entailing excessive cost *or* best available techniques not entailing excessive cost
BBU	Federal Association of Citizens' Initiatives for Environmental Protection (Bundesverband Bürgerinitiativen Umweltschutz)
BEUC	European Bureau of Consumers' Associations
BGA	Federal Health Office (Bundesgesundheitsamt)
BMI	Federal Interior Ministry (Bundesministerium des Innern)
BMJ	Federal Justice Ministry (Bundesministerium für Justiz)
BMJF[G]	Federal Ministry for Youth and Family (Bundesministerium für Jugend und Familie [Gesundheit])
BMU	Federal Ministry for the Environment, Nature Protection and Nuclear Safety (Bundesministerium für Umwelt, Naturschutz und Reaktorsicherheit)
BMV	Federal Ministry for Transport (Bundesministerium für Verkehr)
BMW	Bayerische Motorenwerke
BMWi	Federal Ministry for Economics (Bundesministerium für Wirtschaft)
BPEO	best practicable environmental option
BPM	best practicable means
BUND	Federal Association for Environmental and Nature Protection Germany (Bundesverband für Umwelt- und Naturschutz Deutschland)
CCMC	Committee of Common Market Automobile Constructors
CDU	Christian Democratic Party of Germany (Christlich Demokratische Partei Deutschlands)
CEC	Council of the European Communities

Abbreviations

CLEAR	Campaign for Lead-Free Air
CO	carbon monoxide
CO_2	carbon dioxide
CONCAWE	European Oil Industries' European Organisation for Environmental and Health Protection
COREPER	Committee of Permanent Representatives
CP	comparative politics
CSU	Christian Social Union (Christlich Soziale Union)
D	Germany (Deutschland)
DEFRA	Department of the Environment, Food and Rural Affairs
DETR	Department of the Environment, Transport and the Regions
DG	Directorate General
DHSS	Department of Health and Social Security
DNR	German Nature Circle (Deutscher Naturschutzring)
DoE	Department of the Environment
DoT	Department of Transport
EA	Environment Agency (for England and Wales)
EAP	Environmental Action Programme
EC	European Communities or European Community
ECAS	European Citizen Action Service
ECE	(United Nations) Economic Commission for Europe
ECE-R	Economic Commission for Europe Regulations
ECJ	European Court of Justice
E. coli	*Eschericia coli*
ECOSOC	Economic and Social Committee
EEA	European Environment Agency
EEB	European Environmental Bureau
EEC	European Economic Community
EFTA	European Free Trade Agreement
EP	European Parliament
EPHA	European Public Health Alliance
EPP	European People's Party
EQOs	environmental quality objectives
ERGA	European Regulations, Global Approach – Air Pollution
FCEC	(British) Federation of Civil Engineering Contractors
FDP	Liberal Democratic Party (Freie Demokratische Partei)
FEEE	Foundation for Environmental Education in Europe
FIA	Association of International Automobile Clubs (Féderation Internationale de l'Automobile)
FoE	Friends of the Earth
FTP	Federal Transport Procedure
g/l	grammes per litre
GM	General Motors
HC	unburnt hydrocarbons

HCEC	House of Commons Environment Committee
HLSCEC	House of Lords Select Committee on the European Communities
HoC	House of Commons
HoL	House of Lords
IEEP	Institute for European Environmental Policy
IR	international relations
ISO	International Standards Organisation
LAWA	German *Länder* Water Working Group (Länder Arbeitsgemeinschaft Wasser)
LRTAP	Long Range Transboundary Air Pollution
MAFF	Ministry of Agriculture, Fisheries and Food
MCS	Marine Conservation Society
MVEG	Motor Vehicle Emissions Group
NO_x	Nitrogen oxides
NRA	National Rivers Authority
O_3	Ozone
OFWAT	Office of Water Services
OJ	Official Journal (of the European Communities)
Pb	Lead
PDS	Party of Democratic Socialism (Partei des Demokratischen Sozialismus)
pH	numeric value showing the degree of acidity or alkalinity
PHLS	Public Health Laboratory Service
PM	particulate matter
ppm	parts per million
QMV	qualified majority voting
RAC	Royal Automobile Club
RCEP	Royal Commission on Environmental Pollution
SEA	Single European Act
SMMT	Society of Motor Vehicle Manufacturers
SO_2	sulphur dioxide
SPD	Social Democratic Party of Germany (*Sozialdemokratische Partei Deutschlands*)
SRU	Council of Environmental Experts (Sachverständigenrat für Umweltfragen)
UBA	Federal Environmental Agency (Umweltbundesamt)
UEL	uniform emission limit
UN	United Nations
UNECE	United Nations Economic Commissions for Europe
UNEP	United Nations Environmental Programme
USEPA	United States Environmental Protection Agency
USITC	United States International Trade Commission
UV	ultraviolet

VDA	Association of the German Automobile Industry (Verband der deutschen Automobilindustrie)
VDI	Association of German Industry (Verband der deutschen Industrie)
WHO	World Health Organisation
WRC	Water Research Centre
WSA	Water Services Association
WWF	World Wide Fund for Nature

List of interviewees

The name and institutional affiliation of interviewees as well as the place where the interview took place are given below. The dates of the interviews are not stated in order to guarantee promised non-attributability.

Arp, Henning: Commission, DG Environment, member of Commissioner Wallström's cabinet; Brussels, Belgium

Barthel, Friedhelm: Volkswagen AG; Wolfsburg, Germany

Basler, Armin: BMU, head of Chemicals and Water Issues; Bonn, Germany

Bauer, Max: former BMU official; Bonn, Germany

Becker, Klaus: UBA, head of Air Pollutants from Traffic Unit; Berlin, Germany

Bengtson, Pernilla: Commission, DG Environment, member of Commissioner Wallström's cabinet; Brussels, Belgium

Berendes, Konrad: BMU official; Bonn, Germany

Betts, Peter: DETR official and former environmental counsellor in the UK's Permanent Representation; London, UK

Beyer, Bernd: UBA official; Berlin, Germany

Bird, Collin: DETR official in the private office of the Environmental Minister Michael Meacher, London, UK

Bird, Peter: EA–NRA official; Bristol, UK

Blaukat, Udo: Association of Publicly Owned Local Utilities Companies (Verband der kommunalen Unternehmen); Cologne, Germany

Blöch, Herbert: Commission, DG Environment, head of the Water Unit; Brussels, Belgium

Bongaerts, Jan: Institute for European Environmental Policy; Bonn, Germany

Bonsall, Joe: DoE–DETR, head of Water Quality Division; London, UK

Bosenius, Udo: BMU official; Bonn, Germany

Breier, Siegfried: environmental attaché in the Permanent Representation of the Federal Republic of Germany; Brussels, Belgium

Mr Breitwieser: Adam Opel AG; Rüsselsheim, Germany

Brusasco-Mackenzie, Margaret: Commission, head of International Division in DG Environment; Brussels, Belgium

Cashman, Liam: Commission, DG Environment's Legal Unit; Brussels, Belgium

Clinton-Davis, Stanley: former Environment and Transport commissioner; London, UK

Cock, Josephine: DTI official; London, UK

Collins, Ken: MEP and chairperson of the Environmental Committee of the European Parliament; Strathclyde, UK

Mr Csicsaky: Social Ministry of Lower Saxony; Hannover, Germany (telephone interview)

Cucchi, Carlo: Committee of Common Market Automobile Constructors (ACEA); Brussels, Belgium

Czepuck, Andreas: BMU official; Bonn, Germany

Ms Dau: Social Ministry of Mecklemburg West Pommerania; Schwerin, Germany (telephone interview)

Mr Dick: Vauxhall; Luton, UK (telephone interview)

Ditsch, Karl-Friedrich: BMV official; Bonn, Germany

Dröll, Peter: Commission, DG Environment official; Brussels, Belgium

Dunmore, Jane: CLEAR; London, UK (written communication)

Earnshaw, David: (former) research assistant to Ken Collins, MEP; Brussels, Belgium and Strathclyde, UK

Featherstone, Simon: environmental counsellor in the UK Permanent Representation; Brussels, Belgium

Feldthus Andersen, Lene: Foundation for Environmental Education in Europe; Copenhagen, Denmark

Fendick, Malcolm: Department of Transport–DETR, (former) head of Traffic Pollution Unit; London, UK

Ferguson, Malcom: Institute for European Environmental Policy; London, UK

Finn, Bolding Thomsen: Foundation for Environmental Education in Europe; Copenhagen, Denmark

Frank, Detlef: Bayerische Motorenwerke (BMW); Munich, Germany

Franke, Klaus-Dieter: Allgemeiner Deutscher Automobil Club (ADAC); Munich, Germany

Friedrich, Axel: UBA, head of the Environment and Transport Division; Berlin, Germany

Gaede, Wolfgang: Council Secretariat, head of Environmental Division; Brussels, Belgium

Gerbrandy, Gerben Jan: assistant to Mr Eisma, MEP; Brussels, Belgium

Greening, Paul: Commission, DG Industry; Brussels, Belgium

Gruden, Dusan: Porsche AG, head of Environment Division; Stuttgart, Germany

Haigh, Nigel: head of the London office of the Institute of European Environmental Policy; London, UK

Härdtl, Wighard: state secretary in the Ministry for Economic Co-operation and Development and former spokesman for Interior Minister Friedrich Zimmermann; Bonn, Germany

Harrison, Peter: Perkins Technology; London, UK
Hauschulz, Gerhard: Mercedes-Benz; Stuttgart, Germany
Havemeister, Gerd: Institute for Hygiene and Environmental Medicine, University of Kiel; Kiel, Germany
Hawkins, Michael: Ford Motor Companies; Basildon, UK
Hedström, Anna: environmental attaché in the Swedish Permanent Representation; Brussels, Belgium
Heinemann, Mechthild: BMU official; Bonn, Germany
Henley, Nicholas: Commission, DG Environment official; Brussels, Belgium
Henssler, Herbert: Commission, DG Industry official; Brussels, Belgium
Herrmann, Petra: assistant to Bernd Lange, MEP; Brussels, Belgium
Hey, Christian: EEB, European Policy director; Brussels, Belgium
Höller, Christiane: University of Kiel, Institute for Hygiene and Environmental Medicine; Kiel, Germany
Holman, Claire: environmental consultant; Bristol, UK (telephone interview)
Ms Homp: Tourist Board, Schleswig Holstein; Kiel, Germany (telephone interview)
Hull, Robert: Commission, DG Environment, head of Policy Co-ordination; Brussels, Belgium
Hutchison, Kate: Marine Conservation Society; Ross-on-Wye, UK (telephone interview)
Irberger, Sture: environmental attaché in the Swedish Permanent Representation; Brussels, Belgium
Jekel, Heidi: BMU official and former environmental attaché in the German Permanent Representation; Bonn, Germany
Karlsson, Jan: Swedish Environmental Protection Agency, head of Transport Section; Stockholm, Sweden
Kemper, Gerd: BMU official; Bonn, Germany
Kivimäki, Iris: assistant to Heidi Hautala, MEP; Brussels, Belgium
Klatte, Ernst: EEA official; Copenhagen, Denmark
Knobling, Ansgar: (Environment and Social) Ministry official Schleswig-Holstein, and EU representative of the Bundesrat on Bathing Water Issues; Kiel, Germany
Knobloch, Tore-Peter: BMU official; Bonn, Germany
Krämer, Ludwig: Commission, (former) head of DG Environment's Legal Unit; Brussels, Belgium
Krapp, Herbert: environmental attaché in the German Permanent Representation; Brussels, Belgium
Lange, Bernd: MEP; Brussels, Belgium
Ms Langer: Commission, DG Environment, head of the Water Unit; Brussels, Belgium
Lindemann, Christian: BMU official; Berlin, Germany
Long, Tony: WWF, head of the Brussels office; Brussels, Belgium

Lopez-Pila, Juan: UBA–BGA official; Berlin, Germany
Loretto, Cait: Marine Conservation Society; Ross-on Wye, UK
Macrory, Richard: environmental lawyer, and member of the Royal
    Commission on Environmental Pollution; London, UK
Maier, Eddie: Commission, DG Science official; Brussels, Belgium
Malek, Otto: BMU, head of the Water Division; Bonn, Germany
Margaria, Giovanni: European Automobile Manufacturers' Association
    (ACEA), director Emissions and Fuels; Brussels, Belgium
Mr May: Rover Group, Ltd; London, UK
McDonald, Elizabeth: DETR official; London, UK
Mehlhorn, Bernd: UBA official; Berlin, Germany
Mehrländer, Horst: BMWi official; Bonn, Germany
Möbs, Hans: BMU, under state secretary; Bonn, Germany
Mückenhausen, Peter: BMV official; Bonn, Germany
Müller, Edda: BMU official, and environmental minister,
    Schleswig-Holstein; Bonn, Germany
Murphy, Patrick: Commission, DG Environment official; Brussels, Belgium
Mr Muttelsee: BMWi official; Bonn, Germany
Mwers, Karen: Automobile Association; Basingstoke, UK (written
    communication)
Ms Nagl: environmental counsellor in the Austrian Permanent
    Representation; Brussels, Belgium
Neild, Chloe: Institute for European Environmental Policy; London, UK
Papadopoulos, Ierotheos: Commission, DG Environment official; Brussels,
    Belgium
Paton, Alisdair: Scottish Office; London, UK
Perby, Harald: Swedish Ministry of the Environment official; Stockholm,
    Sweden
Plowman, John: DoE, head of the European Division; London, UK
Räth, Bernd: DNR; Bonn, Germany
Rebernig, Georg: environmental counsellor in the Austrian Permanent
    Representation; Brussels, Belgium
Rocker, Werner: Ministry for the Environment, Planning and Agriculture,
    North Rhine Westfalia; Düsseldorf, Germany
Rodt, Stephan: UBA official responsible for car emissions; Berlin, Germany
Mr Romer: German FEEE representative; Schwerin, Germany (telephone
    interview)
Röscheisen, Helmut: DNR, head of the Bonn office; Bonn, Germany
Sach, Karsten: BMU official and Environmental counsellor in the German
    Permanent Representation; Brussels, Belgium
Saunders, Bruce: SMMT; London, UK
Schaarschmidt, René: BMV official; Bonn, Germany
Scheiner-Bobis, Katrin: BMU official; Bonn, Germany

Schneider, Regina: EEB; Brussels, Belgium

Schröder, Dietrich: BMV official; Bonn, Germany

Simpson, Alec: Commission, DG Environment and former DoE official; Brussels, Belgium

Mr Smith: Clyde River Purification Board; London, UK

Stamm, Rolf: CDU, German Bundestag and former BMV official; Bonn, Germany

Stanton, Jose: Tidy Britain Group–Going for Green; Norwich, UK (telephone interview)

Stockart, Karolin: Council Secretariat official; Brussels, Belgium

Stratenwerth, Thomas: BMU, head of the European Unit; Bonn, Germany

Strecker, Kurt: BMU official; Bonn, Germany

Stubbs, John: Automobile Association; Basingstoke, UK

Tappe, Matthias: UBA official; Berlin, Germany

Taschner, Karola: European Environmental Bureau, scientific advisor; Brussels, Belgium

Thomsen, Finn Bolding: FEEE representative; Copenhagen, Denmark

Tindale, Steven: DETR official; London, UK

Tripp, David: DETR official; London, UK

Van Maele, Bert: Commission, DG Environment official; Brussels, Belgium

Vanke, Jeremy: Royal Automobile Club; London, UK

Mr Vehse: Commission, DG Industry, member of Industry commissioner Martin Bangemann's cabinet; Brussels, Belgium

Vittinghoff, Kurt: MEP; Brussels, Belgium

Vygen, Hendrick: BMU, head of the European Unit; Bonn, Germany

Wakeman, John: Lucas; London, UK

Waldegrave, William: minister at the Treasury and member of Parliament, former Parliamentary under-secretary of state and minister in the DoE; London, UK

Weigelt, Ulla: environmental attaché in the Swedish Permanent Representation; Brussels, Belgium

Weir, Fiona: Friends of the Earth; London, UK

Westheide, Eberhard: BMU, head of the Transport and Environment Division; Bonn, Germany

Williamson, David: Institute for European Environmental Policy, deputy director; London, UK

Yarnold, Ian: DETR official; London, UK

Part I

British and German environmental policy in Europe

This book assesses the strengths and weaknesses of the European Union's environmental policy and policy-making process. It analyses how member governmental, European Union (EU) institutional and non-governmental actors have tried to influence the common environmental policy since 1972. One major focus is on the question of whether distinct national and supranational approaches to environmental policy and policy-making can be identified. In order to keep such a task manageable within the confines of this book, and to provide sufficient analytical depth, two case studies – on car emission regulation (Part II) and bathing water protection (Part III) in two member states, Britain and Germany – have been selected for detailed analysis.

Part I explains the wider environmental policy-making framework in Britain, Germany and the EU. Chapter 1 assesses the main factors which help to explain the adoption of environmental policy measures at the domestic level. It identifies and explains the core differences between the British and German environmental regulatory styles within both the historical and the wider European contexts. Chapter 2 offers a critical assessment of the most important EU integration and politics theories while putting forward the main theoretical approach used for this book, together with a number of propositions which will be empirically tested. Chapter 3 explains the main features of the EU environmental governance system and identifies the core actors of the EU environmental policy network, thus setting the scene for a more detailed assessment provided in Parts II and III.

For reasons of simplicity, the terms 'Britain' and 'United Kingdom' (UK) are used interchangeably (despite the fact that the UK includes also Northern Ireland). The term 'Germany' refers to the Federal Republic of Germany (FRG) both pre- and post-unification. The environmental policies of the new German *Länder* (that is, the states of the former East Germany – German Democratic Republic (GDR) – which was not itself an EU member state) are assessed only since unification took place in 1990.

Any study on the EU which takes a long-term perspective is faced with terminological problems resulting from several name changes. This book assesses a topic of great complexity. I have therefore opted for simplicity regarding the use of the term 'European Union', which here refers also to the European Communities (EC) and the European Economic Community (EEC), although this may upset (legal) purists. Similarly, the directorate generals (DGs) of the European Commission are referred to by name rather than Roman numbers (for example, DG Environment instead of DG XI), as has become custom since the late 1990s. When reference is made to legal provisions of EC/EEC Treaties the numbering introduced by the 1999 Amsterdam Treaty is used, although the old numbers are given in brackets.

1
Environmental pressures and regulatory styles

Britain and Germany are conventionally portrayed as exhibiting mark-edly different national environmental policy approaches, and are frequently located at opposite ends of the environmental leader–laggard dimension. During much of the 1970s and 1980s, Britain was described as an environmental laggard, or even the 'dirty man of Europe',[1] while Germany was usually portrayed as an environmental leader state.[2] It is therefore no surprise that these two member states have often been identified as the chief opponents in EU environmental policy-making.[3]

However, post-unification Germany has lost much of its environ-mental leader status and has found itself under pressure from the EU to reform its traditional approach to pollution control.[4] Britain, on the other hand, has shown a more constructive attitude *vis-à-vis* EU environmental policy since the 1990s.[5] Some observers have even claimed that, in the 1990s, the British government has brought about a shift in the Commission's approach to EU environmental policy.[6]

In 1995, one senior German Federal Environmental Ministry (Bun-desumweltministerium – BMU) official conceded that 'Germany has lost its status as the EU's "environmental forerunner" (*umweltpoliti-scher Vorreiter*)', but was quick to add that 'Germany must re-occupy this position!'[7] (The term 'forerunner', as distinct from 'front-runner', is frequently used by German officials when referring to a member state which goes out ahead of the others, preparing the ground for those that will follow in its footsteps.[8]) In the same year, one of his British counterparts from the Department of the Environment (DoE), which has formed part of the Department of the Environment, Trans-port and the Regions (DETR) since 1997, and the Department of Environment, Food and Rural Affairs since 2001, provided the following written statement:

[The] comment about Britain and Germany being classically portrayed as at opposing ends of the [leader–laggard] spectrum and exhibiting different national approaches would certainly have been true a few years ago. However, my personal impression is that the two countries are now much closer in approach, each having moved some way towards the other.[9]

Two observations can be made from these comments: first, a state's position on the environmental leader–laggard dimension may vary over time; second, national environmental policy approaches do not remain immutable, although usually they are adapted only incrementally. The claim that both Britain and Germany have moved some way towards one another contradicts the argument, put forward in an important study by Adrienne Héritier and colleagues, that within the

Table 1.1 *Explanatory variables for domestic and EU environmental policy action*

Domestic environmental policy action	
Ecological vulnerability	State of the environment
Economic capacity	State of the economy
Political salience	Public environmental awareness, level of environmental group activity, party political competition about 'green' issues, and media attention to environmental issues
Environmental regulatory style	Institutional responsiveness and problem perception, preferred mode of policy-making, and environmental standard-setting philosophy
European Union environmental policy action	
Transborder economic issues	National environmental regulations can act as barriers to trade, so must be harmonised within the internal market. Member states may seek to export their national environmental standards and approaches
Transborder environmental issues	Member states need to coordinate their policy measures in order to tackle transborder pollution
Political legitimacy and task expansion	Common environmental policy measures can raise the quality of life of citizens and may generate political support for the EU and its institutional actors

EU member states 'displace one another as front-runners, leaving the rest of the field to adjust as need be'.[10]

However, before these issues can be assessed, it is necessary first to examine the main factors which have led to the adoption of (or resistence to) environmental policy measures. The main explanatory variables put forward in the environmental policy literature are complex and contested.[11] However, as table 1.1 illustrates, the level of ecological vulnerability, political salience of environmental issues and economic capacity, as well as a responsive environmental regulatory style, are widely seen as important variables which help to explain the adoption of (ambitious) national environmental policy measures.

Because the EU is not a state, even if it exhibits certain state-like characteristics, the adoption of common environmental policy measures is often explained with reference to different factors, the most important of which (see table 1.1) can be summarised as follows.[12] First, different national environmental standards pose a threat to the functioning of the internal market when they act as barriers to trade and must therefore be harmonised (or approximated through a process of mutual recognition). Second, the EU offers a policy-making arena for tackling transnational environmental problems which cannot be solved by member states acting in isolation. It also provides member governments, which are concerned about the existence of a 'level playing field' and/or administrative adaptation costs, with the opportunity structures to export their standards and/or preferred national problem-solving philosophies to the EU level. Third, many EU environmental policy measures are aimed at enhancing the 'quality of life' of its citizens. These measures often generate wide public support and therefore help to increase the political legitimacy of the EU, especially at times of high public environmental awareness.

As will be explained in chapter 2, competing theories exist as to which factors (functional spill-over, intergovernmental adjustment or a federalisation of the EU) are the main driving forces behind the EU's environmental policy. However, before this can be done it is necessary to assess the main explanatory variables applicable for British and German environmental policies which have more deeply engrained institutional and historical roots than EU environmental policy.

Ecological vulnerability

The ecological vulnerability of a state depends most of all on its physical environment and how it has been affected by anthropogenic activities.

Britain's island status

One does not have to push the importance of Britain's island status as far as Samuel Finer has in arguing that it has had a profound bearing on its political institutions.[13] However, strong winds, short and fast-flowing rivers and a scouring sea have had a major impact on British environmental policy. Classic air and water pollutants are relatively quickly dispersed and diluted. They will be rendered harmless if the natural carrying capacity (that is, the self-restoring capacity) of the environment is not exceeded. However, a dilute-and-disperse policy can also be used to externalise the cost of pollution control measures by shifting the problem to other countries or international commons (such as the High Seas). Examples include a 'high chimney' policy for coal-fired power stations to disperse sulphur dioxide emissions and a 'long sea outfall' policy to dilute sewage discharges.

The UK shares land borders with only one other state – the Republic of Ireland – with which transnational environmental problems are not, however, an important political issue. One DoE official argued that 'geography is the key which unlocks many of the differences between Britain and the continental member states'.[14] On the other hand, Britain's island status offers little extra protection against global environmental threats such as climate change and the depletion of the stratospheric ozone layer. This is arguably one reason why Prime Minister Margaret Thatcher chose the issue of climate change, in a speech before the Royal Society in 1988, to announce that the precautionary principle would have to play a role in British environmental policy.

Germany at the centre of Europe

Germany is a continental state located at the centre of Europe which, post-unification, shares land borders with nine other states, six of which are member states. In comparison to Britain, Germany suffers from a much higher degree of imported pollution. Some of its rivers (such as the Rhine and Elbe) originate outside German territory, while the disappearance of the Iron Curtain has made Germany a major transit country between Western and Eastern Europe and further increased pollution from transport.

However, Germany is not a classic environmental 'victim state' either, as it also exports a significant amount of pollution. Up until the early 1980s, Germany relied on a high chimney policy, and for a long time used its most important rivers as 'natural sewers'. It was only in 1982 that Germany adopted an environmental leader role at the EU and international level.[15] However, the economic cost of unification is widely seen as one important factor which has dampened Germany's desire for costly environmental policy measures.

Air and water pollution in Britain and Germany

Water of a certain quality must be available in sufficient quantities for anthropogenic usages, and those usages, in turn, put pressure on water resources. In comparison to Britain, Germany extracts a much higher percentage of its fresh water resources.[16] This is mainly due to Germany's intensive industrial usage. The fact that, in the 1990s, water shortages have not occurred in Germany, while they have in Britain where the 'annual precipitation is high and withdrawal per capita is low compared to many OECD countries',[17] is an indication of serious underinvestment within the British water sector in previous decades.[18] On the other hand, the overall number of inhabitants connected to the sewerage system in Britain stood at 82 per cent in 1980 and rose a further four percentage points by 1995. However, in the 1980s, Germany began to overtake Britain with regard to both the number of people served by sewers and the level of treatment provided.[19]

Sulphur dioxide (SO_2) and nitrogen oxide (NO_x) are classic air pollutants and a major cause of acid rain. Nitrogen oxide, for which road transport became the biggest single source in both Britain and Germany in the 1980s and 1990s, is also a precursor substance for tropospheric ozone (O_3, or summer smog) which can damage plants and poses a health threat. Carbon dioxide (CO_2), which is released when fossil fuel is burned, is widely regarded as the most important climate-change gas. In the early 1990s, the OECD published national environmental performance reports about Britain and Germany which concluded that Germany's record in reducing air pollutants was a formidable one, even though it had been achieved without taking the most cost-efficient pollution abatement measures.[20] At the time, the OECD's verdict on Britain was less positive: 'compared with most other European OECD countries, UK emissions of SO_x, NO_x and CO [carbon monoxide] per capita and per unit GDP remain high'.[21]

Between 1970 and 1990, CO_2 emissions declined by approximately 13 and 10 percentage points for Britain and Germany respectively. However, a large part of Britain's reduction in CO_2 emissions was not the result of environmental policy measures but the unintentional consequence of a politically motivated dash for gas. In the 1980s, the Thatcher government encouraged a switch from coal-fired power stations to gas for economic reasons, but also in order to break the political influence of the left-wing miners' unions. Similarly, it was the near collapse, following unification, of the manufacturing industry in the former East Germany that has led to a steep reduction of CO_2 emissions in the new German *Länder* since 1989. These examples illustrate that it is important also to assess the wider political context when environmental policies are explained.

Pollution indicators in the European Union

The EU's internal market spans a physical environment which is considerably more varied than that of any single member state. Similarly, the population density and the level of economic development vary between different member states; so do the pressures on the physical environment. Because the EU does not have a territory, as do its constituent member states, pollution indicators published by the Commission and the European Environment Agency (EEA) usually refer to national data and EU averages. Another reason for this is that the EEA's remit is 'to record, collate and assess data on the state of the environment ... in all Member States'.[22] However, it is the member governments which collect the data and implement the environmental policy measures called for under EU laws.

Economic capacity

The cost to a state's economy of a particular environmental policy measure is widely seen as an important variable which helps to explain a government's stance on (domestic, EU and international) environmental issues. There is agreement that governments are less likely to favour stringent environmental regulations during an economic crisis.[23] The main reason for this is that pollution abatement measures are conventionally seen as a cost burden for the economy. If this conventional wisdom is to be believed, one would expect the most serious Anglo-German conflicts over EU environmental policy measures to occur when the economic fortunes of these two member states diverge significantly.[24]

Britain's post-Second World War economic performance is a poorer one overall than is Germany's.[25] However, Germany's sluggish (post-unification) economic performance in the 1990s is reflected in the recent *Standort Deutschland* debate (that is, Germany as a production and investment location)[26] which questioned the future of the German economic model (*Modell Deutschland*).[27] Britain's economic performance, on the other hand, improved during the 1990s although it has not caught up with Germany in terms of GDP levels.

However, the conventional wisdom about a trade-off between economic prosperity and environmental protection has been challenged. Empirical data has shown that a decoupling of economic growth and environmental pollution levels can be achieved (at least within certain sectors).[28] Advocates of the concept of 'ecological modernisation', which became more widely accepted as a macro political norm among policy makers in Germany than in Britain, have even argued that stringent pollution abatement measures can be beneficial in economic terms because they may help to modernise the economy.[29]

Ecological modernisation in Germany

Empirical evidence shows that pollution abatement technology has provided a significant number of jobs in Germany. In the 1990s, Germany has been a leading exporter of environmental technology with a world market share of around 20 per cent. The German Federal Environmental Agency (Umweltbundesamt – UBA) estimated that the export value of German environmental abatement technology amounted to DM31.5 billion in 1994 (at 1994 prices).[30] In the same year, some 500,000 people worked in the environmental protection sector.[31]

It is difficult to gauge the overall effect of environmental regulations on the German economy because there is as yet no 'green' GDP. On the other hand, frequent criticism that Germany conducts a successful industrial policy through the adoption of stringent domestic environmental regulations could be interpreted as indirect evidence that 'environmental protection pays'. One BMU official explained:

> Foreigners often complain that we are not really interested in environmental protection but out to gain an economic advantage for our

industry. This is plainly wrong but possibly a side effect. We tell them ... that it is correct that an ambitious environmental policy also leads to economic benefits. It forces industry to develop technologies for which additional demand will later be created through EU or national legislation as other governments start to recognise that these technologies are needed on environmental grounds. Environmental abatement technology therefore is an excellent export industry.[32]

However, officials in the Economics Ministry (Bundeswirtschafts-ministerium – BMWi) often hold a very different view:

German environmental policy is conducted against industry. It is a policy which is hostile to industry (*industriefeindliche Politik*). I can honestly tell you that in the Economics Ministry our hair sometimes goes grey worrying about what the Environmental Minister is up to ... We have seen several regulations which are unjustifiable on objective grounds, where we in the Economics Ministry have said, this is hysteria and not objective policy (*Sachpolitik*)![33]

In 1992 another BMWi official commented:

Stricter domestic environmental laws cause competitive problems for German industry. One has to face up to this ... Industry is often too cowardly to stand up against the BMU in public because it fears a bad press. Instead they come to us for help. In the Economics Ministry we are concerned about the *Standort Deutschland*. We will try to achieve [an EU-wide] harmonisation of standards [and] Brussels is often our last hope when it comes to toning down some of the extreme measures put forward by the BMU.[34]

The macro-political guiding norm of a 'social market economy' (*soziale Marktwirtschaft*), which allows the state to set the framework conditions (*Ordnungspolitik*) for interactions with and between private actors, has become deeply engrained in post-Second World War German economic policy-making.[35] In the early 1970s and 1980s, there was considerable cross-party support to further develop this norm into one of a 'social and ecological market economy' (*soziale und ökologische Marktwirtschaft*).[36] However, the *Standort Deutschland* debate has forced advocates of ecological modernisation onto the defensive.

The extent to which the wider economic and political context has changed for environmental policy-making in Germany can be illustrated by the following episode. In the late 1980s, the BMU wanted to organise a public debate about ecological taxes, but was unable to recruit a prominent industrialist prepared to speak out against eco-taxes.[37] In 1998, a new Social Democratic Party/Alliance '90–Greens (SPD–Green or 'Red–Green') coalition government was elected. When it introduced the first stage of the ecological tax reform in 1999, all of the main industry associations issued fiercely worded press statements against eco-taxes. In 2000 the all-party support for eco-taxes finally broke down when the main opposition parties – Christian Democractic Union (CDU), Christian Social Union (CSU) and Liberals (FDP) – demanded the withdrawl of the eco-tax reform. Chancellor Gerhard Schröder (SPD) remained committed to the eco-tax reform although his support waned after massive public protests against high oil prices in 2000.

Ecological modernisation in Britain
Traditional Labour Party ideology, as well as the dominant monetarist economic theory of Thatcherite Britain, made it difficult for advocates of the ecological modernisation concept to gain support among British policy makers.[38] Until the late 1980s, various British governments perceived pollution abatement measures mainly as a cost burden to industry, acceptable only if scientific proof exists that serious environmental damage would occur in the absence of such regulations.

It is not surprising, therefore, that a 1993 report sponsored by the Department of Trade and Industry (DTI) stated that 'much of the growth seen within the [British environmental technology] market over recent years can be attributed to measures needed for compliance under [EU] directives'.[39] This is not to deny that individual DoE–DETR–DEFRA secretaries of state (such as Chris Patten, John Gummer and John Prescott) and junior environmental ministers (such as William Waldegrave and Michael Meacher) made attempts (largely in vain) to introduce core aspects of the concept of ecological modernisation into British environmental policy.[40]

It was only in the late 1980s that the Conservative government under Prime Minister Margaret Thatcher began to shift its view. This occurred mainly for two reasons. First, in the late 1980s a wave of environmental awareness and 'green consumerism' swept through Britain. Second, as environmental policy matured it was no longer necessary to rely exclusively on 'command and control' regulations.[41] However, although less interventionist market instruments (such as eco-taxes) were often praised in ministerial speeches, they were rarely adopted until the late 1990s.[42]

In contrast to the UBA's periodic reports on Germany's state of the environment (*Daten zur Umwelt*), the British DoE–DETR's annual *Digest of Environmental Statistics* does not provide any information on the importance of pollution abatement technology for the domestic economy.[43] As late as 1996, DTI officials were unable to provide the author with detailed figures about British exports of pollution abatement technology.[44] However, they supplied extracts from a commissioned report which stated that the 'UK market is estimated at $8bn in 1992, and is estimated to reach almost $13bn by 2000, equivalent to growth of 6% p.a.'.[45]

The wider political context changed in Britain with the election of a ('New') Labour government in May 1997. Environmental protection formed part of Labour's 'New Deal'[46] and was one of the major themes under its highly successful EU Presidency in 1998.[47] However, following its re-election in June 2001, Prime Minister Tony Blair decided again to split up DETR, which had been founded only in 1997, and amalgamated its environment sections with much of the former Ministry of Agriculture, Food and Fisheries (MAFF) to form the newly established DEFRA. This administrative reform has widely been seen as a (moderate) down-grading of environmental issues by the Labour government. This is illustrated by the fact that the old DETR was headed by a Secretary of State, John Prescott, who also acted as Deputy Prime Minister and (at least initially) had considerable weight within the cabinet. DEFRA's Secretary of State, Margaret Beckett, does not have such political standing and had little option but to give immediate political priority to agricultural issues following the crises in agriculture triggered by the foot-and-mouth epidemic which broke out only a few months before the election in 2001. The Labour government under Prime Minister Tony Blair continued with the use of eco-taxes on petrol which had been introduced by its Conservative predecessor in order to reduce consumption. However, the steep rise in petrol prices led to massive public protests in the summer of 2000 and led to (moderate) concessions in the 2001 Budget put forward by the Chancellor Gordon Brown.[48]

Ecological modernisation in the EU
The fourth and particularly the fifth Environmental Action Pro-gramme (EAP) mentioned core aspects of the concept of ecological modernisation.[49] However, the closest the EU has come to an endorsement of this concept is in chapter 10 of the Commission's 1994

White Paper entitled *Growth, Competitiveness, Employment. The Challenges and Ways Forward into the 21st Century*.[50] So far, the 1994 White Paper, which was strongly endorsed by DG Environment, has had little impact on EU policies. On the contrary, the Commission-sponsored 'Molitor Report',[51] which was published in 1995, turned back the clock. It was rooted in the conventional wisdom that stringent pollution abatement measures and economic growth are mutually exclusive aims while giving preference to the latter.

The Commission's proposal for a sixth EAP, which was published in January 2001, also contained few explicit references to ecological modernisation while emphasising the need for 'non-regulatory methods'.[52] It was severely criticised by environmental NGOs, the European Parliament (EP) and the Environmental Council for failing to put forward unambiguous objectives.[53] However, conflicting signals emerged from the Commission in 2001. While the draft for the sixth EAP was widely condemned as unambitious and devoid of clear targets, the same cannot be said about the Commission's ambitious Sustainable Development strategy which was published only a few months later.[54]

Political salience

The political salience of environmental issues depends on a range of interrelated factors such as environmental awareness, media coverage, support for environmental groups and the politicisation of environmental issues among political parties. The relative importance of these variables is contested and cannot be assessed within this book.

Environmental awareness

Environmental catastrophes attract media attention and trigger a rise in public environmental awareness. They often provide a 'window of opportunity' for policy entrepreneurs to push through stringent measures which, at other times, would have been vetoed or severely watered down.[55]

However, Ronald Inglehart has challenged the explanation that support for environmental groups and protection are functions of the level of environmental degradation.[56] Inglehart has claimed instead that generations socialised in affluent liberal democracies develop 'postmaterialist' values (such as a desire to protect the environment) once their basic material needs are satisfied. Put simply, postmaterialist theory predicts that support for environmental protection depends most of all on the level of affluence within highly industrialised liberal democracies.

Table 1.2 shows that between 1986 and 1999, the average number of people who thought that environmental problems were 'an urgent and immediate problem' has been consistently lower in Britain than the EU average while Germany has been consistently above the EU average. Anglo-German differences amounted to 18 and 17 per cent in 1986 and 1988 respectively. However, the gap narrowed to 7, 5 and 4 percentage points in 1992, 1995 and 1999 respectively.

Table 1.2 *Environmental awareness in %, 1986–99*

	1986	1988	1992	1995	1999
EU average	72	74	85	82	69
Britain	62	67	82	80	66
Germany	80	84	89	85	70
(Former) West Germany	80	84	88	84	70
(Former) East Germany	n/a	n/a	95	88	69

Note: The figures are rounded. Table 1.2 presents the data for the number of people who chose answer (a) to the following question: 'Many people are concerned about protecting the environment and fighting pollution. In your opinion is this: (a) an immediate and urgent problem; (b) more a problem for the future; (c) not really a problem; (d) don't know?'
Sources: Eurobarometer (1995); CEC (1999e: 5, 1999f: 13)

These findings are broadly compatible with Inglehart's theory, if one accepts that Britain's and Germany's overall economic performances diverged significantly for much of the 1980s and converged somewhat during the 1990s, when Britain's economic fortunes improved and post-unification Germany found it difficult to adjust to global economic competition.[57] However, table 1.2 also shows that in the immediate post-unification years, the less wealthy population in the former East Germany, which had suffered from a high degree of environmental degradation under the old Communist regime, attributed more urgency to resolving environmental problems than did the more prosperous population of the old German *Länder*.[58] On the other hand, in the new German *Länder* there was a drop of 7 percentage points between 1992 and 1995 and another reduction of 19 percentage points between 1995 and 1999 which can be explained at least partly by the fact that the worst (visible) pollution problems have been successfully tackled while continued economic insecurity has weakened support for stringent environmental measures.

Environmental groups

Public policy scholars often subscribe to the view that 'Britain has the oldest, strongest, best-organised and most widely supported environmental lobby in the world'.[59] However, Germany's environmental movement is also well funded and has enjoyed wide support since the late 1960s.[60] In comparison to their British and German counterparts, EU-wide environmental umbrella groups are younger, more heterogenous and often suffer funding problems.

Party politics

The fact that Britain lacks an electorally successful 'green' party is usually attributed to its ('first past the post') electoral system.[61] The British Green Party nevertheless achieved a 15 per cent polling in the 1989 Euro-elections. However, this proved to be an outlier result. Britain's Green Party has contributed little to the politicisation of environmental issues within mainstream party politics, which remained low up until the late 1980s.[62]

The German Greens have been represented in the national parliament (*Bundestag*) since 1983. The mainstream parties in Germany (CDU/CSU, SPD and FDP) have all stressed to varying degrees, the importance of environmental issues in their party programmes.[63] In 1998, the Green Party together with the SPD formed the first ever 'Red–Green' government in Germany.

The media

The media are important for raising environmental awareness. The German media have covered environmental issues extensively, and many broadsheets have employed environmental correspondents since the 1970s. Environmental issues have also received wide coverage in the British media, although environmental correspondents did not become a common feature in broadsheets until the 1980s.

Environmental regulatory style

Policy styles

According to the *policy style* concept, policy actors in different governance systems do not necessarily propose the same course of action when faced with similar policy problems. The policy style concept was developed to identify 'standard operating procedures' and legitimising norms which guide policy makers in their efforts to solve public policy problems. It was initially used to capture national differences. However, it has been argued that, in principle, it can also be applied to the analysis of EU policy-making.[64]

The policy style concept as pioneered by Jeremy Richardson and colleagues puts forward a classification of public policy-making along two dimensions:[65] first, a government's approach to problem-solving can range from reactive to anticipatory; second, a government's relationship with other core non-governmental actors may vary between consensual and impositional. The policy style concept therefore rejects Lowi's claim that 'policy determines politics'[66] and instead argues that 'different countries adopt different policy responses to problems such as air or water pollution, nuclear energy, housing or health problems'.[67]

The traditional British policy style has often been described as flexible, informal, consensual, incremental and devoid of long-term objectives.[68] These labels fit the following assessment of British environmental policy-making as put forward by Eric Ashby and Mary Anderson:

> British legislation must appear to our fellow Europeans to be pragmatic, piecemeal, ad hoc, the product of expedience, not principle: a policy to be described as a non-policy. Yet British policy has deep roots in history. It is the product of nearly two centuries of evolution in which impracticable ideas have been eliminated, Utopian aspirations have been discarded, and the policies which have survived have been proved to work.[69]

German governments are also said to have favoured consensus and consultation, although the latter is characterised by 'corporatist' elements because it mainly extends to employers and unions. The 'opportunity structures' or access points during the policy formulation phase are often seen as relatively closed for environmental groups, which instead have to make use of the courts during the 'post-decisional' phase, that is, after the adoption of legislation.[70] German

public policy is often portrayed as highly legalistic, the result of a
'concretisation' of constitutional and general legal principles within
a 'state of law' (*Rechtsstaat*).[71] Compared to Britain, Germany is said
to have developed 'a more active and anticipatory style of problem
solving' because of the more important role it attributes to the state
in public policy-making.[72]

However, Kenneth Dyson has argued that in Germany 'a given
policy sector or a particular case may display various styles as well
as shifts in the dominant style over time'.[73] Such findings reduce the
general explanatory power of the policy style concept. Within the
context of German public policy-making, Klaus von Beyme has therefore warned that '[b]road generalisations about a national style of
policy-making tend to obscure historical changes over time, variations
between fields of policy and the differences between the role of various
parties'.[74]

A closer look at British developments also reveals differences across
sectors and shifts over time.[75] Scholars who set out to identify an EU
policy style usually concede that there is in fact a 'multiple model of
EC policy-making'.[76]

Environmental policy styles
The policy style concept of the 1980s has made a revival within the
environmental policy literature of the 1990s, which emphasised the
importance of the leader–laggard dimension for EU environmental
policy.[77] Mikael Andersen and Duncan Liefferink, drawing on work
by Jeremy Richardson and David Vogel, put forward the following
argument:

> Each nation has a distinct regulatory style which is a function of its
> more general policy style, and which causes the environment to be
> regulated in the same way as other areas of corporate conduct ... It
> can sometimes be more difficult to define a common EU policy given
> such differences in regulatory traditions, than it is to reconcile different
> opinions about the level of environmental protection.[78]

Andersen and Liefferink therefore accepted David Vogel's claim that
'environmental policy [can be used] as a basis for generalising about
the politics and administration of government regulation'.[79]

The environmental regulatory style approach advanced in this book
takes a more nuanced view. While accepting that national regulatory
styles play an important role and must be reconciled on the EU level, it

is argued that attention should also be paid to sectoral and sub-sectoral differences which, according to the government–industry literature of 1980s, may at least occasionally play a more important role than national differences.[80] The author of this book agrees with Charles Anderson's view that policy-making 'is not simply problem-solving. It is also a matter of setting up and defining problems in the first place'.[81] However, this author also accepts Lynton Caldwell's argument that 'environmental policy making may be understood as an effort to reconcile behaviour with knowledge; neither is immutable'.[82]

The policy style concept is a useful analytical tool. However, it has used too broad a brush to highlight differences between standard operating procedures in various governance systems and paid too little attention to 'action-guiding'[83] norms at the sectoral level. It therefore needs refining in order to provide a more robust analytical framework which is able to capture the specific characteristics of environmental policy. It is for these reasons that use is made of a more focused 'environmental regulatory style' concept in this book, which emphasises the importance of different environmental standard-setting philosophies.

Environmental standard-setting philosophies

The preferred British and German environmental standard-setting philosophies are often portrayed as exhibiting mutually exclusive national features. Britain is conventionally portrayed as having shown a marked preference for environmental quality objectives (EQOs), the best practicable means (BPM) principle and, more recently, the best practicable environmental option (BPEO). British governments are said to have insisted that scientific proof must exist before remedial action, which must be cost-effective, can be taken.[84] Furthermore, British environmental policy is often described as a science-driven attempt to 'optimise pollution'[85] by taking advantage of the carrying capacity of the environment.

Germany is commonly said to favour uniform emission limits (UELs) which are set at the source of pollution and derived from the principle of best available technology (BAT). Germany's reliance on the BAT principle has been encouraged by its early adoption of the precautionary principle (*Vorsorgeprinzip*). The latter legitimises the adoption of pollution abatement measures in the absence of scientific proof if there is a (significant) risk that (irreversible) environmental damage would otherwise occur.

Table 1.3 lists some of the key standard-setting principles which can be commonly found in the Anglo-German environmental policy literature.[86]

Table 1.3 *British and German standard-setting philosophies*

Britain	Germany
Environmental quality objectives (EQOs)	Uniform emission limits (UELs)
Best practicable means (BPM) or best practicable environmental option (BPEO)	Best Available Technology (BAT)
Scientific proof	Precautionary principle

Some scholars have argued that EQOs and UELs are mutually exclusive.[87] However, this author belongs to a school of thought which has argued that emission limits and EQOs can and should be combined.[88] This is not to deny that locally variable EQOs and EU-wide UELs can only be combined in the form of a 'parallel approach'.[89] However, EQOs are not as variable as their advocates have claimed, while emission limits are not *necessarily* uniform.

The argument advanced in this book is therefore that environmental pollution/quality can be measured principally in two *complementary* ways: first, as harmful emissions discharged from a particular source into the environment: and, second, by monitoring the quality of the receiving environment. Historically, comprehensive emission data from point sources (such as factories) became available more widely and at an earlier stage than ambient environmental quality data which require extensive monitoring (or complex computer modelling).

Environmental quality objectives and uniform emission limits
It is necessary first to explain the core features of the EQO and UEL approaches before national and supranational preferences can be assessed.

Emission limits and EQOs are both usually defined for different environmental media (that is, air, water and soil). Other types of standard (such as biological and exposure standards) exist but have not led to major Anglo-German disputes (at the EU level).[90]

Figure 1.1 illustrates that (uniform) emission limits focus on the sources of pollution while EQOs focus on the receiving environment.[91] (Uniform) emission limits stipulate the legally permitted discharge level for a certain substance from a particular source. EQOs, on the other hand, specify health related and/or environmental targets which are defined as threshold levels beyond which a pollutant should not be detectable.

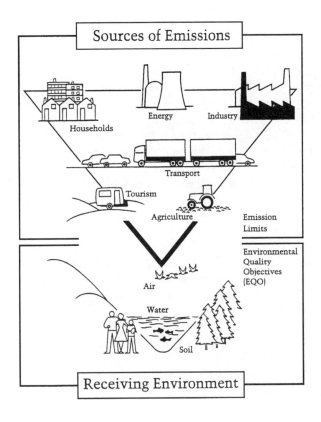

Figure 1.1 *Emission limits and environmental quality objectives*

EQOs are usually based on the assumption that discharges of a certain substance result in polluting effects only once they reach a certain threshold level which exceeds the natural carrying capacity of the environment; when adequately dispersed, many substances will not irreversibly harm the environment and/or human health. EQOs are said to be science-driven and aim to 'optimise pollution'. However, there is no safe threshold level for highly toxic substances. In any case, most EQOs merely prescribe a certain risk level which is deemed acceptable rather than an absolute threshold level below which no health and/or environmental damage will occur. The risk is often considerably higher for vulnerable people (such as the eldery, sick and children) and species threatened by extinction. It is therefore doubtful whether an EQO-derived approach can best be described as a science-driven approach because the level of pollution deemed to be an acceptable risk within a particular governance system may change over time as it is dependent on wider economic and social factors over which scientists have no control.

EQO- and UEL-centred approaches each have different advantages and deficiencies. UELs are easier to monitor than EQOs, especially at the EU and the international level.[92] They also encourage the adoption of the latest pollution abatement technology if they are derived from the BAT principle. As Albert Weale has pointed out, '[t]he idea is ... to dynamize the setting of emission limit values by tightening standards in the light of emerging technological possibilities'.[93] The danger is that such an approach can lead to 'technical fixes' which fail to solve the problem while delaying urgently needed behavioural changes. However, as the British Royal Commission on Environmental Pollution (RCEP) has argued: 'It would be dangerous if arguments against "technical fixes" prevented full advantage being taken of technology's potential contribution to the efficient and appropriate use of resources.'[94]

EQOs, on the other hand, lend themselves more easily to determining the most cost-effective policy measures, particularly when combined with the 'critical loads' concept. The critical loads concept was pioneered by Sweden within the negotiations for the UN's Long Range Transboundary Air Pollution (LRTAP) convention to reduce below a critical threshold level highly acidified soils, lakes and rivers.[95] It quickly gained support in Britain, while many German officials have remained largely unconvinced about its merits. One of the arguments often put forward against the EQO–critical loads concept is that it can be used to justify 'filling up' the environment with potential pollutants in order to save money on costly pollution abatement measures.[96] It has also been criticised for downplaying the risk of unknown long-term effects, bioaccumulation and synergistic reactions.[97]

The exclusive adoption of either emission limits or EQOs will lead to serious deficiencies in efforts to control pollution. Once the threshold level of a particular EQO is breached, it is necessary to trace the sources of the pollutants and reduce their discharge level. On the other hand, even stringent BAT-derived UELs may not be sufficient to prevent detrimental health effects and grave environmental pollution. It may therefore be necessary to adopt more far-reaching behavioural and/or structural changes.

Evolution of British preferences for EQOs

EQOs can be used in a variegated manner in order to allow for more lenient emission standards for local or regional areas which exhibit low ecological vulnerability. It is not difficult to see why British policy makers should regard EQOs as the more attractive approach. Compared to Germany, Britain suffers overall from low ecological vulnerability and stands less chance of gaining economically from stringent UELs because its pollution abatement technology industry is less developed.

However, a closer look at historical developments in Britain and Germany reveals that both these states have used a mix of EQOs and emission limits.[98] Traditionally, British water pollution control measures relied more strongly on EQOs, while air pollution abatement measures were based mainly on emission limits; in Germany the development was the other way around. National distinctions (instead of environmental media and issue-specific differences) only became more important once the first major items of common environmental legislation arrived on the EU's agenda in the 1970s.[99]

Much of early EU environmental legislation focused on water pollution abatement. It was here that the first acrimonious disputes about EQOs and UELs took place between Britain and Germany. Germany became the most outspoken advocate of BAT-derived UELs which were resisted by British policy makers on the grounds that they were alien to a long and successful tradition of (water) pollution control based on EQOs.[100] However, Nigel Haigh has pointed out that

> [t]he words environmental quality objectives (EQOs) are nowhere to be found in any official document to describe a tool for pollution control before the EEC's first Action Programme on the Environment of November 1973. This does not mean that it did not exist either in a vague form or quite precisely … It can be said with certainty that the EQO idea formed no part of British air pollution policy before Community membership.[101]

A similar view has been expressed by a DoE official:

> The practice evolved into a philosophy of quality objectives which were
> to become the basis for all pollution control and management. But
> interestingly the concept was not formalised in legislation until 1989.
> No national water quality objectives were produced until the mid 1980s
> – and then only in response to European Community requirements.[102]

Andrew Jordan and John Greenaway have even argued that Britain's sewage policy amounted initially to little more than 'a set of politically and economically expedient tools, which were only worked up into a broader "philosophy" in the late 1970s by British officials to justify the status quo to foreign observers'. [103]

It is a common misperception that EQOs can be implemented without reference to emission limits.[104] It is true that EQOs do not usually stipulate UELs. However, in practice, 'normal' discharge standards (or 'consents') are adopted in order to facilitate the work of the regulator and/or inspector on the ground. For example, prior to EU legislation, no statutory emission limits existed in Britain with regard to sewage discharges. However, a Royal Commission on Sewage Disposal, set up as long ago as the late nineteenth century, had recommended a 'normal' discharge standard (defined as organic oxygen consuming matter) which had been widely applied.[105] This 'normal' standard was replaced by a more formalised discharge consent system in the 1974 Control of Pollution Act until privatisation of the water industry and EU legislation brought about the adoption of statutory legislation.[106]

The traditional informality of British (pollution control) practice often kept 'normal' standards hidden from outsiders. This allowed for flexibility during the implementation phase and 'insider deals' between the regulator and the regulated, who did not have to fear public scrutiny. Proponents of this approach praised the fact that it allowed for tailor-made agreements which took account of cost-effectiveness considerations or, as one DETR official put it, 'horses for courses'.[107] Opponents, on the other hand, criticised the lack of transparency.[108]

Evolution of German preferences for emisssion limits
In Germany, UELs were first developed for water discharges, although initially not derived from the BAT principle. It was only in the 1980s when the Water Management Act (Wasserhaushaltsgesetz) was revised that the BAT principle was stipulated in combination with a waste

water tax.[109] Subsequent demands for EU-wide UELs were not made solely because such an approach guaranteed a higher level of environmental protection; it also helped German industry to achieve a level playing field with its competitors.[110] However, stringent BAT-derived UELs were also demanded by environmental groups which were opposed to 'environmental dumping'.[111]

Much of German environmental legislation is now based on emission limits which are often derived from the BAT principle on a country-wide basis (although there are important exceptions). However, in practice, many *uniform* emission limits stipulated derogations and escape clauses. Even where this is not the case, practical implementation is often less than uniform, a point highlighted by Jochen Hucke:

> Germany is often pictured as a country in which law enforcement is characterised by a system of strict regulations, clear and binding orders and obedient compliance in the Prussian tradition executed by a well-organised and efficient administration, much as was described by Max Weber in his ideal type of 'traditional bureaucracy', able to impose its authoritative will on a by-and-large law abiding public. Drawing on ... a study of air and water pollution control in the Federal Republic of Germany (FRG), we argue that even here, beneath the surface of seemingly clear and authoritative regulatory standards, the actual practice of implementation involves a substantial amount of bargaining over the terms of regulatory actions between enforcement agencies and their 'clientele' rather than the command and control compliance usually assumed.[112]

The implementation deficit with regard to UELs, particularly during the early years of German environmental policy, in the 1980s, is well documented.[113] It was only in the 1990s that the EU's implementation deficit in the environmental policy field became fully apparent.

EU preferences

It has been argued that, following successful lobbying by the German government in the early 1980s, the Commission switched to UELs from its initial preference for EQOs, but returned to its original EQO approach in the 1990s.[114] However, a closer look at EU environmental legislation reveals that it resembles a patchwork which contains both (uniform) emission limits and EQOs rather than expressing a clear preference for either of the two approaches.[115]

The politicians and officials interviewed generally recognised that, overall, Britain shows a greater preference for EQOs and Germany a stronger preference for (uniform) emission limits. Several Anglo-German disputes on the EU level have centred on this issue.[116] However, over time attempts have been made to bridge differences at the EU level and both Britain and Germany have each moved some way towards the other.

In the early 1970s, Britain vetoed a proposal which was based on UELs, for a directive on waste water discharges from the wood pulp industry. It also insisted that the 1975 directive on the discharge of dangerous substances into the aquatic environment should stipulate a 'parallel approach' which allowed member states to choose between UELs and EQOs.[117] In 1975 the German *Länder*, which have the competencies for water management, issued the 'Mainz Paper' (*Mainzer Papier*) which stipulated the need for minimum UELs based on the state of the waste water technology.[118]

However, in 1988 Germany used its EU Presidency to organise an informal Ministerial water seminar in Frankfurt, the conclusions of which stated that UELs and EQOs can and should be used in a 'combined approach'.[119] In the same year, the DoE issued a consultation paper entitled *The Red List* which stated that for dangerous substances

> technology-based emission standards, based on best available technology not entailing excessive cost ('batneec'), will be applied to discharges to water ... the Government considers it is necessary to ... minimise inputs to all parts of the environment as part of a more precautionary approach to water pollution.[120]

In the 1990s, the EU Commission made use of the combined approach.[121] This was possible largely because, as Ruth Levitt has argued, '[t]he differences [between EQOs and (uniform) emission limits] are matters of nuance and interpretation rather than fundamental and irreconcilable positions'.[122] This was also acknowledged in the DoE's *Red List*, which stated: 'increasingly it has come to be recognised that the best way to protect the aquatic environment is through a combination of the two approaches'.[123]

Evolution of the BPM, BPEO and BATNEEC principles in Britain
British environmental policy has traditionally relied on the BPM principle, which has been supplanted more recently by the principles of the best practicable environmental option (BPEO) and the best available techniques not entailing excessive costs (BATNEEC).[124]

The BPM principle was introduced to British environmental policy in all but name in the 1874 Alkali Act which, according to Stuart Bell,

> saw the introduction of the first proper emission standards in British legislation by specifying actual amounts of certain substances per cubic metre of emitted gas. If these emission limits were being met, then it was presumed that any legislation was being complied with and that the best practicable means were being used.[125]

However, the implementation of these emission limits occurred in a flexible manner. The first Chief Inspector of the Alkali Inspectorate, Angus Smith, believed in an implementation style characterised by persuasion and cooperation.[126] Smith and his successors had no alternative as they could not rely on prosecutions to enforce these standards. The courts only played a secondary role in British environmental policy-making prior to 1989. This was the year that the National Rivers Authority (NRA) was set up, introducing a more adversarial implementation style to British environmental policy.

The BPEO is widely seen as an extension of the BPM principle. However, it introduced some new elements, such as the need to consider the environment in the round rather than from a media-specific perspective.[127] In 1988, the RCEP's *Twelfth Report* defined the BPEO as follows: 'The BPEO procedure establishes, for a given set of objectives, the option that provides the most benefit or least damage to the environment as a whole, at acceptable cost, in the long run as well as in the short term.'[128]

The need for an integrated approach to pollution control was already mentioned by the RCEP in its *Fifth Report* published in 1976.[129] It was ignored by the government for a long time but finally triggered the setting up of a unified Environment Agency in 1996.[130] Britain's Environment Agency ensures implementation of the integrated pollution control approach and grants authorisation to industrial processes only if they comply with the BATNEEC principle. Importantly, the British BATNEEC principle stipulates the best available *techniques* rather than, as the German BAT principle does, the best available *technology*. This implies that the best available technology may not necessarily constitute the best available technique for resolving a particular environmental problem. The BATNEEC principle therefore further elaborates the BPEO principle, and both principles were incorporated into the 1995 Environmental Act.

Evolution of the BAT principle in Germany
The origins of the BAT principle can be traced to nineteenth-century
Prussian trade ordinances (Gewerbeordnungen) and the duty of the
authorities to protect citizens against physical harm within their
territory (*Polizeyrecht*).[131] The BAT principle's modern-day definition
became enshrined in the 1974 Federal Ambient Environmental Quality
Protection Act (Bundesimmissionsschutzgesetz) which has been called
the *Magna Carta* of German environmental policy.[132]

The German BAT principle evolved over time and the following
more differentiated principles were also invoked:[133] first, the less ambitious generally recognised rules of technology (*allgemein
annerkannten Regeln der Technik*); second, the best available scientific
and technological knowledge (*Stand von Wissenschaft und Technik*),
which is more ambitious than BAT; third, the best available scientific
knowledge (*Stand der wissenschaftlichen Erkenntnis*), which demands
the application of the most sophisticated technology and is applicable
under the atomic and genetic technology laws. Considering the important role technological principles have played in German
environmental policy, it is not surprising that Albert Weale has argued
that '*Vorsprung durch Technik* would not be an inappropriate motto
for the process of policy-making'.[134]

The adoption of the precautionary principle in the national Environmental Programme in 1971 greatly facilitated implementation of
the BAT principle. Pushed to the extreme, the combined precautionary
and BAT principles could in theory legitimise the adoption of the
best available technology regardless of the state of the environment.
However, the 1971 German Environmental Programme also introduced the principles of proportionality (*Verhältnismäßigkeitsprinzip*)
and cooperation (*Kooperationsprinzip*) which, in the words of one
German critic, have all too often turned the BAT principle into 'a
soft cushion' (*ein sanftes Ruhekissen*) [135] for industry.

The BAT principle leaves room for interpretation and includes
consideration of the cost implications as well as wider societal
benefits; its application does not lead to a quasi-automatic adoption
of the best technology available on the market.[136]

The specification of what constitutes the BAT traditionally
had been left to professional associations such as the Association of
German Engineers (Verband der Deutschen Ingenieure) and the German
Association of the Gas and Water Sector (Deutscher Verein des
Gas- und Wasserfaches), which have existed since the nineteenth

century. The technical standard-setting process remained largely a self-regulatory process for industry up until the politicisation of environmental issues in the early 1970s. It opened up the relatively closed technical environmental standard-setting process to new actors such the UBA and (federal and *Länder*) Environmental Ministry officials. However, environmental groups and the general public have remained largely excluded.[137] Citizens and environmental groups eager to influence the standard-setting process had little option but to challenge a particular technical standard through the courts, although, since the late 1990s, greater use has been made of wider consultation processes.[138] Germany's federal set-up provides additional opportunity structures for the Green Party to gain access to Parliament. However, it makes participation of environmental groups more complicated, as they must also try to influence the *Länder* governments which have formed working groups on environmental issues that meet behind closed doors without public participation.

The EU patchwork

The EU is not constrained to the same degree by deeply embedded action-guiding norms, mainly because it is still a relatively young governance system. Another important reason is that the EU must accommodate different national preferences and environmental regulatory styles. The EU's EAPs and environmental legislation make frequent reference to both the BAT and BATNEEC principles, the latter of which is often defined as 'best available technologies not entailing excessive cost', although the definition 'best available *techniques* not entailing excessive cost' is also frequently used. The BATNEEC principle appeared first in EU legislation in the context of emissions to air from industrial plants (84/360/EEC). The RCEP pointed out in its *Twenty-First Report*:

> The draft of this Directive would have required use of 'state of the art' technology, and was amended following pressure from the UK. In this Directive, the 'T' stands for 'technology'. In the 1990 Act the UK used 'techniques' to ensure BATNEEC could be given as wide an interpretation as the earlier term 'best practicable means' (BPM).[139]

Joanne Scott has pointed out that the more recent directive on integrated pollution prevention and control (IPPC) stipulated that

> BAT (unlike BATNEEC in the 1984 [industrial plants] 'framework' directive) applies, not as a direct means of regulating the behaviour of

plants, but rather as a tool to inform the national standard-setter in the
formulation of emission limit values ... Such is the definition of BAT
in this directive, and the range of criteria to be taken into account in
its application, that BAT-derived emission standards can be anticipated
to vary as between both industrial sector and locality.[140]

It would not have been difficult to find additional examples which
point to complex and sometimes contradictory EU compromises. The
BATNEEC principle seems to offer relatively wide scope for different
interpretations by various actors. The former Environmental Commissioner Stanley Clinton-Davis even warned that, 'in too many
ways the BATNEEC principle has been replaced by another acronym
– CATNIP, the Cheapest Available Technology Not Involving
Prosecution'. [141]

Conclusion

Chapter 1 has identified ecological vulnerability, economic capacity,
political salience and environmental regulatory styles as important
explanatory variables for (a government's stance on) domestic environmental policy measures. It has been argued that Germany suffers
overall from higher ecological vulnerability than Britain. Moreover,
a correlation exists between Britain and Germany's divergent economic capacities and Anglo-German differences about the adoption of
ambitious environmental policy measures. The concept of ecological
modernisation – which was accepted at an earlier stage, and more
widely in Germany than in Britain – helps to explain why differences
in the problem perceptions of core British and German policy actors
persisted although the economic context variables became less dissimilar in the 1990s. The EU and Britain have so far made only
hesitant attempts to endorse the concept of ecological modernisation,
which, on the other hand, has also lost support in Germany, as can
be seen from the *Standort Deutschland* debate.

The ecological vulnerability and economic capacity of a state are
unreliable guides for establishing whether a member government
will adopt domestic pollution abatement action and/or push for
ambitious environmental standards at the EU level. The political
salience of environmental issues and a responsive national environmental regulatory style are also important factors.

This chapter has identified the core features of the British, German
and, to a lesser degree, the EU environmental regulatory styles. It has

been argued that the differences between the EQOs and (uniform) emission limits approach should not be exaggerated, and that they are in fact, at least in principle, complementary. However, this has not prevented the British and German governments from opposing each other's preferred standard-setting philosophies at the EU level on the grounds that they do not fit in with long-established national traditions.

The differences between the British BPM, BPEO and BATNEEC principles and the German BAT principle have been found to be significant. The EU's BATNEEC principle is a compromise between British and German preferences (as well as the preferences of other member states and EU institutional actors). This can be seen from the fact that the EU's use of the BATNEEC principle in various directives allows for both the adoption of the best available *techniques* (which is closer to the British BPM principle) as well as the best available *technology* (which is closer to the German BAT principle).

How different national and supranational (standard-setting) preferences are accommodated within the EU's environmental governance system will be a central focus of chapter 3 and the case studies. However, before this can be done it is necessary to explain the chosen theoretical approach within the context of the wider theory debate about multi-level EU policy-making.

Notes

1 Lodge (1989); Rose (1990); Weale (1992a: 69).
2 Collier and Golub (1997); Holzinger (1994); Johnson and Corcelle (1989: 8) and Sbragia (1996) all argue that Britain and Germany are environmental laggard and leader states respectively.
3 Boehmer-Christiansen and Skea (1991); Boehmer-Christiansen and Weidner (1995); Héritier *et al.* (1994, 1996); Sbragia (1996).
4 Andersen and Liefferink (eds) (1997); Demmke (1994: 47); Héritier *et al.* (1994, 1996); Müller-Brandeck-Bocquet (1996); Pehle (1997, 1998).
5 Haigh (1996); A. Jordan (2000, 2002).
6 Héritier *et al.* (1994, 1996); Knill (1996); Pehle (1998).
7 Interview in 1995.
8 See also Liefferink and Anderson (1998a).
9 Letter from DoE official dated 31 July 1995.
10 Héritier *et al.*'s argument (1996: 1) would only be compatible with the above comment by the DoE official if Britain and Germany were moving

towards each other in order to adjust to the environmental regulatory style of another member state.

11 Andersen and Liefferink (eds) (1997); Boehmer-Christiansen and Skea (1991); Caldwell (1984, 1990); Dryzek (1997); Jänicke and Weidner (eds) (1995, 1997); A. Jordan (1999b); Sprinz and Vaahtoranta (1994); Underdal and Hanf (eds) (1999); Weale (1992a); Weale *et al.* (1996, 2000); Zito (2000).

12 Andersen and Liefferink (eds) (1997); Héritier *et al.* (1994, 1996); Holzinger (1994); A. Jordan (1999b); Knill and Lenschow (eds) (2000); Liefferink and Anderson (1998a, 1998b); Weale *et al.* (2000); Wurzel (1993); Zito (2000).

13 Finer (1984: 135).

14 Interview in 1993.

15 Weale (1992a, 1992b).

16 DETR (1997); EEA (1998a, 1998b); OECD (1993, 1994); UBA (1997a).

17 OECD (1994: 47).

18 Kinnersley (1988, 1994); Maloney and Richardson (1995); OECD (1994: 47–64).

19 EEA (1995b, 1998b).

20 OECD (1993).

21 OECD (1994: 95).

22 Article 2 of *Directive 1210/90/EEC*.

23 See Haigh (1996) for the British case and Müller (1986) for the German.

24 On the other hand, significant sectoral variations may exist; see Wilks and Wright (eds) (1987).

25 OECD (1993, 1994).

26 BMWi (1993); Wurzel (1996a: 286–7).

27 Dyson (ed.) (1992); *The Economist*, 4 May 1996, 21.

28 CEC (2001); EEA (1998a, 1998b); UBA (1997b).

29 Andersen (1994); Andersen and Sprenger (eds) (2000); Hajer (1995); Heseltine (1992); Jänicke (1993); Jänicke and Weidner (1995, 1997); Schröder (1989); Töpfer (1989a, 1989c); Weale (1992a, 1993); Weale *et al.* (2000); Weizsäcker (1997).

30 UBA (1997b: 61).

31 UBA (1997a: 50). It should however be pointed out that 128,000 of these jobs were state sponsored (*Arbeitsbetschaffungsmaßnahmen*) to reduce unemployment.

32 Interview in 1992.

33 Interview in 1992.

34 Interview in 1992 when Klaus Töpfer, who skilfully used the media for generating public support for stringent environmental policy measures, was still environmental minister.

35 Dyson (ed.) (1992); Bulmer and Paterson (1987).

36 Hartkopf and Bohne (1983: 84); Töpfer (1989a), Schröder (1989).
37 Interview in 1993.
38 Hajer (1995).
39 Fax message from the DTI dated 2 April 1996.
40 Haigh (1996); Hajer (1995).
41 John Dryzek (1997: 82) has argued that neoliberals successfully used the derogative label 'command and control' within the public policy discourse to discredit traditional environmental regulation.
42 OECD (1994: 110).
43 DETR (1997, 1998c); DoE (1996).
44 Interviews and written communications with DTI officials in 1995–96.
45 Fax message from the DTI dated 2 April 1996. The figures refer to 1996 prices.
46 DETR (1998a, 1998b).
47 Wurzel (2001).
48 *Financial Times*, 8 March 2001.
49 CEC (1987) and CEC (1993d). See also Weale *et al.* (2000).
50 CEC (1994a).
51 CEC (1995c).
52 CEC (2001a: 61).
53 *ENDS Daily*, 10 January, 1 March, 14 March and 20 March 2001.
54 CEC (2001b).
55 Hucke (1981); Kingdon (1995); Sabatier and Jenkins-Smith (eds) (1993).
56 Inglehart (1971, 1977).
57 Hodges and Woolcock (1993).
58 Rehbinder (1992).
59 Dalton (1994); Jordan and Maloney (1997); McCormick (1991: 34).
60 Dalton (1994); Hey and Brendle (1994).
61 See, however, Kitschelt (1993).
62 Holzinger (1994: 164–7); Robinson (1992).
63 Malunat (1987). The reformed former East German Communist Party, the Party of Democratic Socialism (PDS), also stresses the need to protect the environment.
64 Mazey and Richardson (1993b).
65 See Richardson (ed.) (1982).
66 Lowi (1964).
67 Richardson and Watts (1986: 4).
68 Hayward (1974); Richardson (ed.) (1982).
69 Ashby and Anderson (1981: 152–3)
70 Kitschelt (1986); Rose-Ackermann (1995).
71 Dyson (1982); Dyson (ed.) (1992).
72 Beyme (1985: 5) who refers to Richardson (ed.) (1982).
73 Dyson (1982: 21).

74 Beyme (1985: 5).
75 Marsh and Rhodes (eds) (1992); Wilks and Wright (eds) (1987).
76 Mazey and Richardson (1993b: 256).
77 Andersen and Liefferink (eds) (1997); Héritier (1995); Héritier *et al.* (1994, 1996); Kelemen (1995); Liefferink and Andersen (1998a, 1998b); Sbragia (1996); Weale (1992a, 1992b); Weale *et al.* (1996, 2000).
78 Andersen and Liefferink (1997: 6).
79 Vogel (1986: 24).
80 Grant *et al.* (1988); Wilks and Wright (eds) (1987).
81 Anderson (1978: 23) as cited in Hayward (1991: 385).
82 Caldwell (1990: 15).
83 Weale (1993: 200).
84 Boehmer-Christiansen and Skea (1991); Héritier *et al.* (1994, 1996); RCEP (1998).
85 Ashby and Anderson (1981: 152–3).
86 Boehmer-Christiansen and Skea (1991); Boehmer-Christiansen and Weidner (1995); Héritier *et al.* (1994, 1996); Sbragia (1996, 2000).
87 Golub (1994); Héritier (1996); Héritier *et al.* (1994, 1996); Sbragia (1996).
88 Haigh (1987: 22–3); Haigh (ed.) (1995: 3.5); Merkel (1996: 248); Rehbinder and Stewart (1985a); Wurzel (1993: 191–4).
89 This approach was taken under the dangerous substances water directive (76/464/EEC).
90 Haigh (ed.) (1995: 34–5); RCEP (1998); Scott (1998: 25–37); Wurzel (1993: 191–4).
91 Figure 1.1 shows the sectors as identified in the fifth EAP (CEC 1993d) and adds households as a source.
92 Gündling (1991); Weale (1992b).
93 Weale (1992b: 54).
94 RCEP (1998: 35).
95 Levy (1993).
96 Interview with UBA official in 1993.
97 Bioaccumulation takes place when the level of a toxic substance accumulates through the food chain. Synergistic effects take place when the harm caused by pollutants is increased when they react with other pollutants.
98 Weale *et al.* (1991: 63). For the German case see also Bechmann (1984); Bohne (1992); Hartkopf and Bohne (1983); and Wey (1982). For the British case see Ball and Bell (1995); Bell (1997); Haigh (1982); Haigh (ed.) (1995); and Holdgate (1983).
99 Wurzel (1993: 191, 1996a: 283).
100 Bungarten (1978); Golub (1994).
101 Haigh (1982).
102 Osborn (1990: 3).

103 Jordan and Greenaway (1999: 686).
104 Golub (1994); Héritier (1996); Héritier *et al.* (1994, 1996); Sbragia (1996).
105 Haigh (1982: 3); Holdgate (1983: 9); Kinnersley (1988); NRA (1991); OECD (1994: 56). See also chapter 9.
106 Jordan and Greenaway (1999); Kinnersley (1988, 1994).
107 Interview in 2001. See also Ashby and Anderson (1981: 152–3).
108 Pearce (1981); Rose (1990).
109 Paragraph 7a of the Water Management Act. See also Andersen (1994).
110 Grant *et al.* (1988).
111 EEB (1987).
112 Hucke (1981: 130).
113 Mayntz (ed.) (1980).
114 Héritier (1996); Héritier *et al.* (1994, 1996); Liefferink (1996).
115 Haigh (ed.) (1995: 3.1); Rehbinder and Stewart (1985a: 17).
116 Bungarten (1978).
117 *Council Directive 76/464/EEC* of May 1976 on pollution caused by dangerous substances discharged into the aquatic environment of the Community, OJ No. L 129, 18 May.
118 LAWA (1975).
119 Presidency Conclusions (1988). See Weale *et al.* (2000); Wurzel (1996a).
120 DoE (1988: 1 and 3).
121 COM(93) 680, final.
122 Levitt (1980: 94).
123 DoE (1988: 5).
124 Bell (1997); Ball and Bell (1995); RCEP (1998); Weale *et al.* (1991, 2000).
125 Bell (1997: 339).
126 Ashby and Anderson (1981); Weale (1996b: 112).
127 Weale *et al.* (1991).
128 RCEP (1988) as cited in Bell (1997: 306). See also RCEP (1998).
129 RCEP (1976).
130 Bell (1997: 306–7); Haigh (1996); Weale (1997).
131 Bohne (1992); Hartkopf and Bohne (1983); Weale *et al.* (1991). The *Polizeyrecht* included the duty to uphold law and order but also to protect the population against disease.
132 Interior Minister Gerhart Baum as cited in Müller (1986: 272).
133 Kloepfer (1998); Merkel (1996); Schulte (1999: 44–5).
134 Weale (1992b: 179).
135 Bechmann (1984: 127).
136 Interviews with BMU and UBA officials in 1992 and 1998. See also Weale *et al.* (2000).
137 Rose-Ackerman (1995).
138 Interview with BMU and UBA officials in 1998.
139 RCEP (1998: 37–8).

140 Scott (1998: 28), who refers to *Directive 96/61/EEC*.

141 Written communication from Lord Stanley Clinton-Davis dated 15 November 1996. He added: 'I have never associated the British Government directly with this.'

Theorising multilevel European Union policy-making

Following its inception in the early 1970s, EU environmental policy quickly developed into one of the most popular common policies and is frequently held up as a model for international cooperation elsewhere.[1] However, there is considerable disagreement about whether EU environmental policy has led to a trading-up of member state environmental standards or has encouraged lowest common denominator solutions.[2] Empirical evidence can be found to support both schools of thought, leading some scholars to conclude that the EU's record is in fact a mixed one.[3]

It is also unclear to what degree, if any, member state environmental standard-setting philosophies and policy-making procedures have been 'Europeanised' as a consequence of EU membership. Some studies suggest that the policy space for (unilateral) national action has been severely constrained;[4] others have argued that the degree of national convergence within the EU is not very high when the entire policy cycle (including implementation) is looked at.[5]

There has long been agreement that early EU environmental policy measures were largely driven by member state initiatives.[6] More recently, Adrienne Héritier and colleagues, Alberta Sbragia and David Vogel have argued that environmental leader and/or highly regulatory member states export their national environmental standards and regulatory styles.[7] Highly regulatory member states are not necessarily environmentally progressive states interested in the adoption of ambitious environmental policy measures, but may instead have a well-developed body of national environmental legislation on which they would like to see EU environmental policy measures modelled in order to reduce adaptation costs which result from the introduction of novel procedures, dissimilar regulatory philosophies and different standards.[8]

In essence this amounts to the claim that EU environmental policy measures are little more than national environmental policy measures dressed up as European legislation. This view, which is in line with intergovernmentalist theory, is rejected by scholars who have argued that EU environmental policy measures are typically complex compromises (with derogations, phased in deadlines, fudged action-guiding principles, etc.) drawn up to accommodate the central demands of the core policy actors. Albert Weale has claimed that:

> [EU] environmental standards ... are neither a reflection of a dominant coalition of countries pushing their own national style of regulation ... nor a merry-go-round in which different countries have a go at imposing their own national style in a sector that is of particular importance to them. Instead, they are the aggregated and transformed standards of their original champions modified under the need to secure political accommodation from powerful veto players.[9]

The main reason why conflicting interpretations have emerged about which type of actor dominates EU environmental policy-making is that scholars have borrowed different theoretical lenses from competing theories of EU integration and politics. It is to these theories I now turn.

Theories of European integration and politics

There is no single generally acknowledged theory of the EU. This is unsurprising, as political science is essentially a multi-theoretical discipline.[10] Different theoretical perspectives may actually help increase our understanding because they shed light on different aspects of the EU. However, there is also the danger that terminological inflation and conceptual confusion will hinder the development of empirically grounded theory development. According to different studies, the EU constitutes: a federation,[11] a multi-tiered state,[12] a regulatory state,[13] a supranational Community,[14] a multi-level political system,[15] a poly-centric system,[16] a regime,[17] less than a federation but more than a regime,[18] a network,[19] and a forum for problem-solving.[20]

It would not have been difficult to further extend this list, which covers almost the entire intergovernmentalist–federalist divide. Most political scientists would probably agree that the EU constitutes a unique political entity (although realists and neo-Marxists would argue that the EU's unique features are epiphenomenal). Some scholars have therefore suggested that the EU should be treated as *sui generis* or as an atypical outlier,[21] while others have argued that over time the EU may develop from 'anomaly to archetype',[22] thus providing a model for regional integration elsewhere.

This book is not the place to put forward a detailed assessment of EU theories.[23] However, the core features of the two most influential macro-theoretical concepts – intergovernmentalism and neofunction-alism – are briefly assessed before the middle-range theoretical approach used in this book is explained.

Early theories of EU integration and politics

International relations (IR) dominated the early research on the EU, while comparative politics (CP) concepts have come to be increasingly used by EU scholars since the 1990s. Realist-inspired intergovernmen-talism and pluralist-derived neofunctionalism initially gained most influence among IR theories focusing on the EU.

Intergovernmentalism

For classical realist theory, states constitute unitary actors which behave as power maximisers in an anarchic international political system. States need to fend for their survival as there is no over-arching authority which can enforce international rules. Classical realist approaches argue that the EU's institutional structure is inher-ently unstable as it depends on either an external threat, an internal hegemon or a fragile balance of power for its existence.

Neorealist – liberal intergovernmentalist, interdependence and regime – theories have modified some of the core assumptions put forward by classical realist authors. However, all neorealists still argue that the EU is an international organisation which provides merely a bargaining arena for member states. EU institutional actors (such as the Commission) cannot develop independent 'European' preferences because they are dominated by national interests. From a neorealist perspective, the outcome of the EU policy-making process can best be explained by reference to the national interest(s) of the most powerful member state(s). Moreover, cooperation within the EU is seen to depend on reciprocity and is limited to technical or 'low politics' issues.

Neofunctionalism

Neofunctionalist scholars draw heavily on the functionalist notion of *spill-over* to explain the integration process. Spill-over effects are said to occur on a sector by sector basis (functional spill-over or scope expansion) before spilling over into the political realm (political spill-over or level expansion). Neofunctionalists predict that successful technical cooperation within a limited number of 'low politics' sectors (such as coal and steel) would create strong political pressures both to extend co-operation to other sectors and to deepen European integration.

Early neofunctionalists saw the Commission as a European government-in-waiting. They argued that national interest groups would soon bypass their domestic governments and gradually shift their attention (and loyalties) to the EU level. They identified an integration process which was driven by a small supranational bureaucracy (the Commission) and non-governmental elites (interest groups) from which governments and the public were largely excluded. This process is now commonly referred to as the 'Monnet method'[24] or 'integration by stealth'.[25] However, neofunctionalists were forced to build into their theory retarding elements (such as 'spill-back' pressures or 'dramatic political actors') to account for the 1966 Luxembourg Compromise which guaranteed member governments the right to invoke a veto on grounds of 'vital national interests'.[26]

The fact that early intergovernmentalists largely ignored EU environmental policy is hardly surprising, considering that it is a relatively technical 'low politics' area. However, it is ironic that the pioneer of neofunctionalist theory, Ernst Haas, announced the 'obsolescence of integration theory' in the early 1970s at around the same time as the EU moved into a new policy field (environmental policy) not explicitly mentioned in its treaties.[27] Many neofunctionalists followed Haas's advice and therefore missed the opportunity to test empirically the claim that EU environmental policy constitutes 'a relatively technical policy area where one would expect neofunctionalism to perform relatively well'.[28]

The relaunch of integration theories
The relaunch of the internal market project ('1992') formed part of the 1987 Single European Act (SEA), which started a new integrationist phase. It also triggered a relaunch of traditional (macro) theories as well as producing novel (middle-range) approaches, particularly from a CP perspective.[29] However, the 'no' vote in the first Danish referendum on the Treaty on European Union (Maastricht Treaty) in 1992 threw political elites and academics alike into new confusion.[30]

Relaunched intergovernmentalist and neofunctionalist theories have continued to provide different explanations of what drives EU policy-making at the systemic level, although the distinction between IR and CP concepts has become blurred.[31] Intergovernmentalists have remained adamant that the EU provides little more than a bargaining arena for governments which remain in control of the policy-making process.[32] Their main research focus has been on the 'history making'[33] decisions such as the Rome Treaty, the SEA, the Maastricht Treaty and the Amsterdam Treaty, all of which were negotiated and agreed on by member governments. However, some neorealists, for example Robert Keohane and Stanley Hoffmann, have argued that the EU 'has gone well beyond any known "international organization" ... [and were] struck by the distinctiveness of the Community among contemporary international organizations'.[34] New neofunctionalists, on the other hand, argue that Treaty amendments merely formalised and constitutionalised a degree of integration which had already been reached in between the history-making intergovernmental bargains.[35]

For many EU scholars it became increasingly clear that the EU's governance system has been shaped by both intergovernmental and supranational actors.[36] For Paul Taylor the EU is based on an equilibrium between governments and supranational actors which can be readjusted to new context variables but not relinquished in favour of one type of actor without fundamental changes to the existing institutions and procedures.[37] EU environmental policy scholars have also turned their attention to the mutual dependencies between member-governmental and EU institutional actors.[38] Albert Weale has argued that '[a]lthough EU rule-making institutions can be said to have a life of their own in the environmental policy field, they still need to be connected to the life-support machine of the nation states if they are to function at all'.[39]

For a long time there was an 'intellectual apartheid'[40] between IR and CP approaches which made the recognition of the mutual dependency (or partial autonomy) of intergovernmental and supranational (as well as non-governmental) actors difficult.[41] However, since the 1990s a somewhat tentative dialogue has developed between these two sub-disciplines of political science.[42] This development is of importance for the analysis of environmental policy where the traditional distinction between foreign and domestic politics has increasingly been challenged.[43]

The following three developments stand out from the recently revived theories of EU integration and politics.

1 IR neorealist (liberal intergovernmentalism, interdependence and regime) theories and CP neopluralist (policy network, new institutionalism and multi-level) approaches have developed somewhat similar research agendas.
2 The analytical tools of recent theories have become sufficiently differentiated as to be able to capture the increased complexity of the EU governance system.
3 The fact that CP approaches increasingly play a more prominent role can be interpreted as evidence that many scholars conceptualise the EU as a multi-level governance system which has matured sufficiently as to render helpful (middle-range) theories originally developed for the analysis of domestic and/or comparative politics.

The arrival of the environment on the research agenda

Prior to these EU theoretical developments, environmental issues had already arrived on both the IR and CP research agendas. It is therefore necessary briefly to examine the most important rival concepts in this research area before outlining the theoretical approach and specific propositions put forward in this book.

Regime theories Neorealist theories have been widely used for the study of international environmental politics.[44] They are still state-centred approaches and their main analytical focus remains national interests.[45] However, regime theoretical approaches acknowledge that, under conditions of reciprocity, it is rational for governments to cooperate with other states in order to resolve collective action problems which are beyond their national problem-solving capacity. Many environmental problems are transborder issues and fall into this category.

Stephen Krasner has put forward the following influential definition of what constitutes a regime:

> Regimes can be defined as sets of implicit or explicit principles, norms, rules, and decision-making procedures around which actors' expectations converge in a given area of international relations. Principles are beliefs of fact, causation, and rectitude. Norms are standards of behaviour defined in terms of rights and obligations. Rules are specific prescriptions or proscriptions for action. Decision-making procedures are prevailing practices for making and implementing collective choice.[46]

Modifications of Krasner's definition can be found in several regime theoretical approaches used to analyse international environmental politics. Oran Young, who drew on Douglas North's new institutionalist approach,[47] defined regimes as

> constellations of agreed-upon principles, norms, rules and decision-making procedures that govern the interactions of actors in specific issue areas. As such, they provide the rules of the game that define the character of recognised social practices ... Organisations, by contrast, are material entities possessing offices, personnel, equipment, budgets, and legal personality. They play important roles in implementing and administering the provisions of many, though by no means all, international regimes.[48]

Young remains firmly within the neorealist school of thought when he attributes merely implementation and administrative powers to international organisations.

EU environmental policy has not as yet been assessed from a regime theoretical perspective by any major study, although several EU environmental policy studies have made reference to regime theory.[49] The main reason for this can be found in William Wallace's often quoted dictum that the EU is '[l]ess than a federation, [but] more than a regime'.[50]

However, both the EU and the member states are affected by or have entered into international environmental regimes such as the Convention on Long Range Transboundary Air Pollution (LRTAP) and the Climate Change Conventions.[51] Member governments can try to influence environmental policy from 'outside' the EU by signing up to international agreements or forming alliances with non-member states.[52]

However, Mikael Andersen and Duncan Liefferink have argued that,

> environmental policy has probably become one of the most internationalised policy fields with a universal tool-kit and policy concepts and strategies ranging from sustainable development to life cycle analysis. Nevertheless, comparative research has often pointed to substantial variations in the approaches to environmental policy across different countries.[53]

These differences are captured best by CP theories.

Policy network analysis There is a certain resemblance between regime theoretical and policy network approaches. However, regime theory has concentrated on the IR level, while policy network analysis has traditionally focused on the 'rules of the game' at the domestic politics level. Policy network analysis takes into account the fragmentation and sectoralisation of policy-making within highly developed liberal democracies.[54] This is one of the reasons why it is a particularly promising approach for the assessment of EU policy-making which is organised largely along functional and sectoral lines. Moreover, policy network approaches have recently been used to assess EU environmental policy-making.[55]

The policy network analysis was initially developed within CP as a critique of both classical pluralist approaches (which had claimed that public policy essentially reflected the outcome of interest group competition) and corporatist approaches (which argued that some governments deliberately granted representational monopolies to a limited number of interest groups, such as employers and unions, to participate in the public policy-making process).[56] By contrast, policy network scholars instead stress the mutual (but often asymmetrical) dependencies of governmental and private interest group actors within a certain policy sector.

It is necessary to define briefly the terminology used in this book because there is considerable dispute about the best analytic use of the policy network concept.[57] For the majority of scholars, policy networks oscillate between two poles on a continuum that extends from tightly structured and less permeable *policy communities* to relatively open and fluid *issue networks*.[58] In this book *policy network* is used as the generic term that embraces both policy communities and issue networks. A policy community is characterised by a limited number of core actors ('insiders') who, within a particular policy (sub)sector, are relatively insulated from other actors of the wider *policy universe* which consists of numerous other (sub)sectoral policy networks. The core actors of a policy community are 'sometimes in conflict, often in agreement, but always in touch and operating within a shared framework'.[59] Issue networks, on the other hand, are characterised by a larger number of actors, high permeability, *ad hoc* participation and limited consensus on the core beliefs between the main actors. Policy communities are relatively stable and enduring whereas issue networks are usually unstable and ephemeral.

The core actors of a policy network may not share the same beliefs but they have in common a shared interest in a particular policy issue. Policy networks are characterised more by horizontal than by

hierarchical governance structures; in analytical terms they are therefore located *between* markets and hierarchies. Solutions acceptable to
core actors holding veto powers must be found. The question of who
is in the driving seat – public or private actors – is often a difficult
one to answer and must be established empirically. Policy communities
and, to a lesser degree, issue networks, are occasionally dominated by
private actors such as transnational corporations. Susan Strange
and John Stopford, for example, have argued that a new 'triangular
diplomacy' is emerging in which transnational corporations negotiate
directly with foreign governments rather than through their domestic
government.[60]

However, scholars who use a neopluralist concept ('structured
pluralism' is the term preferred by Jack Hayward)[61] for analysing
public policy have argued that public actors do not necessarily become
puppets of powerful private interest groups; on the contrary, it may be
more appropriate to talk of 'pressured groups' rather than pressure
politics.[62] Seen from a neopluralist perspective, policy networks not
only reduce the 'transaction costs' (by providing a negotiating and
bargaining arena) but increase the 'steering capacity' of governance
actors.[63]

EU policy networks According to Thomas Risse-Kappen,

> there is growing convergence among international and comparative
> politics scholars conceptualising the EU as a multilevel structure of
> governance where private, governmental, transnational and suprana-
> tional actors deal with each other in highly complex networks of varying
> density, as well as horizontal and vertical depth.[64]

EU policy networks are said to differ from national policy networks
in four major respects.[65] First, they are less stable and often exist over
a relatively short period of time. Second, they are less institutionalised,
with contacts between the core policy actors less frequent. Third,
there is usually a higher number of actors involved whose interests
and problem perceptions are more heterogenous. Sonia Mazey and
Jeremy Richardson have argued that EU environmental policy-making
'is best characterised as policy-making through loose, open, and
extended issue networks, rather than through well defined, stable,
and exclusive policy communities'.[66] However, Simon Hix has warned
that fragmentation should not be confused with pluralism:

> the vision of the EC as a pluralist dream is slightly misleading ... the

decision-making process is fragmented into separate interest areas, and each area is controlled by 'special interest coalitions'. The access of all interest groups to EC policy channels is far from equal, despite the common policy of subsidizing non-economic interests.[67]

Fourth, the Commission plays a central role, especially during the policy-formulation stage.

The policy network approach as a research method

The question of whether the policy network approach has matured into a middle-range *theory* is a contested one. Put simply, scholars who argue that the policy network analysis constitutes an explanatory theory claim that 'networks affect policy outcomes',[68] while their critics deny this.[69] However, some critics even accept that the policy network analysis offers a useful research *method* for identifying the core policy actors and mapping out their interaction patterns.[70] The policy network analysis focuses primarily at the (sub)sectoral or meso-level and proceeds in a bottom–up fashion. Its research strategy can therefore be seen as one of backward mapping. It takes the policy output as a starting-point for identifying the core policy actors together with their interests, strategies and guiding norms. In this book, the policy network approach is used primarily as a research *method*, although the aim is also to contribute to theoretical under-standing of EU environmental policy and policy-making.

The starting-point of the case studies (Parts II and III) is EU environmental legislation because, as Eberhard Bohne has argued, 'each law constitutes an autonomous action guiding system (*autonomes Handlungssystem*) which ... may form part of a wider action guiding system ... The empirical social sciences have used the term network for such interlocking systems'.[71] Similarly, Stephen Woolcock and colleagues have argued that '[e]very regulatory regime or set of stand-ards represents a form of national social contract that reflects a particular consensus or balance between competing interests ... [I]ndividual governments are generally reluctant to see them eroded by EC proposals'.[72]

However, the EU may also be used by governments to overcome the resistance of powerful domestic veto actors, although this may create new dependencies and unintended effects which become clear only at a much later stage. As new institutionalist scholars have pointed out, member governments may find themselves 'locked in' once EU legislation has been adopted.[73] In any case, the adoption and revision of (national and EU) environmental legislation usually requires considerable technical and scientific expertise, which makes the 'science-politics interface' a particularly important one for environmental policy.[74]

Epistemic communities
The need for technical and scientific expertise opens up channels of influence for epistemic communities, which have been defined by Peter Haas as

> networks of knowledge-based communities with an authoritative claim to policy-relevant knowledge within their domain of expertise ... Their members share knowledge about the causation of social or physical phenomena in an area for which they have a reputation for competence, and a common set of normative beliefs about what actions will benefit human welfare in such a domain.[75]

Helen Wallace has pointed out that the debate within the EU about epistemic communities is '[i]n some sense ... a reprise of the Monnet approach to European integration. For Monnet and his colleagues it was important to provide a framework through which the "brightest and the best" could be enabled to pioneer new ideas for collective and supranational policies.'[76]

Peter Haas stresses the importance of knowledge and ideas in claiming that

> when epistemic communities are widely spread, even in the absence of leadership by a strong state, environmentally effective regimes are possible ... As epistemic communities obtain and consolidate influence in different governments, national preferences and policies will come to reflect the epistemic beliefs.[77]

However, agreement within epistemic communities is not usually sufficient to trigger policy change. More broadly based advocacy coalitions which embrace a wider set of political and social actors are needed.[78]

Advocacy coalitions
Paul Sabatier has pioneered the advocacy coalition framework. He defines an advocacy coalition as '[p]eople from a variety of positions, elected and agency officials, interest group leaders, researchers, who [1] share a particular belief system – a set of basic values, causal assumptions, and problem perceptions – and who [2] show a non-trivial degree of co-ordinated activity over time'.[79]

Sabatier argues that advocacy coalitions are value based and aim to translate their beliefs into general policy programmes and specific policy measures. Their policy beliefs are structured into hierarchical layers made up of deep core, near core and secondary beliefs. According to the advocacy coalition framework, '[p]olicy change is best understood as the product of competition between several advocacy coalitions'.[80] However, Sabatier argues that 'while minority coalitions can seek to improve their relative position through augmenting their resources and "outlearning" their adversaries, their basic hope of gaining power within the sub-system resides in waiting for some external event to significantly increase their political resources.'[81] To bring about policy change, advocacy coalitions will therefore usually have to rely on factors exogenous to the (sub)sector within which they operate, although events such as environmental accidents may create 'policy windows'.[82]

Rival advocacy coalitions engage in a 'dialogue of the deaf'[83] in relation to their near core and core beliefs. Unlike epistemic communities, advocacy coalitions are therefore not interested in establishing a consensus about 'scientific truths'. On the contrary: For [advocacy coalitions], learning is an instrumental process: far from a disinterested search for truth, it is a means of achieving *a priori* beliefs'.[84]

Typically, environmental advocacy coalitions that press for more stringent pollution abatement measures are opposed by economic feasibility coalitions which warn of the negative economic consequences of such measures.[85] Disputes between rival advocacy coalitions are mediated by policy brokers 'whose dominant concerns are with keeping the level of political conflict within acceptable limits and reaching some "reasonable" solution to the problem'.[86] Senior civil servants often take on such a brokering role.

Within the EU, one might expect the Commission to become a policy broker which mediates between rival advocacy coalitions made up of environmental leader and laggard states together with their respective constituencies. However, there are at least two unresolved theoretical problems. First, the advocacy coalition framework is essentially a (classic) pluralist approach which leaves little room for the independent preferences of governance actors (such as member governments and EU institutions). Andrew Jordan and John Greenaway have warned that 'Sabatier allows for a plurality of [advocacy coalitions] in a system, but the more one multiplies the number the more everything begins to look like old-style American pluralism spiced up'.[87] Second, the Commission is more commonly described as a policy entrepreneur than as a neutral policy broker.[88] And other EU institutional actors, such as the European Parliament (EP) and the European Court of Justice (ECJ), have also taken on a role which goes well beyond that of mediator.

Environmental policy is a highly technical and knowledge-intensive policy field in which new scientific findings and policy ideas are awarded a high premium. Ideas therefore matter for environmental policy-making.[89] However, Albert Weale has pointed out:

> If ideas have power, they only do so in the context of the specific institutional and historical circumstances in which they are located. Properly to understand the power of ideas, therefore, we need also to understand how the context of policy discourse constrains and facilitates certain constructions of policy rather than others, and how, in context, ideas and policy principles are adapted and interpreted.[90]

Theoretical approach and main research questions

This book presents new empirical findings and aims to make a contribution within the theory debate about EU environmental policy which, according to Duncan Liefferink and Arthur Mol, 'has hardly begun'.[91] It therefore sets out to test a number of specific propositions.

The (middle-range) theoretical approach used is best labelled neo-pluralist (or structured pluralist) policy network analysis. The label *neopluralist* refers to the fact that, in line with (new) institutionalist approaches, steering capacity is attributed to public actors (such as member governments and the Commission). Moreover, it assumes that policy-making will usually develop in terms of evolutionary path-dependent policy learning[92] although it also allows for lesson-drawing across borders[93] as well as 'revolutionary' learning or policy u-turns as a result of policy failure (such as an environmental catastrophe) and shocks exogenous to the policy (sub)sector (such as an economic crisis).[94]

On the other hand, the research focus on *policy networks* emphasises that mutual dependencies exist between public and private actors which may not always take the form of (highly) institutionalised relations. The approach taken here therefore also differs from both intergovernmentalist approaches (which argue that member states are in control of EU policy-making) and neofunctionalist theory (which argues that the Commission and the interest groups are the driving forces behind EU policies and integrationist moves).

Main research propositions
If, as was argued in chapter 1, distinct national environmental regulatory styles guide the actions of core national policy actors, there are principally three alternative ways in which they can be accommodated at the EU level. First, a process of regulatory competition between the (environmental leader and/or highly regulatory) member states determines who will be able to export its national regulatory style to the EU level and to other member states.[95] This view is, in principle, compatible with the core assumptions of intergovernmentalist theory.

Second, an EU 'operating system' will emerge which both continuously widens the range and scope of environmental issues under its jurisdiction and gradually overrides national preferences and regulatory styles. If this is the case, it is only a matter of time before the EU will develop its own supranational environmental regulatory style.[96] This alternative fits neofunctionalist predictions.

Third, EU environmental policy measures constitute complex compromise proposals originally put forward by policy entrepreneurs but modified by the need to secure acceptance from those governance and non-governmental actors with veto powers.[97] This alternative fits the neopluralist policy network perspective.

In line with the neopluralist policy network approach, the following three main propositions will be empirically tested in this study.
1 EU environmental policy measures are typically the aggregated and transformed proposals of policy entrepreneurs modified by the need to secure political accommodation from 'policy spoilers' or veto actors.
2 Differences in national environmental regulatory styles matter during the EU environmental policy-making process and help to explain the actions of member governments.
3 Conflicts about EU environmental policy frequently cut across the boundaries of institutional and non-governmental actors, and at least occasionally, also across member governments and beyond national borders.

Cross-country and cross-sectoral longitudinal case study research
The case studies on car emission and bathing water regulations will

be analysed over their entire policy cycle. For analytical purposes the stages of this cycle can be disaggregated into:

- agenda setting
- policy formulation
- decision-making
- implementation
- evaluation and
- revision

although in practice the different phases often overlap.[98] The underlying assumption is that the EU has developed institutional arrangements, procedural mechanisms and policy instruments which make it more appropriate to talk of an EU 'environmental governance system'[99] rather than of 'foreign environmental policy'.[100] This is not to argue that the 'EU's would-be polity'[101] has already developed into a polity. However, the EU has acquired certain state-like characteristics such as a parliament, a court and qualified majority voting (QMV) as a decisional rule, while, at the same time, member states have lost some qualities traditionally associated with sovereign states. And, arguably, this is nowhere more evident than in the environmental field, where national problem-solving capacities are limited for two main reasons. First, pollution does not stop at national borders. And, second, the creation of an internal market is incompatible with the adoption of national pollution abatement measures which constitute barriers to trade.

This study takes a longitudinal perspective (over a period of more than three decades) for three main reasons.[102] First, different types of actors may dominate different phases of the policy-making process. A research focus which excludes the *post-decisional* implementation, evaluation and revision phases may therefore provide a distorted picture of which type of actor dominates policy-making.[103] Second, there is growing recognition that policy formulation and implementation are inextricably linked.[104] The well-known implementation deficit in EU environmental policy may not be the result solely of member states defending their national interests and domestic environmental regulatory styles.[105] Poorly drafted EU legislation or complex political compromises may turn out to be difficult or even impossible to implement on the ground.[106] Third, environmentally harmful effects of anthropogenic activities often become detectable only after a considerable time lag. Equally, pollution abatement measures frequently become fully effective only years after their implementation.

Research methods
The findings of this book are based on more than 100 interviews (in Britain, Brussels, Germany and Luxembourg) and extensive archive studies, as well as an analysis of the relevant primary documents and secondary literature. While it was relatively easy to find officials in Brussels and Germany willing to grant access to unpublished archival material, this was not the case in Britain, although British officials were very willing to be interviewed. However, environmental groups, research institutes and newspaper archives provided rich pickings in terms of leaked government documents, confirming Jack Hayward's claim that 'in Britain the "leak" is the counterpart of the rule of secrecy'.[107] Interviews with German officials were conducted in German and have been translated by the author. German primary documents and secondary sources cited have also been translated. However, occasionally a German key term has been given in brackets when it refers to a specific meaning which is difficult to translate.

Case studies
Car emissions can cause serious health and environmental problems. In 1998 the DETR estimated that every year, in Britain alone, 24,000 people die prematurely as a result of excessive traffic fumes.[108] Cars are a widely traded product for which different national standards may cause a barrier to trade. The car emission regulations case study should therefore provide important insights into how conflicting (public) environmental objectives and (private) economic interests are reconciled at the EU level.

The EU's bathing water directive is concerned with a very different regulatory issue.[109] It aims to protect the aquatic environment for a particular human activity (bathing) and has, therefore, also been referred to as a 'quality of life' measure.[110] Differing national bathing water standards do not present a direct threat to the functioning of the internal market. The first EU car emission directive was agreed in 1970; the adoption of the bathing water directive followed five years later. Both measures therefore belong to the first generation of EU environmental policy measures. However, while the 1970 car emission directive has since been revised numerous times, the 1975 bathing water directive has remained in force without substantive revision for more than twenty-five years. The two case studies should therefore shed light on the factors that drive and constrain the revision of EU environmental policy, allowing questions about 'non decision-making'[111] and policy 'lock in'[112] to be addressed. The fact that car emission and bathing water regulations are two very different environmental policy issues should make it possible to assess whether there is evidence that environmental regulatory styles guide the actions of the core actors in different policy (sub)sectors. The recent EU environmental policy literature has paid increasing attention to different national environmental regulatory styles.[113] However, little research effort has so far been spent on the assessment of cross-sectoral and/or cross-media (for example, air and water) differences and similarities.[114] The choice of Britain and Germany as the two member states under consideration should allow for a particularly interesting comparison, as these two member states are often portrayed as exhibiting markedly different national environmental regulatory styles. However, before the case studies can be assessed, it is necessary first to identify the core actors and to explain the main features of the EU environmental governance system, while keeping in mind the theoretical approach and propositions outlined above.

Notes

1 Brenton (1994: 107); Caldwell (1984: 43); Hurrell and Kingsbury (1992: 36); Sands (1991); Vogel (1995: 81).

2 The trading-up claim is supported by Arp (1995), Eichener (1997), Héritier (1995), Krämer (1995: 61), Sbragia (1996) and Vogel (1995, 1997). The lowest common denominator argument can be found in Bungarten (1978: 126), Prittwitz (1984: 439), Scharpf (1988: 241) and Strübel (1992).

3 Andersen and Liefferink (eds) (1997); Holzinger (1994); Liefferink and Andersen (eds) (1997); Rehbinder and Stewart (1985a); Scharpf (1996); Weale (1992a, 1996a); Weale *et al.* (1996, 2000); Wurzel (1996a, 2001).

4 Haigh (1992, 1996); A. Jordan (1999a, 1999b, 2002); Héritier *et al.* (1994, 1996); Sbragia (1996).

5 Weale *et al.* (1991, 1996, 2000); Andersen and Liefferink (eds) (1997).

6 Bungarten (1978); Moltke (1987); Rehbinder and Stewart (1985a, 1985b).

7 Héritier (1995, 1996); Héritier *et al.* (1994, 1996); Sbragia (1996); Vogel (1993, 1995, 1997).

8 Börzel (2000); Héritier (1996); Héritier *et al.* (1994, 1996); Knill and Lenschow (eds) (2000).

9 Weale (1996a: 607).

10 Strange (1988: 7–22); Weale (1992a: 37–67).

11 Pinder (1991: 18).
12 Bulmer (1994: 351).
13 Majone (1994).
14 Nugent (1994: 431–2).
15 A. Jordan (2000, 2002); Marks *et al.* (1996); Scharpf (1994: 227); Weale *et al.* (2000).
16 Arp (1995).
17 Mol and Liefferink (1993: 28–31); Weale (1992a: 33).
18 W. Wallace (1987).
19 Keohane and Hoffmann (1991: 10).
20 H. Wallace (1987: 44).
21 Risse-Kappen (1996: 56).
22 Burley (1993: 233).
23 For a review see Cram (1996) and Rosamond (2000).
24 Featherstone (1994); Hayward (1996); Monnet (1980).
25 Hayward (1996); Weale (1999).
26 Nugent (1994: 144).
27 E. Haas (1975). The EU's first Environmental Action Programme (CEC 1973) was published in December 1973.
28 A. Jordan (1997: 46). See also Taylor (1983: 215).
29 Hayward (ed.) (1996); Hix (1994, 1998); Jachtenfuchs and Kohler-Koch (eds) (1996); A. Jordan (1997, 1998a, 1998b); Page (1997); Peters (1992, 1996, 1997); Peterson (1995a, 1995b, 1997); Sbragia (ed.) (1992).
30 A second referendum, in May 1993, produced a slim majority in favour of the Maastricht Treaty, which subsequently came into force in November 1993.
31 However, this claim is rejected by both realist IR and pluralist CP approaches.
32 Moravcsik (1991, 1993).
33 Peterson (1995a).
34 Keohane and Hoffman (1991: 10–11).
35 Sandholtz (1992).
36 Weale *at al.* (2000).
37 Taylor (1996).
38 Andersen and Liefferink (eds) (1997); Arp (1995); Héritier *et al.* (1994, 1996); Holzinger (1994); Knill and Lenschow (eds) (2000); Liefferink and Andersen (eds) (1997); Weale *et al.* (1996, 2000); Wurzel (1996a, 2000, 2001); Zito (2000).
39 Weale (1996a: 602).
40 Bulmer (1994: 355).
41 Almond (1989); Rustow and Erickson (eds) (1991: 448).
42 Armstrong and Bulmer (1998: 50); Hix (1994 , 1998); Hurrell and Menon

(1996); A. Jordan (1997); Risse-Kappen (1996); Schumann (1996: 39); H. Wallace (1996a: 11).
43 Weale (1992a: 32).
44 Rowlands (1992, 1994); Young (1989, 1993).
45 Strange (1983).
46 Krasner (1983: 2).
47 North (1990).
48 Young (1993: 145).
49 Liefferink *et al.* (eds) (1993); Weale (1992a: 190–207).
50 W. Wallace (1987).
51 Underdal and Hanf (eds) (1999).
52 Hurrell and Menon (1996: 391).
53 Andersen and Liefferink (1997: 19).
54 Hayward (1991); Marin and Mayntz (eds) (1991); Marsh and Rhodes (eds) (1992); Wilks and Wright (eds) (1987).
55 Arp (1995); Demmke (1994); Héritier (1993); Héritier *et al.* (1994, 1996); Huber (1997); Liefferink (1996); Peterson and Bomberg (1999); Porter (1997); Richardson (1994).
56 The classical definition of pluralism and corporatism can be found in Schmitter (1974).
57 Simon Bulmer (1994: 83) has called it the 'Kama Sutra' problem.
58 Börzel (1998); Héritier (ed.) (1993); G. Jordan (1990); Marin and Mayntz (eds) (1991); Marsh and Rhodes (eds) (1992). However, Hayward (1991) and Wilks and Wright (eds) (1987) use the term policy network to assess the interaction patterns between different policy communities.
59 Heclo and Wildavsky (1974: xv).
60 Strange and Stopford (1991).
61 Hayward (1986, 1991).
62 Hayward (1986: 39–55, 1991: 401).
63 Marin and Mayntz (1991).
64 Risse-Kappen (1996: 62).
65 Demmke (1994); Héritier (1993: 435); Héritier *et al.* (1996: 7); Liefferink (1996); Peterson (1992, 1995a, 1995b); Peterson and Bomberg (1999); Porter (1997).
66 Mazey and Richardson (1992: 112).
67 Hix (1994: 13).
68 Josselin (1996: 298); Marsh and Rhodes (1993: 262); Peterson (1995a).
69 Dowding (1995). See also Beyme (1997).
70 Beyme (1997).
71 Bohne (1992: 191).
72 Woolcock *et al.* (1991: 5).
73 Armstrong and Bulmer (1998); A. Jordan (1999a, 2000, 2002); Pierson (1998); Pierson and Leibfried (1995: 10); Sandholtz and Stone Sweet (eds) (1998).

74 Hajer (1995: 140).
75 P. Haas (1995: 179).
76 H. Wallace (1996a: 22).
77 P. Haas (1995: 188).
78 Dudley and Richardson (1996: 69); Rowlands (1992, 1995); Sabatier (1993, 1998).
79 Sabatier (1998: 115).
80 Jenkins-Smith and Sabatier (1993: 6). See also Sabatier (1993, 1998, 1999).
81 Sabatier (1993: 35).
82 Hucke (1985: 384); Jenkins-Smith and Sabatier (1993); Kingdon (1995: 165); Sabatier (1993, 1998, 1999).
83 Jenkins-Smith and Sabatier (1993: 48).
84 Jordan and Greenaway (1999); Schumann (1996).
85 Sabatier (1998).
86 Sabatier (1993: 27).
87 Jordan and Greenaway (1999).
88 Arp (1995): Héritier *et al.* (1994, 1996); Majone (1994); Majone (ed.) (1996).
89 Jachtenfuchs (1995); P. Haas (1990, 1992, 1995); H. Wallace (1996a); Weale (1993).
90 Weale (1993: 200).
91 Mol and Liefferink (1993: 99).
92 Armstrong and Bulmer (1998); Kitschelt (1991: 459); Pierson (1998).
93 Dolowitz and Marsh (2000).
94 Sabatier (1993, 1998).
95 Héritier (1996); Héritier *et al.* (1994, 1996); Sbragia (1996); Vogel (1995).
96 Mazey and Richardson (1993b).
97 Similarly Weale (1996a: 607).
98 Héritier (ed.) (1993).
99 Bulmer (1994); Weale *et al.* (2000).
100 Prittwitz (1984).
101 Lindberg and Scheingold (1970).
102 Paul Sabatier (1993, 1998, 1999) convincingly argues that public policy should be studied over a period of at least one decade.
103 A. Jordan (1997); Richardson (1996b); Taylor (1991: 78); H. Wallace (1996b: 15).
104 Demmke (1994: 22); Siedentopf and Ziller (eds) (1988).
105 Heritier *et al.* (1994, 1996); Knill and Lenschow (1998).
106 HoL (1992, 1997); Weale *et al.* (2000: 324).
107 Hayward (1991: 386).
108 DETR (1998a: Foreword).
109 *Directive 76/160/EEC*, OJ No. L 31, 5 February 1976, p. 1.
110 Haigh (ed.) (1995: 4.3).

111 Bachrach and Baratz (1962).
112 A. Jordan (1999a); Pierson (1998).
113 Andersen and Liefferink (eds) (1997); Héritier *et al.* (1994 , 1996); Liefferink and Andersen (eds) (1997); Sbragia (1996); Weale *et al.* (1991, 1996, 2000); Wurzel (1996a, 2001). See already Bungarten (1978).
114 However, see Bungarten (1978); Weale *et al.* (1991, 2000).

3

The European Union environmental governance system

EU policy-making is organised primarily along functional lines. With the exception of the European Council and the ECJ, all official EU institutions are geared towards a sectoral mode of decision-making. This helps to avoid politically divisive grand-scale zero-sum conflicts (where the winner takes all), but can give rise to disjointed decision-making which is unable to take into consideration the requirements of a cross-cutting policy such as environmental policy.[1]

The legal fiction of the Council of Ministers as a collective decision-making body still exists, although in practice it has given way to a 'hydra-headed conglomerate of a dozen or more functional Councils'.[2] As a rule, EU environmental policy measures are negotiated by the Environmental Council, although other technical councils increasingly have to deal with environmental requirements which, since the Single European Act (SEA) came into force in 1987, must be integrated into other EU policies.[3] The Commission, which has the formal right to initiate EU legislation, adopts its proposals by common consent within the College of Commissioners. However, most of the drafting for environmental proposals usually will have been undertaken by officials from the Directorate General for Environment (DG Environment). The EP initially had only consultative powers but was given real legislative clout with the introduction of the cooperation and co-decision procedures. The EP adopts its position on a particular environmental dossier by majority voting within plenary sessions. However, the rapporteur's report from Environmental Committee often gets approval subject to modifications in the plenum.

It is possible to conceptualise the Environment Council, the DG Environment and the EP's Environmental Committee as part of an EU-wide environmental policy network, despite existing institutional rivalries and differences in policy aims and problem-solving strategies. Another core actor is the ECJ whose pro-integrationist case law greatly helped to pave the way for a common environmental policy which was not explicitly mentioned in the EC/EEC Treaty prior to 1987. The EEA, which was formally set up only in 1996, has also been trying hard to become a core actor. Non-governmental actors, including environmental groups (such as the EEB) and corporate actors affected by EU environmental legislation, also form part of the EU environmental policy network.

The Economic and Social Committee (ECOSOC) and the Committee of Regions are official EU institutions which must be consulted before common environmental legislation can be adopted. However, both institutions have remained on the periphery of the EU environmental policy network.

European Council

The European Council, which is made up of the heads of state and government, cannot itself adopt legislation, although it can resolve political stalemate paralysing decision-making in one of the technical councils (such as the Environmental Council). It can also launch new political initiatives. The official signal for the start of the common environmental policy was given by the heads of state and government at their Paris meeting in October 1972.[4]

However, the European Council can also put the brakes on European integration. The Edinburgh European Council, which took place under the British Presidency in December 1992, issued a declaration on the principle of subsidiarity which was aimed at curtailing the legislative activism of the Commission and technical councils. The British and French governments subsequently jointly submitted an unofficial hit-list containing twenty-four items of EU legislation earmarked for repatriation; seven of these were environmental policy measures, including the bathing water directive. The German government also drew up a hit-list but it was much shorter and contained only one environmental item (a directive on zoos). However, the BMU had to fight hard to dissuade the Economics Ministry from listing the bathing water directive, which had been included on an earlier BMWi internal draft.[5] In the end, only the proposal for a directive on zoos was withdrawn and no existing item of EU environmental legislation was repatriated.[6] EU environmental policy nevertheless entered a

defensive phase in 1992 from which it had still not fully recovered at
the beginning of the twenty-first century.

Environmental Council

The Environmental Council is a latecomer in comparison to most
other technical Councils. However, the frequency of its meetings has
increased since its inauguration in 1973 (see figure 3.1).

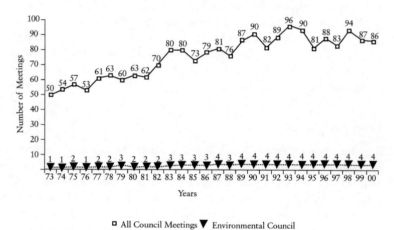

□ All Council Meetings   ▼ Environmental Council

Figure 3.1 *Number of Council of Minister meetings, 1973–2000*

Source: Council Secretariat

Helen Wallace has argued that

> The Council is both a European institution and the prisoner of the
> member states, or perhaps rather of the member governments ... The
> remarkable growth of the Council with its vertical segments and hori-
> zontal layers reveals two paradoxical trends. On the one hand, the
> extension of policy authority to a process of European governance
> demands more and more of the energy of delegates from the member
> governments in the Council, better Councils, with ministerial partici-
> pants and thousands of national officials. The intensity and intimacy
> of their involvement is unparalleled at the transnational level. Yet, on
> the other hand, this engagement is also an effort to control the content
> and direction of European policies and to subject the Commission to
> continuous and detailed scrutiny.[7]

The Council meetings are prepared by the Brussels-based Committee of Permanent Representation (COREPER) officials and Council working groups which are dominated by national officials. This has led to a well-documented process of *engrenage* during which national bureaucracies have become increasingly drawn into the EU policy-making process.[8]

Germany's Environmental Council representation

The German Environmental minister's entourage for Council meetings has often reached the 'size of a football team'.[9] Since it was set up in 1986, the BMU – and before then the Interior Ministry (BMI) – has been the lead department on environmental dossiers negotiated within the Environmental Council. However, for economically important dossiers the BMWi usually has also been represented. Frequently, other ministries and (since a constitutional change in 1992) the German *Länder* have also insisted on direct representation.

The size of the German delegation can largely be explained by the relative independence enjoyed by individual ministries which creates the need for other ministers and especially the chancellor, who issues the policy guidelines (*Richtlinienkompetenz*), to keep cabinet colleagues in check.[10] One BMU official pointed out that 'representatives from other Ministries are sent to Environmental Council meetings to write down every word said by the Environment Minister. If he has not towed the line agreed on by the Cabinet they will rush home to go and tell the Chancellor.'[11] British officials in particular are often critical of what they perceive as the inability of the German government to arrive at a clear national position for Council negotiations.[12]

Conflicts between the BMU and BMWi in the environmental field are due to both institutional and party ideological factors. The BMWi has traditionally perceived itself as the champion of the social market economy and industry's ally. The BMU, which was set up only in 1986, started to embrace the concept of ecological modernisation, particularly during Klaus Töpfer's (CDU) reign as minister (1987–94) as well as under its first Green Environmental minister, Jürgen Trittin, who came to office in 1998, although the latter has shown little interest in EU environmental policy.[13]

Under the Centre–Right (CDU/CSU/FDP) coalition government between 1982–98, the BMU was always headed by a CDU politician while the BMWi was in the hands of the FDP. The FDP had a strong environmental profile until 1982 when it left the Centre–Left (SPD–FDP) coalition which had lasted from 1969 to 1982.[14] Within the succeeding Centre–Right coalition government, the Liberals toned down their 'green' credentials.[15]

In 1998 a Red–Green (SPD–Alliance '90/Greens) coalition government came to power. This has not put an end to party ideological conflicts between the BMWi and BMU. Werner Müller, who is a former manager without party affiliation, was nominated by the SPD to become Economics Minister and Jürgen Trittin, from (the fundamentalist wing of) the Green party, was made Environmental Minister. Chancellor Schröder (SPD) occasionally intervened on behalf of the BMWi in order to halt what he perceived as Trittin's anti-business political stance. This conflict occasionally even spilled over on to the EU level.[16]

Another domestic institutional actor which usually also plays a central role during the domestic and EU environmental policy-making process is the Federal Environmental Agency (UBA). The UBA, which was founded in 1974, undertakes much of the technical and scientific work on environmental issues for the German government. Formally, the UBA is answerable to the BMU, although it has a reputation for being a fairly independently minded agency which does not hesitate to criticise the government.

Britain's Environmental Council representation
Britain is generally seen as having a well co-ordinated national position at the EU level.[17] In Britain the 'first past the post' electoral system rarely produces coalition governments, a feature which makes it easier to keep a 'prime ministerial lid' on inter-ministerial disputes and ensures that they cannot spill over on to the EU level.[18] Under consecutive Conservative governments (1979–97), intra-party ideological conflicts about Britain's role within the EU gradually intensified, with the 'Eurosceptics' increasingly gaining the upper hand. Some EU environmental policy issues were therefore framed by Britain's Conservative governments in such a way that they were relegated to secondary importance while sovereignty and EU integration issues took on primary importance. One example is Britain's stern opposition to the Commission's proposal for an EU-wide CO_2/energy tax, although this faded marginally when a Labour government under Prime Minister Tony Blair came to power in 1997.

Up to the late 1980s, the politicisation of environmental issues was low, which explains why the House of Lords played a more important role overall than the House of Commons in scrutinising EU environmental law.[19] The House of Lords Select Committee on the European Communities (HLSCEC) and, to a lesser degree, the House of Commons Environmental Committee (HCEC) frequently criticised the British government for its failure to adopt a more constructive position on EU environmental policy.[20]

Conflicts between the Deptartment of Trade and Industry (DTI), which took on a sponsoring role for Industry, and the DoE–DETR–DEFRA are common. However, in comparison to the German BMU, the DoE in particular was in a much weaker position at the domestic and EU levels for three major reasons. First, for a long time the adoption of environmental policy measures was favoured by British governments only once they had passed the cost-effectiveness test imposed by the powerful Treasury and the prime minister. The Treasury's important role in the environmental policy field can be explained by Britain's relatively poor economic performance until the 1990s and the dominant monetarist ideology under various Conservative governments which perceived environmental regulation mainly as a cost burden for industry. Second, the DoE was 'not a ministry whose sole, or even primary purpose [was] the protection of the environment'.[21] The environmental section of the DoE was relatively small, and other issues (such as the controversial 'poll tax') attracted considerably more attention from the DoE's Secretaries of State.[22] The various departmental reorganisations, which involved the amalgamation of the environment sections of the former DoE into DETR in 1997 and DEFRA in 2001 (see Chapter 1), brought about no fundamental change in this regard. DETR and DEFRA's Secretaries of State remained pre-occupied with topics other than environmental and the junior Environment Minister, Michael Meacher, failed to get Cabinet representation. Third, on several important EU environmental dossiers – such as the car emission dossiers of which the Department of Transport (DoT) was in charge – the DoE was not actually the lead department although the dossier was negotiated within the Environmental Council.

A unified Environmental Agency for England and Wales was set up only in 1996; Scotland and Northern Ireland have their own regulatory agencies. Prior to the Environmental Agency, competences were scattered between various agencies. Environment Agency officials often complain that they are held at arms length by the DoE–DETR–DEFRA as regards direct participation in Council negotiations.[23]

Decision-making within the Environmental Council
EU environmental legislation is adopted by the Environmental Council. Since the SEA came into force in 1987, qualified majority voting (QMV) became applicable under the internal market provision.[24] It was extended (subject to certain exceptions)[25] to include the environmental chapter by various Treaty amendments which have since taken place.[26]

The 1987 SEA is often portrayed as a major breakthrough for EU environmental policy-making because it (re)introduced QMV. However, Josef Weiler's argument about the 'shadow of the vote',[27] that is, the threat of a vote being called at any time during a Council meeting, carries little weight in the Environmental Council, where formal voting rarely takes place.[28] Weiler has further argued that the absence of a formal vote makes little difference because the Presidency informally counts the votes while negotiations are in progress until the necessary majority exists, at which point it declares the dossier as adopted. However, Helen Wallace has countered this argument by pointing out that the SEA brought about a more subtle change, in that

> the definition of consensus-building shifted from being a wooden insistence on unanimity to being a process of persuading the reluctant to shift position or to abandon opposition. This resulted less from insistence on votes than from the proponents of a policy working harder to accommodate the concerns of the reluctant within their preferred policy.[29]

Helen Wallace's argument explains well the plethora of tailor-made derogations, escape clauses and the phasing in of implementation deadlines which are characteristic of much of the EU's environmental legislation. It also resolves the puzzle of why there was no significant increase in the number of items of EU environmental legislation adopted in the years immediately after the SEA came into force, in 1987, as can be seen from figure 3.2.

Commission

The Commission has the formal monopoly to initiate EU legislation and can take member states to the ECJ. It therefore occupies a central node within the EU policy network.[30] However, the Council occasionally puts pressure on the Commission to (re)submit a proposal, while the 1999 Maastricht Treaty granted the EP the right to request legislative proposals.

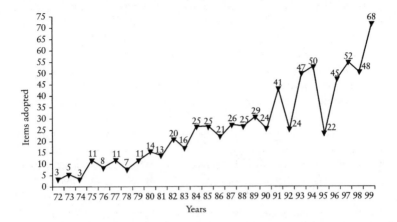

Figure 3.2 *EU environmental legislation adopted during 1972–99*

Sources: Haigh (ed.)(1995) and written communication from the IEEP in 2000

Internal organisation and the politics of staffing

In the late 1990s twenty commissioners were in charge of twenty-three DGs. Tensions between different commissioners and DGs are a common feature of EU policy-making. In the environmental field they have occurred between DG Environment and DG Industry in particular.

The Commission's reliance on seconded national officials and consultants is partly due to internal recruitment patterns, which favour generalists.[31] DG Environment has built up an extensive array of *ad hoc* and permanent (advisory, consultation and management) committees to gain the expertise needed for the drafting of often highly technical environmental policy proposals.

The parachuting in of national civil servants to strategic positions within the Commission is a well known fact.[32] The British government has a reputation for being a master of this art, while German civil servants are more reluctant to accept temporary postings to Brussels.[33] As Andrew Jordan has shown, in the 1990s the British government took measures (such as fast-track promotion) which encouraged civil servants to work temporarily for an EU institution in Brussels in order to gain a better understanding of EU policy-making.[34] The German government, on the other hand, failed to adopt similar measures.

In the 1980s, German nationals occupied several heads of unit posts within DG Environment. However, their numbers dropped after the resignation and downgrading of several German DG Environment heads of unit in the 1990s which caused considerable concern within the BMU and made headlines in the German press.[35] The German 'underrepresentation' within DG Environment was even the subject of a meeting between German understate secretaries responsible for European Affairs (Europaunterstaatssekretäre) in 1996.[36]

The recent shift in DG Environment's preferred environmental regulatory style towards the increased use of procedural measures, framework directives and EQOs based on cost-effective considerations in place of UELs derived from the BAT principle was, at least partly, attributed by several BMU and UBA officials to the lack of adequate German representation within DG Environment.[37] Some German BMU officials detected a distinctly 'British flavour' to certain proposals coming out of DG Environment in the 1990s.[38]

Several BMU and UBA officials expressed particular concern about the downgrading of the Legal Unit within DG Environment, not least because its energetic head Ludwig Krämer was moved sideways to the Waste Unit. In early 2001, Krämer, who to the dismay of the packaging industry in particular refused to temper his environmental zeal, was once again moved - this time to a newly created (relatively small) unit entitled Environmental Governance. Krämer's latest move was instigated within a major reorganisation of DG Environment that was carried out under its outgoing British director general, Jim Currie, who was considerably more open to industry concerns than most of his predecessors. Krämer arrived at DG Environment in the mid-1980s and soon became nicknamed 'the Sheriff'[39] because of his uncompromising stance *vis-à-vis* member governments which had failed to implement EU environmental legislation. British officials who were used to a more pragmatic and consensual domestic implementation style soon became highly irritated by what they saw as Krämer's inflexibility.[40]

However, Krämer, who took a tough stance towards all member governments in breach of EU laws, did not have many friends within the German federal or *Länder* governments either (apart from BMU and UBA officials), because no member state wants to be seen as having flouted the rules. The highly regarded *Environment Watch: Western Europe* put forward the following observation:

Krämer's unit had its heyday between 1989 and 1992 as the environment commissioner at the time, Carlo Ripa di Meana, aggressively and publicly pursued member states over alleged infringements of environmental legislation, sometimes holding news conferences on the issue with Krämer at his side. But since Britain started to push for greater subsidiarity in the EU environmental policy and other areas in 1992, the Commission has been reluctant to risk antagonizing member states and has kept a strikingly lower profile in infringement cases.[41]

Environmental commissioners

Commissioners take an oath to act in the 'European interest' and to 'neither seek nor take instructions from any government'.[42] However, the fact that, up until the European Council in Nice in 2000, the five big member states (Britain, France, Germany, Italy and Spain) refused to give up their second commissioner (the other member states can nominate only one commissioner) revealed the extent to which member governments value public service in the 'European interest' being carried out by their nationals.

Karl-Heinz Narjes (1981–85) and Stanley Clinton Davis (1985–89) have been the only German and British nationals respectively who have held the office of environmental commissioner up to now. Narjes jointly held the environment (DG Environment) and industry (DG Industry) portfolios, while Clinton-Davis was commissioner in charge of DGs Environment and Transport. Considering the political salience of environmental issues in Germany, it is surprising that Narjes has been the only German environmental commissioner until now.

It is not only the nationality of the commissioner which matters; his/her party affiliation is important, as can be seen from the frosty relationship between Stanley Clinton-Davis (Labour) and William Waldegrave (Conservative), both of whom were British nationals (the one serving as EU commissioner and the other as a junior minster in the DoE). However, the impact which the party affiliation of particular commissioners has on a Commission proposal is difficult to predict (which is not the same as saying that it does not matter) because they are adopted by common consent.

The flamboyant Italian Carlo Ripa di Meana (1989–92) achieved the highest public profile of any environmental commissioner up to now. At a time of high public environmental awareness, he tried to enlist the help of national environmental groups to aggressively pursue his strategy of shaming member governments into improving their implementation record. This strategy both raised his own public profile and gave him added legitimacy, as he could claim that he acted on behalf of EU citizens who had asked the Commission for help. Ripa di Meana relied heavily on the legal expertise of Ludwig Krämer, and these two men were soon on a collision course with the British government in particular.

The Commission's tough stance on implementation coincided with British environmental policy coming out of a defensive phase. The DoE's Secretaries of State Chris Patten (1989–90) and Michael Heseltine (1990–92) showed a more constructive attitude towards EU environmental policy.[43] Chris Patten and Michael Heseltine both belonged to the dwindling pro-European wing of the Conservative Party and therefore felt aggrieved that their efforts were not being rewarded by the Commission.[44]

British politicians and officials have often maintained that Britain's implementation record is generally a good one, and certainly better than that of most member states.[45] However, the data in table 3.1, which is taken from the Commission's *Annual Reports on Monitoring the Application of Community Law*, shows a somewhat different picture.[46] As regards timely transposition of environmental directives (that is, the adoption of national laws to implement EU legislation), the UK does not belong to the top achievers. Out of twelve EU member states (EU–12), the UK was ranked fourth in 1992, joint-seventh in 1990, 1993 and 1994, and eighth in 1991. Out of fifteen member states (EU–15), the UK was ranked seventh in 1995 and 1996. Germany did somewhat better in the EU–12 ranking by finishing joint-fourth in 1990 and 1991, joint-fifth in 1992 and 1993 and sixth in 1994; in the EU–15 rankings, Germany was joint-second and fifth in 1996 and 1995 respectively.

However, a member state's formal transposition record says little about what happens on the ground. The DG Environment officials interviewed accepted that, overall, Britain's practical implementation record is a good one.[47] On the other hand, Britain's transposition record on environmental directives is worse than its transposition record for the total number of all EU directives applicable. This suggests that in Britain environmental directives have not been taken as seriously as have the internal market directives which make up the bulk of the total number of directives listed in table 3.1; for Germany, it has been the other way round.

Adrienne Héritier and colleagues have argued that in the 1990s the

Table 3.1 *Transposition (%) of EU directives*

| | Timely transposition of environmental directives[a] | | | | | | |
Member state	1990	1991	1992	1993	1994	1995	1996
Britain	91[95]	85[95]	93[93]	90[92]	82[89]	93[95]	94[94]
Germany	92[95]	92[93]	92[90]	91[89]	91[91]	94[93]	96[94]
Belgium	86[92]	81[88]	94[91]	91[91]	85[90]	83[89]	86[93]
Denmark	99[97]	98[97]	99[96]	98[95]	100[98]	98[98]	96[98]
Greece	79[85]	76[90]	86[88]	84[88]	85[87]	88[90]	91[91]
Spain	92[94]	92[92]	91[90]	90[90]	86[91]	90[93]	94[95]
France	92[94]	89[95]	96[93]	95[89]	94[92]	95[93]	93[92]
Ireland	87[91]	84[89]	90[91]	88[89]	97[92]	95[93]	96[93]
Italy	63[82]	59[77]	83[89]	81[89]	76[88]	85[89]	85[90]
Luxembourg	89[90]	86[87]	92[88]	92[91]	93[94]	92[94]	96[93]
Netherlands	97[93]	95[90]	97[93]	92[92]	98[94]	98[97]	98[97]
Portugal	95[84]	94[86]	89[89]	90[92]	82[97]	87[90]	94[92]
Austria	–	–	–	–	–	92[84]	94[88]
Finland	–	–	–	–	–	87[71]	86[81]
Sweden	–	–	–	–	–	94[93]	95[94]

Note: The figures are rounded. [a] Figures in brackets refer to the timely transposition of the total of EU directives applicable
Sources: CEC (1991a: III and 82; 1992a: III and 66; 1993a: 7 and 139; 1994a: 7 and 83; 1995a: VI and 72; 1996a: 2 and 91; 1997a: 17 and 107)

British government brought about a change in the Commission's preference from BAT-derived UELs to cost-effective measures derived from EQOs as well as framework directives.[48]

However, there were also other reasons why DG Environment altered its preferred standard-setting approach, the most important of which can be summarised as follows: first, the debate about the principle of subsidiarity led to a search for less intrusive policy measures; second, severe economic recession in Europe made the Commission and member governments more cost-conscious about the (short-term) effects of environmental regulations; third, by the 1990s, EU environmental policy had matured as a policy field and was undergoing a review within a changed political context; fourth, DG Environment's internal re-organisation, which was partly a reaction to the changed wider policy and political context, facilitated a new approach to EU environmental policy.[49]

The departure of Environmental Commissioner Ripa di Meana and the Dutch Director-General Laurens Brinkhorst, who resigned in 1992 and 1995 respectively, left DG Environment's Legal Unit, and especially its head Ludwig Krämer, open to attacks from powerful opponents. The Legal Unit was subsequently downgraded within DG Environment and Krämer was moved 'sideways', against his will. On 3 February 1995 *Environment Watch: Western Europe* reported:

> Krämer's effective demotion after 10 years in the job and the downgrading of his unit are widely seen as politically motivated revenge by national governments for his strict interpretation of EU environmental laws and his uncompromising pursuit in the European Court of Justice of member states that fail to properly transpose or implement them.

British government officials were pleased with DG Environment's new organisational outlook.[50] And one DG Industry official commented: 'I would have sacked Krämer a long time ago if I had been his boss.'[51]

Sixty prominent European environmental lawyers, including several eminent lawyers from Britain (such as Richard Macrory, who later became a member of the RCEP), thought differently and signed a declaration to get Krämer reinstated.[52] All efforts to reverse the Commission's decision came to no avail. The EEB, which is a Brussels-based umbrella group representing more than 100 groups, presented Krämer with its Twelve Stars Award 1995 after his departure from the Legal Unit. The EEB's eulogy stated: 'In an era of deregulation, the EEB wants to underline the importance of civil servants' role. Citizens are expecting civil servants to be loyal to the people. The work done by Mr Krämer is of the kind that would contribute significantly to reconcile civil society and public authorities.'[53]

The fuss and fury about Krämer's actions reflected a conflict about the role of Commission officials within the EU environmental policy-making process as well as a deep-seated dispute about different environmental regulatory styles.

European Parliament

The EP's Environmental Committee has often been seen as DG Environment's natural ally.[54] Prior to the SEA, the EP only had a consultation right, although it tried to act as an agenda-setter.[55] The introduction of the cooperation and the co-decision procedures has increased its powers and altered the EP's relationship *vis-à-vis* other EU institutions. The co-decision procedure in particular has increased the EP's influence at the expense of the Commission because in the Conciliation Committee the EP and Council negotiate directly with each other. The Conciliation Committee has been used only sparingly, although it is most widely used in the environmental field where the EP wants to keep a high public profile.[56]

As a rule, party ideological distinctions have overriden national differences within the EP since the 1990s. However, the exceptions tend to get ever more numerous the more important in economic terms, a particular environmental dossier is for a particular member state. The British case is special due to the fact that until 1992 MEPs from the Conservative Party remained aloof from the European People's Party (EPP) which represents mainstream continental Christian Democracy rather than *laissez-faire* and/or libertarian values which dominated the British Conservatives during much of the 1980s and 1990s. British Labour MEPs, on the other hand, joined the Socialist Party group when Britain became an EU member state and held a number of influential posts within the environmental field. Ken Collins was the chairperson of the EP's Environmental Committee for fifteen years, until he retired in 1999. His post was taken over by Caroline Jackson (UK, Conservatives), who became the first chairperson of the Environmental Committee from the EPP. The German Socialist Beate Weber (1984–89) was the only other chairperson since the EP's Environmental Committee was set up in 1979.

The EP suffers from what David Judge and colleagues have called the 'technological deficit'.[57] MEPs therefore often approach national environmental agencies or environmental groups for information on environmental dossiers.

Non-governmental actors

Neofunctionalist theory predicted that over time, interest groups would gradually shift their attention to the European level and in particular the Commission.[58] However, empirical research has shown that (well-resourced) interest groups often conduct lobbying at both the domestic and EU levels.[59]

Environmental lobby
The EEB, which was founded in 1974, is the most important player
among the Brussels-based environmental lobby. However, Friends
of the Earth (FOE) (1986), Greenpeace (1988), the World Wide Fund
for Nature (WWF) and Climate Action Network (both 1989), Transport & Environment (1992) and BirdLife International (1993) have
also all opened their own Brussels offices.[60] The EEB and the new
arrivals meet up regularly to coordinate their strategies.

The EEB's activities are financed by its constituent member groups,
the Commission and sympathetic member governments. The EEB has
close links with the EP's Environmental Committee. The links between
the EEB and DG Environment had been close until the early 1990s,
when it changed somewhat, partly because of DG Environment's
'softly, softly' approach. Another reason was that environmental
NGOs pushed harder for the integration of environmental requirements into other policy areas and therefore had more direct contact
with officials from other DGs.[61]

In the early 1990s, Christian Hey and Uwe Brendle argued that
German environmental groups are less compromising with regard to
their principled beliefs and less interested in direct lobbying than their
British counterparts, who tend to be more success-oriented campaig-
ners.[62] However, the attitudes of German environmental groups have
since changed. The German Nature Circle (Deutscher Naturschutzring – DNR) has edited the well-researched monthly *EU
Rundschreiben* (*EU Circular*) which focuses mainly on EU environmental policy. The growing attention paid to EU environmental policy
by German environmental groups is due both to the increased importance of the EU for German environmental policy and the fact
that post-unification Germany has lost much of its environmental
leader status.

The activism of British environmental groups at the EU level is
often explained as a function of the low priority awarded to environmental issues in Britain.[63] However, Tony Long and others have
pointed out that British environmental groups have always been highly
active regardless of the attitude of the government of the day.[64] British
environmental groups launched the highest number of complaints
about alleged non-implementation of EU environmental legislation in
the late 1980s and early 1990s (although this was no longer the case
in the late 1990s).[65]

Epistemic communities

Epistemic communities can play an important role in environmental policy-making.[66] However, they have been largely ignored within the existing EU environmental policy literature, although policy actors rely heavily on new scientific findings and policy ideas when trying to influence EU environmental policy-making. It is therefore not surprising that there was an upsurge in environmental research institutes, think-tanks and consultancies as the importance of EU environmental policy increased.

EU institutional actors (and especially the Commission and the EP) but also NGOs often have to rely on outside experts for highly technical EU dossiers. These experts can, in turn, act as policy entrepreneurs or policy spoilers, for which they often quickly get an EU-wide reputation. Often 'trusted relationships' develop between EU institutional actors and policy experts which allows the former to informally ask for feedback on highly technical dossiers during the policy-formulation stage.

The British House of Lords has criticised the Commission's consultation process for its lack of transparency.[67] This is not to argue that the British and German governments always rely on transparent consultation processes. However, independent environmental agencies and expert councils such as the British Environment Agency and the RCEP, as well as the German UBA and the Environmental Expert Council (Sachverständigenrat für Umweltfragen – SRU), which attract widespread attention in the domestic media when they criticise government policies, are missing at the European level or have different functions.

In 1993, the Commission set up a consultative forum on environmental issues which is made up mainly of industry and union representatives, scientists, environmental groups and local authority officials. However, its membership is very heterogenous and its workplan is largely unstructured. The EEA has been unable to take up a more activist role partly because DG Environment has kept it at arms length for fear that it may take away some of the Commission's powers.[68]

European media

Advocacy coalitions, as defined by Paul Sabatier, include actors as varied as elected politicians, agency officials, interest group leaders, researchers and journalists.[69] All of these actors are present at the EU level. However, one of the weakest core actors within the EU environmental policy advocacy coalition is the media. There is no

EU-wide popular press or television, and it is difficult to envisage such a development in the near future. There is only an embryonic European media which caters for a small elite. This places at a structural disadvantage environmental groups which (in contrast to corporate actors) often rely heavily on the media to generate public and political support for their aims.

The industrial lobby

The involvement of corporate actors in EU environmental policy-making will be assessed in more detail in the case studies, as it can vary considerably from sector to sector. At this stage, it is sufficient to note that corporate actors play a very important role in EU policy-making, as can be seen from the fact that the relaunch of the internal market project ('1992') has been attributed to interest group pressure.[70]

In comparison to environmental groups, industry is significantly better organised and resourced at the EU level. Most major national and transnational companies have their own Brussels offices in addition to sector-specific and industry-wide European umbrella groups. It should not, however, be overlooked that industry is not a homogenous actor either. Industrial Euro-umbrella groups have remained weak despite attempts by the Commission to foster transborder links and to grant them privileged access.[71]

Splits within industry have often occurred between those corporate actors which specialise in pollution abatement technology and others which are unable or unwilling to invest in more advanced environmental technologies. The main line of conflict within EU environmental policy-making may therefore not always run between environmental NGOs and industry but between reform-minded NGOs and 'corporate environmental leaders', on the one hand, and radical environmental groups and 'corporate environmental laggards', on the other. Paradoxically, hard-nosed industrialists who show little concern about the environment may find themselves in the same camp as radical environmentalists, both arguing that tinkering with the market system will not lead to an improvement of living conditions within the EU.

Linking the different levels and actors

EU environmental policy-making is a multilevel activity for which special instruments, procedures and programmes have been devised over time to link the core policy actors who operate on different levels.

Legal instruments

There are three main legal instruments by means of which binding EU environmental legislation can be adopted: directives; regulations; and decisions. Regulations and decisions are directly applicable. However, the overwhelming majority of EU environmental legislation consists of directives which must be formally transposed by national legislation ('formal transposition') before they are implemented on the ground ('practical implementation'). Directives grant member governments considerable flexibility as regards the integration of EU legislation into the existing body of national environmental laws.[72] Directives became the most commonly used legal instrument mainly because environmental policy was not explicitly mentioned in the EC/EEC Treaty prior to the SEA, which came into force in 1987. Common environmental policy measures therefore had to be based primarily on the internal market provision, which allowed for the harmonisation of member state legislation that posed a threat to the functioning of the internal market.[73] The contested 'implied powers' doctrine, which was contained in another Treaty provision, was the other main alternative legal base.[74]

Another legal provision which granted member governments the right to adopt 'prohibitions or restrictions on imports, exports or goods in transit ... on the grounds of the protection of health and life of humans, animals or plants', could have provided the most important legal base for nationally more stringent environmental measures.[75] However, the dominant legal view was that this provision could be used only in exceptional circumstances (such as an environmental catastrophe) because the free movement of goods, services and people constituted the primary objective on which the EC/EEC Treaty was based.[76]

The EU's adoption rate for legal measures in the environmental field amounted to more than 100 items of legislation prior to 1987, while it stood at almost 700 legal measures by the end of 1999 (see figure 3.1). One of the reasons why the EU was able to move quickly into the environmental field without explicit legal provisions was the Information and Standstill Agreement.

The Information and Standstill Agreement

The Paris Summit, on 19–20 October 1972, is usually credited with having signalled the official start of a common environmental policy.[77] The ministers responsible for environmental issues met for the first

time in Bonn, on 30–31 October 1972 where they adopted a number
of general principles (such as 'the polluter pays' principle) which later
found their way into the first EAP. They also agreed that EU environmental measures could be derived from one of three sources: first,
the Information and Standstill Agreement; second, the EAP; and, third,
the application of appropriate Treaty provisions.[78]

It was the attempt to revitalise the internal market project (or
'negative integration') in the late 1960s which forced the Commission
to pay more attention to national environmental legislation which
threatened the functioning of the internal market. In 1969, the Programme for the Elimination of Technical Obstacles to Trade was
adopted in conjunction with a legally non-binding Information and
Standstill Agreement (Standstill Agreement), the latter of which obliged
member governments to inform the Commission about draft national
legislation with a potential impact on the internal market.[79] Draft
national legislation notified under the Standstill Agreement had to be
put on hold for up to twelve months to allow the Commission to
come up with a proposal for EU legislation instead.

The Standstill Agreement was amended in 1973 to specifically
include draft national environmental legislation after the French
government blocked attempts to amend the Treaty to include explicit
environmental provisions. France was opposed to the extension of
the Commission's powers, and the Standstill Agreement left member
governments in the driving seat.[80] Eckard Rehbinder and Richard
Stewart have therefore argued that during the early phase of EU
environmental policy '[s]trongly environmentalist member states were
more or less able to set the pace and direction for Community action
by unilaterally proposing strong national environmental legislation,
which forced the Community to react with measures of its own'.[81]

More recently other scholars have claimed that the Standstill
Agreement still allows environmental leader states and/or highly
regulatory states to set the EU's agenda.[82] However, this argument
overlooks the fact that the Standstill Agreement was merely a
'gentlemen's agreement' which has never been widely applied by
member governments.[83] It quickly produced a paradoxical effect in
that the more national legislation was notified to the Commission
the less likely the Commission was on average to react to any one
particular national item of legislation. This can be seen from situation reports on the first EAP, which stated that the Commission
had proposed nine common measures on the basis of thirty-three

Table 3.2 *Notifications of national environmental legislation, 1973–77*

Member states	Draft legislation	Administrative measures	International agreements	Others	Total
Britain	6	0	0	0	6
Germany	28	2	2	2	34
Belgium	1	3	1	0	5
Denmark	1	24	4	0	29
France	26	6	3	6	41
Ireland	2	0	0	0	2
Italy	4	0	2	0	6
Netherlands	6	17	0	0	23
Luxembourg	1	0	0	0	1
Total	75	52	12	8	147

Source: SRU (1978: 513)

notifications by June 1974 while the figure merely rose to 16 out of 60 notifications by October 1974.[84] This can be largely attributed to the Commission's limited staff resources and the fact that the Environmental Council is not 'a legal sausage machine'[85] the output of which can be increased easily at the will of ministers. In many cases the Environmental Council was therefore unable to live up to the promise it had given under the first EAP to adopt (or reject) all Commission proposals within nine months.

The Commission put on a brave face when it declared that the Standstill Agreement would make it possible to 'profit from the experience obtained by the Member States and to build cross-links between national laws via Community legislation'.[86] However, these cross-links were not fostered to the same degree with all member states, as can be seen from the data in table 3.2. The environmental leader states Denmark, Germany, and the Netherlands (but also France, which had proposed the extension of the Standstill Agreement) put forward many more notifications than any of the other member states. Britain's low notification rate fits its image as a laggard state and reluctant European partner, but is also due to the fact that statutory legal provisions were largely absent from the British environmental regulatory style up to the late 1980s.

The Environmental Action Programmes

For Eckhard Rehbinder and Richard Stewart, it is '[t]he environmental program of 1973 ... which marks the beginning of a true common environmental policy'.[87] The EAPs define the general policy principles and indicate the medium- to long-term policy aims. However, the first three EAPs in particular lacked clearly defined objectives and failed to stipulate deadlines. They also constituted more of a hotchpotch of ideas and issues which were fashionable at the time and showed little strategic thinking.

At times the EAPs even stipulated unrealistic tasks, one of which was the adoption of environmental legislation derived from EQOs.[88] It was an impossible task mainly because comprehensive ambient environmental quality data simply did not exist at that time. It is telling that the EU's first *State of the Environment Report* was published only in 1977, that is, after the adoption of the second EAP.[89] However, the title of this report was a misnomer as it consisted of little more than a list of pressing environmental problems. The only realistic way of adopting pollution control measures in the absence of reliable ambient environmental quality data was therefore to base them on an emission limits approach which was, in some cases, derived from the BAT principle. Unsurprisingly, most of the early EU environmental legislation was in fact based on an emission limits approach or a parallel approach, as was the case for the dangerous substances directive (76/464/EEC).[90]

Duncan Liefferink has argued that the legally non-binding character of the EAPs made it possible to obtain the inclusion of a broad range of policy issues and measures in the programmes which, strictly speaking, had no legal base under the EC/EEC Treaty.[91] On the other hand, the EAPs' lack of legal clout has meant that they are not widely known outside DG Environment. One DG Industry official responsible for the car emission regulation dossiers commented: 'I have never looked at any of these [Environmental] Action Programmes. Once we [in DG Industry] have sorted out the technical details we leave it up to DG Environment to fill into the "whereas" sections [which state the legal and programmatic basis of a particular Commission proposal] however they like'.[92]

Conclusion

Chapter 3 has identified the EU environmental policy networks' core actors (European Council, Environmental Council, member governments,

Commission, EP, ECJ and non-governmental actors) at the systemic level and assessed their functions within the EU environmental policy-making process. It has been argued that EU environmental policy-making is a multi-level activity for which special tools (such as directives and the legally non-binding Standstill Agreement) have been devised in order to link the activities of the core policy actors who operate on different levels.

Member governments and the Commission are often seen as the most important policy entrepreneurs in the EU environmental policy field. Chapter 3 has shown that this generally holds true, although other institutional actors, the EP in particular, and non-governmental actors can also play an important role. However, successful policy entrepreneurs must overcome the resistance of a wide range of policy spoilers and/or veto actors. Chapter 3 has argued that broader political context variables exogenous to the environmental field (such as the debate about the principle of subsidiarity) can play an important role in determining whether policy entrepreneurs or spoilers/veto actors will succeed. It has also shown that different environmental regulatory styles play an important role during the EU environmental policy-making process.

This chapter has alerted the reader to the fact that policy disputes occasionally cut across EU institutional and non-governmental boundaries as well as national borders. In cases like this, it may be useful to talk of environmental advocacy coalitions which are opposed by economic feasibility coalitions (the latter of which recruit some of their core members from the wider 'policy universe', including the heads of state and government as represented in the European Council). This will be assessed in more detail in the case studies. However, chapter 3 was unable to show that EU environmental advocacy coalitions remain stable over a relatively long period of time. There were relatively strong links between DG Environment and the EP's environmental committee, as well as the EEB during the 1980s, although these weakened in the 1990s.

Deep-seated disputes about EU environmental policy, which may be harbingers of policy change, often cut across EU institutional and non-governmental boundaries, and at least occasionally also across national boundaries. These disputes become apparent within policy networks whose core actors share a common interest in a particular policy issue and/or problem, although they rarely share the same policy aims and problem-solving strategies.

Mikael Andersen and Duncan Liefferink have warned that 'there is not a single and universal network surrounding EU environmental policy, but rather different clusters of networks for different issues'.[93] The policy network analysis is therefore arguably most useful in analytical terms on the (sub)sectoral level where tightly knit policy communities are said to be more common and more differentiated. The degree to which this is indeed the case will be a major focus within the case studies which are assessed in Parts II and III.

Notes

1 Wurzel (1996a: 275, 2001).
2 Pinder (1991: 25).
3 Article 174, EC Treaty (formerly Article 130R, EC/EEC Treaty).
4 *EC Bulletin* 10 (1972: 15–16).
5 Interview with BMU official in 1993.
6 A. Jordan *et al.* (1999).
7 H. Wallace (1996b: 59).
8 Peters (1992, 1997); H. Wallace (1984, 1990a); Wessels (1997).
9 Interview with a German official in 1992. See also Pehle (1997: 198).
10 Wurzel (2000).
11 Interview with a BMU official in 1993.
12 Interviews with DoE officials over 1992–97.
13 See Wurzel (2000).
14 Malunat (1987); Müller (1986).
15 Jahn (1997).
16 Rüdig (2000); Wurzel (2000). Alliance '90/Greens (Forum '90/Die Grünen) is the result of the merger of the (East German) Alliance '90 and the (West German) Green Party which took place following unification.
17 Interviews with German, Austrian, Swedish and Finnish permanent representation officials in 1998.
18 Aspinwall (2000).
19 Weale (1996b, 1997).
20 Haigh (1996).
21 Weale (1996b: 108).
22 A. Jordan (2000, 2002); Weale (1996b).
23 Interviews in 2000.
24 Article 95 EC Treaty (formerly Article 100A EC/EEC Treaty).
25 Article 175 EC Treaty (formerly Article 130S(2) EC/EEC Treaty).
26 Articles 174–6 EC Treaty (formerly Articles 130R–T EC/EEC Treaty).
27 Weiler (1991).

28 H. Wallace (1996b); Weale (1996a); Wurzel (1996a).
29 H. Wallace (1996b: 54).
30 Arp (1995: 213); Majone (1994).
31 Arp (1995); Page (1997).
32 Page (1997).
33 Interviews over 1993–97.
34 A. Jordan (2000, 2002).
35 *Der Spiegel*, 7 September 1992.
36 Interview with BMU official in 1996.
37 Interviews during 1996–97.
38 Interviews with BMU officials during 1995–97.
39 Interview with Stanley Clinton-Davis in 1995.
40 Interviews with British officials over 1992–96.
41 *Environment Watch: Western Europe*, 4: (3): 3.
42 Article 213 EC Treaty (formerly Article 157 EC/EEC Treaty).
43 Jordan and Greenaway (1999).
44 Interview with DoE officials during 1992–93.
45 Interviews with DoE officials over 1992–97.
46 Since 1998, the Commission's implementation reports no longer provide separate data for environmental directives.
47 Interviews during 1992–94 and in 1999.
48 Héritier (1996); Héritier *et al.* (1994, 1996). See also Liefferink (1996).
49 Friedrich *et al.* (2000); Williams (1995).
50 Interviews in 1996.
51 Interview in 1996.
52 *Environment Watch: Western Europe*, 3 February 1995.
53 EEB (1996: 7).
54 Earnshaw and Judge (1995); Judge *et al.* (1994).
55 Earnshaw and Judge (1995, 1996); Judge *et al.* (1994: 32); Tsebelis (1994); Tsebelis and Garret (1997).
56 Interview with the EP's Environmental Committee Chairperson Ken Collins in 1996. See also Wurzel (1996a: 278–9).
57 Judge *et al.* (1994: 46).
58 Haas (1964); Lindberg and Scheingold (1970).
59 Mazey and Richardson (eds) (1993); McLaughlin *et al.* (1993).
60 Long (1998); Webster (1998).
61 Interviews with EEB and WWF representatives in 1998.
62 Hey and Brendle (1994). See also McCormick (1991).
63 Hey and Brendle (1994).
64 Long (1998); McCormick (1991); Mazey and Richardson (1992).
65 Interviews with DG Environment officials over 1992–96 and in 1998.
66 P. Haas (1992).
67 HoL (1997).

68 Interview with an EEA official in 1997.
69 Sabatier (1998, 1999); Sabatier and Jenkins-Smith (eds) (1993).
70 Sandholtz and Zysman (1989).
71 Greenwood (1997); Kohler-Koch (1994); Mazey and Richardson (1992, 1993a, 1993b).
72 However, the ECJ has developed the doctrine of 'direct effect' according to which directives may become directly applicable.
73 Article 95 EC Treaty (formerly Article 100A EC/EEC Treaty).
74 Article 308 EC Treaty (formerly Article 235 EC/EEC Treaty).
75 Article 30 EC Treaty (formerly 36 EC/EEC Treaty).
76 However, see Krämer (1990a, 1990b, 1995).
77 *EC Bulletin* 10 (1972: 15–16).
78 OJ No. C 112/6, 20 December 1973, 7.
79 OJ No. C 76, 17 June 1969, 1 as amended by OJ No. C 117, 31 December 1973, 1.
80 Bungarten (1978: 138).
81 Rehbinder and Stewart (1985a: 17).
82 Héritier (1996); Héritier *et al.* (1994, 1996); Sbragia (1996); Vogel (1995).
83 See Bungarten (1978: 129); Krämer (1995); Rehbinder and Stewart (1985a: 16); Wurzel (1993).
84 SEC(74) 2297, 21 June 1974, 1; and SEC(74) 3889, 26 September 1974, 1.
85 Interview with DoE official in 1993.
86 SEC(74) 2297, 21 June 1974, 10.
87 Rehbinder and Stewart (1985a: 18).
88 CEC (1973: 15–18).
89 CEC (1977a, 1977b).
90 See also chapter 1.
91 Liefferink (1996).
92 Interview in 1992.
93 Andersen and Liefferink (not dated: 21).

Part II
Car emission regulation

The first EU car emission directive (*70/120/EEC*) was agreed on in March 1970.[1] It harmonised German (1968) and French (1969) draft national exhaust emissions legislation which had been passed on to the Commission under the Standstill Agreement of the 1969 general programme for the elimination of technical barriers to trade ...[2] *Directive 70/120/EEC* was adopted by the Internal Market Council three years before the Environmental Council met for the first time.

Since 1970, *Directive 70/120/EEC* has been amended more than ten times on the basis of the internal market provisions of the EC/EEC Treaty.[3] Over time the health and environmental requirements have become more stringent and important although the tension between internal market requirements (elimination of barriers to trade) and environmental protection (ambitious environmental standards) has not subsided. Initially, only petrol cars were regulated while directives targeting diesel cars and the lead content in petrol followed at a later stage.[4] EU emission abatement measures were then extended to cover lorries, vans, motor cycles, off-road vehicle (such as tractors) and heavy machinery tools. This may appear like environmental regulatory overzealousness and an intrusion by the EU into the 'nooks and crannies' of member state affairs. However, the importance of also tackling sources other than cars becomes clear when one considers, for example, that a petrol lawnmower operated for one hour generates as much air pollution as a new car equipped with a three-way catalytic converter and driven for several thousand kilometres.[5] Despite hard-won EU car emission standards and considerable advances in emission abatement technologies, road traffic related pollution continues to give rise to serious health and environmental problems at the beginning of the twenty-first century, after more than thirty years of EU regulatory activities.

Over time, car emission pollutants were also targeted by ambient air quality directives which set health targets and EQOs for air pollutants such as sulphur dioxide (SO_2) and lead (Pb). However, EU car emission standards were not explicitly linked to the achievement of specific health targets and EQOs until the 1990s. Table II.1 lists the EU's car emission and fuel directives as well as the relevant ambient air quality directives.

Table II.1 *EU car emission, fuel and ambient air quality directives*

UNECE car emission regulations and corresponding EU legislation

Petrol cars ECE-R[a] 15–00 of 1.8.1970 transposed into EU *Directive 70/220/EEC*

ECE-R 15–01 of 11.12.1975 transposed into EU *Directive 74/290/EEC*

ECE-R 15–02 of 1.3.1977 transposed into EU *Directive 77/102/EEC*

ECE-R 15–03 of 6.3.1978 transposed into EU *Directive 78/665/EEC*

ECE-R 15–04 of 20.10.1981 transposed into EU *Directive 83/351/EEC*

EU legislation on car emission and fuel standards

Petrol cars *Directive 88/76/EEC* (1985 Luxembourg Compromise) published on 9.2.1988

Directive 89/458/EEC (small cars directive) published on 3.8.1989

Directive 91/441/EEC (consolidated directive or Euro I) published on 30.8.1991

Directive 93/59/EEC (light commercial vehicles) published on 28.7.1993

Directive 94/12/EC (Euro II standards) published on 19.4.1994

Diesel cars *Directive 72/306/EEC* published on 20.8.1972

Directive 88/77/EEC published on 9.2.1988

Directive 89/491/EEC published on 15.8.1989

Directive 91/542/EEC published on 25.10.1991

Fuels *Directive 78/611/EEC* (lead content in petrol) published on 22.7.1978

Directive 85/210/EEC (introduction of unleaded petrol) published on 3.4.1985

Auto-Oil I Programme The Commission publishes the Auto-Oil I Programme on 18 June 1996. The Council and EP adopts a directive (*96/0163/EC*) on mandatory car emission limits for 2000 (Euro III) and 2005 (Euro IV), a directive (*96/0614/EC*) on fuel quality and a directive on vans in June 1998

| Auto-Oil II Programme | In 1997, the Commission initiates the Auto-Oil II Programme which is radically altered after the adoption of mandatory Euro IV standards in June 1998. Commission publishes the Auto-Oil II Programme in October 2000. In early 2001 the Commission announces more stringent sulphur standards for fuels |

EU ambient air quality standards related to pollution from passenger cars

Ambient air quality standards	*Directive 80/779/EEC* (sulphur dioxide and suspended particulates) of 30.8.1980
	Directive 82/884/EEC (lead) published on 31.12.1982
	Directive 85/203/EEC (nitrogen oxides) published on 27.3.1985
	Directive 92/72/EEC (tropospheric ozone) published on 13.10.1992
	Directive 94/63/EEC (volatile organic compounds) published on 31.12.1994

Note: a ECE-Regulation

Part II of this book focuses on the most important phases and critical junctures of EU car emission policy-making. In line with the methodological approach outlined in chapter 2, car emission legislation is treated as reflecting complex compromises agreed on as a result of the need to accommodate the demands of both policy entrepreneurs and policy spoilers/veto actors. The legislative output was taken as a starting-point for identifying the core actors, their interests, strategies, problem perception and preferred standard-setting philosophies. In doing this Part II assesses the role of both policy entrepreneurs and environmental regulatory styles for a policy sector which is of great importance for the EU in environmental and economic terms.

David Vogel has argued that a 'ratcheting upward' of regulatory standards in competing political jurisdictions takes place due to the 'California effect'.[6] California was allowed to take the lead in establishing stricter emission standards in USA. The American standards, in turn, quickly became the benchmark for leading world markets.[7] Chapter 4 therefore traces the origins of car emission regulation inside and outside of Europe, while focusing on Germany in particular. It explains why the main policy-making arena for member state car emission regulations shifted from the United Nations (UN) Economic Commission for Europe (ECE) to the EU level in the early 1980s. Chapter 5 assesses why different EU policy actors favoured two mutually exclusive car emission abatement technologies (the three-way catalytic converter *and* the lean-burn engine) and how the conflict was resolved in the late 1980s. Chapter 6 focuses on the Auto-Oil Programmes which were widely seen as having put forward a new approach to EU car emission policy-making for the twenty-first century.

Notes

1 OJ No. L 76, 6 April 1970.
2 OJ No. C 76, 17 June 1969, 1.
3 Article 95 EC Treaty (formerly Article 100A EC/EEC Treaty and Article 100 EEC Treaty).
4 *Directive 72/306/EEC*, OJ No. L 190, 20 August 1972, and *Directive 78/611/EEC*, OJ No. L 197, 22 July 1978, respectively.
5 *Economist*, 4 March 1995.
6 Vogel (1995: 259, 1997).
7 Vogel (1995, 1997).

4

The origins of car emission regulation

Problem pressures

Car emissions can give rise to serious health problems and environmental damage.[1] The main pollutants traditionally regulated are carbon monoxide (CO), unburnt hydrocarbons (HC) − most of which are volatile organic compounds (VOCs) − and nitrogen oxides (NO_x). Some of these primary pollutants contribute towards secondary pollution such as acid rain, winter smog and high levels of tropospheric ozone (O_3) concentrations (summer smog). Depending on the fuel used, cars may also emit harmful lead, sulphur dioxide (SO_2), benzene or particulate emissions. Carbon dioxide (CO_2), which is widely recognised as a major climate change gas, is formed when fossil fuel is burned.

Table 4.1 lists some of the most important health and environmental problems which can be generated by car emissions. The amount of air pollutants released by cars depends on a range of factors, such as the number of vehicles and their kilometrage. Table 4.2 presents the data for CO, NO_x, VOCs and CO_2 emissions from road transport sources in Britain and Germany between 1970 and 1994. It shows an increase in main traffic-related pollutants in both Britain and Germany despite a tightening of EU car emission regulations since 1970.

Table 4.1 *Health and environmental effects of car emission pollution*

Primary pollutants	Health and environmental risks
Carbon monoxide (CO)	Health risks mainly in urban areas
Volatile organic compounds (VOCs)	Health and environmental risks. Precursor substance for tropospheric ozone (summer smog)
Unburnt hydrocarbons (HC)	Most unburnt hydrocarbons are VOCs and trigger similar detrimental effects
Nitrogen oxides (NO_x)	Precursor substance for winter smog and tropospheric ozone. Contributes towards acid rain
Lead (Pb) in petrol	Health risks
Benzene (in petrol)	Health risks: carcinogenic
Particulates (in diesel)	Health risks: carcinogenic
Sulphur dioxide (SO_2)	Environmental and health risks
Carbon Dioxide (CO_2)	Climate change gas
Secondary pollution	*Primary car pollutants involved*
Winter smog	SO_2 and smoke particles. Health and environmental hazard
Tropospheric ozone (summer smog)	NO_x and VOC react under strong sunlight to form ozone (O_3). Health and environmental hazard
Acid rain	NO_x and SO_2 can cause damage to the environment and buildings
Climate change	CO_2 is a climate change gas

Sources: EEA (1997) and UBA (1997a) and interview information

Table 4.2 *Total emissions from road transport in Britain and Germany, 1970–94*

Country	1970	1975	1980	1983	1985	1990	1992	1994
Carbon monoxide (CO) in 1000 tonnes								
UK[a]	3,300	n/a	4,600	4,400	4,900	5,600	5,200	4,500
	[n/a]	[6,800]	[7,900]	[8,100]				
D	7,400	8,700	7,500	n/a	6,200	5,200	4,100	3,400
Nitrogen oxides (NO$_x$) in 1000 tonnes								
UK[a]	650	n/a	890	959	1,100	1,400	1,300	1,200
	[n/a]	[430]	[490]	[508]				
D	550	810	1,100	n/a	1,200	1,100	1,000	900
Volatile organic compounds (VOCs) in 1000 tonnes								
UK[a]	645	n/a	900	n/a	1,000	1,200	1,100	964
	[n/a]	[450]	[530]	[540]				
D	702	854	943	n/a	933	800	637	506
Carbon dioxide (CO$_2$) emissions in million tonnes								
UK	62	n/a	76	92	95	121	121	n/a
D	68	84	105	n/a	110	150	160	160

Note: [a] The DoT changed its methodology for measuring in-service performance in 1983. The figures in square brackets refer to data published before the changes were made retrospectively
Sources: Adapted from DETR (1997: 9–42), DoT (1986, 1993 and 1995) and UBA (1997a)

As table 4.2 shows, road traffic related CO, NO$_x$ and VOC emissions started to decline in Germany in the 1980s, but in Britain this has only occurred since 1990. By 1994 Germany had almost halved its CO emissions from an all-time high in 1985, while in Britain there was a more moderate decline which set in at a later stage. Nitrogen oxide emissions, which were not regulated until 1977, declined more recently and more gradually in both states.

The reduction of NO$_x$ emissions became a key political issue in Germany when they were identified as a major contributing factor responsible for the 'dying forests' (*Waldsterben*). The British government revised its national traffic related NO$_x$ (and CO) emissions in the mid-1980s after the Department of Transport (DoT) adopted a new methodology for measuring the in-service performance of cars.[2]

This resulted in almost a doubling of the traffic-related NO_x emissions in Britain and brought them in line with NO_x emissions in Germany.

Table 4.3 *Relative contribution of traffic-related emissions (as %) in Britain and Germany, 1983–94*

Member state	1983	1985	1990	1994
Carbon monoxide (CO)				
UK	84	84	90	75[a]
D	68	69	60	59
Former West Germany	68	69	70	61
Former East Germany	23	24	39	48
Volatile organic compounds (VOCs)				
UK	42	43	47	30[a]
D	37	38	45	32
Former West Germany	37	38	36	28
Former East Germany	46	48	64	49
Nitrogen oxides (NO_x)				
UK	39	43	51	49[a]
D	41	45	46	47
Former West Germany	41	45	55	50
Former East Germany	12	12	21	37
Carbon dioxide (CO_2)				
UK	24	26	33	34
D	13	15	15	18
Former West Germany	13	15	19	19
Former East Germany	4	3	6	13

Note: [a] Percentages for 1995
Source: Adapted from DETR (1997) and UBA (1997a)

Despite increasingly more stringent EU standards, the relative contribution from road traffic sources towards the national totals of CO, VOCs, NO_x and CO_2 emissions remained high in both Britain and Germany until the 1990s (table 4.3). In 1994, road traffic sources amounted to almost 75 and 59 per cent of the total CO emissions in Britain and Germany respectively (although the 1990s levels are no

longer considered a serious health hazard).[3] In the mid-1990s, about
one third of all VOCs (and thus also of hydrocarbons HCs) originated
from traffic sources in Britain and Germany and breaches of tropospheric ozone standards were common. About half of all NO_x
emissions, which contribute towards acid rain and the formation of
tropospheric ozone, originated from traffic sources in Britain and
Germany in the mid-1990s. Of more recent concern has been the rise
of CO_2 emissions which are released when fossil fuel is burned. The
contribution of road traffic towards CO_2 emissions has increased
considerably in Britain and Germany. Britain's poor public transport
system goes some way towards explaining why its average annual
distance travelled by car is one of the highest within the EU.[4] In 1993,
it stood at 16,000 kilometres in Britain compared to 14,000 kilometres
in Germany.[5]

The adoption of more sophisticated car emission abatement technology in modern cars, which quickly replaced the technologically
outdated East German (Trabant and Wartburg) cars after unification
failed to prevent a rise in some car emission pollutants (CO_2 emissions
in particular) in the new German *Länder*, where the number of
cars and their kilometrage increased rapidly after unification.[6] Technological modernisation is therefore not always sufficient to reduce
environmental pollution.

Table 4.4 *Numbers of cars (millions) registered in Britain and
Germany, 1950–99*

	1950	1958	1960	1965	1970	1975	1980	1985	1990	1995	1999
Britain	2.4	4.8	5.8	8.9	11.4	14.1	16.3	18.3	22.5	24.3	26.8
Germany	n/a	2.8	4.0	8.1	13.0	15.0	23.2	25.9	30.7[a]	40.5	42.4

Note: [a] The figure for 1990 refers to the former West Germany only
Sources: DpT (1995), VDA (1995a, 1995b and 2000a) and SMMT and VDA
telephone information in 2001

As table 4.4 shows, car registration was higher in Britain than in
Germany until the 1960s, when it changed due to Germany's rising
economic prosperity and Britain's relative economic decline. However,
car ownership has remained relatively low in Europe compared to
America which adopted the first national pollution abatement
measures.

The origins of car emission regulation

From the 1970s the USA became the benchmark for car emission regulations, with Europe and Japan initially lagging behind.[7] David Vogel has argued that Germany's role within the EU is similar to that of California in American as regards car emission policy-making.[8] It is therefore useful to analyse the main features of early American car emission regulations before developments in Europe are assessed.

America takes the lead

In 1959 California adopted its first major car emission regulations. From the 1950s onwards, the infamous Los Angeles smog became more frequent due to a steep rise in the number of cars and their kilometrage. The climatic and geographic condition of the Los Angeles Basin, which suffers from poor air circulation, especially during summer, made matters worse. California stipulated urban ambient air quality targets (health targets and EQOs) which were then translated into emission limits for cars and other sources of pollution. However, in order not to impose too high a cost on the automobile industry, the adopted car emission limit values did not go beyond what could be achieved with the BAT, although even stricter standards would have been necessary to achieve the agreed targets.

The 1970 Clean Air Act Amendments (or 'Muskie laws'),[9] radically altered America's approach to car emission regulation. The Muskie laws introduced a *technology-forcing* approach by stipulating 90 per cent reduction targets for CO and HC emissions by 1975 (compared to 1970 levels) and NO_x emissions by 1976 (compared to 1971). Reduction targets of this magnitude could no longer be achieved by the BAT and engine internal optimisation. Instead, they forced automobile companies to invest heavily in research and development for new technologies.

The Muskie laws introduced a waiver which allowed the authorities to grant derogations where good faith efforts by corporate actors failed to achieve compliance.[10] The original 1975–76 deadlines were extended several times until the development of the three-way catalytic converter made compliance with the 90 per cent reduction targets from 1970 levels possible. The three-way catalytic converter did not become a required standard feature for new cars in the USA until 1983 (US 1983 standards), although California was allowed to proceed at a faster pace. Importantly, California's forerunner status was not perceived as a threat to the functioning of the internal (American) market, unlike nationally more stringent car emission standards in the EU.[11]

Japan follows the American lead

Japan adopted major car emission regulations in the 1960s, although these did not bring about the desired improvement in air quality.[12] Air pollution reached record levels in the 1970s when Tokyo's authorities issued some thirty smog warnings annually. Japan's largest cities therefore lobbied the government to adopt car emission standards similar to the American Muskie laws.[13] However, Japan's automobile industry put up fierce resistance, arguing that the American standards were unnecessarily stringent for Japanese conditions and would prevent the development of promising engine internal abatement technologies, such as the lean-burn engine.

Tokue Shibata, who in the 1970s chaired the car emission expert group of Japan's largest cities, has argued that Toyota and Nissan in particular used the lean-burn argument merely as a delaying tactic. However, Kanehira Maruo has claimed that Japan's automobile industry had a genuine interest in the lean-burn technology which promised to bring about a simultaneous reduction in emissions and fuel consumption.[14] Suffice it to note that in 1975 the Japanese government decided to follow the American lead by adopting car emission standards as stringent as the Muskie laws.[15]

Early car emission regulations in Germany

In Germany, warnings about the detrimental impact on health of car emissions can be traced to the 1920s.[16] However, political pressure to tackle car emissions only mounted when the number of cars increased steeply after the 'economic miracle' (*Wirtschaftswunder*) of the 1950s. The government was initially reluctant to act because the motor car had become a symbol of prosperity and freedom.[17] Moreover, the strongly export-oriented automobile industry played an important part in Germany's economic revival after the Second World War.

Severe smog episodes in Germany's industrial heartland, the Ruhr area in North Rhine Westphalia, led to the adoption of early industrial air pollution control measures, at times serving as a model for federal legislation.[18] However, cars largely escaped emission regulations up until the 1960s. In 1960, the Road Traffic Licensing Ordinance (Straßenverkehrszulassungsverordnung) was amended to stipulate the

BAT principle for vehicle emission requirements. However, its inter-pretation was left to the Association of the German Automobile Industry (Verband der Deutschen Automobilindustrie – VDA) which merely drew up voluntary guidelines to pre-empt the legislation de-manded by a cross-party interparliamentary working group since the 1950s.[19] The first car emission legislation, which regulated merely CO emissions, came into force only in July 1969.[20]

In Germany the starting-point of modern day environmental pol-icy is 1969 when a newly elected Centre–Left (SPD–FDP) coalition government adopted an Immediate Environmental Programme (Sofort-programm Umwelt).[21] It announced a two-step reduction in the maximum lead content in petrol to 0.4 grammes per litre (g/l) by 1972 and 0.15g/l by 1976. It also advocated the possible introduction of unleaded petrol by 1980.[22] The more comprehensive Environmental Programme, which followed three years later, confirmed the two-step reduction of lead in petrol but failed to mentioned the introduction of unleaded petrol.[23]

The 1971 Environmental Programme announced the reduction of car emissions from petrol cars to one-tenth by 1980 compared to 1969 levels.[24] The 90 per cent reduction target was identical to that of the Muskie laws. This was no coincidence, because developments in America had an important influence on German environmental pol-icy at the time.[25] However, the German government refrained from adopting the American technology-forcing strategy, opting for the traditional BAT principle instead.

In 1972, the government convened a meeting at Baiersbronn be-tween the Ministries of the Interior (BMI), Transport (BMV) and Economics (BMWi) and representatives of the automobile and oil industries to discuss the implementation of the 1971 Environmental Programme.[26] The Baiersbronn meeting was in line with similar cor-poratist consultation exercises in other sectors. It was triggered by the government's need for reliable data to calculate the emission limit values for the 90 per cent reduction target. The Federal Environmental Agency (UBA), which now calculates these kinds of data, was not established until 1974. The automobile and oil industries argued that the 90 per cent reduction target was unachievable without the intro-duction of unleaded petrol and the three-way catalytic converter, which both industries were fiercely opposed to on cost grounds and for fear of breaking up the European market. Aware of the fact that the government had publicly committed itself to emission reductions, the automobile industry accepted 80 per cent reduction targets for CO and HC emissions by 1984. However, it rejected as unrealistic a similar target for NO_x emissions.

The Lead in Petrol Law (Benzinbleigesetz) was the first measure adopted under the 1971 Environmental Programme. It reduced the maximum lead content in petrol to 0.4g/l by 1 January 1972. The government weathered fierce industry opposition and concerns from the EU Commission when it further reduced the maximum lead content to 0.15g/l by 1 January 1976.[27] However, it refrained from using the BAT principle, which had become enshrined in the 1974 Federal Ambient Environmental Quality Protection Act (Bundesimmissionsachutzgesetz),[28] to press for the unilateral introduction of unleaded petrol. Instead, the German government pressed for more stringent measures at the European level.

Britain's failure to adopt car emission standards
The Clean Air Act was adopted four years after a severe smog episode killed some 4,000 people in London in December 1952.[29] It resulted in a gradual tightening of air pollution control measures, bringing about a decline in winter smog incidents. Car ownership was still relatively low, and little was known about the detrimental effects of car emissions in the 1950s. However, car emissions did not become a priority issue in Britain even when scientific knowledge had improved and America, Japan and Germany began to adopt car emission reduction targets.

Lord Ashby, a chairperson of the Royal Commission on Environmental Pollution (RCEP), and Mary Anderson still maintained in 1982 that

> In Britain there is no evidence that any of the emissions from automobiles are as serious a hazard to health as are the emissions from domestic fires burning soft coal. The amount of carbon monoxide you inhale in a busy street rarely reaches the amount inhaled after smoking three or four cigarettes; nor does carbon monoxide accumulate in the atmosphere, as carbon dioxide does ... As for lead, the amount you inhale from car exhausts, though under suspicion that it might have long-term sub-clinical effects on children, is only about a quarter of the amount you absorb from other sources.[30]

One British automobile industry representative later defended the British reluctance to accept more stringent EU car emission limits with the following arguments: 'The ... Clean Air Acts of the 1950s had virtually removed industrial smog from Britain (something the US and Germany have not fully achieved) and automobile exhaust was not thought a serious problem'.[31]

Car emission regulations were pushed on to the political agenda in Britain largely as a result of developments at the European level.

ECE car emission regulations

Until the 1980s the UN ECE rather than the EU provided the main regulatory arena for car emission policy-making in Europe. The ECE was set up in Geneva in 1947 to deal with pan-European trade and social issues, and environmental issues became part of its remit only at a later stage.[32]

However, within the ECE car emissions were initially perceived merely as a road safety issue (because black smoke from exhaust pipes can impair the vision of drivers) [33] and an urban health problem. ECE regulations formed part of the type approval measures (that is, the technical requirements which a car must fulfil before it can be approved for sale in another country). The fact that most West and East European countries were represented in Geneva made the ECE an attractive regulatory arena, although decision-making was slow and produced little more than lowest-common-denominator solutions due to unanimous voting requirements.[34]

Until the 1990s, the Commission held only observer status within the ECE because 'member governments jealously guarded their negotiating rights and made sure that the Commission ended up sitting at the children's table (*Katzentisch*)'.[35] Over time the Commission assumed a more important coordinating role for delegations from the EU, which nevertheless spoke with different voices at the ECE. The same Commission and member government officials attending the ECE meetings in Geneva usually also participated in Commission and Council committee meetings on car emissions in Brussels. Industry representatives also attended some ECE meetings, but had no voting rights. However, it was an open secret that some governments relied heavily on the expertise of their domestic automobile producers.[36]

The adoption of the test cycle
In the 1960s, the French government became increasingly concerned about air pollution in Paris. It submitted to the ECE a test cycle, which simulates car exhaust emission performance under laboratory

conditions, for adoption in 1965.[37] Britain and Germany, both of which at the time had strongly export-oriented domestic car industries, instead favoured the adoption of the American test cycle for the ECE because it would have lowered the cost of the type approval for producers exporting to America. However, France, which exported few cars outside Europe, indicated that it would veto the American test cycle. The other ECE contracting parties therefore accepted in principle the French test cycle. However, the British government successfully pressed for the lowering of the average speed of 21.2kmph (based on 1950s Paris road traffic) to 18.9kmph.[38]

The test cycle is as important as the emission limit values assigned to it: a lenient test cycle devalues stringent emission limits. Ideally, a test cycle should simulate real-world driving conditions. However, engines can be constructed in such a way that they perform markedly better under predetermined test conditions than on the road. This is known as 'cycle beating'. Incidents have occurred where manufacturers made the emission abatement equipment shut off altogether outside the range covered by the test cycle.[39] As a rule, the lower the average and top speeds the easier it will be to comply with the emission limit values.

Table 4.5 *ECE and US test cycles compared*

	ECE test cycle	US 1975 FTP test cycle
Length (km)	4.052	12.067
Average speed (kmph)	18.9	31.67
Maximum speed (kmph)	50	91.2
Evaporative emissions	–	2 g per test
Durability requirements (km)	–	80,000

Source: UBA unpublished mimeo

The ECE test cycle, which remained applicable until the early 1990s (subject to minor modifications), was considerably more lenient than the Federal Transport Procedure (FTP) 1975 test which came into force for all American states in 1975. As table 4.5 shows, the ECE test cycle was much shorter and stipulated significantly lower speeds. It also failed to cover evaporative emissions and durability requirements for emission abatement devices.

Critics of the catalytic converter were quick to point out that the American test 'favoured the catalytic converter because it stipulated fairly high speeds early on so as to quickly heat up the catalyst to its optimal operating temperature'.[40] However, unlike the American FTP 1975 test, the ECE test disregarded the first 40 seconds of the cold-start phase when emissions are very high because the engine is not yet warmed up.

The adoption of emission limits

In the 1950s, CO emissions reached health-threatening concentration levels in many urban areas. However, the first two ECE car emission regulations, ECE-Regulations (ECE-R) 15–00 and 15–01, were adopted only in 1970 and 1975 respectively. They set limits for CO and HC emissions; NO_x was first regulated by ECE-R 15–02 in 1977.

The ECE's car emission limits stipulated moderate reduction targets which could usually be complied with by corporate environmental laggards. ECE-R 15–01 reduced CO emissions by 20 per cent and HC emissions by 15 per cent compared to the requirements of ECE-R 15–00. The next two steps (ECE-R 15–02 and ECE-R 15–03) further reduced CO and HC emissions by similar percentage ranges. However, the emission reduction gains from individual cars were more than offset by a steep rise in the total number of cars and their increased average kilometrage.

ECE signatories were allowed to delay transposition of agreed limit values into national legislation, but had to permit the type approval and sale of imported cars which complied with the ECE regulations. ECE regulations were therefore *optional* rather than mandatory. ECE-R 15–00 to 15–03 were speedily transposed into EU directives, which also remained *optional* directives.

Environmental leader states

Growing public concern and new scientific findings about the detrimental health and environmental effects of car emissions led Austria, Germany, Switzerland and Sweden to push for more stringent standards in the 1970s.[41] However, these attempts were vetoed by environmental laggards within the ECE. In the early 1980s several European Free Trade Agreement (EFTA) states, including Austria, Finland, Norway, Switzerland and Sweden, therefore opted out of the ECE's car emission regulations and instead adopted modified versions of the American standards. This was welcomed by environmental groups, but was criticised by Europe's car and oil industries for being unjustified on scientific grounds and for breaking up the European market.[42]

The Danish, Dutch and German governments wanted to adopt standards similar to those of the EFTA states, with whom they formed the Stockholm Group. The Stockholm Group 'was based on a German idea although it was formally initiated by Sweden'.[43] It was set up to provide assistance to European governments wanting to adopt the American standards but which had little domestic expertise.[44] One DG Industry official called participation in the Stockholm Group by member governments an 'unfriendly act'.[45] Austria, Finland, Norway, Liechtenstein, Sweden and Switzerland but also Denmark (which was an EU member state) became full members of the Stockholm Group, while Germany and the Netherlands (as well as America and Canada) held observer status.

In 1978, the Swiss and German governments submitted relatively ambitious proposals to the ECE. The German proposal had been worked out by the UBA in the face of opposition from the German automobile industry.[46] It suggested reduction rates of 50–70 per cent (compared to those of ECE-R 15–03). This would have required emission limits of between 30 and 48 grammes per test for CO and 10 grammes per test for HC + NO_x emissions, depending on the weight of the vehicles.[47]

Table 4.6 *Emission limits of ECE Regulation 15–04*

Reference weight category in kilogrammes	Emission limit in grammes per test	
	CO	HC + NO_x
>2150	110	28
2150–1930	101	26.5
1930–1700	93	25
1700–1470	87	23.5
1470–1250	76	22
1250–1020	67	20.5
<1020	58	19

Source: Becker (1988)

Table 4.6 shows that ECE-R 15–04, which was adopted in 1981, stipulated values that were considerably more lenient than those of the German proposal. It also illustrates that ECE regulations differentiated emission limit values according to weight categories, with heavier cars being allowed to comply with more lenient standards. The transposition of the lenient ECE-R 15–04 limit values into EU legislation (*Directive 83/351/EEC*) was delayed by more than two years because the British, French and Italian governments insisted on more lead time for their car industries. However, the Danish, Dutch and German governments considered the limit values too lenient. From 1980 onwards, some UBA officials edged the German government towards demanding the introduction of the three-way catalytic converter which, however, required the availability of unleaded petrol.

The introduction of unleaded petrol

The elimination of lead in petrol was demanded on health grounds and/or in order to make possible the introduction of the three-way catalytic converter in Europe.[48] Lead was added in refineries to prevent the engine from knocking and to raise its performance. Additives other than lead were available but not used, mainly for cost reasons. The toxicity of lead has been known for centuries, but traffic-related airborne lead concentrations only became a concern when the number of cars increased dramatically.

The reduction of lead levels in petrol

The first EAP (1973) listed lead as a substance for which EU action was deemed necessary.[49] In 1975, the Commission published the following proposals: first, biological standards for lead in human blood; second, minimum ambient air quality standards for lead; and, third, a maximum level of lead in petrol. However, the proposal of biological standards for lead in blood merely resulted in a one-off screening exercise of 1,800 volunteers.[50] The directive on ambient air quality standards for lead (82/884/EEC) was not adopted until 1982, being blocked by the British government for several years on the grounds that there was insufficient scientific evidence to justify the proposed standard.[51]

In 1976, the Commission put forward a proposal which would have granted member governments the option of adopting either 0.4g/l or 0.15g/l as maximum limit values for the lead content in petrol by 1978. The Commission's proposal was triggered by the German Lead in Petrol Law which stipulated a maximum lead level of 0.15g/l by

1976. Nigel Haigh has argued that the adoption of *Directive 78/661/EEC* in May 1978 'shows that in favourable circumstances a determined Member State can pull the rest of the Community along behind it so that higher environmental standards are achieved throughout the Community more quickly than if the Member State had proceeded at [its] own pace'.[52] However, the German government neither acted as a pusher state in the way Haigh has suggested nor adopted a first-mover strategy as identified by Adrienne Héritier and colleagues.[53] Instead, the German government opted for a (defensive) forerunner strategy, as explained by Duncan Liefferink and Mikael Andersen.[54] The German government was determined to go ahead with national legislation regardless of whether or not the EU would follow. It was convinced that it could rely on Article 30 EC Treaty (formerly Article 36 EC/EEC Treaty) which allows for stricter national health and environmental standards in exceptional circumstances. The Commission decided not to take court action and, as one UBA official explained, instead 'put forward its own proposal which stipulated a maximum lead level of 0.4g/l and a lower limit of 0.15g/l as an option for individual member states. The lower limit value, which automatically sanctioned the German Lead in Petrol Law, was an option so to speak. It was not the rule.'[55]

In Britain, even the higher 0.4g/l lead limit was criticised as unnecessarily stringent by several speakers in the House of Commons (HoC).[56] British Conservative MEPs also expressed concern during the EP's plenary session on 10 November 1975. The Eurosceptic James Spicer, who spoke on behalf of the European Conservative Group (which was made up solely of British Conservative MEPs), explained that his group would be voting against the proposed directive 'because of the cost entailed and the absence of proof that there was any harm to health from lead in petrol'.[57] A few months earlier, the European Conservative Group had opposed the bathing water directive on similar grounds.[58]

Directive 78/661/EEC was not simply the German Lead in Petrol law dressed up as European legislation. The Environmental Council made important changes to the Commission's proposal. For example, it put back by four years the proposed 1977 implementation deadline at the insistence of the British government.[59] Moreover, the 0.15g/l limit value was made a minimum limit value, which later prevented the introduction of unleaded petrol.[60] Nigel Haigh has pointed out that

[t]he provision in the Directive to prevent a limit of less than 0.15g/l ...
was put in at the suggestion of the British government among others,
presumably to ensure that no barriers to trade in motor cars would be
created by any one Member State insisting on lead free petrol. As a
result the ... Directive lost some of its claim to be an environmental
protection measure.[61]

From the early 1970s onwards, the DoE and the Department of
Health in Britain became increasingly concerned about the detrimental
health effects of lead in petrol. However, these concerns were overruled by the Department of Energy, the DoT and the Treasury which
feared an increase in oil consumption (and thus a negative effect on
Britain's flagging economy) as a result of reducing lead levels in petrol.
In the late 1970s, the DoT carried out a study in cooperation with
the oil industry which identified a lead limit value of 0.45g/l by 1981
as the most cost-effective solution. It explicitly rejected the (German)
0.15g/l limit value on cost grounds.[62]

However, in May 1981, the British Environmental Minister Tom
King announced a reduction in the maximum lead content in petrol
to 0.15g/l by 1985 at the latest. King justified the new limit value
by referring to the BPM principle when he argued that it would
'reduce by about two-thirds lead emissions from cars some 10 years
earlier than any other *practicable* method'.[63] The shift in the British
government's position was triggered by public opinion and the
findings of the DHSS-sponsored Lawther report on lead in the environment.[64] However, *The Times* concluded that the new maximum
lead level

> smelled of departmental compromise. Those, such as the Treasury and
> the Department of Energy, who worried about the cost of eliminating
> toxic lead argued for a minimal reduction. Those who were convinced
> of the danger to children's health (and the cost of treating lead poi-
> soning) could only in logic argue for the rapid and major reduction or
> elimination of lead in petrol. The outcome was a familiar compromise,
> unsatisfactory in view of the dangers involved. If the medical case
> against lead holds, then 1985 is too long and 0.15 grammes per litre ...
> is too high. Moreover, there is no commitment beyond 1985, whereas
> the United States, Japan, Australia, Germany and Sweden are com-
> mitted to a transition to completely lead-free petrol. Our motor car
> exporters will then no longer have access to those markets, unless they
> adjust in line.[65]

The unleaded petrol directive
The directive (*85/210/EEC*) to introduce unleaded petrol was agreed
in principle by the Environmental Council on 6–7 December 1984,
less than six months after the Commission had issued its proposal.
It was formally adopted by the Environmental Council only on 20–21
March 1985 because the EP had not issued its (legally non-binding)
opinion on time. However, the Council's short negotiation phase
disguises the political controversy which surrounded the introduction
of unleaded petrol.

In 1982, a confidential report was leaked to *The Times* in which
the Department of Health's Chief Medical Officer Henry Yellowlees
warned that lead could damage the health of children in particular.[66] The Conservation Society, which had been demanding the
introduction of unleaded petrol since 1973, set up the Campaign
Against Lead in Petrol in 1977. But it was the Campaign for Lead-Free
Air (CLEAR), founded in 1982 by Des Wilson, which caught the
attention of both media and politicians.[67] However, prior to 1985,
British environmental groups did not link their demands for the
introduction of unleaded petrol to the adoption of the three-way
catalytic converter.[68]

In April 1983, the British government came out in support of the
introduction of unleaded petrol on the day when the RCEP published
its *Ninth Report* which recommended the introduction of unleaded
petrol.[69] The British government subsequently asked the Commission
to revise the EU's existing 0.15g/l minimum lead level for petrol.
However, the British government's support for unleaded petrol was
exclusively based on health considerations and did not extend to the
introduction of the three-way catalytic converter.

The German government submitted a memorandum to the Environmental Council which demanded the introduction of unleaded
petrol and more stringent car emission standards in May 1983.[70]
Britain and Germany therefore pushed for the introduction of unleaded petrol at the EU level at around the same time. However, the
German government explicitly linked the introduction of unleaded
petrol to the adoption of the three-way catalytic converter in July
1983. Germany's demands were supported in principle by the Danish,
Dutch and Greek governments. The EP, supported by the European
Environmental Bureau (EEB) and the Bureau of European Consumers'
Associations (BEUC), had favoured the early introduction of unleaded
petrol since February 1982.

Europe's oil and automobile industries, on the other hand, raised doubts about the scientific evidence and warned about the cost implications. The French and Italian governments were also opposed to taking lead out of petrol.

European Regulations, Global Approach – Air Pollution
Faced with conflicting demands from different policy actors, a largely defunct ECE car emission policy-making process and limited in-house expertise, the EU Commission decided to set up an *ad hoc* advisory group called European Regulations, Global Approach – Air Pollution (ERGA). However, 'Global Approach' was a misnomer, as ERGA dealt with urban air pollution. It assessed the effect of car emission abatement technologies on petrol consumption and the cost implications of various technologies.[71]

Nigel Haigh has argued that the Commission set up ERGA because it was '[u]nder pressure from a number of sources concerned at the ad hoc approach to vehicle emissions that paid little attention to the possible economic consequences for the important automobile industry in the Community'.[72] This was also the view of the British government and Europe's automobile producers.[73] However, it was not shared by the Danish, German, Greek and Dutch governments, all of which insisted (to varying degrees) that BAT-derived emission standards would benefit both the environment and the international competitiveness of Europe's automobile industry.

The ERGA I report, published in August 1983, stated that in order to arrive at 'rational emission limits' it was necessary to estimate their likely impact on air quality.[74] This was the first half-hearted attempt at the EU level explicitly to relate car emission limits to EQOs. According to one British automobile industry representative, '[t]he UK as a matter of fact had quite a lead in [the ERGA process which was] going to look at the true objective air quality ... and working back from that what vehicles should be made to do'.[75] One DoT official therefore complained:

> My colleagues here [in the DoT] were trying to get some science-based objective view about what level emissions should be ... The ERGA report did try to establish some sort of scientific and technical basis. I think there was great disappointment here that having the ERGA report produced at the technical level it was immediately disregarded on the political level in Germany.[76]

British officials were adamant that the ERGA process pointed towards the adoption of the lean-burn engine as the most cost-effective car emission abatement technology. However, the recommendations put forward in the ERGA I report remained vague. One British automobile industry representative, who supported the lean-burn engine, conceded that the ERGA process 'indicated that it was probably impossible to define an absolute threshold level for each of the pollutants. Thus a pragmatic approach to establish a level of protection which was both desirable and attainable was adopted, which means what the politicians are likely to agree to.'[77]

The British government tried to use the ERGA process to fend off the BAT-derived proposal which Germany had submitted to the ECE in 1978 and resubmitted to the EU in 1982. However, in 1983, the German government went even further and demanded the introduction of the three-way catalytic converter, arguing that it now constituted the BAT.

The ERGA process was biased against the three-way catalytic converter. The offer by the British catalytic converter company Johnson Matthey to give evidence to ERGA II working groups was turned down on the grounds that 'the Committee felt there was nothing further that they could add to the depositions already laid before, and considered by ERGA I'.[78] On the other hand, the lead additive producer Associated Octel was given the opportunity to distribute a paper which criticised the *Ninth Report* of the RCEP for supporting the introduction of unleaded petrol.[79]

Access to the ERGA working groups was controlled by a steering committee which was made up mainly of DG Industry officials, although DGs Environment, Transport and Energy were also represented. A French Ministry of Transport official, Bernard Gauvin, who had already chaired the ECE's car emission working group meetings, was made chair of the ERGA steering committee. He was an outspoken critic of the three-way catalytic converter.

Participation in ERGA was restricted to Commission and member government officials and representatives from the European umbrella groups of the automobile and oil industries. The automobile industry usually sent representatives from the Committee of Common Market Automobile Constructors (CCMC), which was the European association of the member states' automobile producers, and representatives from the Comité de Liaison de la Construction Automobile des Pays des Communautés Européennes (CLCA), which was the European peak organisation of the national associations for the automobile producers. The oil industry was primarily represented by the Oil Companies' European Organisation for Environmental and Health Protection (CONCAWE).

Environmental and consumer groups were viewed warily as outsiders as can be seen from the following written statement made by one DG Environment official in 1984:

> Presence of 'outsider' at [ERGA] meeting ... Representative of German Consumers found in the meeting with CONCAWE, CCMC, CLCA ... He has agreed, with no reservation, to maintain the confidentiality of what he heard and received. He fully realises the 'system' for transmission of proposals from Commission to Council ... He must, per se, have realised he was out of 'order' ... No further action needed but await other Consumer Union approaches![80]

This statement illustrates well the Commission's initial bias in favour of producer groups at the expense of public interest groups. It shows that NGOs were not considered for membership of the emerging EU car emission policy community. It was only from 1987 onwards and after considerable lobbying efforts (which included a plea for assistance to the Dutch and German governments) that the EEB and BEUC were invited to Commission car emission working groups.

With the benefit of hindsight it is possible to argue that the ERGA process used a somewhat similar approach to that of the Auto-Oil I Programme published by the Commission in 1996 (that is, cost-effective limit values derived from urban ambient air quality objectives).[81] However, when the ERGA process was conducted, EU ambient air quality standards only existed for SO_2, suspended particulates and lead. Only Germany, the Netherlands and Italy had national EQOs in place for CO and NO_x emissions.[82] ERGA therefore also considered World Health Organization (WHO) standards for HC and tropospheric ozone.

Ironically, Britain, which was one of the strongest supporters of the ERGA approach, had no statutory ambient air quality standards in place, and its air quality monitoring system was only rudimentary.[83] Between 1972 and 1989; Britain cut the number of sampling sites which measured NO_x concentrations from 56 to 21.[84] In 1988 there were only fifteen sites which continuously monitored ozone concentrations.[85] Carbon monoxide concentrations were not regularly monitored in Britain prior to 1983, although periodic samples from one site in central

London showed that the alert level was being exceeded regularly.[86] Germany, which is often portrayed as relying on emission limits rather than EQOs, had 126 sites in place for measuring NO_x concentrations in 1982. The British government undertook modelling exercises which 'aimed to determine the effect of different vehicle emission standard scenarios on ground level ozone'.[87] However, this did not amount to a coherent EQO-derived air pollution strategy; the beginnings of such a strategy were almost a decade later, when in the early 1990s independent expert panels on air quality standards were set up.[88]

The publication of the ERGA II report coincided with the Commission putting forward in May 1984; a proposal for a directive to introduce unleaded petrol. The British Conservative MEP Alexander Sherlock was the EP's rapporteur for the directive on unleaded petrol and the directive to reduce car emissions, which were considered together by the EP.[89] Part I of the Sherlock report, which dealt with unleaded petrol, was uncontroversial. However, Part II, which focused on car emissions, produced fierce disputes amongst MEPs.[90] A large majority of MEPs supported the introduction of unleaded petrol (*Directive 85/210/EEC*) from 1 January 1986. *Directive 85/210/EEC* was adopted by the Environmental Council on 20/21 March 1985 and largely made redundant the recommendations of the ERGA II report.

Anglo-German implementation differences
Britain and Germany's implementation records for *Directive 85/210/EEC* differ significantly, as can be see from figure 4.1.

In 1983, Britain was the first member state to demand the introduction of unleaded petrol. However, five years later, the market share of unleaded petrol made up only 1 per cent of the total petrol sales in Britain. It rose to 19 per cent in 1989, the year for which *Directive 85/210/EEC* stipulated that member governments must 'ensure the availability and balanced distribution of unleaded petrol'.[91]

The slow uptake of unleaded petrol in Britain was due to a number of factors. First, the British government initially relied almost exclusively on moral persuasion measures (such as the printing of leaflets and advertising), criticised as insufficient by the HoC Environment Committee (HCEC) and environmental groups.[92] Second, fiscal incentives to encourage the uptake of unleaded petrol were introduced only in 1987, but initially they failed to equate the price of unleaded with leaded premium petrol.[93] It was only from 1989 onwards that tax incentives for unleaded petrol were increased significantly. Third, the

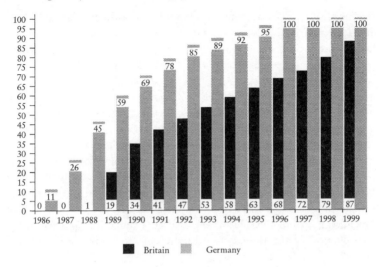

Figure 4.1 *Uptake of unleaded petrol (in %) in Britain and Germany, 1986–99*

Note: The percentage figures are rounded
Sources: DETR (1997: 43, 1988: 51, 2000: 59) and UBA written communications in 1999 and 2001

Society of Motor Vehicle Manufacturers (SMMT), which is the umbrella association of Britain's automobile producers and importers, warned car owners not to use unleaded petrol.[94] The main motorist organisations, the Automobile Association (AA) and the Royal Automobile Association (RAC), also failed to support the use of unleaded petrol prior to 1986.[95] Fourth, cars equipped with a three-way catalytic converter were not widely sold in Britain until 1989. Fifth, regular leaded petrol was not banned.

In 1984 the DoT and DoE argued that 'the remaining lead in petrol should be phased out as soon as practicable'.[96] In 1989, less than 20 per cent of all petrol sold in Britain was unleaded. In the early 1990s one sampling station in London occasionally recorded lead concentration levels which were three times the permitted ambient air quality level set in *Directive 82/884/EEC*.[97] However, between 1980 and 1997, the estimated lead emissions from cars in Britain declined from 7.5 to 0.8 tonnes annually.[98]

In Germany, unleaded petrol reached a domestic market share of almost 60 per cent in 1989; it rose to almost 100 per cent by 1996 (see figure 4.1). The German government encouraged the uptake of unleaded petrol by adopting a range of different policy instruments. First, it negotiated a voluntary agreement with the oil industry, which would make unleaded petrol widely available from 1986 onwards. Second, it introduced tax incentives for unleaded petrol of four pfennigs per litre in 1985, increased to seven pfennigs in 1986 (at 1986 prices).[99] Third, it banned the sale of leaded regular petrol. Fourth, it encouraged the uptake of three-way catalytic converter cars (which have to run on unleaded petrol) with fiscal incentives.

Environmental groups and Germany's main motorist organisation, General German Automobile Association (ADAC), campaigned in favour of unleaded petrol. The umbrella group of the German automobile industry, VDA, gave up its resistance to the introduction of unleaded petrol in 1983. However, the VDA remained opposed to the introduction of the three-way catalytic converter until well into the late 1980s.

Conclusion

Until the early 1980s, EU institutional actors played only a secondary role during ECE negotiations, which were conducted by member governments. However, the Commission gradually acquired a coordinating role by organising meetings in Brussels prior to ECE negotiations in Geneva, where national officials nevertheless spoke with different voices. DG Industry was the lead department within the Commission because the ECE (and later the EU) negotiations were conducted within the context of type approval agreements. DG Environment, which was set up in 1981, and its predecessor, the Commission's Environment and Consumer Protection Service, played only a minor role during this phase of EU car emission policy-making. As car emissions became politically more salient, the same government, Commission and industry experts started to meet more frequently and gradually began to form what could be termed a more tightly knit EU car emissions policy community. The EP and environmental and consumer NGOs were excluded from the ECE and EU's car emission policy-making process.

Germany and other environmental leader states made several attempts to significantly tighten car emission regulations within the ECE framework. When they failed, the EFTA states opted out and adopted (modified versions of) the American standards, which had become the benchmark for Europe. Germany actively supported this move by helping to set up the Stockholm Group, which provided technical assistance.

Britain, on the other hand, was one of the driving forces behind the ERGA process which had been set up by the Commission in order to arrive at car emission proposals acceptable to all core policy actors. However, the ERGA process, whose aim it was to arrive at cost-effective measures derived from EQOs, was biased against the introduction of ambitious car emission standards, as can be seen from the selective evidence assessed and the exclusion of public interest groups in favour of producer groups.

The British government was initially opposed to the introduciton of unleaded petrol. However, it changed its position, and Britain and Germany pushed for the adoption of unleaded petrol at the EU level at around the same time. However, the British government was slow to implement the directive on unleaded petrol, and remained opposed to the introduction of the American car emission standards which would have required the adoption of the three-way catalytic converter.

Notes

1 EEA (1995a, 1997, 2000); RCEP (1994, 1997); SRU (1973, 1983).
2 DoT (1986: 119).
3 Interviews with UBA and DoE officials in 1997.
4 Greenpeace (1990); RCEP (1994, 1997).
5 VDA (1995a: 338–42).
6 UBA (1997a).
7 Arp (1995); Berg (1982); Holzinger (1994); Vogel (1995); Weale (1996a: 598).
8 Vogel (1995, 1997).
9 Senator Muskie (Democrat) was the driving force behind the 1970 Amendments.
10 Berg (1982); Rehbinder and Stewart (1985a: 113–5).
11 Vogel (1995, 1997).
12 Berg (1982: 444–90).
13 Berg (1982: 444); Shibata (1979: 147); Winzer (1990: 51–4).
14 Maruo (1992); Shibata (1979: 146–50).
15 However, the emission limits were based on a different test cycle.
16 UBA (1985: 3).
17 Klenke (1995); Weale et al. (2000: 398).
18 Weale et al. (1991: 40–6, 2000); Wey (1982: 181–94).

19 Klenke (1995: 71–6); E. Müller (1986: 53–4).
20 UBA (1985: 4).
21 E. Müller (1986); Weale *et al.* (2000).
22 Berg (1985: 9); Winzer (1990: 80).
23 E. Müller (1986: 51); SRU (1973); Winzer (1990: 78–9).
24 BMI (1972).
25 Bechmann (1984); E. Müller (1986); Weale *et al.* (1991, 2000).
26 Boehmer-Christiansen and Weidner (1995: 46); Winzer (1990: 69).
27 Hartkopf and Bohne (1983).
28 Paragraph 38 specifically linked the reduction of car emissions to the BAT principle.
29 Ashby and Anderson (1981: 104).
30 Ashby and Anderson (1981: 143).
31 Cutting (1987: 46)
32 Arp (1995); Berg (1982); Holzinger (1994).
33 Barthel (1991: 68).
34 Friedrich *et al.* (1998a,1998b, 2000). Levy (1993) takes a more optimistic view.
35 Interview with a BMWi official in 1992.
36 The Italian government once distributed a position paper using official Fiat letter heads (Interview in 1993).
37 Berg (1985: 6).
38 Berg (1985: 7).
39 Walsh (1987: 25).
40 Interview with DG Industry official in 1993.
41 Becker (1988); Berg (1982).
42 Barthel (1991); VDA (1983: 48).
43 Interview with a Swedish official in 1998.
44 Interviews in 1993 and 1998. See also Arp (1995: 52–3); Liefferink (1996: 107).
45 Interview in 1992.
46 Becker (1989: 43); VDA (1981: 45).
47 Becker (1988: 43).
48 Until the early 1980s, European producers worked unsuccessfully on the development of lead-resistant catalysts (Klenke 1995: 105).
49 CEC (1973: 13).
50 Johnson and Corcelle (1995: 132–3).
51 Haigh (1987: 199); Johnson and Corcelle (1995: 133).
52 Haigh (1987: 203).
53 Héritier (1996); Héritier *et al.* (1994; 1996). The first-mover strategy is explained in chapter 2.
54 Liefferink and Andersen (1998a).
55 Interview in 1992.

56 Haigh (1987: 204–5).
57 Haigh (1987: 204).
58 See chapter 7.
59 Haigh (1987: 204–5); *The Times*, 11 February 1982.
60 A number of exemptions were also introduced.
61 Haigh (ed.) (1995: ch. 6, section 7, page 3).
62 DoT (1979).
63 Italics added; cited in press statement by the Office of the European Commission in London, dated 28 May 1981.
64 DHSS (1980).
65 *The Times*, 9 February 1982.
66 *The Times*, 9 February 1982.
67 Interview with William Waldegrave in 1996.
68 Interview with FoE campaigner in 1993; Wilson (1983).
69 RCEP (1983).
70 Westheide (1987: 33).
71 CEC (1983d); VDA (1974: 49).
72 Haigh (1987: 206).
73 Cutting (1987).
74 CEC (1983d: 8).
75 Interview in 1993.
76 Interview in 1993.
77 Cutting (1987: 44).
78 Commission of the European Communities XI/A/2 Ref: ERG-II-SCPS 3/DR of 11 October 1983.
79 ERGA-II-WG 3.2/D.
80 Interview information from Commission official in 1993.
81 Written communication from a DoT official dated 21 June 1996.
82 CEC (1983d: 42).
83 RCEP (1994: 35–6).
84 Arp (1995: 77).
85 HoC (1988: column 275).
86 *New Scientist*, 13 May 1989, p. 45.
87 Written evidence from DoT official dated 21 June 1996. See also HoC (1988).
88 DoE (1994a, 1994b, 1995).
89 EP Working Document 2–1–1-/84/A.
90 Arp (1995); Holzinger (1994: 215–22).
91 Article 1 of *Directive 85/210/EEC*.
92 HoC (1988) and Greenpeace (1990).
93 HoC (1988: 436).
94 HoC (1988: 436).
95 Written communications from the AA and the RAC dated 14 September 1993 and 7 September 1993 respectively.

96 DoT and DoE (1984).
97 DETR (1997: 45).
98 DETR (1998c: 51).
99 HoC (1988: 447).

5

The catalytic converter versus the lean-burn engine controversy

On 21 July 1983 the German government announced the introduction of unleaded petrol and the three-way catalytic converter for all new cars by 1 January 1986. The decision was confirmed in principle in a statement issued on 26 October 1983 which, however, no longer explicitly referred to the three-way catalytic converter. Instead the October statement demanded 'the reduction of pollutants in car exhausts through the use of the best available technology. For this purpose the existent American car emission limits and test cycle shall be introduced.' [1] This amounted to a threat from the German government to go it alone despite its assurances that it would seek an EU-wide solution.

Subsequently, EU car emission policy-making became a high politics issue which at times threatened to escalate into a trade war. [2] The main dispute during 1983–91 centred around two mutually exclusive car emission abatement technologies: the three-way catalytic converter and the lean-burn engine. It ended with the phasing in of emission standards which, in practice, required the adoption of the three-way catalytic converter, initially only for large cars over 2 litres (the 1985 Luxembourg Compromise), then also for small cars under 1.4 litres (the 1989 small cars directive) and finally for all new cars (the 1991 consolidated directive). [3]

Germany's pusher role

Germany did not become an environmental leader state at the EU and the international level until 1982. [4] Germany's more progressive international stance became apparent for the first time during a conference on acidification in Stockholm in June 1982, that is, a few months before the faltering Centre–Left coalition government (SPD–FDP) collapsed in October 1982. [5] Up until then, Britain and Germany had been allies in rejecting demands to significantly reduce the SO_2 and NO_x emissions which contributed towards acid rain in Northern Europe. To the surprise of many observers (including the British government)[6] the new Centre–Right (CDU/CSU–FDP) coalition government did not opt for a more cautious environmental policy.[7]

Waldsterben as threat and window of opportunity
The German government had been unable to achieve by 1980 its 90 per cent car emission reduction target (from 1969 levels), as stipulated in the 1971 Environmental Programme.[8] The Interior minister Gerhart Baum (FDP) submitted relatively ambitious German proposals to the ECE in 1978 and to the EU in 1982. However, Baum was unable to push for the adoption of unleaded petrol and the three-way catalytic converter because of fierce resistance from the automobile and oil industries and the lack of backing from Chancellor Helmut Schmidt (SPD), who showed little interest in environmental issues. It was left to Baum's successor Friedrich Zimmermann (CSU) to brush aside objections from industry and cabinet colleagues who were reluctant to use the threat of going it alone. The cabinet's decisions in July and October 1983 were very much the result of Zimmermann's personal initiative, which one BMU–BMI official described as 'a forced ride (*Parforceritt*) through the cabinet'.[9]

Zimmermann's move was influenced by growing public concern about dying forests (*Waldsterben*). It presented him with a 'policy window' to outmanoeuvre opponents of the three-way catalytic converter.[10] Within the Centre–Right coalition government, Friedrich Zimmermann, Ignaz Kiechle and Werner Dollinger were chosen as Ministers of the Interior, Agriculture and Transport respectively. All three politicians were members of the conservative CSU in Bavaria, a *Land* with a high forest density and tourism.

The media had already been focusing on the *Waldsterben* issue for some years. A series of articles about *Waldsterben* which appeared in the influential weekly *Der Spiegel* in 1981, had been largely based on information supplied by the UBA.[11] Environmental groups such as the German Nature Circle (Deutscher Naturschutzring – DNR) and the German Association for the Alps (Deutscher Alpenverein), the Federal Association of Citizens' Initiatives for Environmental Protection (Bundesverband Bürgerinitiativen Umweltschutz – BBU) and the Federal Association for Environmental and Nature Protection Germany (Bundesverband für Umwelt- und Naturschutz Deutschland – BUND) had also already conducted campaigns. In 1983, the Council of Environmental Experts (SRU) published a special report on forest damage and air pollution which concluded that immediate action was needed to curb car emissions.[12] The electoral success of the Green Party, which entered the national Parliament (Bundestag) for the first time in 1983, further increased the pressure on the federal government.

The choice of Zimmermann, the CSU's foreign policy and defence specialist, as Interior minister in Chancellor Helmut Kohl's (CDU) new Centre–Right coalition government came as a surprise to many observers. According to his spokesman at the time,

> Zimmermann had been tipped as Defence Minister and had to act from a standing position. He quickly decided that his priorities should be law and order and the environment, the latter of which took the opposition by surprise. Zimmermann wanted to show a high profile [in the run up to March 1983 elections]. He quickly identified air pollution as his first priority and water pollution, especially the North Sea, as his second priority issue. Internal BMI plans for a Large Combustion Ordinance already existed under the old [SPD–FDP] coalition government but did not get anywhere under Chancellor Helmut Schmidt and [Economics Minister] Otto Graf Lambsdorff.[13]

Encouraged by the success he had achieved with the Large Combustion Ordinance, Zimmermann then decided to tackle traffic and household sources. Car emission regulations did not become one of Zimmermann's priorities until 1983. The Large Combustion Ordinance initially remained a domestic issue because it is a process standard and therefore did not constitute a barrier to trade. However, car emission regulations are product standards which must be harmonised under the EU's internal market provision. The threat to adopt unilateral action therefore brought the German government into conflict with the Commission as well as with the British, French and Italian governments, all of whom threatened court action. However, the opposition parties in the Bundestag, the SPD and the newly elected Green Party, urged the government to go it alone, reflecting how important environmental pollution (and *Waldsterben* in particular) had become as a political issue by 1983.[14]

The lack of speed limits

The (three-way) catalytic converter had been in use in America and Japan since the 1970s. However, driving conditions in Europe differed, particularly in Germany where there are no general speed limits on motorways. According to a Commission study the average speed on German motorways was, however, only 5kmph higher than in France and Italy, and 15kmph higher than in the Netherlands and Belgium, because drivers in these countries regularly ignored speed limits.[15] The German government's refusal to adopt speed limits was due to fears that this would damage its high-performance car producers (BMW, Mercedes and Porsche).[16] Japanese car companies advertised their products with slogans such as 'tested on German motorways'.[17] And Porsche invited affluent American customers to its Stuttgart headquarters where they were issued with maps showing stretches of motorway without speed limits.[18]

Under pressure from environmental groups, the opposition parties (SPD and Greens) in the *Bundestag* and the French and Italian governments, the German government set up a speed limit test programme in 1984. The British government stayed out of this dispute because it considered speed limts a subsidiarity issue.[19] The test programme came to the conclusion that a speed limit of 100kmph would lead to only marginal environmental gains and was unacceptable to the public, although several German officials privately conceded that the programme was biased against speed limits.[20] Follow-up (desk) studies by the UBA concluded that a speed limit of 130kmph would lead to a reduction in the overall level of car emission related CO, HC and NO_x of 1–7 per cent.[21] These are small margins compared to the 90 per cent reduction capacity of the three-way catalytic converter. However, the German government's refusal to adopt speed limits damaged its credibility during EU negotiations.

Establishing the three-way catalytic converter as the BAT option
Some UBA officials (such as Axel Friedrich who later became the head of the Environment and Transport Division) blamed car emissions for acid rain and forest damage, and demanded the introduction of the three-way catalytic converter as early as 1980. However, prior to 1983 they were reprimanded by their superiors.[22]

The ADAC, which, unlike the UBA, was against speed limits, became increasingly concerned that the car was being branded by environmentalists as the 'environment's enemy number one' and motorists as 'killers of the environment' (*Umweltmörder*).[23] The ADAC had long suspected that the automobile industry's claims about the alleged poor performance of the three-way catalytic converter were exaggerated. For the ADAC 'there came a point when we said:

"Enough is enough! Our friends in industry have poked fun at us for long enough. We will now run our own tests to find out what the three-way catalytic converter can do." '[24] ADAC membership stood at 7.3 million in 1983. It therefore wielded considerable influence and had the necessary financial muscle.

UBA officials and ADAC representatives set up a joint programme in Berlin to test the three-way catalytic converter under German driving conditions. An earlier attempt to conduct such a test in Munich had to be abandoned after the automobile industry (and BMW in particular) exerted pressure on the ADAC.

Fifteen Volkswagen Golfs, the most widely sold car in Germany at the time, were selected for the UBA–ADAC test programme in 1983. Five Golfs were equipped with a three-way catalytic converter, another five had conventional engines which were run on leaded petrol and the remaining five also had conventional engines but were run on unleaded petrol. The five three-way catalytic converter equipped Golfs had to be bought in America (where they were sold under the name Volkswagen Rabbit) and exported to Germany, because Volkswagen, which until 1985 was fiercely opposed to the introduction of the three-way catalytic converter, refused to cooperate.

In contrast to claims by the German automobile industry, the test results showed that the three-way catalytic converter was a highly effective and reliable technology which did not increase fuel consumption. On the contrary, the adoption of electronic fuel management led to lower petrol consumption in comparison to Golfs with carburettor technology. The UBA and the ADAC rejected VDA claims that the cost of the three-way catalytic converter would amount to up to about DM5,000 over the lifetime of a vehicle. The UBA put the cost of the three-way catalyst as low as DM150. The ADAC estimated that installing the entire three-way catalytic converter system (including indirect fuel injection and the lambda sensor) would amount to about DM1,500 for a typical medium-sized car.[25]

The UBA and the ADAC not only exposed as unfounded the alleged deficiencies of the three-way catalytic converter but presented it as the BAT option already available on the world's leading markets. It appealed to environmentally concerned citizens and drew on the notion of ecological modernisation which assumes that stringent environmental standards can be beneficial for business. German producers, who advertised their international success as based on *Vorsprung durch Technik*,[26] were put on the defensive. One representative of a

German automobile company conceded: 'There came a point when the three-way catalytic converter was equated with innovation ... and cars not equipped with it were seen as technologically inferior ... The media then started to ask why is it available in America and Japan but not in Germany?'[27]

The argument that Germany's automobile industry 'made common cause with German environmentalists to demand that Europe adopt American standards'[28] is flawed. Germany's car industry was fiercely opposed to the introduction of the US 1983 standards, although the producers of large cars were somewhat less obstructive.[29] Environmental groups, on the other hand, wanted more far-reaching behavioural and transport policy changes, which fits Christian Hey and Uwe Brendle's claim that German environmental groups were highly principled in their aims and strategies during the 1980s.[30] The German government therefore faced an uphill struggle in convincing consumers of the benefits of three-way catalytic converter equipped cars. For this reason, the BMI immediately embarked on plans to financially support the purchase of cars equipped with the three-way catalytic converter.

The adoption of tax incentives
Friedrich Zimmermann wanted to ensure that car sales would not plummet as a result of stringent emission standards. He therefore 'favoured an effective and simple allowance similar to that of child benefit'.[31] However, the BMI's initial plan to introduce a direct subsidy (*Kaufhilfe*) based on industry's inflated cost figures ran into insurmountable difficulties. It was opposed by the Finance Minister Gerhard Stoltenberg (CDU), who warned that such a subsidy was economically inefficient and could set a dangerous precedent.[32] Stoltenberg instead proposed the introduction of fiscal incentives in the form of a tax allowance deductible from road tax (*Kraftfahrzeugsteuer*).

The Economics Minister Manfred Bangemann (FDP), who later became EU Industry Commissioner (1985–99), strongly advised against direct subsidies after taking a sounding from EU Commissioners who were open-minded about fiscal tax incentives. This helped the Finance Ministry to get its proposal adopted in cabinet on 19 September 1984; four months later the fiscal incentives were extended to the retrofitting of old cars with catalytic converters.[33]

The British, French and Italian governments were opposed to the German (as well as to the Danish, Dutch and Greek) fiscal incentives,

Table 5.1 *German car exports and imports in 1983*

Member state	Exports		Imports		Net balance of trade	
	Number	Value [a]	Number	Value [a]	Number	Value [a]
Britain	467,000	6.5	8,000	0.2	459,000	6.3
France	266,000	3.7	180,000	1.8	86,000	1.8
Italy	200,000	3.0	104,000	0.9	96,000	2.1
Total	933,000	13.2	292,000	2.9	641,000	10.2

Notes: The numbers are rounded and may therefore not add up; value [a] in billion DM
Sources: VDA and BMU (undated memos)

and they called on DG Industry for support. However, DG Industry lost an internal Commission battle against DG Environment, which was backed by DG Competition and the Legal Service. In April 1985, the Commission issued a statement that it would not object to fiscal incentives in Germany which took effect in July 1985.[34] However, the Commission insisted that fiscal incentives had to be lower than the cost of the pollution abatement technology adopted and closely monitored their level in Germany because its large car market has a considerable 'pulling effect'.[35]

The introduction of fiscal incentives increased rifts which had appeared within the VDA. BMW and Mercedes became less opposed to the three-way catalytic converter, something which could not be said of Volkswagen, Opel and Ford-Germany. Initially, Volkswagen was the most vociferous opponent of the US 1983 standards (although this was later denied by the company).[36] Ironically, Volkswagen was the only automobile company in which the German state held a direct stake, and *Land* officials from Lower Saxony were represented on its supervisory board. In its attempt to prevent the introduction of the US 1983 standards within the EU, Volkswagen enlisted the help of the British government. DoT officials accepted invitations to visit Volkswagen's headquarters in Wolfsburg (Germany).[37] On the other hand, the British catalytic converter producer Johnson Matthey visited Germany to put across to BMI and UBA officials its case in favour of the three-way catalytic converter.

The German government (and the BMWi in particular) was worried that the introduction of fiscal incentives would trigger retaliatory action.[38] Table 5.1 shows that the German automobile industry achieved a trade surplus of more than DM10.2 billion in 1983 (at 1983 prices) over those member states whose governments favoured the lean-burn engine. In 1983, Germany's exports to Britain were particularly high, with 467,000 cars, while imports from Britain had almost come to a halt at a mere 8,000 vehicles.[39]

Britain's reaction to the German initiative
The British government and British industry rejected the demand for US 1983 standards as an overreaction which had more to do with the German love affair with forests than it did with a science-driven environmental policy.[40] One British automobile industry representative interviewed argued:

> To me the turning point was 1983. Up to that point it had been a very rational process of deciding what the next step in the emission regulations was going to be ... But then – bang! In 1983 the German Environmental Minister was saying: 'Oooh! Our trees are all dying!' Shock, horror and dismay! And ever since there has been political turmoil. I mean literally. Ever since, the Germans, backed up of course by the Danes, the Dutch and Greeks, pressed for [US 1983 standards] ... Also countries like Switzerland, Austria, Norway, Finland and Sweden were all going down the American route.[41]

It was only from the late 1980s onwards, and after having retrospectively revised upwards the traffic-related NO_x emissions, that the British government conceded that acid rain, tropospheric ozone and forest damage constituted a serious domestic problem. The revised figures showed that by 1984 road traffic had overtaken power stations as the largest source of NO_x. However, acid rain and high levels of tropospheric ozone, for which NO_x emissions are a precursor substance, remained a low priority until the late 1980s, when, according to the Environmental Minister William Waldegrave, 'the real battle within Whitehall was fought over large combustion plants rather than cars'. [42]

British environmental groups initially focused mainly on power stations in their campaign against acid rain.[43] Unlike the German groups, they lacked such a potent symbol as widescale forest damage: wooded areas totalled only 2.1 million hectares in Britain in the early 1980s, in contrast to 7.4 million hectares in Germany.[44] However, the percentage of damaged trees was actually higher in Britain than in Germany for much of the 1980s, as can be seen from Table 5.2.

Table 5.2 *Defoliation (in %) of trees in Britain and Germany, 1986–96*

		1986	1987	1988	1989	1990	1991	1992	1993	1994	1995	1996
Britain	Conifers											
		n/a	23.0	27.0	34.0	45.0	51.5	52.7	16.8	15.0	13.0	13.9
	Broadleaves											
		n/a	20.0	20.0	21.0	28.8	65.6	67.8	17.1	12.4	14.5	15.0
Germany	Conifers											
		19.5	15.9	14.0	13.2	15.0	24.8	23.8	21.4	21.6	18.3	16.7
	Broadleaves											
		16.8	19.2	16.5	20.4	23.8	26.5	32.0	29.9	30.1	29.9	30.8

Source: EEA (1998b: 55–6)

The Forestry Commission in Britain, initially rejected the idea of tree-health surveys, the first of which was undertaken by Friends of the Earth (FoE) with the help of German forestry experts.[45] Confronted with the alarming results from the FoE survey, the Forestry Commission conducted its own surveys which also showed an increase (albeit a significantly lower one) in the number of defoliated trees. However, the Forestry Commission and the British government remained adamant that there was no scientific proof of a causal link between car emissions and damaged forest.

One DoT official interviewed commented on Anglo-German differences in perception of the problem in the 1980s: 'In Germany there was a fixation on acid rain and forest damage. The Germans therefore focused on the NO_x issue ... We saw energy consumption as an environmental concern. We thought that something more energy efficient must be better, all else being equal.'[46] However, he added that

> by 1989 our genuine environmental concern in the UK had changed focus. We then realised that urban air quality and NO_x levels were important. There is absolutely no doubt in my mind now that the sort of environmental improvement that was offered by lean-burn would not be good enough to meet our environmental needs now. We do need three-way catalytic converters but at the time we were not convinced.[47]

Trade implications

Katharina Holzinger has argued that the British government's support
for the lean-burn engine is best explained by reference to Ford-UK
and Rover–British Leyland's economic interest in this technology.[48]
Holzinger's argument is confirmed by a House of Commons statement
made by the Environmental Minister William Waldegrave in 1985: 'It
is noticeable ... that Ford has recently made a large investment in this
country in lean burn engine technology, aimed at the large market in
the European Community as well as the British market ... Of course,
as in the past, the interests of the British motor industry will be close
to our hearts.'[49] And Lord Brabazon of Tara, even argued: 'I am in
no doubt that the advantages of lean-burn will mean that almost all
manufacturers will have to adopt this technology sooner or later; but
I am pleased to report that United Kingdom engineers from several
organisations are at the forefront of these developments.'[50]

The British government pinned its hopes on the lean-burn engine
at a time when the domestic automobile industry was in dire straits.
In 1982, overall car production in Britain had declined to levels of
output last seen in the 1950s and stood at only 0.88 million units,
while the balance of trade for motor cars reached a deficit of £1.4
billion (at 1982 prices).[51] In particular, Rover–British Leyland, which
became nicknamed '*British Elend*' (British misery) in Germany,[52] had
been on a downward spiral since the 1950s. British Leyland was
part-privatised and renamed Rover in 1986; it was not fully privatised
until 1988.[53] Rover and the economically more successful Ford-UK
were staunch proponents of the lean-burn engine.

However, Henning Arp has claimed that the British government

> was not a mere instrument of business ... For their part, the adminis-
> tration, led by the Prime Minister, was convinced of the merits of the
> new technology. Its commitment to the lean-burn rationale cannot be
> explained simply with reference to industry pressure. Rather, it was the
> lean-burn rationale which convinced government, and made it a 'true
> believer'.[54]

The lean-burn engine as the BPM option

One of the reasons why the British government uncritically accepted
the claims by corporate advocates of the lean-burn engine technology
was that Ford-UK and, to a lesser degree, Rover–British Leyland went
to great lengths to present the lean-burn engine as a cost-efficient
technology which best suited the traditional British environmental

regulatory style. Ford-UK, responsible for emission control within Ford-Europe, ran an aggressive lobbying campaign. Rover saw little need to engage in similarly overt lobbying but instead relied on its status as a (partly) state-owned company.[55]

One core lobbying document distributed by Ford-UK in 1983 labelled the lean-burn engine technology a 'lifetime concept ... because Lean-Burn engines inherently emit low levels of pollutants due to their design principles without the need for additional equipment'.[56] It omitted to mention that lean-burn engines required an oxidation catalyst to comply with EU car emission legislation. In June 1984, William Waldegrave was still justifying Britain's opposition to the catalyst at a UNECE conference in Munich as follows:

> [I]t is our conviction that many of the [pollution] control systems now available are far from ideal both from environmental and financial standpoints. I include in this list the three way catalytic systems available to curb emissions from petrol engined vehicles ... We seek new technologies that achieve pollution abatement as an integral part of design rather than add on curative devices.[57]

It is ironic that Ford-UK became the most vociferous proponent of the lean-burn engine in Britain, branding the three-way catalytic converter a complex and expensive 'hang-on' technology which had a poor in-service record in the USA. It claimed that 'the Ford position is to expose the reality of the Catalyst, and promote the "Lean-Burn" concept with all its real-world advantages'.[58] Ford-UK's criticisms went so far that its American parent company felt it had to draw a line. One industry representative recalled the following scene during a meeting of the SMMT:

> We reached the point where the crucial element in the argument for the lean-burn was the data available from the United States about the shortcomings of the three-way catalyst technology ... There came a point when in fact Ford-US leaned on Ford-UK and said: 'Sorry, you cannot say that our three-way catalytic converters do not work in the United States. Shut up!'[59]

Ford-UK also heavily lobbied the Commission, arguing that the lean-burn engine was a 'European response to a European situation'.[60] It warned the Environmental Commissioner Clinton-Davis that DG Environment's preference for 'the US '83 standards would lead to massive job losses in Europe'.[61]

The DoT did commission some studies but the British government did not fundamentally challenge the technological feasibility of the lean-burn technology, which, after all, was only at a developmental stage. However, this did not prevent William Waldegrave from arguing that

> emission controls in this country have gradually developed as technology advances have pushed forward the definition of what is cost-effective. These have now brought us to the lean burn engine which ... promises both emission reductions and fuel savings. The Government wish to encourage this development, and therefore have no intention to impose standards in this country that would require manufacturers to use expensive three-way catalyst technology instead.[62]

However, for the British government, Ford-UK and Rover's failure to deliver the promised low-emission lean-burn engine 'became an embarrassment from a certain point onwards'.[63] In 1987, the DoT finally carried out its own two-year test programme at the Transport Research Centre. The DoT bought six Toyota cars which, at the time, had the most developed lean-burn engines. Two of them were equipped with US three-way catalytic converters, two had conventional petrol engines which complied with existent EU emission legislation and two were lean-burn engines with an oxidation catalyst. DoT officials 'were surprised how good the three-way catalytic converter was'[64] when they saw the test results. However, as was pointed out by one DoT official,

> [i]t is wrong to think that there was any sort of gradual softening of the UK attitude towards three-way catalysts ... the turning point was in 1989 when the European Parliament overturned the common position adopted by Council ... and introduced standards that effectively meant fitting a three-way catalyst to cars under 1.4 litres. Once that decision had been imposed, there was little left to fight for.[65]

The only major domestic policy actor in Britain (apart from Johnson Matthey) to advocate the adoption of the three-way catalytic converter prior to the late 1980s was the House of Lords Select Committee on the European Communities (HLSCEC).[66] In April 1985, Lord Nathan argued that 'the lean-burn engine requires at least equally sophisticated control mechanisms to maintain good driveability and an oxidation catalyst is required'.[67] And the Earl of Shannon warned that

> lean-burn will do little in the place where it is most required: that is, in the urban driving cycle where one is continuously accelerating and braking ... Unless there is a quantum leap in lean-burn technology ...

the motor industry could well find itself going up a technological blind alley. If they feel they can just scrape by now, any later tightening up of the emission standards will put this course right out of court, even with an oxidation catalyst.[68]

It was only from the late 1980s onwards that Britain's FoE and Greenpeace in Britain started to support the three-way catalytic converter.[69] In 1988, Greenpeace ran a campaign branding Ford-UK as a corporate environmental laggard and FoE launched a campaign to boycott Peugeot which had important production sites in Britain and, under its President Jacques Calvet, became the most hardline corporate opponent of even the most moderate EU car emission legislation.[70]

The EEB and FoE jointly organised an international seminar, 'The Clean Car: A Challenge for Europe', in London on 12 March 1987.[71] However, it left unconvinced those representatives of the British automobile industry, the DoT, the DTI, the DoE and the Department of Energy who attended. The lean-burn engine also received continued support from the main motorist organisations, the AA and RAC,[72] as well as most of the media.[73] In 1988, the HCEC, which had traditionally been a progressive actor in British environmental policy-making, still backed the lean-burn engine 'as the best practicable means ... to limit NO_x and hydrocarbons',[74] although it was 'appalled ... at the standard of evidence received from motor car companies'.[75] Car emission regulations did not develop into a partisan political issue, despite the fact that individual Labour and Liberal Democrat MPs favoured the three-way catalytic converter.[76]

According to one DoT official, the lean-burn engine received the personal backing of Margaret Thatcher, because the

> chief scientist of the cabinet office made a presentation explaining the technology ... Margaret Thatcher was a chemist, a scientist, who understood the technical issues. She concluded on the basis of what she had been told that lean-burn was the way to go. For her, the three-way catalytic converter was a wasteful approach.[77]

However, the lean-burn engine also fitted the Thatcher government's low-cost approach to pollution control. Margaret Thatcher perceived (environmental) regulations mainly as red tape and a costly burden on industry. The German government was widely – but wrongly – seen in Britain as 'having been persuaded by their manufacturers, on competitive grounds, to press for catalysts'.[78] It is therefore reasonable to assume that Thatcher, who held anti-German sentiments,[79] suspected Germany of wanting to achieve a technological hegemony within the automobile sector in Europe.

In order to understand the complex and highly politicised EU negotiations between 1983 and 1991, it is necessary to explain the most important environmental and economic implications of the prinicipal technological options.

Car emission policy-making as technology choice

EU car emission directives do not prescribe a particular technology. However, certain limit values and test cycle requirements may favour particular technological options. In the 1980s the EU was concerned with a number of technical options for reducing car emissions (non-technical measures such as improved public transport were left to member states). These options are considered under the headings which follow.

The catalytic converter

The catalytic converter consists of a metal casing into which is inserted a ceramic or metal honeycomb structure coated with precious metals (platinum, rhodium and sometimes also palladium). The catalyst works effectively only when sufficiently heated up, which means that emissions are not treated during the first few minutes of a journey following a cold start.[80] A car fitted with a catalytic converter must run on unleaded petrol because lead renders ineffective the precious metals.

In the early 1980s there were principally three types of catalytic converter available in Europe. The fully regulated (closed-loop) three-way catalytic converter, which made possible compliance with the US 1983 standards, was able to reduce CO, HC and NO_x emissions by up to 90 per cent while using platinum to oxidize CO and HC (into CO_2 and water) and rhodium to reduce NO_x (into nitrogen – N_2). It constituted the BAT option. In this book, for reasons of simplicity, the closed-loop catalytic converter is referred to as the three-way catalytic converter.

In order to allow for a simultaneous oxidation and reduction within the fully regulated three-way catalytic converter, the engine must run on or close to an air:fuel ratio of 14.7:1.0. This air:fuel ratio is called 'lambda 1' (or the stoichiometric point) and leads to the complete combustion of the fuel. Lambda 1 can be attained during acceleration phases and full-load conditions only with electronic fuel injection (and a lambda sensor).[81]

In the 1980s, fuel injection was a standard feature only for large and sports cars; small and medium-sized cars instead relied on carburettor technology. Mercedes discontinued the use of carburettor technology for all of its models in 1979, while Volkswagen and Rover–British Leyland, relied on it until well into the 1980s.[82]

In 1987 approximately 35 per cent of all new cars sold in the EU were fitted with fuel injection.[83] However, in the small-car category (under 1.4 litres), only 7 per cent were equipped with fuel injections.[84] The adoption of the three-way catalytic converter therefore triggered a higher increase in the price of small (and medium-sized) cars, both in absolute and relative terms compared to the price of large cars. This was one reason why the producers of small cars, which cater for a very price-sensitive market segment, were more strongly opposed to the introduction of the three-way catalytic converter than the producers of large cars, whose purchasers tend to be more affluent.[85] However, over time, the producers of small and medium-sized cars would probably have made the switch from carburettor technology to fuel injection as the more advanced technology leading to lower fuel consumption.[86]

The second principal type of catalyst was the unregulated (open-loop) catalytic converter, which does not rely on electronic fuel injection. It can therefore be fitted to cars with carburettors. However, unregulated three-way catalytic converters can reduce CO, HC and NO_x emissions by only approximately 50–60 per cent.

The third type of catalyst is the (open-loop) oxidation catalyst, which can reduce CO and HC emissions by approximately 90 per cent. However, it leaves NO_x emissions untreated. It is technologically the simplest type of catalytic converter and can also be used with carburettor technology.

The British government initially had been opposed to the adoption of any type of catalyst. However, in 1985, it supported the adoption of the lean-burn engine in combination with the oxidation catalyst as the BPM option. It is impossible to identify an exact date for this policy change as British ministers and officials issued contradictory statements (some opposing all types of catalyst, others welcoming the oxidation catalyst) during the first half of 1985.[87]

The first generation of catalytic converters had been fitted to cars in the USA in the 1970s, and had suffered from teething problems and increased fuel consumption. Moreover, the failure by the American government to adopt fiscal incentives for unleaded petrol encouraged deliberate misfuelling with cheaper leaded petrol. The early negative American experience was often cited by proponents of the lean-burn engine: they also raised doubts about the availability of precious metals and questioned whether electronic fuel-injection systems would be attainable for all producers.[88]

The availability of precious metals
Most platinum reserves are located in South Africa and the former USSR; some can be found in Canada and America. The world's leading catalytic converter manufacturer Johnson Matthey is a British company, although it is controlled by the South African mining company Rustenburg. For British environmental groups 'the South African connection was very important' and the main reason why they 'kept a healthy distance from Johnson Matthey'.[89] At the time, groups such as FoE and Greenpeace supported a trade embargo against the apartheid-ridden South Africa.

German environmental groups were not faced with the same dilemma. First, the main German catalytic converter manufacturer Degussa had no direct South African connections. Second, most German environmental groups initially focused on curbing car usage rather than on technological options. Early on, only the more traditional groups, such as the DNR and the German Alps Association supported the introduction of the three-way catalytic converter.

The availability of the lambda sensor
The German company Bosch had a quasi-monopoly on electronic fuel-injection devices and the lambda sensor in continental Europe in the early 1980s. This caused concern among French and Italian car producers in particular.[90] However, Germany's Volkswagen, Opel and Ford-Germany were also worried that Bosch might give preference to its long-standing customers Mercedes, BMW and Porsche which used electronic fuel-injection for American export models.[91] The British government and manufacturers downplayed Bosch's dominant position.[92]

Experience of exporting to America
During EU negotiations, much was made of the fact that the producers of large cars had gained a competitive advantage due to their American

export experience.[93] In the 1980s, the French manufacturers Peugeot[94] and Renault, as well as Italy's Fiat, produced only small and medium-sized cars. The picture was more complicated for Britain and Germany. The largest volume producers in Britain (Ford-UK, Vauxhall and Rover–British Leyland) and Germany (Volkswagen, Opel and Ford-Germany) also specialised in small and medium-sized cars. On the other hand, Britain's Rolls Royce, Bentley and Jaguar, as well as Germany's Mercedes,[95] BMW and Porsche, produced only large cars. However, Britain's manufacturers of large cars produced and exported significantly fewer cars than their German competitors. In 1983, German producers exported twenty-seven models equipped with three-way catalytic converters to America while the export total for all the remaining EU manufacturers amounted to just ten.[96]

The data in table 5.3 reveals that between 1970 and 1983 the EU's large car producers expanded their exports to America while the majority of small and medium-sized car producers were in retreat.[97] One of the reasons was that Europe's small car producers increasingly lost out to competition from Japanese companies, which were quicker to adapt to stringent American emission regulations that were similar to domestic regulations.

European producers of small and medium-sized cars were concerned that adoption of the US 1983 standards by the EU might give Japanese producers (which also specialised in small and medium-sized cars) a competitive advantage. In 1986, William Waldegrave argued during a House of Commons debate:

> Viscount Davignon, the former Industry Commissioner, made a formidable remark before he retired. Of the German proposals to provide fiscal incentives for those cars that cause little pollution [i.e. comply with the US 1983 standards] he said that it was the first time that a European country had introduced proposals that would directly subsidise Japanese industry. We must take account of such considerations.[98]

Ironically, Japanese producers were later well behind most European small car producers in offering cars equipped with three-way catalytic converters on the German market.[99]

The lean-burn engine

All British and German automobile producers undertook research on the lean-burn engine technology.[100] However, the producers of large cars soon abandoned the lean-burn engine technology because of

Table 5.3 *European car exports to America*

	1970	1975	1980	1983
German companies				
Volkswagen	569,696	267,718	90,923	61,275
Audi	8,054	50,784	42,483	46,995
Mercedes–Benz	25,055	42,233	51,340	73,692
BMW	14,584	19,419	37,015	59,243
Porsche	13,653	16,224	10,493	21,199
German total	734,237	490,694	300,849	262,404
British companies				
British Leyland	71,259	70,839	30,010	15,815
Rolls Royce–Bentley	340	756	n/a	n/a
British total[a]	86,035	74,277	30,010	15,815
Italian companies				
Fiat	38,095	101,522	39,924	6,729
Alfa Romeo	1,417	5,342	2,997	2,995
Italian total	39,512	107,390	42,921	9,724
French companies				
Peugeot	4,996	11,850	12,807	15,241
Citroën	1,209	–	–	–
Renault	20,732	5,780	24,567	28,198
French total	32,972	17,630	37,374	43,439

Note: [a] The British total includes unit figures for Jensen, Lotus, Rootes and Delorean
Source: United States International Trade Commission (1984)

concerns about inferior driveability and poor emission performance during acceleration and high-speed phases. However, Ford-UK, Rover, Volkswagen, Peugeot, Renault and Fiat remained proponents of the lean-burn engine for much longer.

Lean-burn engines aim to achieve both a reasonable emission reduction and a lower fuel consumption. The lean-burn engine is based on the concept that the greater the air:fuel ratio (that is, the 'leaner' the mixture) the greater the fuel savings. Genuine lean-burn engines operate at an air:fuel ratio of 21:1 at which point CO, HC and NO_x emissions are reduced by approximately 50–70 per cent compared to conventional petrol engines without the three-way catalytic converter.[101] However, such a lean mixture has (to date) proved unachievable because it causes the engine to misfire and stall.

Lean-burn engines need to run on an air:fuel ratio which is as close as possible to 21:1 while cars equipped with a three-way catalytic converter need a stoichiometric air:fuel ratio of 14.7:1.0. This makes the two concepts incompatible.

In the early 1980s, lean-burn engines were produced that were able to run on an air:fuel ratio of 18:1 at a constant speed of 90 kmph.[102] These engines were able to comply with ECE-R 15–04 but not the US 1983 standards. The first generation of lean-burn engines produced very high NO_x and HC emissions during acceleration phases and under full-load conditions. Adding an oxidation catalyst reduced HC emissions but left the high NO_x emissions unaffected.

Corporate proponents of the lean-burn engine technology argued that – given more lead-time for research and development – the lean-burn engine would soon be able to deliver both significant fuel efficiency improvement and reasonable emission reduction at a reasonable cost.

The diesel engine

Some manufacturers tried to benefit from consumer insecurity about future EU emission legislation by promoting the diesel as a 'green' car, since on average a diesel car needs less fuel than an equivalent petrol car.[103] However, diesel fuel contains a higher average carbon content and more energy is needed in the refinery to produce 1 litre of low-sulphur diesel fuel than is required for 1 litre of unleaded petrol. To gain a net CO_2 reduction, a diesel car needs a fuel consumption which is at least 13 per cent lower than that of an equivalent petrol car.[104] Moreover, diesel cars produce higher NO_x emissions than petrol cars equipped with a three-way catalytic converter.

In America and Japan, diesel cars almost disappeared from the market in the 1970s after the adoption of stringent limit values for carcinogenic particulates, although this was disputed by the car industry.[105] The EU introduced relatively lenient particulate limit values in the late 1980s. The German government demanded the BAT option for both petrol and diesel cars. However, after heavy lobbying from Mercedes and Volkswagen, fiscal incentives were granted not only for the three-way catalytic converter but for diesel cars which met the lenient EU particulate limits.

EU negotiations

The arduous negotiations at the EU level between 1983 and 1991, which led to the phasing in of the three-way catalytic converter have been well documented and analysed in studies by Katharina Holzinger and Henning Arp.[106] This chapter therefore focuses mainly on how Anglo-German differences were reconciled during the EU negotiations while presenting new empirical findings.

Germany's demands for the US 1983 standards were supported by Denmark, Greece and the Netherlands, while Britain found allies in the French and Italian governments. However, William Waldegrave, who skilfully negotiated the car emission dossiers for the British government between 1983 and 1988, has argued that 'there was no permanent alliance. The car emission directives were unlike the large combustion directive where the UK was isolated. On car emissions, alliances were shifting depending on the issue ... which made these negotiations extraordinarily complex.'[107]

Table 5.4 presents an overview of the different car categories, emission limit values and implementation dates adopted under the 1985 Luxembourg Compromise, the 1989 small cars directive and the 1991 consolidated directive. It also states the limit values for a diesel car directive which was adopted in 1991.[108] For petrol cars, the cheapest technological compliance option is listed.

The 1985 Luxembourg Compromise is best seen as an 'overall package'[109] which defused the highly divisive three-way catalytic converter v. lean-burn engine controversy through a series of compromise deals which accommodated the core demands of the central policy actors.[110] It put forward a multifaceted approach which differentiated car emission limit values according to three categories, set variable implementation deadlines and stipulated a raft of tailor-made derogations that took into account the difficulties certain producers had with particular car models. For example, the British government managed to get Land Rover cars reclassified as 'off-road' vehicles which were allowed to comply with significantly more lenient values.[111]

Table 5.4 *EU car emission directives, 1987–91*

1985 Luxembourg Compromise (Directive 88/76/EEC):

Category	Grammes per ECE test CO	HC + NO$_x$	NO$_x$	Implementation New models	All cars	Cheapest technological option
>2 litres	25	6.5	3.5	1.10.1988	1.10.1989	Three-way catalytic converter
1.4–2 litres	30	8	–	1.10.1991	1.10.1993	Lean-burn and ox-cat
<1.4 litres:						
1st stage	45	15	6	1.10.1990	1.10.1991	Engine optimisation
2nd stage	Limit values to be decided by 1987			1.10.1992	1.10.1993	–

1989 Small cars directive (89/458/EEC):

Category	Grammes per ECE test CO	HC + NO$_x$	NO$_x$	Implementation New models	All cars	Cheapest technological option
<1.4 litres	19	5	–	1.10.1992	1.10.1993	Three-way catalyst

1991 Consolidated directive (91/441/EEC):

Category	Grammes per (new) test CO	HC + NO$_x$	PM	Implementation New models	All cars	Cheapest technological option
All petrol cars	3.16	1.13	–	1.10.1992	1.10.1993	Three-way catalyst

1991 Diesel directive (91/542/EEC):

Category	Grammes per test CO	HC + NO$_x$	PM	Implementation New models	All cars
All diesel cars	3.16	1.13	0.18	1.10.1992	1.10.1993

Notes: The limit values for *Directives 88/76/EEC* and *89/458/EEC* are not comparable with *Directive 91/441/EEC* because different test cycles are applicable. Derogations are not listed. Ox-cat stands for oxidation catalyst
Sources: Adapted from *Directives 88/76/EEC, 89/458/EEC, 91/441/EEC* and *91/542/EEC* and interview information

Germany made bigger concessions than Britain if the 1985 Luxembourg Compromise is considered in isolation. However, by 1991, the
German demands put forward in 1983 had been largely fulfilled. With
the benefit of hindsight, one German BMU official claimed:

> I am glad that we did not run over the British. If the EU had adopted
> standards [through the 1985 Luxembourg Compromise] which would
> have ruled out the development of the lean-burn engine, I am sure a
> myth would have been created that this technology was killed off by
> Germany's drive for the three-way catalyst.[112]

Britain's favoured technological option, the lean-burn engine,
was not lost because the British government was outvoted in the
Environmental Council. The 1989 small cars directive and the 1991
consolidated directive were both adopted unanimously, although
qualified majority voting (QMV), applied after the SEA, came into
force in 1987. Only the 1985 Luxembourg Compromise was adopted
by QMV in 1987 against the votes of Denmark and Greece, neither of
which were car producer states. One German Environmental Council
participant explained:

> On issues which are as sensitive as this one there is no real combative
> voting (*Kampfabstimmung*) where one tries to massively outvote, for
> example, the French government. In Brussels it is important to somehow
> accommodate, if at all possible, all interests ... It would not have been
> necessary to adopt some of the car emission directives unanimously.
> However, it looked good and no one felt pushed to the wall.[113]

This is not to argue that tough bargaining did not play a part in the
Council negotiations. On the contrary, attempts to outmanoeuvre
other policy actors were an important feature of EU car emission
policy-making in the 1980s when 'few subjects have caused as much
bitterness as the "clean cars" dossier'.[114]

The EP as an emerging actor

The adoption of the three-way catalytic converter for new cars would
have been delayed by several years had it not been for the EP. The
cooperation procedure (which grants the EP a veto right if it can
muster the necessary majority in the second reading) was applicable
for all three car emission directives mentioned above. However, the EP
managed to flex its muscles only with regard to the 1989 small cars
directive, which some observers have called a 'surprising success'[115]
and the 'most spectacular use so far of [its] ... new constitutional

powers'.[116] This must be contrasted with the humiliating defeat which the Environmental Committee had to accept when the EP's plenary session failed to reach the quorum needed to adopt its second reading amendments for the 1991 consolidated directive that would have significantly tightened the emission limits. For Ken Collins (Socialist, UK), this event constituted his 'biggest failure' as the EP's longest-serving Environmental Committee chairperson and 'a disaster . . . because the Environmental Committee did not properly recognise that it was not enough for environmentally minded people to agree with each other'.[117]

The EP's success during the second reading amendments of the 1989 small cars directive can be explained by four factors.[118] First, the vote in the plenum took place a few weeks before the Euro elections in 1989, at a time when environmental awareness was high. Second, the EP could count on the support of the Danish and Greek governments which had pledged not to overrule the Parliament in Council. Third, Environmental Commissioner Carlo Ripa di Meana managed to push environmental issues high up on the Commission's agenda (largely against the will of the Commission President Jacques Delors).[119] And, fourth, the fiscal incentives in the large German and, to a lesser degree, the small Danish, Dutch and Greek markets forced all major car producers to offer cars equipped with a three-way catalytic converter for these member states if they did not want to lose market shares. This greatly helped the EP's rapporteur Kurt Vittinghoff (Socialist, Germany) to persuade wavering MEPs about the feasibility of his second reading amendments. Vittinghoff has claimed that all he needed to do before the decisive vote in the Environmental Committee in March 1989 'was to cut out and photocopy adverts in German magazines in which Renault, Peugeot, Fiat and the German producers praised their three-way catalytic converter equipped small cars'.[120]

However, the massive majority in favour of Vittinghoff's amendments in the EP's plenum (309 for; 5 against; and 5 abstentions) would not have been possible without the upsurge of public environmental awareness which had swept through Western Europe in the late 1980s.

The 1985 Luxembourg Compromise

Back in 1984, when EU car emission negotiations threatened to escalate into a trade war, one DG Industry official assessed the situation as follows:

The only recipe possible for getting out of such a stalemate situation – where no group will move to the position of the other – consists in attempting to find a formula in which further concessions are done by all concerned though not being considered as an abandonment of fundamental principles.[121]

The 1985 Luxembourg Compromise tried to achieve this by putting forward a multifaceted approach. The principal decision to adopt such an approach was taken by a special Environmental Council on 21–22 March 1985. The precise limit values were agreed by all member states, (apart from Denmark and Greece, which insisted on more stringent standards), at the Environmental Council meeting in Luxembourg on 27 June 1985. Strictly speaking, this agreement, which was reached on 28 June 1985 at 7.30 a.m. after seventeen hours of continuous and ill-tempered negotiations, might be more accurately described as the '1985 Luxembourg Near-Agreement'. However, after the SEA came into force, the 1985 Luxembourg Agreement was formally adopted by QMV (against the votes of Denmark and Greece) as *Directive 88/76/EEC* on 3 December 1987.

The EP did not attempt to use its new second reading powers to tighten the 1985 Luxembourg Compromise, although many MEPs severely criticised the leniency of the standards. Most MEPs were afraid of unravelling the extraordinarily complex compromise and wanted to give sufficient lead-time to industry. The EP was split mainly along national rather than party political lines, particularly during the first reading.[122] Alexander Sherlock (European Democrat, UK) was the rapporteur for the first and second readings. His first report triggered over 150 amendments, mainly from Danish, Dutch and German MEPs demanding more stringent measures.[123]

The Commission as broker and policy facilitator
After Germany had threatened to adopt the American standards unilaterally, the Commission put forward a two-staged approach in July 1984, which, it claimed, would produce EU car emission standards *equivalent to* (that is, not identical with) the US 1983 standards by 1995.[124] However, the UBA estimated that the Commission's first-stage limit values would have allowed cars in the EU to emit twice the amount of pollutants per kilometre compared to America.[125]

The Commission's proposed limit values for the first stage became known as the Davignon values;[126] they did not fulfil German demands and threw a lifeline for the lean-burn engine. The Commission's second-stage proposal was published only on 29 November 1984. It proposed that the Council should agree before 31 December 1988 on limit values within ranges that spanned the demands put forward by the environmental leaders and laggards.[127]

In order to defuse the conflict which threatened to escalate in 1984, additional negotiating fora were established at both the Council and the Commission level. In late 1984 the Council set up the Council High Level Working Group on car emissions; and in January 1985 the Commission founded the Motor Vehicle Emission Group (MVEG) as an *ad hoc* working group. The MVEG was the 'child of a political emergency situation'[128] the initial task of which was to provide technical information requested by the Council High Level Working Group.[129]

The Motor Vehicle Emissions Group
The MVEG, whose proceedings were similar to the ERGA working groups (explained in chapter 4), played a central role during 1985–91. An official from the French Transport Ministry, Bernard Gauvin, who had already chaired the ERGA steering committee and was an outspoken critic of the US 1983 standards, was the MVEG's chairperson from 1985 to 1996. MVEG meetings were attended by Commission and member government officials and representatives from the European associations of the oil and automobile industries (CONCAWE, CCMC and CLCA). The European umbrella group FIA (Association of International Automobile Clubs) and the most important supplier companies were also represented from the start. Europe's main environmental and consumer NGOs (EEB and BEUC) gained access only in September 1987.

The Commission rarely disregarded a consensus which emerged from within the MVEG because it quickly became a pre-negotiating forum for Council negotiations: the same national experts who attended the MVEG usually also participated in Council working groups. Political and economic interests played an important role within the MVEG, although they were often hidden behind technical arguments.[130] One MVEG participant explained: 'There was plenty of politics in the MVEG meetings. National diplomats merely added a different flavour to COREPER and Council Environmental Working Group meetings which otherwise differed little from MVEG meetings.'[131]

The MVEG has met approximately every two months since its

inaugural meeting on 14 January 1985.[132] The average number of delegates remained fairly stable during the first five years but rose from 41 to 52 between 1990 and 1996. Germany usually sent the largest delegation, with up to eight officials from three different ministries (BMU–BMI, BMWi and BMV) and the UBA; occasionally the Association for Technical Instructions (Technischer Überwachungsverein – TÜV), which undertakes emission testing, was also represented. According to one British automobile industry representative: 'The UBA is usually the most gung-ho while the Economics Ministry often makes very sensible comments when you talk to them in the corridor.'[133] It is no coincidence that the Environmental Ministry was the lead department for MVEG delegations in those member states which demanded the adoption of the US 1983 standards, while the Transport Ministry headed the national delegation in Britain, France and Italy, which insisted on less stringent standards.[134]

Germany and the Netherlands were most active as regards the submission of technical MVEG discussion papers. Britain, France and Italy also regularly submitted papers, while Denmark only occasionally made a written contribution. The Commission put forward only a limited number of technical papers, almost all of which were drafted by DG Industry. The EEB also submitted some technical papers.[135]

The CCMC was set up in 1972 because the 'European car manufacturers felt there was a need to talk directly to the Commission'.[136] It complemented the lobbying activities of the CLCA, which was made up of the national automobile associations (such as the SMMT and the VDA).[137] CCMC members were Britain's Rover–British Leyland, Rolls Royce and Jaguar and Germany's BMW, Mercedes, Porsche and Volkswagen as well as Italy's Fiat and France's PSA (Peugeot/Citroën) and Renault. However, Japanese producers with production facilities in Britain and the American daughter companies, Ford-Europe and Opel/Vauxhall, were excluded from the CCMC. One Ford-UK representative felt that this 'allowed us to take up a distinct Ford position without having to compromise, although on balance it is better to be inside'.[138]

Decisions were taken unanimously within the CLCA and CCMC. This granted veto powers to corporate environmental laggards. All companies represented within the CCMC initially rejected the US 1983 standards on cost and scientific grounds. However, Peugeot's president, Jacques Calvet, took such a hard line that the other European manufacturers, increasingly concerned about their image at a time of rising environmental awareness, collectively resigned from the CCMC and set up the Association of European Automobile Constructors (ACEA) in 1991.[139] ACEA combined the functions of the CCMC and the CLCA and admitted Ford-Europe, Opel–Vauxhall, Volvo and Saab as members. Peugeot joined ACEA in the late 1990s, although Japanese producers have remained excluded.

The EEB and the BEUC ran campaigns in favour of BAT-derived car emission standards.[140] However, these groups suffered from underfunding and much of the work was initially left to the EEB's scientific advisor Karola Taschner, a German national who relied heavily on the UBA for expertise. A former American EPA car emission expert, Michael Walsh, wrote for no fee several technical papers for the EEB in the mid-1980s. A British consultant, Claire Holman, who was paid for by FoE England, worked for the EEB in the late 1980s and early 1990s.

In early 1984, DG Environment officials put forward an internal proposal which demanded 'the use of the best available technology'[141] for all major sources of air pollution. However, DG Environment's proposal never made it beyond the cabinet of Commissioner Karl-Heinz Narjes, who was a (CSU-nominated) German national in charge of both DG Environment and DG Industry between 1980 and 1984. It was only under the (Labour-nominated) British Commissioner Stanley Clinton-Davis, who became responsible for DG Environment and DG Transport in 1985, that DG Environment launched an 'attack on DG Industry'[142] in order to expand its competences and bring about more ambitious EU car emission standards. It is for this reason that the British Junior Environmental Minister William Waldegrave felt that 'things went more smoothly under Narjes than Clinton-Davis'.[143]

The rise in environmental awareness forced DG Industry into supporting the BAT principle although its desk officials worked on the basis of the following curious definition:

> Generally, technical solutions are considered to conform to the state of the art if they are progressive and have proved their reliability in practice or, at least, if their use does not present too much technical and economic risk for the motor industry as a whole. In other words, the state of the art is a compromise between what is, at present, technically feasible in special cases and what is general technical practice.[144]

This interpretation of the 'state of the art', which amounted to an adoption of the best available technologies not entailing excessive cost (BATNEEC) principle at the EU level, was very different from the German government's understanding of the BAT principle, and one that came closer to the British BPM principle.

The importance of national economic interests
The decision to use engine size as the reference-point for the differentiated approach gradually emerged out of the many meetings which took place in early 1985. It 'was used because it constituted a well established criterion on which most member states based their road tax charges. It had nothing to do with technology or science but was a purely political decision to get out of a tricky situation.' [145] The cut-off points between the different categories (under 1.4 litres, between 1.4 and 2 litres and above 2 litres) reflected the economic interests of the main producer states (Germany, France, Italy and Britain).[146]

Table 5.5 shows that Germany had the highest share of large cars (over 2 litres) with regard to both registration and production output. The car fleets and production output in Italy and France were skewed towards the small-car sector (under 1.4 litres) while Britain had a particular economic interest in the medium-sized category where much of Ford-UK and Rover's output could be found.

The definition of large cars (over 2 litres) was uncontroversial. However, the cut-off point for the small-car category was hotly disputed. The German government favoured 1.0 litre as the cut-off point, while Britain and France wanted to see it extended to 1.3 litres. However, the Italian government insisted on 1.4 litres.

The Council negotiations
The March 1985 Environmental Council reached agreement on four general principles:
1 emission limits should be set according to three categories of engine size (small, medium and large);
2 the EU standards should be *equivalent to* the US 1983 standards;
3 the emission limits should be achievable through different technologies and at a reasonable cost; and
4 a more representative European test cycle should be adopted by the end of 1987.

The ministers were hopeful that the political compromise could be quickly translated into technical regulations. However, one DG

Table 5.5 *Registration and production of cars in the main producer states in 1983*

State	Registered cars according to engine capacity (in %) [Production of cars according to engine size (in %)]		
	>2 litres	1.4–2 litres	<1.4 litres
Germany	13[17]	50[52]	37[31]
Britain	7[5]	42[34]	51[61]
France	3[2]	30[27]	67[71]
Italy	1[1]	15[25]	84[74]
EU average	4[n/a]	34[n/a]	60[n/a]

Note: In 1983 Germany, Britain, France and Italy had registered 23, 18, 20 and 19 million cars respectively
Sources: Commission and BMU (undated memos)

Industry official noted: 'The deliberations of the [MVEG] ... have clearly shown the customary tendency by experts to unfasten the package that the Ministers have attempted to fasten'.[147] This contradicts the widely held view that Commission working groups (and the EU policy-formulation phase in general) are characterised by problem-solving during which technical and scientific experts show a greater propensity for arriving at common solutions compared to more the conflictual political bargaining which is supposed to dominate Council negotiations during the adoption phase.[148]

The British negotiator in the Environmental Council, William Waldegrave, agreed to the 1985 Luxembourg Compromise only *ad referendum*, while arguing that as a junior minister he needed clearance from the cabinet for his stance. However, this was mainly a negotiating ploy. The British government formally agreed to the compromise in early July 1985 following a meeting called by Prime Minister Thatcher which turned into 'a sort of court'.[149] It found that Waldegrave had 'stayed well within [his] instructions and that [he] could have gone even a bit further'.[150] It overruled the DTI's Secretary of State Norman Tebbit, who had been so concerned about the struggling Rover–British Leyland company that he phoned Waldegrave the day before the June Environmental Council meeting to demand a robust defence of British economic interests.[151]

The small cars directive

The 1985 Luxembourg Compromise stipulated that the Council should decide on a second stage to supplant the lenient first-stage emission limits for small cars by 1987. However, this decision was delayed until 1989, by which time the German, Dutch, Danish and Greek fiscal incentives had started to bite. The British government (and the UK automobile industry) [152] was opposed to fiscal incentives on the grounds that this would lead to a distortion of the internal market. The British government unsuccessfully lobbied the Commission to take legal action and even delivered an *aide memoire* in protest to the German government on 15 May 1985 (one day after France had taken the same step).

The importance of fiscal incentives was recognised by one DoT official, who stated:

> Tax incentives in Germany played a crucial role. By creating a market for three-way catalysts in Germany in the absence of mandatory standards, all the motor industry that wanted to sell cars in Germany had to produce vehicles that complied. In the end this resulted in companies such as Ford withdrawing their criticism of three-way catalyst technology simply because they had to sell it and support it in the German market. Thus, if nothing else, the German tax incentives had the effect of effectively silencing the motor industry's vociferous criticism of three-way catalyst technology.[153]

In the 1980s, the small car producers gradually switched from carburettor to fuel-injection technology and introduced a limited number of models equipped with a three-way catalytic converter. Opel-Germany switched its entire output to three-way catalytic converters before the 1989 small cars directive was adopted, while Ford-UK and Rover–British Leyland were the last to make the transition.[154]

At the start of the small cars directive's negotiations, Britain and Germany again found themselves in opposite camps. Britain (supported by France, Italy and Spain) initially proposed the following limit values for small cars: CO: 35 and HC + NO$_x$: 12g/test (abbreviated as 35–12). The German government (supported by Denmark, Greece and the Netherlands) pushed for 20–5. The main obstacle was the HC + NO$_x$ limit value, for which the British and German governments were prepared to accept 8g/test by late 1988.

Britain's new policy stance was seen by some observers as a 'U-turn' [155] and fits the general trend of the 'greening' of British politics that took place in the late 1980s. The softening of Germany's position has been explained by Holzinger and Arp with reference to a rare package deal in EU environmental policy-making. According to their interpretation, Germany accepted less stringent limit values for small cars in order to get the large combustion directive adopted during its EU Presidency in 1988.[156]

However, there is no empirical evidence that the German Environmental Minister Klaus Töpfer (CDU) who was a strident supporter of the three-way catalytic converter,[157] struck such a deal, the existence of which was denied by all the policy actors interviewed.[158] Environmental Commissioner Clinton-Davis even had to persuade Töpfer not to break up one decisive Council meeting, during the German Presidency, because of the lack of movement shown by the French and Spanish governments. Italy gave up its opposition to stringent emission limits for small cars after another tailormade derogation was agreed which, in effect, exempted Fiat's Panda model on the grounds that it was a 'low powered' vehicle used only for short journeys. Incidentally, the Environmental Council meeting on 27–8 June 1985 which agreed this derogation also adopted measures to protect the elephant.[159] One British official therefore amused his minister with the following statement: 'Today we have saved the elephant and the Panda!'[160]

Germany's readiness to accept less ambitious car emission limit values was partly due to the pressure to act as a broker that the office of the Presidency exerts on its incumbent.[161] Also, time was on Germany's side since the adoption of fiscal incentives. And the German government could rely on the EP to try everything possible to tighten the Council's common position. Kurt Vittinghoff (Socialist, Germany), who was the Environmental Committee's rapporteur for the 1989 small cars directive, was seen among British officials and automobile representatives as 'somewhat of an environmental extremist [who] ... played a numbers game – [as] all he wanted was to see the numbers [for emission limits] come down'.[162] Vittinghoff has rejected this accusation, although he stated that his experience as a former union representative taught him to demand more than what was realistically achievable in order to get what was necessary. Vittinghoff explained:

> Several British MEPs repeatedly told me that 'the best is the enemy of the good'. This makes one wonder about whether one has prevented something good by asking for the best. I can honestly say that I do not believe that I ever prevented something good with my demands ... which were always realistic and achievable. The only unrealistic thing

was to expect that the Council and the Commission would accept all of my demands. From visits to the main automobile producers I knew that engineers and union representatives often wanted much tighter standards than their management.[163]

However, in 1989 the Environmental Commissioner Ripa di Meana not only accepted most of Vittinghoff's second reading amendments but tightened them even further. The Environmental commissioner held a joint press conference with Kurt Vittinghoff in which he announced that the Commission was prepared to accept 19–5 (rather than the EP's 20–5) as the common position for the second reading. Carlo Ripa di Meana, later nicknamed 'Carlo the Ripper'[164] by the British Prime Minister John Major, would not have been able to persuade his fellow commissioners to accept BAT-derived car emission standards without the unprecedented upsurge in public environmental awareness that occurred in the early 1990s.

Member governments who were opposed to stringent limit values grudgingly accepted the EP's and the Commission's common position because it was impossible (due to the Danish and Greek position) to overturn it unanimously in Council, in which case the proposal would have lapsed. The automobile industry viewed the latter scenario as the worst option because, as one British industry representative explained: 'We prefer slightly more stringent standards which give us more lead time compared to more lenient standards which stipulate short implementation deadlines'.[165]

The 1989 small cars directive was adopted after another marathon negotiating session of the Environmental Council on 8–9 June 1989.[166] It was the first EU car emission directive that was *mandatory* rather than *optional*. However, because small cars now had to comply with the most stringent emission limits it was decided to adopt a consolidated directive to bring into line the emission limits for all cars, regardless of their engine size. The 1989 small cars directive was therefore never implemented, but it 'was like the bursting of a dam for the three-way catalytic converter'.[167]

The consolidated directive

The adoption of the consolidated directive should have been a formality as the emission limit values had already been agreed and required only technical translation. DG Industry invited officials from Britain, Germany, France, Italy and Belgium for this task. However, the EP again tried to tighten the emission limits and stipulate additional requirements (such as durability requirements which were already in force in America and most EFTA states).[168] The Commission would have been prepared to accept some of the EP's demands.[169] However, after massive lobbying by the automobile industry, the EP this time failed to achieve the necessary quorum during the second reading, which meant that the first reading's common position was adopted unamended.

Conclusion

From 1983 onwards the EU (rather than the ECE) became the central decision-making arena for car emission regulations for member states. Member governments and corporate actors remained the driving force, although the Commission increasingly adopted a brokering role. The EP succeeded in pushing through most of its demands only with regard to the 1989 small car emissions directive. Germany's leader role and its insistence on BAT-derived EU car emission standards were decisive in bringing about the phasinig in of the three-way catalytic converter. Despite the applicability of QMV, all directives were adopted unanimously, with the exception of the 1985 Luxembourg Compromise which resulted in a multifaceted approach that took account of the core demands of those environmental leaders and environmental laggards with important car production facilities.

Germany's demands regarding the principal technological options preferred (the three-way catalytic converter *or* the lean-burn engine) split the actors of the EU car emission policy network into two rival camps and led to the formation of opposing advocacy coalitions. The alliances varied considerably, however, between different directives or even between different provisions of the same directive. The German demands for the adoption of the US 1983 car emission standards received support from the Danish, Dutch and Greek governments. These member governments were supported by a majority of MEPs as well as the European environmental and consumer groups (the EEB and the BEUC). However, the British, French and Italian governments, as well as the European associations of the automobile industry (the CCMC and the CLCA) and the oil industry (CONCAWE), were fiercely opposed to their introduction. The Commission, which was internally divided, tried to come up with compromise proposals that would preserve the unity of the internal market.

The action-guiding norms of diverse national environmental

regulatory styles have been an important influence on the behaviour of member governments and help to explain how the problem was perceived and also the selection of preferred policy options. This is not to downplay the importance of economic interests, which figured prominently in the demands put forward by national governments. During the 1980s, an EU car emission regulatory style developed key features, which can be summarised as follows.[170]

1 EU car emission regulations covered a limited range of pollutants.

2 Limit values were tightened according to a step-by-step process in line with technological advancements, although the standards adopted usually took account of the core demands of the environmental laggards. This explains why the EU followed the USA's lead (in adopting the three-way catalytic converter) though with a delay of almost ten years.

3 Member governments dominated the EU policy-making process, although they had to take seriously EP demands following the introduction of the cooperation procedure.

4 The Commission took on a brokering role and tried to balance the conflicting demands for the creation of an internal market ('negative integration') and a high level of environmental protection ('positive integration'). DG Industry, which saw the automobile industry as its natural ally, was mainly concerned with the prevention of barriers to trade. DG Environment, which formed close links with environmental and consumer NGOs during the 1980s, pushed for BAT-derived EU car emission limits.

5 Some NGOs (such as the EEB) gained access to the EU's car emission policy community, although they could not match the technical expertise of the corporate actors which exerted considerable pressure on EU decision makers due to the importance of the automobile and oil industries for Europe's economy.

This chapter has shown the increasing importance of EU institutional actors (such as the Commission and the EP in particular) and of non-governmental actors (such as car producers and environmental NGOs) in the EU car emission policy-making process. The automobile and oil industries yielded considerable influence, while environmental NGOs gained access to the MVEG only in the late 1980s onwards – a time when environmental awareness surged in most member states. Importantly, direct cross-border lobbying took place and there is strong empirical evidence that conflicts often cut across governmental, EU institutional, NGO and corporate actors.

Notes

1 BMI press release dated 27 October 1983.
2 Interviews with British, German and EU officials during 1991–93. See also *Financial Times*, 21 March 1985.
3 See *Directives 88/76/EEC, 89/458/EEC* and *91/441/EEC* respectively.
4 Boehmer-Christiansen and Skea (1991); Weale (1992: 67); Weale *et al.* (2000); Weidner (1989: 9).
5 Interview with BMU and UBA officials in 1992–93.
6 Interviews with British officials and William Waldegrave over 1991–96.
7 Weidner (1989: 2–4).
8 See chapter 4.
9 Interview in 1993. Zimmermann's role was confirmed by BMU–BMI and UBA officials interviewed.
10 Arp (1995: 72–81); Boehmer-Christiansen and Weidner (1995); Holzinger (1994: 194–201); Turner (1988); Weale *et al.* (2000); Westheide (1987); Winzer (1990).
11 Interview in 1992.
12 SRU (1983).
13 Interview with Wighard Härdtl in 1996. Lambsdorff was on the economic Right of the FDP and opposed to stringent environmental regulations.
14 Bundestag (1983, 1984).
15 DGVII/496/85-EH, 15 October 1985.
16 Boehmer-Christiansen and Weidner (1995); Sbragia (1996: 252).
17 Interview with BMU official in 1993.
18 Interview in 1992.
19 Interview in 1993.
20 Interviews in 1992–93.
21 UBA (1992, 1999).
22 Interview in 1993.
23 Interview with an ADAC representative in 1992.
24 Interview in 1992.
25 All figures refer to 1983 prices. Interviews with UBA officials and ADAC representatives during 1991–94.
26 This slogan was popularised by Audi advertising. See Weale (1992b).
27 Interview in 1992.
28 Vogel (1997: 562). See also Vogel (1995: 67).
29 This was confirmed by all BMU–BMI and UBA officials interviewed.
30 Hey and Brendle (1994).
31 Interview with Wighard Härdtl in 1996.
32 *Süddeutsche Zeitung*, 25 August 1984.
33 Becker (1988: 47); Westheide (1987).
34 Commission, press release IP(85)114 of 2 April 1985.

35 Liefferink (1996); Sbragia (1996); Vogel (1995, 1997); Weale *et al.* (2000: 475).
36 Interview with Volkswagen representatives in 1992. However, there were also internal rifts within Volkswagen.
37 Interviews in 1993. See also Arp (1995).
38 Interviews in 1992. See also VDA (1984: 51).
39 VDA (1984: 15).
40 Interviews over 1992–96.
41 Interview in 1993.
42 Interview in 1996.
43 Boehmer-Christiansen and Skea (1991); Hajer (1995).
44 CEC (1989b: 98).
45 Arp (1995: 137–8); Hajer (1995: 132–8); HoC (1988: column 432).
46 Interview in 1993.
47 Interview with DoT official in 1993.
48 Holzinger (1994: 185). See also Boehmer-Christiansen and Weidner (1995).
49 *Hansard*, House of Commons debate on 14 January 1986, column 1034.
50 *Hansard*, House of Lords debate on 22 April 1985, column 972.
51 SMMT (1993: 54 and 215).
52 Interview with UBA official in 1993.
53 Arp (1995: 145–7); Wilks (1984).
54 Arp (1995: 164).
55 Interview with representatives from Rover in 1993.
56 Ford of Europe (1983: 10).
57 UNECE (1984: no page numbers).
58 Ford of Europe (1985: 14).
59 Interview in 1993.
60 Interview in 1993.
61 Interview with Clinton-Davis in 1995.
62 *Hansard*, House of Commons debates of 14 January 1986, column 1035.
63 Interview with William Waldegrave in 1996.
64 Interview with a DoT official in 1993.
65 Written evidence from a DoT official dated 21 June 1996.
66 HoL (1985).
67 *Hansard*, House of Lords debate on 22 April 1985, column 954.
68 *Hansard*, House of Lords debate on 22 April 1985, column 954.
69 Interview information with FoE campaigner in 1993.
70 Interview with FoE campaigner in 1993. FoE (1988) and Greenpeace (1990).
71 EEB (ed.) (1987). It was financially supported by the German Goethe Institut.
72 Written evidence from the AA and RAC dated 14 September 1993 and 7 September 1993 respectively.

73 However, the *New Scientist* and the *ENDS Report* favoured the US 1983 car emission standards early on.
74 HoC (1988: lx).
75 HoC (1988: lix).
76 *Hansard*, House of Commons debates of 14 January 1986.
77 Interview in 1993.
78 David Wallace (1995: 153), a DTI official, still makes this claim.
79 Thatcher (1993). Nicholas Ridley, who was the DoE's Secretary of State for the Environment in 1986–89, was a confidante of Margaret Thatcher. In 1990 he was forced to resign as secretary of state at the DTI for making anti-German and anti-EU remarks (Bulmer *et al.* 2000: 65).
80 Over time, catalytic converters that light up more quickly were produced.
81 Other technical options are possible, but are more costly or less reliable.
82 Interviews with Mercedes, Volkswagen and Rover–British Leyland representatives during 1991–93.
83 Searles (1987: 38).
84 Krote and Gruden (1987: 187).
85 Arp (1991, 1995); Holzinger (1994, 1996).
86 Interviews 1991–92.
87 The Opposition Labour MP David Clark attacked the government for this inconsistency (*Hansard*, House of Common debate on 14 January 1986, columns 1038–9).
88 Ford of Europe (1983, 1985).
89 Interview with FoE campaigner in 1993.
90 Arp (1995); Holzinger (1994).
91 Interviews in 1991.
92 Interviews in 1992.
93 Interviews with DG Industry officials in 1993. See also Arp (1995: 149); Holzinger (1994).
94 In the 1980s Peugeot bought Citroën to form PSA Peugeot Citroën.
95 The name Mercedes is used as shorthand for Mercedes–Benz, Daimler Benz and Daimler Chrysler.
96 VDA (1983: 54).
97 The French producers catered mainly for the American small diesel market.
98 *Hansard*, House of Commons debate on 14 January 1986, columns 1047–8.
99 Westheide (1987).
100 Interviews with British and German automobile representatives.
101 The German VDA estimated its emission-reduction capacity as close to 50 per cent (VDA 1985: 54) while the British government and British industry put it at 70 per cent (Interviews in 1993).
102 Cutting (1987: 46).

103 Interview with SMMT and VDA representatives in 1992–93. VDA (1987: 56).
104 Interview with UBA official in 1994. *ENDS Report* 205, February 1992, p. 15.
105 Interviews during 1991–93. VDA (2000b: 147).
106 Arp (1995); Holzinger (1994). See also Arp (1991, 1993); Boehmer-Christiansen and Weidner (1995); Friedrich *et al.* (1998a, 1998b, 2000); Holzinger (1996, 1997); Hubschmid and Moser (1997); Neu (1990); Turner (1988); Vogel (1995, 1997); Weale *et al.* (2000: 397–409); Westheide (1987); Winzer (1990); Wurzel (1999a).
107 Interview with William Waldegrave in 1996. This view was confirmed by BMU and UBA officials interviewed over 1992–97.
108 *Directive 91/542/EEC.*
109 Arp (1993: 164).
110 Holzinger (1994: 383).
111 See William Waldegrave's statement during the House of Commons debate on 14 January 1986 (*Hansard*: column 1035).
112 Interview in 1993.
113 Interview in 1993.
114 *Financial Times*, 10 March 1989.
115 Holzinger (1996).
116 *Financial Times*, 13 April 1989.
117 Interview in 1998. However, German UBA officials blamed Portuguese MEPs for leaving before the vote to catch their flights (Interviews in 1993).
118 See also Holzinger (1994: 384).
119 Ross (1995). See also *Financial Times*, 10 March 1989.
120 Interview in 1993.
121 Interview information from a DG Industry official in 1993.
122 Arp (1995); Holzinger (1994).
123 Holzinger (1994: 218).
124 COM(84) 226 final, 6 July 1984.
125 Becker (1988: 47). See also EEB (1985); Walsh (1987, 1988).
126 The Belgian Industry Commissioner Etienne Davignon became involved in the formulation of the 'lean-burn friendly' first-stage proposal. For one DG Industry official this was due to the fact that French producers and Ford-Europe had important production sites in Belgium (interview in 1993).
127 COM(84) 564 final, 29 November 1984.
128 Arp (1995: 201).
129 See III/71/85-EN (VE/SEC/1).
130 Interviews in 1992–93. Arp (1995); Holzinger (1994).
131 Interview with a DoT official in 1993.

132 Friedrich *et al.* (1998a, 1998b, 2000).
133 Interview in 1993.
134 The HLSCEC was critical of the fact that the DoT rather than the DoE was the lead department (HoL 1985).
135 EEB (1987).
136 Interview with a former CCMC representative in 1992.
137 Arp (1995: 177–82); Holzinger (1994: 210–15); McLaughlin *et al.* (1993).
138 Interview in 1993.
139 Another reason was Calvet's opposition to Japanese imports.
140 EEB (1985, 1987).
141 Interview information from DG Environment official in 1993.
142 Interview with Stanley Clinton-Davis in 1995.
143 Interview with William Waldegrave in 1996.
144 Henssler and Gospage (1987: 71–2).
145 Interview with a German official in 1993.
146 Arp (1995); Holzinger (1994: 176).
147 Interview information in 1993.
148 Eichener (1997); Héritier (1996: 155); Héritier *et al.* (1996); Peters (1992: 119); Peterson (1995a). Arp (1995: 208) also warns that EU car emission legislation does not support these claims.
149 Interview with William Waldegrave in 1996.
150 Interview with William Waldegrave in 1996.
151 Interview in 1996.
152 All of the British automobile industry representatives interviewed opposed fiscal incentives.
153 Written communication dated 21 June 1996.
154 On 10 May 1983 the *Financial Times* reported that Ford-Europe started a crash programme which cost approximately $200 million and involved 400 of its 5,000 European engineers.
155 *Financial Times*, 24 May 1989.
156 Arp (1995: 238); Holzinger (1994: 306–8).
157 Töpfer (1989a, 1989b).
158 Interviews in 1991–96.
159 Council of the European Communities, General Secretariat press release 7803/85 (Presse 108), p. 1.
160 Interview in 1992.
161 Wurzel (1996a, 1996b, 2000).
162 Interview with a SMMT representative in 1992.
163 Interview in 1993.
164 Interview with Stanley Clinton-Davis in 1995.
165 Interview in 1993.
166 Holzinger (1994: 330–6).
167 Interview with a BMU official in 1993.

168 Holzinger (1994); Arp (1995).
169 Interviews with Commission officials in 1992–93.
170 See also Weale *et al.* (2000: 404).

6

The Auto-Oil Programmes

Continuity and change

In the early 1990s EU car emission policy-making entered a calmer phase following the highly politicised conflicts which surrounded the phasing in of the three-way catalytic converter in the 1980s. However, overall the EU's car emission regulation style of the early 1990s constituted an incremental extension of the approach adopted in the 1980s which tightened car emissions on a step-by-step basis in line with technological developments.[1] The two-stage approach first adopted under the 1989 small cars directive was continued. It consisted of a further tightening of car emission limits by setting mandatory standards at the first stage and then more stringent indicative standards at a second stage for which member governments were allowed to grant fiscal incentives to encourage the early introduction of less polluting cars. The 1991 consolidated directive (91/441/EEC) stipulated mandatory emission limits (Euro I) which made the three-way catalytic converter a standard feature for all new petrol-powered cars registered within the EU by 1 July 1992, while also putting forward the two-step approach mentioned above. In the 1990s, EU car emission regulations began to cover issues such as better test procedures and greater durability requirements for pollution abatement equipment.

Setting the scene for the Auto-Oil I Programme
In 1994 *Directive 94/12/EC* further tightened the limit values for petrol and diesel cars (see table 6.1). It again put forward a two-stage approach which consisted of mandatory limit values for 1996 (Euro II) and more stringent indicative limit values for 2000 (Euro III). Since Euro II, different limit values have been adopted for petrol and diesel

cars which have been allowed to comply with more lenient HC and
NO$_x$ emissions on the grounds that they are more fuel efficient than
petrol cars. The Euro II diesel limit values for particulates, which are
a serious health hazard, were considerably more lenient than those
in force in the USA or Japan.[2]

Table 6.1 *Euro II emission limits (in g/test)*

	Emission limits					
	CO	HC + NO$_x$	NO$_x$	HC	Particulates	Implementation
Petrol cars	2.2	0.6	–	–	–	1996 for new
	2.7[a]	–	0.252[a]	0.341[a]	–	models; 1997 for all new cars
Diesel cars[b]	1.06	0.71	0.63	–	0.08	1996 for new models; 1997 for all new cars

Notes: [a] Corrected values based on a new test procedure
[b] More lenient values were stipulated for direct injection diesel cars until 1999
Source: *Directive 94/12/EC*

The German government unsuccessfully pushed for more stringent
mandatory petrol and diesel limit values for 1996 (Euro II) and failed
to get the indicative (petrol and diesel) limit values for 2000 (Euro
III) changed to mandatory standards.[3] The EP's Environmental Committee, and especially its rapporteur Kurt Vittinghoff (Germany,
Socialist), also favoured a significant tightening of the (mandatory
and indicative) limit values and the adoption of maintenance and
inspection requirements for exhaust gas abatement devices.[4] However,
the Environmental Committee failed to get the necessary quorum in
the EP's plenum during the second reading after intense lobbying from
the automobile industry, arguing that 'the "best available technology"
approach was imposing costs which would outweigh the additional
benefits to be gained'.[5]

The German government raised concerns about the wording of
Article 4 in *Directive 94/12/EC* which stated that the Commission
should base its new car and fuel emission reduction proposals on *air
quality objectives* and *cost-effectiveness* considerations.[6] However, the
German government voted in favour of *Directive 94/12/EC* in 1994
because it did not want to delay the adoption of the new mandatory

Euro III limits which became applicable on 1 January 1996.⁷ With the benefit of hindsight it can be argued that the German government (and the BMU in particular), which favoured BAT-derived car emission and fuel standards, underestimated the significance of Article 4 in *Directive 94/12/EC* which was later used repeatedly by the Commission to legitimise its 'new approach' under the Auto-Oil I Programme that was already well under way by 1994.

The Auto Emissions 2000 Symposium
Since November 1991, DG Environment officials considered the adoption of an Auto-Oil Programme along similar lines to the US Auto-Oil Air Quality Improvement Research Programme, which had been initiated in April 1990.⁸ However, the main impetus for the Auto-Oil I Programme came from the Commission-sponsored Auto Emissions 2000 Symposium in Brussels on 21–2 September 1992.⁹ The range of speakers at the symposium spanned the entire party political–corporate spectrum. It included environmental hawks such as Kurt Vittinghoff MEP, who stressed the need for BAT-derived EU car emission limits on environmental grounds and to improve the competitive edge of Europe's automobile industry in the global marketplace, as well as corporate environmental laggards who warned that a continuation of the EU's regulatory approach of the 1980s would lead to mounting costs and few tangible benefits for the environment.¹⁰ Almost all of the representatives of the automobile and oil industries demanded the adoption of EQO-derived cost-effective EU car emission and fuel standards; for one German BMU official this amounted to a concerted action by corporate actors.¹¹

However, in 1992 DG Industry was still unconvinced of the need for a new (EQO-derived cost-effectiveness) approach to EU car emission policy; this was instead championed mainly by DG Environment which received the support of DG Energy.¹² DGs Energy and Environment were the driving forces behind the European Programme on Emissions, Fuels and Engine Technologies (EPEFE) which was signed between the Commission and the European umbrella groups of the automobile industry (ACEA) and oil industry (EUROPIA) on 19 July 1993.¹³ EPEFE became an integral part of the Commission's Auto-Oil I Programme, the procedural arrangements and overall scope of which emerged only gradually.¹⁴

The Auto-Oil I Programme

The Commission published the Auto-Oil I Programme in June 1996.[15] It originally put forward three proposals:
1 a directive on car emissions;
2 a directive on the quality of (petrol and diesel) fuels; and
3 a legally non-binding communication on a future strategy to control atmospheric emissions from road transport.

The Commission's car emissions directive stipulated mandatory limits for 2000 (Euro III) and indicative limits for 2005 (Euro IV). The proposed fuels directive put forward only mandatory standards for 2000 while not setting any indicative standards for 2005. The Commission's aim was to propose indicative standards for fuels for 2005 and to review the 2005 indicative values for car emissions on the basis of the findings of the Auto-Oil II Programme which it launched in January 1997.

For the Commission, the Auto-Oil I Programme constituted 'a ground-breaking initiative in which the resources and expertise of two major industries were combined in collaboration with the services of the Commission'.[16] DG Environment officials consistently used a policy discourse which praised the close collaboration between the Commission and the automobile and oil industries while promoting the Auto-Oil Programme as 'the more rational approach' to EU car emission policy compared to the BAT-derived step-by-step approach of the 1980s.[17]

In order to understand why several member governments, the overwhelming majority of MEPs and environmental and consumer NGOs severely criticised the Commission's new approach both on procedural and substantive grounds, it is necessary to assess the shortcomings both of the main studies on which it was based as well as the policy formulation process within which they were conducted.

The Auto-Oil I Programme was based on three interrelated studies:
• EPEFE focused on the effects of different engine technologies and fuel properties on the emission performance of cars. It was jointly financed and carried out by ACEA and EUROPIA.
• Computer models to predict tropospheric ozone concentrations across the EU and urban ambient air quality in seven European cities.[18] DG Environment was the lead department for these studies.

- Cost-effectiveness studies for different packages of (vehicle technology and fuel quality as well as some non-technical) measures on the basis of largely confidential data supplied by the automobile and oil industries. These studies, for which DG Industry took overall responsibility, were carried out by the accountancy firm Touche Ross.

The Auto-Oil I Programme instigated a novel 'tripartite dialogue' between the Commission (mainly DGs Environment, Industry and Energy) and the automobile and oil industries from which other stakeholders (such as member governments and environmental and consumer groups) were excluded. Overall co-ordination of these studies was managed through a tripartite working group chaired by DG Environment.[19] This meant that DG Industry, which had been the Commission's lead department on car emission regulation, lost out to DG Environment which greatly raised its own profile by becoming *chef de files* of the Auto-Oil I Programme.

DG Industry was hesitant to endorse the new approach because it feared that it would lead to the abolition of a level playing field across the EU for cars and fuels while risking the fragmentation of the internal market.[20] However, DG Industry's reluctance was also fuelled by its fear of losing its dominant position within the Commission on the EU car emission dossiers. Historically, EU car emission regulations had been dealt with in the context of the harmonisation process of national type approval requirements for which DG Industry had become the Commission's lead department. However, DG Environment could legitimately claim overall responsibility for a programme the main aim of which was to arrive at the most cost-effective policy measures for achieving a selected number of urban ambient air quality targets and EU-wide tropospheric ozone standards. The adoption of EU ambient air quality directives in the 1990s presented DG Environment with an opportunity to outmanoeuvre DG Industry. This explains why DG Industry officials later expressed considerable *Schadenfreude* when the Auto-Oil I Programme ran into difficulties.[21]

DG Environment had tried to extend its influence on the car emission dossiers following the appointment of Clinton-Davis as Environmental (and Transport) commissioner in 1985. Clinton-Davis described DG Environment's efforts as 'an attack' on DG Industry.[22] Further evidence for the argument that the Auto-Oil I Programme was at least partly the result of a turf battle between different DGs is provided by the fact that DG Transport, which in 1992 had issued a Green Paper on transport entitled *Sustainable Mobility*, was largely kept out of the policy-formulation process of the Auto-Oil I Programme.[23] The disagreements between DGs Environment and Industry were recognised by one British automobile industry representative, who generally favoured the tripartite dialogue of Auto-Oil I Programme but regretted the 'open warfare' between these two DGs.[24]

However, the Auto-Oil Programme also triggered considerable rifts within the German government. The BMU and UBA were opposed to the Commission's new approach, while the BMWi broadly welcomed the emphasis on cost-effectiveness and greater cooperation with industry as became apparent during the first working group meeting of the Auto-Oil II Programme in January 1997. The BMU representative, who headed the German delegation, argued against a follow-up programme for the Auto-Oil I Programme while pointing out that sufficient data already existed for the adoption of mandatory car emission and fuel standards for 2005. He prematurely left the meeting in protest after strongly criticising the Commission's new approach. However, the rest of the football-team-sized German delegation stayed on. To the surprise of all delegates present and the amusement of all but the remaining BMU and UBA delegates, one German Economics Ministry (BMWi) official expressed support for the continuation of the Auto-Oil I Programme while praising the Commission's new approach. This seriously undermined the credibility of Germany's boycott threat.[25] However, the UBA did later boycott some Auto-Oil II Programme working group meetings.[26]

The disunity of the German delegation was greeted with relief by DG Environment officials who had become concerned that its 'most important project launched in the early 1990s'[27] might be sunk at the inaugural meeting of the Auto-Oil II Programme. Beforehand, DG Environment had informally asked officials in environmental leader states whether they would join Germany's boycott.[28] This was not the case, partly because the German Environmental Minister Angela Merkel (CDU) had failed to actively rally support from other member governments. Another reason was that, in the 1990s, some environmental leader states, like Sweden which had joined the EU in 1995, showed considerable interest in adopting a more flexible EQO-derived approach to car emission regulations. The Swedish government therefore considered the Auto-Oil Programme a useful exercise, although it favoured considerably more stringent (car emission and fuel) standards than those proposed by the Commission.[29] The British government was strongly in favour of the Commission's new EQO-derived cost-effectiveness approach. After all, Britain had played a leading role within the ERGA (European Regulations, Global Approach – Air Regulation) committees which had been set up by the Commission as advisory *ad hoc* committees during the early 1980s and assessed cost-effectiveness approaches along similar lines.[30]

The Auto-Oil II Programme therefore went ahead, although its agenda had to be radically altered when, in June 1998, the Environmental Council and the EP adopted mandatory car emission limits and fuel standards for 2005, thus ignoring the Commission's suggestion first to await the findings of the Auto-Oil II Programme.

Main innovations of the Auto-Oil Programmes
The Commission's new approach exhibited the following procedural and conceptual innovations. First, procedurally the tripartite dialogue fostered closer cooperation between the Commission and corporate actors in possession of much of the expertise necessary for drawing up highly complex technical regulations.

Second, there were sound conceptual reasons explicitly to link car emission limits and fuel standards while making their levels dependent on the achievement of health targets and EQOs. The reader may recall the argument, put forward in chapter 1, that even BAT-derived standards may not be sufficient for solving pressing environmental and health problems.

Third, over time ever more stringent uniform emission limits (UELs) will produce diminishing margins of return. In other words it becomes increasingly more expensive to reduce the remaining pollution. The automobile and oil industries forcefully argued that this point had been reached by the early 1990s. DG Environment agreed with the corporate actors on this issue and abandoned its preference for the BAT approach. DG Environment favoured the adoption of relatively ambitious standards, but had overestimated its own capacity to successfully conclude such a resource-intensive and complex programme as the Auto-Oil I Programme while underestimating the knowledge and power resources of the corporate actors involved.

Weaknesses of the Auto-Oil I Programme approach
The main procedural weakness was the exclusion of member governments, environmental and consumer NGOs and the supplier

industry.[31] These stakeholders were represented in the Motor Vehicle Emissions Group (MVEG) which, prior to the launch of the Auto-Oil I Programme, was the Commission's main technical advisory committee.[32] The MVEG, which was only occasionally briefed about the findings of the Auto-Oil I Programme, was sidelined by the Commission in favour of the tripartite dialogue for three main reasons:

1 It was concerned that its new conceptual approach to EU car emission regulations would otherwise be rejected by the 'old guard' within the MVEG.[33]

2 The tripartite dialogue was in line with DG Environment's desire since the mid-1990s to move away from 'command and control' legislation in favour of a more cooperative approach to environmental policy-making.[34] The Commission tried to legitimise its closed cooperation with industry by referring to the principle of shared responsibility as outlined in the fifth EAP.[35] However, this amounted to a *post hoc* justification because the fifth EAP was adopted only after the initiation of the Auto-Oil I Programme.

3 More importantly, the tripartite dialogue did not actually reflect the principle of shared responsibility as outlined in the fifth EAP, which explicitly mentioned the general populace and public authorities as important stakeholders.[36] The origins of the principle of shared responsibility can be traced to the 1987 Brundtland Report and the UN's Earth Summit in 1992, both of which influenced the fifth EAP, where it was defined as the inclusion of *all* stakeholders concerned.[37]

The main substantive and conceptual weaknesses of the studies for the Commission's Auto-Oil I Programme can be summarised as follows. First, it focused primarily on human health targets in urban areas and tropospheric ozone (summer smog) across the EU while excluding consideration of pressing environmental issues such as acid rain and climate change.

Second, the choice of 2010 as the cut-off point for the cost-effectiveness studies introduced a bias against pollution abatement measures which could have brought about significant health and environmental benefits within a much shorter time span.

Third, some of the air quality modelling studies used a measurement area (or grid) which was so wide that it seriously underestimated the detrimental health and environmental effects of the pollution predicted for 2010.

Table 6.2 *Air quality targets for the Auto-Oil I Programme*

| | | Pollutants | | |
| | | *Urban* | *Urban* | *Tropospheric* |
Urban NO$_2$	*Urban CO*	*benzene*	*particulates*	*ozone*
Targets for 2010	200μg/m^3 as a maximum hourly value	10mg/m^3 as a maximum hourly value	10μg/m^3 as an annual mean	50μg/m^3 as a 24-hour rolling average	180μg/m^3 as a 1-hour 99 percentile value

Source: Adapted from CEC (1996d)

The urban health targets and EQOs adopted for the Commission's Auto-Oil I Programme are listed in table 6.2. They were taken from existing EU directives and WHO standards. By putting forward a target value of 10 microgrammes per cubic metre (μg/m^3) for benzene, the Commission abandoned its 'more rational' approach based on 'sound science' as benzene is a carcinogenic substance for which no safe limit values exist.[38] The benzene target adopted for the Auto-Oil I Programme was derived from a draft proposal for a benzene directive for which the Commission had the BATNEEC principle in mind.

Fourth, the narrow cost-effectiveness approach failed to take into account wider social costs such as hospital treatment and increased mortality rates caused by car emissions. It made no attempt to balance the expected costs for industry and car users against the health and environmental benefits for society at large.

Fifth, the Auto-Oil I Programme studies failed to take account of the findings of important studies that predicted a significant increase in traffic pollution within the next few years. In the mid-1990s the European Environment Agency (EEA) and the British Royal Commission on Environmental Pollution (RCEP) published reports suggesting drastic measures to curb pollution from road traffic.[39]

It is therefore no surprise that both the Council and the EP demanded significantly more ambitious standards, as can be seen from tables 6.3 and 6.4. Often Commission environmental proposals are aimed somewhere in between the anticipated policy stance of the cost-conscious Council and that of the environmentally minded EP. However, this was not the case for a single limit value of the proposals put forward under the Commission's Auto-Oil I Programme.

Table 6.3 *Car emission limits for 2005*

	Commission proposal	EP 1st reading	Council	EP 2nd reading	Conciliation Committee
Parameters					
Petrol cars: limit values in g/km by 2005					
CO	1.00 indicative	1.00 mandatory	1.00 indicative	1.00 mandatory	1.00 mandatory
HC	0.10 indicative	0.10 mandatory	0.10 indicative	0.10 mandatory	0.10 mandatory
NO_x	0.08 indicative	0.08 mandatory	0.08 indicative	0.08 mandatory	0.08 mandatory
Diesel cars: limit values in g/km by 2005					
CO	0.5 indicative	0.5 mandatory	0.5 indicative	0.5 mandatory	0.5 mandatory
HC	–	0.07 mandatory	–	0.07 mandatory	–
NO_x	0.25 indicative	0.19 mandatory	0.25 indicative	0.19 mandatory	0.25 mandatory
$HC + NO_x$	0.30 indicative	–	0.30 indicative	–	0.30 mandatory
Particulates	0.025 indicative	0.02 mandatory	0.025 indicative	0.02 mandatory	0.025 mandatory

Sources: Commission, Council and European Parliament

Publication of the Commission's Auto-Oil I Programme met with a mixed response. The oil industry strongly welcomed the Commission's proposals while the automobile industry criticised what it perceived to be an unfair cost-burden sharing. The Commission estimated that its car emissions and fuels proposal for 2000 would have amounted to an annual cost of approximately ECU3.1 billion for the car industry and ECU765 million for the oil industry; while national governments would have had to bear an annual cost of about ECU555 million for inspection and maintenance measures. However, for the average motorist the annual extra costs would have amounted to between only ECU1.7 and 2.3 for less polluting reformulated fuels and between ECU145 and 290 for a new less polluting car.[40] Environmental NGOs were therefore quick to point out that the cost

Table 6.4 *Controversial fuel standards for 2000 and 2005*

Parameter	Limits	Commission	EP 1st reading	Council	EP 2nd reading	Conciliation Committee
Mandatory values for petrol fuels for 2000						
Sulphur	max. ppm	200	30	150	150	150
Aromatics	max. vol%	45	35	42	35	42
Benzene	max. vol%	2	1	1	1	1
Values for petrol fuels for 2005						
Sulphur	max. ppm	–	max. 30 mandatory	max. 50 indicative	max. 30 mandatory	max. 50 mandatory
Aromatics	v/v%	–	max. 30 mandatory	max. 35 indicative	max. 30 mandatory	max. 35 mandatory
Mandatory values for diesel cars for 2000						
Sulphur	max. ppm	350	100/50	350	200	350
PAHs	m/m%	11	6/1[a]	11	1	open[a]
Values for diesel cars for 2005						
Sulphur	max. ppm	–	50 mandatory	50 indicative	50 mandatory	50 mandatory[b]
PAHs	m/m%	–	max. 1.0 mandatory	–	max. 1.0 mandatory	open[a]

Notes: PAHs stands for polycyclic aromatic hydrocarbons; ppm means parts per million; v/v means volume percentages; m/m means mass percentage
[a] Derogations possible until 2007
[b] Decision to be taken within the Auto-Oil II Programme
Sources: Commission, Council and European Parliament

implications for car drivers were actually very low considering the detrimental health effects and environmental damage resulting from car emissions.[41]

First reading
The first Environmental Council meeting to discuss the Commission's Auto-Oil I Programme took place on 15 October 1996. Austria, Denmark, Finland, Germany, the Netherlands and Sweden criticised the Commission's proposals as much too lenient, while Greece,

Portugal and Spain in particular raised concerns about the cost implications of the proposed fuel standards. A clear North–South spilt became discernable within the Environmental Council, although Italy demanded more stringent benzene standards. At the time, Britain and France were the only member states to broadly welcome the Commission's proposal. However, subsequent elections in Britain (May 1997) and France (June 1997) brought to power a British Labour and a French Socialist government both of which attributed considerably more importance to curbing traffic emissions than had their Conservative predecessors. Britain and France therefore later abandoned their support for the Commission's proposals.

The co-decision procedure was applicable for the legislative proposals put forward under the Auto-Oil I Programme. During the first reading in 1997, an overwhelming majority of MEPs adopted most of the amendments tabled in reports by the Environmental Committee's rapporteurs – Bernd Lange (Germany, Socialist) on the car emission directive, Noël Mamére (France, Green) on the fuels directive and Doeke Eisma (Netherlands, Liberal) on the legally non-binding future strategy on road transport emissions.[42]

The EP demanded a tightening of car emissions and fuels standards for 2000 and insisted on mandatory standards for 2005. Moreover, the EP rejected the Commission's cost-effectiveness approach and instead proposed the adoption of a cost–benefit analysis which would take into account wider societal costs and benefits.[43] Bernd Lange criticised the tripartite dialogue on the grounds that 'there has been absolutely no transparency and no participation by social groupings, political decision-makers or relevant non-governmental organisations'.[44]

In its common position of October 1997, the Environmental Council also went well beyond the Commission's proposals and accepted some of the EP's demands. However, the EP wanted significantly more stringent standards, and that triggered a second reading.

Second reading
The Maastricht Treaty, which came into force in 1993, requires that the Conciliation Committee be set up under the co-decision procedure, should the Council's and the EP's views still diverge after the second reading. However, for this to happen the EP must, by an absolute majority re-adopt its first-reading amendments during the second reading. For the second reading, Bernd Lange remained the EP's rapporteur on the car emission limit dossier while, on the fuels dossier,

Heidi Hautala (Finland, Green) succeeded Noël Mamére, who left the EP to take up a post in the newly elected French government. Lange and Hautala principally resubmitted for the second reading the EP's first-reading amendments.[45] The German MEP Horst Schnellhart was nominated as a shadow rapporteur. He represented the European People's Party, which was the second largest party grouping (after the Socialists) within the EP. The Environmental Committee's rapporteurs on the car and fuels directives (Lange and Hautala) worked closely with Schnellhart in order to make likely the endorsement of the second-reading amendments by an absolute majority of the EP's plenum.[46] This strategy withstood a massive lobbying campaign by the oil industry against Lange and Hautala's amendments.

In the weeks leading up to the EP's decisive vote in the plenary session, in February 1998, the oil industry's European umbrella organisation EUROPIA ran such an aggressive lobbying campaign that ill-feeling developed among some MEPs.[47] EUROPIA claimed that Lange and Hautala's amendments would 'improve air quality by just one per cent but would cost five times as much as the Commission's original proposals'.[48] The automobile industry, on the other hand, demanded a tightening of the fuel standards both on equity (cost) grounds and because it would facilitate the development of more sophisticated car emission pollution abatement technologies which required very low sulphur fuels.[49] Individual automobile companies (such as Renault) even formed a highly unusual temporary coalition with their long-standing opponents, the Brussels-based environmental and consumer NGOs, in order to help convince MEPs that more stringent fuel standards were needed.[50] The European automobile industry also tried to find allies outside the EU by helping to launch a world fuel charter demanding the availability of (low sulphur) reformulated fuels.

On 18 February 1998 almost all of Lange and Hautala's amendments were accepted by a large majority in the EP's plenum. The only major exception was the sulphur level of petrol fuels for 2000. The EP's tough stance was facilitated by cracks which had appeared within EUROPIA when some Northern European oil companies informed the EP's rapporteurs that more stringent fuel standards were both technically feasible and economically viable.[51]

The Conciliation Committee
The Conciliation Committee had to be set up following the Environmental Council's rejection of most of the EP's second-reading

amendments. The Council and the EP each have fifteen representatives within the Conciliation Committee. However, thirty is far too large a number of negotiators to find compromises on a dossier as complex as the Auto-Oil I Programme. The Environmental Committee's Chairperson Ken Collins explained: 'if you put 15 people on one side, and 15 people on the other, then the only thing you can realistically do is play rugby'.[52] Most of the negotiations were therefore conducted in informal meetings during the British EU Presidency in early 1998, shortly before the Euro elections in July 1998 which allowed MEPs to flag-up their 'green' credentials on dossiers which attracted considerable media attention.

The British Labour government made the environment and transport priority issues during its Presidency in early 1998, having come to power less than a year earlier.[53] However, initially it had not earmarked the Auto-Oil I Programme dossiers, mainly because the EP's vote on the second-reading amendments took place only in February 1998. The British government was encouraged by other member governments to take on the Auto-Oil I dossiers as a matter of urgency.[54] This was welcomed by MEPs, who speculated that Britain, which was not among the most progressive member states on the car emission dossiers in general and the Auto-Oil I Programme in particular, might accept more stringent measures while holding the Presidency.[55] The office of Presidency puts considerable pressure on the incumbent to act as honest broker and accept compromises which it might not embrace when not in office.[56] However, the election of a Labour government in the UK triggered a change of British preferences at the EU level. Two years after the Conservative British government had welcomed the Commission's proposals, Britain abandoned the cost-effectiveness approach.[57]

Spurred on by its rapporteur Bernd Lange, the EP conducted its second reading of a proposal on emission limits on vans within only four weeks, shortly before Easter 1998. This meant that the British Presidency had less than three months to deal with three very complex and highly technical dossiers (cars, vans and fuels), which now made up the Auto-Oil I Programme.

The British Presidency held four formal Conciliation Committee meetings, the first of which took place on 16 April 1998. It also staged three trialogues between the EP's rapporteurs and the Environmental Committee chairperson on the one side and the British deputy permanent representative on the other side; DG Environment's director-general usually also attended these meetings as well as weekly expert meetings held mainly between the EP's rapporteurs and an environmental counsellor from the British permanent representation. They were joined by Commission officials from different DGs. The British Environmental Minister Michael Meacher and the EP's Vice-President Nicole Fontaine conducted the conciliation negotiations only during the last formal committee meeting, on 29 June 1998. This meeting had to resolve only three key issues (in-use compliance measures, cold-start tests and durability requirements) and lasted barely twenty minutes.[58]

The most difficult issue to resolve concerned the new durability requirements. This was due to competition considerations (some companies were much more advanced on this issue) and sovereignty concerns. The British government was reluctant to grant other member governments the power to demand recall actions on British manufactured cars which failed to comply with EU requirements.[59] By the late 1990s, therefore, the main dispute between the Council and the EP had shifted from one about the stringency of future emission limit values to one about how best to ensure the effective functioning of exhaust emissions abatement technology built into cars.

The Conciliation Committee significantly tightened the fuels standards (see table 6.4) and adopted mandatory standards for cars and fuels for 2005. The mandatory limit values set for petrol and diesel cars for 2000 (Euro III) and 2005 (Euro IV), which became enshrined in *Directive 98/69/EC*, are listed in table 6.5.

Table 6.5 *Euro III and IV standards for petrol and diesel cars*

Parameters	Petrol cars by 2000 (Euro III)	Diesel cars by 2000 (Euro III)	Petrol cars by 2005 (Euro IV)	Diesel cars by 2005 (Euro IV)
CO	2.3	0.64	1.0	0.5
HC	0.2	–	0.1	–
NO_x	0.15	0.5	0.08	0.25
$HC + NO_x$	–	0.56	–	0.3
Particulates	–	0.05	–	0.025

Source: *Directive 98/69/EC*

The EP had to make only one major concession, which concerned the sulphur limits for petrol and diesel fuels for 2000. The adopted standards for 2000 and 2005 brought about a significant tightening of the Commission's Auto-Oil I Programme proposals and amounted to a rejection of the cost-effectiveness approach. For Ken Collins (UK, Socialist), it constituted 'the biggest success story without a doubt' during his fifteen years as the EP's longest-serving Environmental Committee chairperson.[60]

Bernd Lange also tried to tighten the standards for a lorries directive for which he became the EP's rapporteur. However, in this case the Council's common position was adopted in 1999, because Lange's amendments failed to command the required majority during the EP's second reading.[61] The lorries directive concluded the Auto-Oil I Programme, which was finally made up of directives for fuels, cars, vans, lorries, and maintenance and inspection requirements.

Pushing for and against a new approach
The EP emerged as the winner from the Conciliation Committee negotiations. The Commission and especially the (corporate laggards within the) oil industry became the biggest losers.[62] The standards adopted therefore came close to those demanded by the environmental leader states within the Council and triggered a near-doubling of costs for oil producers compared to the Commission's original proposals.[63] EUROPIA reacted furiously to the Conciliation Committee outcome, which, it claimed, was based on emotion rather than a rational science-driven approach and would trigger a four-fold cost increase for the oil industry, although this was widely seen as an exaggeration.[64] One Swedish official explained the overreaction by the oil industry as follows: 'The automobile industry had become used to EU regulations for more than 20 years. For the oil industry, however, this process is new and the outcome is [seen as] the end of the oil industry.'[65] The automobile industry, which had favoured the tripartite dialogue but disliked the Commission's proposals, found itself in the winning camp after a determined rearguard lobbying campaign that included the search for allies within the EU beyond the traditional industry–NGO divide as well as outside the EU by getting non EU-producers to sign up to a world fuel charter.

The Commission initially tried to act as a major EU policy entrepreneur when it presented the Environmental Council and the EP with a *fait accompli* in the form of a new approach based on a highly complex and resource-intensive Auto-Oil I Programme, likened by some observers to 'integration by stealth'.[66] The Commission tried to adopt a mediator role during subsequent Conciliation Committee meeting negotiations. However, these negotiations are conducted between the Council and the EP, while the Commission has to look on from the sidelines. The fact that 'fifteen Commission officials' turned up for the first informal trialogue during the Conciliation Committee procedure underlines the strategic importance the Auto-Oil I Programme had for different DGs.[67] When individual DGs put forward contradictory views, they were asked by the EP's Environmental Committee Chairperson Ken Collins to leave the room and to return only after having agreed a common position. The Commission was severely criticised for its procedural innovation (the tripartite dialogue) and saw its substantive policy proposals (for car emissions and fuels directives) significantly tightened. However, cost-effectiveness considerations and the achievement of stipulated health targets and EQOs are likely to become more important for future EU environmental policy. This became apparent during the formulation of the Auto-Oil II Programme.

The Auto-Oil II Programme

In January 1997, the Commission presented the organisational structure and draft work schedule of the Auto-Oil II Programme.[68] After severe criticism of the closed tripartite dialogue used for the Auto-Oil I Programme, the Commission opted for a transparent and very wide-ranging consultation process for the Auto-Oil II Programme. Member governments, environmental NGOs, independent scientists and the supplier industry were represented, in addition to Commission officials (mainly from DGs Industry, Environment, Energy and Transport) and representatives from the automobile and oil industries. The new openness and transparency was widely praised, although some felt the involvement of such a large number of disparate actors constrained chances of finding common ground within a reasonable period of time.[69]

The Commission retained an emphasis on a cost-effective approach to pollution abatement measures based on health targets and EQOs. However, the remit of the Auto-Oil II Programme, which had been initially set up to arrive at cost-effective car and fuel standards for 2005, was radically altered following the 1998 adoption of mandatory standards for 2005 by the Council and the EP. The Commission subsequently adopted the following revised objectives: first, to provide an analytical foundation for the measures outstanding for 2005 (see table 6.4); second, to assess future air quality and establish an analytical framework within which different packages of (technical and non-technical) pollution abatement measures can be assessed using the principles of cost-effectiveness, sound science and transparency; third, to initiate long-term air quality studies covering (in addition to road traffic) emission sources from all sectors.[70]

The theoretical merits of a more integrated approach were recognised by all the policy actors involved. However, the new integrated approach created serious methodological difficulties, either because there were insufficient robust data for some sectors and/or the data were not comparable across the different sectors. For one UBA official, these problems were sufficiently serious to devalue the whole exercise.[71] However, the Commission took a different view, and strongly defended its integrated approach.[72]

Other changes to the overall scope of the Auto-Oil Programme included an extension of the time horizon to 2020 (with several intermittent deadlines) and a widening of the overall geographic scope so that it included three non-EU member states (Estonia, Poland and Switzerland) in addition to member states. The road traffic pollution abatement measures considered for 2005 focused mainly on emission limits for motor cycles and three-wheeled vehicles, improved roadworthiness testing, special fuels for captive fleets (taxis and buses), alternative fuels (such as natural gas and biofuels) and the unresolved specifications for the fuel standards that had been left open in 1998 (see table 6.4). Much of the work was carried out in seven working groups (WG): health targets and EQOs (WG1); vehicle technology (WG2); fuel quality and alternative fuels (WG3); inspection and maintenance (WG4); non-technical measures (WG5); fiscal measures (WG6); and cost-effectiveness analysis (WG7).

The Auto-Oil II Programme was significantly more complex in procedural and conceptual terms than the Auto-Oil I Programme although the Commission felt this was 'a price to pay if one wanted to stick to the principles of sound science, shared responsibility and transparency'.[73] However, some policy actors involved in the Auto-Oil II Programme were less sanguine, arguing that the programme had become so complex as to be almost unmanageable.[74] In 1999, it even looked for a while like the Auto-Oil II Programme policy-formulation process might either grind to a halt or the Commission might again favour a less transparent consultation process with a smaller number of actors in order to make the process more manageable. As a consequence, the MVEG, which had been holding meetings throughout the Auto-Oil I and II Programme processes, again gained in importance.

Table 6.6 *Air quality targets for the Auto-Oil II Programme*

	Pollutant				
	CO (8-hourly rolling average)	NO₂ (annual average)	Benzene (annual average)	PM (annual average)	Tropospheric ozone (8-hourly mean)
Air quality target level	10mg/m³	40μg/m³	5μg/m³	20μg/m³	120μg/m³
Target date	2005	2010	2010	2010	2010

Source: Adapted from CEC (2000e)

The most important health targets and EQOs used for the Auto-Oil II Programme are listed in table 6.6; they were derived from existing and proposed EU directives.[75] The targets for nitrogen dioxide, benzene, particulate matter and tropospheric ozone were more ambitious than those stipulated for the Auto-Oil I Programme.

However, it would be incorrect to argue that the Auto-Oil II Programme considered only health targets and EQOs. The Commission's proposal (COM(99) 125 final) for 'national ceilings for nitrogen oxides and volatile organic compounds were taken as complementary emission reduction targets for "regional" ozone'.[76]

Based on the studies of the Auto-Oil II Programme, the Commission estimated that traditionally regulated road traffic related pollutants (such as CO, HC and NO$_x$) will by 2020 on average fall to less than 20 per cent of their 1995 levels. However, there will be significant variations both in the reduction rates for different pollutants and in their effects on certain regions. Urban health targets will be breached in several European cities, despite marked overall improvements. Targets for particulate matter (from diesel), for tropospheric ozone and, on a localised basis, for nitrogen dioxides will not be met according to the Auto-Oil II Programme studies. They also predicted a rise in CO₂ emissions (which were dealt with outside the Auto-Oil Programmes) until at least 2005.[77] This is partly a consequence of the fact that non-road-traffic-related pollutants from air travel – the fastest growing means of transport during the last few decades – has been hardly regulated at all at the EU level.

The Commission's Auto-Oil II Programme excluded an assessment of whether sulphur specifications for fuels should be reduced to below 50 parts per million (ppm) on the grounds that 50ppm had already been adopted as a mandatory standard by the Environmental Council and the EP. However, lower sulphur fuels were a major source of contention between the oil and automobile industries under the Auto-Oil I Programme.[78] The oil industry was fiercely opposed to a lowering of the sulphur limits while the automobile industry demanded the introduction of ultra-low sulphur or sulphur-free fuels on the grounds that they were necessary for the use of more sophisticated car emission pollution abatement technology. The sulphur limit was the only major concession the EP had to make during the Conciliation Committee procedure when it gave up its demands for a 30ppm limit by 2005 (see table 6.4).

However, lower sulphur fuels were pushed back onto the EU's agenda by the German government which, in a memorandum to the Commission on 16 September 1999 and one to the Environmental Council on 12 October 1999, demanded the EU-wide adoption of a 10ppm limit of sulphur in fuels .[79] In the same year, the BMU made plans within the context of domestic ecological tax reform for the adoption of fiscal incentives aimed at boosting the uptake of fuels containing 10ppm of sulphur.[80] Fuels which contain 10ppm or less of sulphur are usually referred to as sulphur-free fuels. They have been on the market in Sweden and other Nordic countries since the early 1990s.[81] Germany requested EU clearance for the introduction of domestic fiscal incentives for sulphur-free fuels from 2003 [82] while the British Chancellor of the Exchequer Gordon Brown announced a three pence tax cut for ultralow-sulphur fuels in the 2001 Budget.[83] In early 2001 the Commission finally caved in to pressure from some member governments, the automobile industry and environmental NGOs when it announced that it would consider a proposal for ultralow sulphur.[84]

The Auto-Oil II Programme came to the conclusion that 'even the total elimination of traffic emissions whilst keeping non-transport sources unaffected would not be enough to remove all excedences [of the health targets and EQOs] by 2010'.[85] In the Commission's view this finding underlined the need to adopt the most cost-effective measures. For the German government it was further evidence of the need to adopt the BAT principle for regulating road traffic pollution in order to keep detrimental health effects and environmental degradation as low as possible.[86]

Conclusion

The new approach adopted by the Commission for the Auto-Oil I Programme at first sight seems to confirm the argument that, in the 1990s, Britain finally succeeded in persuading the Commission to give up its preference for uniform emission limits derived from the BAT principle, which Germany had demanded ever since the early 1980s, in favour of cost-effective measures derived from EQOs.[87] However, the assessment of the Auto-Oil I and II Programmes in this chapter has revealed a more complex decision-making process. The instigation of the Auto-Oil I Programme was at least partly the result of an internal turf battle within the Commission (mainly between DGs Environment and Industry). Moreover, the EP played a decisive role in the adoption of car emission and fuel standards for 2005 (Euro IV) which were considerably more stringent than those proposed by the Commission. After severe criticism from several member governments (and the German government in particular), the Commission abandoned its tripartite dialogue in favour of a transparent and wide-ranging consultation process during the Auto-Oil II Programme. However, this all but brought to a halt the policy-formulation process undertaken by the actors involved in the Auto-Oil II Programme. As a consequence, the MVEG, the Commission's main advisory committee during the 1980s, gained in importance again.

Chapter 6 has shown that conflicts about the 'new' Auto-Oil Programme approach cut across institutions and member governments which often made reference to their preferred standard-setting philosophy when trying to legitimise their actions. The Auto-Oil Programmes support the view that, since the early 1990s, (together with several member states) the Commission has placed greater emphasis on cost-effectiveness considerations than on standards.

Notes

1 See chapter 5 and Weale *et al.* (2000: 403).
2 DoE (1995); RCEP (1994).

3 Interview with BMU official in 1999.
4 EP (1994).
5 Haigh (ed.) (1995: 6.8).
6 OJ No. L 100/42, 19 May 1994, p. 44.
7 Interview with BMU official in 1999.
8 Arp (1995); Ehret (1998); Friedrich *et al.* (2000: 596).
9 CEC (1996c: 4, 2000e: 6); Friedrich *et al.* (1998a, 1998b, 2000: 596–7); Peake (1997); Wurzel (1999a: 283–4).
10 CEC (1993c).
11 Interview in 1993.
12 Interviews with DG Industry and DG Environment officials in 1992 and 1996–97.
13 ACEA and EUROPIA (1993).
14 Arp (1995); Ehret (1998).
15 CEC (1996c).
16 CEC (1996c: 5).
17 Interviews with DG Environment officials in 1996–98. Arp (1995: 301); CEC (1996c, 2000e); Ehret (1998); Friedrich *et al.* (1998a, 1998b, 2000); Peterson and Bomberg (1999: 178–9); Weale *et al.* (2000: 404–5).
18 Athens, Cologne, The Hague, London, Lyon, Madrid and Milan.
19 Arp (1995: 301).
20 Interviews in 1996. See CEC (1993c: 288).
21 Interviews with DG Industry officials in 1996–97.
22 Interview with Stanley Clinton-Davis in 1995.
23 CEC (1992e).
24 Interview in 1993.
25 Interviews with BMU, UBA, DETR and Swedish Environmental Ministry officials between 1996 and 1998. The German Environment Minister Angela Merkel later wrote a fiercely worded letter of complaint to the Economics Minister Günter Rexrodt.
26 Interview with UBA official in 1999.
27 Interview in 1996.
28 Interview with a Swedish government official in 1997.
29 Molin and Wurzel (2000).
30 See chapter 4.
31 Friedrich *et al.* (1998a, 1998b, 2000).
32 See chapter 5.
33 Interview in 1996. Friedrich *et al.* (2000: 606).
34 Mol *et al.* (eds) (2000); Peterson and Bomberg (1999: 178–9); Weale *et al.* (2000: 404–5).
35 CEC (1996c: 5 and 44).
36 CEC (1993c: 26–7).
37 Brundtland Report (1987); Grubb *et al.* (1993).

38 DoE (1994b); RCEP (1997).
39 EEA (1995c); RCEP (1994).
40 CEC (1996c: 21). All figures refer to 1996 prices.
41 Interview with EEB representatives in 1996.
42 EP (1997a, 1997b, 1997c).
43 EP (1997b: amendment 11, recital 5b).
44 EP (1997b: amendment 9, recital 5).
45 EP (1998a, 1998b).
46 Interview with Bernd Lange in 1999.
47 Interviews with Iiris Kivimäki, assistant to Heidi Hautala and Bernd Lange, and his assistant Petra Hermann in 1998 and 1999.
48 *Environmental Watch: Western Europe*, 20 February 1998, 11.
49 Weale *et al.* (2000: 405).
50 AIT *et al.* (1998); Friedrich *et al.* (2000); Warleigh (2000).
51 Interview in 1998.
52 Ken Collins, quoted in Wurzel (1999b: 8)
53 Wurzel (2001).
54 Interview with a British official in 1999.
55 Interview with Bernd Lange MEP in 1999.
56 Wurzel (1996a, 2000, 2001).
57 Interview with a British official in 1999.
58 Interview in 1998.
59 Interview with DETR official in 1999.
60 Wurzel (1999b: 22).
61 Friedrich *et al.* (2000: 605).
62 *Financial Times* (1997a and 1997b).
63 *Environmental Watch: Western Europe*, 3 July 1998, p. 1.
64 *ENDS Report* 281, June 1998, p. 48. Interviews with BMU, DETR and UBA officials in 1998–99.
65 Interview with a Swedish official in 1998.
66 Friedrich *et al.* (2000), who use Hayward's 1996 term.
67 Interview with Petra Herrman in 1998.
68 CEC (1999d: 5).
69 Interviews with British, German and DG Industry officials as well as an EEB representative during 1999–2001. See also CEC (2000e: 27–8).
70 CEC (2000e).
71 Interview in 1999.
72 CEC (1999d, 2000e).
73 CEC (1999d: 11).
74 Interviews during 1997–2001.
75 See COM(98) 561 final; *Directive 1999/30/EC*; COM(98) 591 final; *Directive 1999/30/EC* and COM(99) 125 respectively.
76 CEC (2000e: 9).

77 CEC (2000e: 4).
78 Weale *et al.* (2000: 405–6).
79 Interview with BMU official in 1999.
80 Interview with BMU official in 1999.
81 See also Weale *et al.* (2000: 405).
82 *ENDS Daily*, 9 March 2001.
83 *Financial Times*, 8 March 2001.
84 *ENDS Daily*, 9 March 2001.
85 CEC (2000e: 13).
86 Interviews with BMU and UBA officials in 1999.
87 Héritier *et al.* (1994, 1996).

Part III
Bathing water protection

At first sight, sewage pollution control appears to constitute a classic 'domestic politics' issue. Alberta Sbragia has argued (with tongue in cheek) that '[i]f "domestic" issues exist at all, one would expect [sewage pollution] to be considered "domestic" rather than "international"'.[1] However, the discharge and dumping of sewage can lead to the eutrophication of the sea and transnational rivers, which in turn, can trigger algae growth which may pose a health risk and produce pollution. A leader in *The Times* on 28 May 1990 therefore argued that 'while the discharge of sewage into shallow water might seem a purely domestic problem, the international community has a legitimate interest in safeguarding the quality of the open sea itself'. Sewage pollution control therefore confirms Albert Weale's claim that environmental issues often render inadequate those traditional political science concepts which rely on the classical distinction between domestic and foreign policy or 'high' and 'low' politics.[2]

Transnational river pollution and the protection of the sea became politically salient issues at the international level in the 1970s.[3] It is therefore unsurprising that much of early EU environmental legislation dealt with water pollution.[4] However, while international environmental regimes focused on global and regional commons (such as the North Sea), EU water legislation also focused on local commons (such as shared lakes) and quality of life issues (such as bathing water standards).[5]

In 1975 the Commission tried to justify its proposal for a bathing water directive by referring to transnational pollution, the internal market (that is the free movement of people) and public demands for amenity standards for bathing waters.[6] However, only a minority of EU bathing waters constitute transborder bathing areas and the risk of tourists falling ill while bathing in other member states created only a tenuous link with the internal market. Some observers have therefore concluded that the *raison d'être* of the bathing water directive lies in its amenity aspects.[7] However, this view was rejected by policy actors who saw the bathing water directive as an important tool for raising the standards of bathing waters, thus lowering the health risk to bathers posed by sewage pollution in particular.

Table III.1 provides an overview of the formal stages of the EU's bathing water policy-making process. It has been drawn up to guide the reader through the assessment of the complex multilevel decision-making processes over a period of more than twenty-five years. EU legislation will be taken as a starting-point for identifying and analysing the core policy actors as well as their interests, strategies, problem perceptions and preferred standard-setting philosophies. In order fully to understand EU bathing water policy it is necessary to assess both the political aspects and the policy–scientific issues while paying attention to the institutional framework and the wider policy network within which the core actors operate.

Table III.1 *Stages of the EU bathing water policy-making process*

Agenda setting, formulation and adoption

UN	WHO organises conferences on bathing water quality in 1972 and 1974
EU	The first EAP mentions the need for common bathing water measures in 1973
	France submits draft national bathing water legislation under the Standstill Agreement on 1 February 1974
	Commission publishes its proposal for a directive on 7 February 1975
	EP debates the directive and adopts its opinion on 13 May 1975
	ECOSOC issues its opinion on 24–25 September 1975
	Environmental Council agrees on the directive on 16 October 1975 and formally adopts it on 8 December 1975
Britain	HoC Select Committee on European Secondary Legislation takes evidence on the proposal on 1 July 1975
	HoL Select Committee on European Secondary Legislation takes evidence on 19 June 1975. It publishes a report on 29 July 1975 and debates the proposal on 13 October 1975
Germany	Federal government issues its statement for the Bundestag on 2 June 1975
	Bundestag Interior Committee publishes its opinion on 26 September 1975
	Bundesrat (EU, Health, Interior and Justice) committees adopt an opinion on the proposal on 2 October 1975

Amendments

EU	EU enlargements trigger minor amendments
	Directives 91/692/EEC and 92/446/EEC require minor changes to the reporting requirements

---

Revision

EU	Commission publishes its proposal for a revised directive on 16 February 1994
	ECOSOC publishes its opinion on 29 July 1994
	Committee of the Regions adopts its opinion on 28 September 1994
	EP adopts its opinion on 11 December 1996
	Environmental Council fails to consider the Commission's proposal
Britain	HoL Select Committee on the European Communities takes evidence on 21 March and 6 December 1994
Germany	Bundesrat adopts its opinion on 21 May 1994
	Federal government issues its statement on 20 June 1994
EU	Commission amends its proposal for a revised bathing water directive in 1997
	Commission withdraws its (1994 and 1997) proposals in late 2000
	Commission publishes a Communication for consultation on a revised directive on 21 December 2000
	Consultation meeting with stakeholders in April 2001
UN	WHO experts adopt draft guidelines for recreational water environments (Annapolis protocol) in 1998

The reasons why the bathing water directive was formulated within a relatively short period and adopted by the Environmental Council in 1975 will be explained in chapter 7 which draws on unpublished empirical evidence. Chapter 8 focuses on the implementation of the bathing water directive in Britain and Germany, and explains why both member states significantly changed their implementation practices after ignoring some of the directive's requirements for several years. Chapter 9 puts forward an analysis of the (stalled) revision process, uncovering the main underlying political and scientific disputes which have formed major stumbling-blocks during the revision process.

Notes

1 Sbragia (1996: 254).
2 Weale (1992a); Weale *et al.* (2000).

3 Brenton (1994: 90).
4 Haigh (ed.) (1995); Jordan *et al.* (1999); Weale *et al.* (2000: 356).
5 Weale *et al.* (2000).
6 CEC (1975a: 2).
7   Haigh (1992); Haigh (ed.) (1995: 4.5).

The origins of bathing water regulation

The public policy literature on the EU bathing water directive is sparse.[1] Moreover, most studies focusing on the origins of the directive have drawn heavily on important contributions by Ruth Levitt and Nigel Haigh who, however, had access to only a limited number of primary sources.[2] Chapter 7 presents new empirical evidence based on unpublished archive material and interviews with core policy actors involved in the policy formulation process of the 1975 bathing water directive.

Agenda-setting and policy formulation

The EU bathing water directive, which was published in February 1976,[3] has remained unchanged for more than twenty-five years. It was agreed in principle by the Environmental Council in October 1975 within a period of little more than eight months following the Commission's formal proposal.[4] The rapidity of the adoption process can be explained by four factors. First, standards for recreational waters had been discussed by the WHO since 1972. Second, the first EAP (1973) had stipulated measures for bathing waters. Third, France had submitted draft national bathing water legislation under the Standstill Agreement in February 1974. Fourth, Italy pushed hard to get the directive adopted during its Presidency in 1975.

The WHO initiative

The WHO's Regional Office for Europe convened meetings in Ostend (Belgium) in 1972 and Bilthoven (Netherlands) in 1974 on recreational water quality for beaches.[5] The Bilthoven meeting formed part of the

WHO's long-term programme in environmental pollution control. Delegates from all but one of the (then) nine EU member states were represented at Bilthoven.[6] The same Commission official who attended the Bilthoven meeting later drafted the proposal for the bathing water directive.

The WHO remains outside the EU decision-making framework. However, the first EAP stipulated that in formulating EU environmental legislation '[m]aximum use will be made of the results already achieved at national and international level, particularly the work done by the WHO'.[7] With the benefit of hindsight, the WHO's Ostend and Bilthoven meetings can be seen as part of the pre-negotiation phase of the EU's bathing water directive. This disproves the claim made by Brendan Moore, a leading British bathing water scientist, that 'the EEC was committed to bathing water standards before these [standards] were discussed at expert level'.[8]

Britain's delegate at the WHO's Bilthoven meeting stressed the

> impracticability of categorizing British beaches in bacteriological terms by means of any realistic sampling programme, because of the great variability of results obtained from one sampling period to the next ... This variability, due to the British coast being scoured by tidal and other sea currents, was contrasted with conditions in the non-tidal Mediterranean.[9]

Similar views were later expressed by the DoE's Environmental Minister Denis Howell, who told the House of Commons:

> I think it is necessary to get clear in our minds what the EEC is mainly on about which I think is the quality of bathing water in the Mediterranean and the Mediterranean countries, which of course is far more inferior in quality and therefore more hazardous than in this country ... There are parts of the Community where the seas are disgraceful and where we would fully support, for our citizens as well as others who are going there on holiday, a cleaning up of the waters.[10]

Britain's delegate at the Bilthoven meeting was adamant that beaches back home did not pose a health risk. He rejected accusations that Britain endorsed the discharge of untreated sewage into estuaries and coastal waters. However, he omitted to mention that Britain discharged millions of tonnes of untreated (or only mechanically treated) sewage into the sea through sea outfalls and by dumping it from ships.[11] The British delegate praised the 1974 reorganisation of the water authorities in England and Wales for having a positive impact on sewage pollution control. However, his claim that 'new water authorities will have sufficient financial and manpower resources to cover the planning, design, construction and operational management of all aspects of sewage and water treatment' [12] was based on wishful thinking rather than fact.[13]

German politicians and officials also considered the quality of their domestic bathing waters to be superior, particularly when compared to Mediterranean beaches.[14] Germany's delegate to the 1974 Bilthoven meeting came from Schleswig-Holstein, which had a high number of bathing areas and a strong interest in tourism. Her report listed the coastal bathing areas and identified problem areas while stressing that

> [b]eaches on either side of sewer outfall points are considered unsuitable for bathing and the sites of discharge are known and labelled as unsuitable by regional authorities ... No standards have so far been drawn up for bathing-waters. Legislation on water resources management is the responsibility of the individual *Länder*.[15]

In 1974 neither Britain nor Germany had in place numerical bathing water standards although the national authorities monitored the quality of some bathing waters.[16] In contrast, France and Denmark, and to a lesser degree Belgium, Greece, Italy and the Netherlands, had adopted numerical standards. The French delegation put forward the most comprehensive report and argued that it would be necessary 'to map carefully every point of the effluent discharge, on the grounds that every beach with a sewer outlet was automatically polluted'.[17] The British delegation disapproved while pointing out that the French claims were not supported by epidemiological data.[18]

The Bilthoven meeting concluded that 'it was generally feasible and desirable to set broad upper limits for the number of faecal indicator organisms in coastal bathing waters'.[19] There was agreement that *Eschericia coli* (*E. coli*) constituted the best indicator organism for faecal contamination of bathing waters. The majority of delegations welcomed the following categorisation for bathing water:

- highly satisfactory: less than 100 *E. coli* counts in 100 millilitres (ml) of water;
- acceptable: consistently less than 1,000 *E. coli* counts in 100ml of water.[20]

The delegates discussed other microbiological, chemical and aesthetic criteria, several of which found their way into the 1975 bathing water directive. However, differences between the national delegations were thinly concealed:

> The only definite conclusion drawn ... is that contact with intact faecal particles in the vicinity of a sewer outfall carries a risk of typhoid or paratyphoid fever being contracted. The apparent lack of wider hazards has not, however, entirely reassured medical scientists, some of whom argue that if the epidemiological and technical methods available to us were more precise a positive correlation between bathing in sewage polluted sea-water might be demonstrated, given the known presence of pathogenic micro-organisms in sea-water ... It was the general consensus ... that there is sufficient evidence to justify a policy of precautionary preventive measures of wastewater pollution in coastal waters used for bathing.[21]

The WHO's Ostend and Bilthoven meetings probably would not have resulted in action in either Britain or Germany without the Commission's proposal for a bathing water directive, which was published on 3 February 1975.[22]

The French initiative

The French government submitted draft national bathing water legislation to the Commission under the Standstill Agreement in February 1974. France established sea-water bathing standards in 1964. It now wanted to adopt similar legislation for inland bathing waters.[23] However, the Commission decided to propose EU bathing water legislation instead, which meant that the French draft national legislation could be put on hold for a period of up to twelve months during which time the Commission and the Council had to adopt common legislation. Following the French notification, the Commission organised a quick succession of meetings with national experts who were often given little prior warning.[24]

France had a national policy for sea-bathing waters already in place and a strong interest in tourism. It could therefore be argued that its notification under the Standstill Agreement constituted an attempt to export French legislation to the EU level.[25] If this was indeed France's intention, the fact that the Commission's desk official in charge of drafting the bathing water proposal was a French-speaking Belgian national whose command of the English language was poor did not hamper the French move.[26] Brendan Moore, who took part in the

WHO's Bilthoven meeting as well as the EU's bathing water working groups, was adamant about the French influence:

> When the study group of national experts was convened in March 1974 to define quality objectives of seawater used for bathing, two constraints on its discussions were applied from the outset. First, health issues were not considered. Secondly, a list of bathing water parameters proposed by the French participants became the framework for the final directive, only the magnitude of the limiting levels of pollutant being effectively left open for discussion.[27]

However, even if one accepts that Moore, an outspoken opponent of numerical bathing water standards, is correct about the French influence on the Commission's proposal, this still leaves open the question of whether the directive, as adopted by the Council, was indeed little more than French national legislation dressed up as an EU directive.

The Commission's initiative

The first EAP identified the need for controlling water used for 'drinking, swimming, farming, pisciculture and industry, beverage industry, [and] recreation'.[28] It stipulated that 'as regards sea water, France, Italy, and United Kingdom Governments will transmit the information at their disposal on sea water for bathing and on quality objectives for beaches'.[29]

To keep up the momentum generated by the first EAP, the Commission set up a Water Quality Working Group in late 1973. It was made up of Commission and national officials who met for several plenary sessions between 1973 and 1976. To cope with the workload, sub-groups on water for fish breeding, sea-water for mussel breeding and sea-water for bathing were set up.

Initially the Commission wanted to put forward two separate proposals for sea-water bathing and fresh-water bathing.[30] This would have been similar to the French national legislation. In January 1974, the Commission invited member governments to attend the first meeting of the sea-water bathing sub-group on 12 March 1974. Meetings on fresh-water bathing took place on 24–25 January, 22 March and 20–21 June 1974. However, at the plenary session of the Water Quality Working Group, on 4–5 July 1974, the Commission presented a merged *Proposal for a Directive Relating to Pollution of Sea Water and Fresh Water for Bathing (Quality Objectives)*, although its

Technical Annexe listed different limit values for sea- and fresh-water bathing.[31]

One German official involved in the Commission's (and later also the Council) Bathing Water Working Groups recalled: 'The Commission's merged proposal came very much as a surprise to member state experts. As far as I can remember no prior consultation took place. It was all done in a terrible rush ... A serious problem was that the minutes of meetings were sometimes available only in French.'[32] The British Environmental Minister Denis Howell put forward a similar complaint when he told the House of Commons Select Committee on the Environment (HCSCE): 'We have lots of reservations about the ... time-scale'.[33]

National delegations felt that the Commission had allocated insufficient time to discuss the scientific issues.[34] Lord Ashby, the chair of the RCEP, warned that the 'standards set out in the annexe are so ill-defined as to be virtually unenforceable';[35] the German Bundesrat took a similar view.[36]

The Commission based its proposal for a bathing water directive on both the internal market provision *and* the implied powers doctrine, as it was aware that the risk of tourists falling ill while bathing in other member states' waters created only a weak link to the free movement of people, which is one of the primary aims of the EC/EEC Treaty.[37] The Commission's emphasis on public demand for common amenity and aesthetic standards was seized upon by the British government, which argued: 'The quality standards in the Annexe to the Directive are in many cases more stringent than required to protect public health or not related to that purpose. They are more in the nature of general water standards covering aspects such as amenity.'[38] However, this view was not shared by the Commission and other member governments. Domestic policy actors in Britain, such as the RCEP, the House of Commons Select Committee on Welsh Affairs, individual scientists and environmental groups began to contest their government's interpretation during the implementation phase of the directive.

At the 1974 Bilthoven meeting, the British delegation had stated its opposition to numerical standards. The Commission's proposal, published on 3 February 1975, therefore looked like it would lead to protracted Council negotiations, or even be vetoed as unanimous agreement was required for the adoption of the directive.

The Italian Presidency's pusher role
Ireland, which held the EU Presidency in the first half of 1975, had
little interest in bathing water legislation but placed the Commission's
proposal on the agenda of two Council Environmental Working
Groups on 5 May and 5 June 1975. Italy, which took over the
Presidency in the second half of 1975, favoured EU legislation and
was keen to be credited with the adoption of the bathing water
directive under its Presidency. Italy's efforts were helped by the fact
that member governments had given a commitment under the first
EAP that the Environmental Council would act within nine months
following publication of a Commission proposal mentioned in this
programme.[39]

The Council Environmental Working Group negotiated the Commission's proposal on 3–4 July and 25 September 1975. The Italian
Presidency wanted to establish as much agreement as possible on the
text of the directive before allowing a debate on the Technical Annexe,
which was not discussed until 25 September 1975. Because time was
pressing and several issues remained unresolved, COREPER II officials
(that is, the permanent representative officials who usually deal only
with major political issues) also became involved in the run up to the
Environmental Council meeting on 16 October 1975. The ministers
dealt mainly with the following key questions.
• What implementation deadline should be set?
• How should transborder pollution be tackled?
• What powers should be granted to the Committee on the Adaptation to Technical Progress?
• Should Bathing Water Reports be published?
All of these questions were resolved at the Environmental Council
meeting in October 1975. However, due to the haste with which the
bathing water dossier was negotiated, editorial changes still had to
be made before it could be formally adopted by the Environmental
Council on 8 December 1975.[40]

The EP's *Report*, which was drafted by the Italian rapporteur Mr
Premoli, had been published on 12 May 1975.[41] ECOSOC issued its
Opinion on 24–25 September 1975.[42] Both documents showed a lack
of technical expertise and the Council did not take up any of the
suggestions made by either ECOSOC or the EP which had only
consultative powers prior to 1987.

The EP's *Report* simply stated: 'As regards the technical and
bacteriological analysis in the directive, the parameters would seem

satisfactory, even if we cannot give a definite judgement at this point. The maximum acceptable limit for faecal colon bacilli would seem satisfactory and the level proposed ideal.'[43] The EP's debate on the Commission's proposal took place on 13 May 1975. It was a low-key affair despite a failed attempt by three British Conservative MEPs to amend the EP's opinion in such a way as to severely limit the scope of the directive.[44]

Textual changes by the Council
The Council made a number of significant changes to the text of the Commission's proposal, the most important of which are summarised in table 7.1.

These changes amounted to a significant narrowing of the scope of the Commission's proposal. The Council also widened a number of existing loopholes and introduced new ones in order to allow for more discretion during the implementation stage. Most important in this regard was the change from the Commission's definition of bathing waters as waters 'in which the competent authorities authorise ... or tolerate bathing' to waters in which bathing is 'authorised ... or not prohibited and is traditionally practised by *a large number* of bathers' [italics added].

Jonathan Golub, Andrew Jordan, Albert Weale and colleagues, and the present author have argued that member governments agreed to early EU environmental legislation relatively speedily because they underestimated the cost implications.[45] However, in the case of the bathing water directive, policy makers in Britain and at German *Länder* level actually exaggerated the cost implications during the policy formulation phase.

When questioned by the House of Lords Select Committee on the European Communities (HLSCEC), Denis Howell made the following cost estimate (at 1975 prices): 'Up to £5,000 per beach per annum [and the] total cost of complying with the directive, including actual improvement of water quality ... is possibly in the region of £100 million'.[46] This was the upper range limit of a 'guesstimate' by the DoE.[47] The German Bundesrat did not put an exact figure on the likely cost of the Commission's proposal but drew 'attention to the burden which the implementation of the directive will cause the *Länder* in terms of finance and personnel'.[48] It was the fears of some member governments about cost implications that triggered some of the amendments outlined in table 7.1.

Table 7.1 *Textual changes to the Commission's proposal by the Council*

Commission proposal	Council text
Article 1(2): Bathing waters are defined as waters 'in which the competent authorities authorise or tolerate bathing'	*Article 1(2)*: Bathing waters are defined as waters in which bathing is 'authorised or not prohibited and is traditionally practiced by a large number of bathers'
Article 2 and Technical Annexe: Differentiated set of limit values for sea and fresh/inland waters as well as water warmer than 20°C. Highly complex sampling regime	*Article 2 and Technical Annexe*: One set of limit values for sea and fresh/inland waters regardless of the temperature. Greatly simplified sampling regime
Article 1(3): The limit values have to be complied with all year round	*Article 1(3)*: The bathing season depends on local practice where no official opening/closing of the season takes place
Article 4: Implementation deadline: eight years	*Article 4*: Implementation deadline: ten years
Article 7: Guide and mandatory limit values	*Article 7*: Insertion of a provision which allows member states to adopt more stringent (guide and mandatory) limit values
Article 8: Waiver provision for exceptional circumstances	*Article 8*: The applicability of the waiver provision for exceptional circumstances was widened
	New Article 13: A new article was inserted to allow for the publication of Bathing Water Reports

Sources: CEC (1975b) and Council (1976)

The British government pressed hard to get the definition of the bathing season (Article 1(2)) changed in order to avoid having to monitor bathing waters all year round. To draw attention to the possible cost implications of the Commission's open-ended definition of the bathing season, the House of Lords cited the example of 'Christmas swimmers'.[49] However, the British government's preference for a narrow definition of the bathing season probably had more to do with the fact that some water authorities discharged increased loads of sewage outside of the main bathing season.

As regards the implementation deadline, the member governments fell into three camps: Denmark, Italy, the Netherlands and Ireland supported the eight-year deadline put forward by the Commission; Belgium, France and Germany advocated an extension to ten years; while Britain was opposed to any specific deadline, seeking instead to leave it to member governments to draw up bathing water improvement schemes that fitted their national priorities.[50] This was in accordance with the dominant British environmental regulatory style at the time which showed an aversion to statutory objectives and fixed deadlines. However, it was also a reflection of the dire financial situation of the British water authorities in the 1970s.[51] A ten-year deadline was finally adopted after Britain secured a widening of the waiver clause.[52] However, the waiver was not used by a single member government.[53]

Another controversial issue concerned transborder pollution. Germany vetoed a proposal from the Netherlands which would have required member states to remedy transfrontier pollution. Germany is a major Rhine upstream polluter and was therefore concerned about possible compensation claims by the Netherlands, which is a Rhine downstream state. The Dutch government also favoured wide-ranging powers and QMV for the Committee on Adaptation to Technical Progress. This was opposed by Britain, Germany and France who demanded a pruning of the committee's powers as proposed by the Commission.[54] In the end, the Commission's position was retained largely unchanged. However, the first meeting of the Adaptation Committee did not take place until June 1996.

The only genuinely new requirement included by the Council in the bathing water directive was the publication of bathing water reports (Article 13). It was proposed by the German Federal government, which ignored concerns raised by the *Länder* that bathing water reports would amount to a misallocation of scant resources better spent on improving sewage treatment facilities – a view which some *Land* officials still held in the early 1990s.[55]

The rationale behind bathing water reports was that they would place member states under public pressure to improve failing bathing waters. In Germany the bathing water directive was negotiated by the Interior Ministry (BMI). However, the idea for bathing water reports was championed by the Ministry for Youth, Family and Health (BMJFG). The BMJFG, which had been responsible for bathing water issues at the federal level until a ministerial reorganisation in 1970, argued that reports would raise awareness about health issues among bathers. The Economics Ministry (BMWi) was quick to support this idea, although it mainly had Germany's tourist industry in mind.

The British government was initially opposed to the publication of bathing water reports. Denis Howell argued that publication of sampling results would result in unrealistic public demands and suggested that monitoring should therefore be carried out 'under the most sensible arrangements with the utmost use of discretion'.[56] The reasons for the British government's decision to withdraw its objections are not entirely clear. However, it is likely that the British government underestimated the future importance of the EU bathing water reports.

Another reason was that Denis Howell wanted to show some good will on a policy issue to which the British government was no longer in principle opposed. Around the same time as the bathing water directive was negotiated, the British government vetoed the proposal for a directive on aquatic discharges from the wood-pulp industry and held up for several months a directive on discharge of dangerous substances into water. It saw little reason to increase tensions with its European partners by opposing the bathing water directive, the scope of which had been narrowed considerably (or, put differently, the loopholes widened) by the Council. Denis Howell stated to the House of Commons:

> The EEC is proposing to create absolute standards which is not exactly the way in which we have operated our environmental legislation and our projects in this country. We prefer to move on more practical grounds than absolute standards; nevertheless ... we are in general support of the direction in which they are moving ... So far as the beaches are concerned we see no difficulty at all in meeting these requirements, although of course one wants to improve even some of our own beaches when resources are available. So far as inland waters are concerned it is rather a different kettle of fish. In some of our inland waters the bacteriological content is such that we could not be happy we could comply with the standards laid down in this directive at the moment.[57]

Britain identified its first inland bathing waters only in 1998.

The 1974–79 Labour government was overall more Eurosceptic than its Conservative predecessor under the Europhile Prime Minister Edward Heath. However, Denis Howell and Baroness Birk, the junior environmental minister, were pro-Europeans. Baroness Birk gave the following reason for her support of the bathing water directive: 'I am a passionate anti-pollutionist and I have always been a pro-European.'[58] The same cannot be said about Prime Minister Margaret Thatcher, who came to power in May 1979, shortly before the deadline for the identification of EU bathing waters expired.

One politically sensitive issue for the British government was the possibility of temporary bathing bans.[59] Such a requirement was not mentioned in the Commission's proposal, nor was it discussed at the Council level. However, the EP had put forward this demand in its *Opinion* in the face of opposition from three British Conservative MEPs.[60] The introduction of bathing prohibitions was criticised by parliamentarians from all political parties in the House of Commons and the House of Lords who argued that prohibitions would be unenforceable because the British people had a right to bathe wherever they wished to do so.[61] However, Lord Diplock exposed this myth during a House of Lords debate in 1975: 'In England the foreshore, with a few exceptions, is the property of the Crown. In England there is no public right of bathing off the foreshore. The position in Scotland may be different.'[62]

Bathing bans did not become a political issue in Germany, where the right to bathe in public lakes, rivers or the sea has become part of the common use (*Gemeingebrauch*) of public goods since the abolition of the Bathing Ordinance (Bade-Polizeiverodnunng) in 1918.[63] Temporary bathing bans had been issued occasionally by the local public health authorities prior to the adoption of the 1975 bathing water directive, and some *Länder* governments actually favoured a bathing ban provision.

Council amendments to the Technical Annexe
The Commission's working groups had spent little time discussing the Technical Annexe. At the time, member government representatives complained that this would force the Council Environmental Working Group and the Environmental Council to waste time on technical details instead of focusing on the remaining political obstacles.

However, the Italian Presidency had made sure that as much consensus as possible on the text of the directive had been reached before it allowed a debate on the Technical Annexe. The lack of time allocated to 'technical details' is surprising, not only because they are often of crucial importance for environmental legislation but because experts had highlighted deficiencies in the Commission's proposal.

The most important changes the Council made to the Technical Annexe can be summarised as:

- the differentiation between sea and fresh water was removed;
- the distinction between water warmer and colder than 20°C was abolished;
- the complex sampling regime was simplified; and
- the limit values for several parameters were changed and one parameter was dropped.

The Commission's rationale for stricter standards in water warmer than 20°C had been based on the tendency of bathers to stay in warmer water for longer and who are thus exposed to a higher health risk if the water is contaminated.[64] This view was supported by the British government, which down-played the counter-argument that some pathogenic organisms die off more quickly in warmer waters and/or strong sunlight.[65] The temperature differentiation was abolished because the average water temperature for a particular bathing area can vary considerably over different years and is known only at the end of the bathing season.

The sampling regime put forward in the Commission's proposal foresaw weekly, fortnightly, monthly, six-monthly and annual samp-ling patterns depending on the results of earlier samples. It also differentiated according to sea and fresh-water bathing, the tempera-ture of the water and the average concentration of bathers per linear kilometre.[66] Unsurprisingly, the Council Environmental Working Group agreed to simplify the sampling regime. However, some of the simplifications led to 'a number of unsatisfactory compromises'.[67]

The Netherlands, which has a few inland sea-water bathing areas (rather than fresh water), pressed for the adoption of a single set of standards for sea and fresh/inland water bathing. However, this had the effect that a few of the parameters put forward solely for fresh water in the Commission's proposal now became applicable also for sea-water, in relation to which they made little sense. One such example is the transparency parameter, which also became applicable to the North and the Baltic Sea where it can not usually be complied with for reasons unrelated to pollution (for example, high turbidity).

When adopting the limit values, the Council generally chose the stricter of the two sets of values put forward in the Commission's proposal for sea and fresh-water bathing, though with two major exceptions: a more lenient guide value was adopted for total coliforms and; the imperative value for faecal streptococci was dropped altogether. The Council also agreed to lower the compliance rate from 90 to 80 per cent for the guide values set for total and faecal coliforms.

The Council accepted all of the parameters put forward in the Commission's proposal, with one minor exception.[68] There was agreement that the microbiological parameters, several of which had already been discussed at the WHO's Bilthoven meeting, were the most important for protecting the health of bathers as they indicate sewage contamination.

Total and faecal coliforms were regarded as the most important microbiological parameters partly because they are easy to sample and inexpensive to analyse. However, the Commission's proposal failed to stipulate the exact coliform species (such as *E. Coli*). This deficiency had been earlier highlighted by Lord Ashby, who argued:

> Coliform bacteria are harmless and benign lodgers in the gut of every one of us. In fact, we pass about 10^{11} – that is, 100,000 million – of them a day. They do not do any harm. Therefore, the only intention of measuring these perfectly harmless organisms in the water is to use them as an index of other bacteria which might or might not be dangerous ... As an index of sewage pollution, counts of coliform are not worthless; they are positively misleading, because they would give people an absolutely spurious impression of scientific accuracy ... This is no plea for dirty beaches – and some of them are revolting! It is not suggesting dragging our feet on the whole problem ... It is a plea not to use expensive and spurious criteria for cleanliness.[69]

Lord Ashby acknowledged that there was a British problem with regard to sewage polluted beaches (something the British government continued to deny until the late 1980s). However, he warned that sewage contamination could not be monitored adequately by the parameters which were subsequently listed in the 1975 bathing water directive.

The consequences of the Commission's and the Council's failure to stipulate precisely the analytical methods for identifying the indicator organisms became fully apparent only during the implementation phase. There is agreement among microbiologists and policy experts

that the analytical reference methods listed in the Technical Annexe
to the bathing water directive are too vague to allow for reproducible
and comparable results.[70] The head of the British Water Research
Centre, A. Gameson, put it as follows:

> the directive states that 'Laboratories which employ other methods must
> ensure that the results are equivalent or comparable to those specified.'
> However, it is difficult to see how this can be complied with when the
> methods 'specified' are not specific, nor are they 'equivalent and com-
> parable' to each other.[71]

Moreover, the methods for handling samples were not specified in
the bathing water directive. This left the door wide open for cheating.
For example, some indicator organisms die off quickly if exposed to
strong sunlight.[72]

Table 7.2 lists the limit values and sampling frequencies of the
parameters set out in the 1975 bathing water directive and compares
them with those put forward in the Commission's 1975 proposal
(listed in italics).

Many of the physico-chemical parameters (see parameters 6–18 in
table 7.2) are of little relevance for an assessment of the health risk
posed to bathers. They were adopted mainly as environmental parameters at a time when the overall ecological quality of waters was
not yet covered by EU legislation. The transparency (11) and dissolved
oxygen (12) parameters can be used as a somewhat crude indicator
for algae blooms which can pose a serious health risk to human and
other organisms.[73] Once an algae bloom has started it is extremely
difficult to control, as algae can grow exponentially, particularly in
water contaminated with sewage, which acts as a nutrient.[74] It is
therefore difficult to follow the reasoning of Lord Nugent of Guildford, chair of the National Water Council in England and Wales,[75]
when he argued: 'These areas where large quantities of sewage sludge
are dumped ... show that not only has the fish life not diminished
but that it has increased. Evidently, there is quite a nutritional value
in effluent so long as you remove toxic elements.'[76] Lord Nugent's
statement had little to do with 'sound science' and much to do with
the fact that dumping provided a cheap solution to sewage disposal.

However, it was not only Britain which initially dragged its feet
during the implementation phase of the bathing water directive: as
chapter 8 shows, Germany's implementation record did not reflect
the environmental leader status it aspired to from 1982 onwards.

Table 7.2 *Parameters of the Council directive and the Commission proposal*

Parameters	Imperative value	Guide value	Sampling frequency
Microbiological parameters			
1 Total coliforms/100ml	10,000 (95% conformity) 10,000 in sea and fresh water	5,000 (80% conformity) 2,000 in sea water 500 in fresh water	Fortnightly [a] Weekly for >10,000 bathers
2 Faecal coliforms/100ml	2,000 (95% conformity) 2,000 in waters >20°C; 5,000 in sea water <20°C	100 (80% conformity) 500 in sea water	Fortnightly [a] Weekly for >10,000 bathers
3 Faecal streptococci/100ml	– 1,000 in sea and 2,000 in fresh water	100 (90%) 100 in sea water	[b] [e]
4 Salmonella/l	0 (95%) 0 in sea and fresh water	– –	[b] [b]
5 Enteroviruses PFU/10l	0 (95%) Viruses: 0 in sea and 1 in fresh water	– –	[b] [b]
Physico-chemical parameters			
6 pH	6–9	–	[b]
7 Colour	No abnormal change No visible change	– –	Fortnightly [a,b] [d]
8 Mineral oils	No odour or visible film No film visible; <0.3mg/l	– <0.2mg/l for fresh water	Fortnightly [a,b] [d]
9 Surface-active substances	No lasting foam No lasting foam; 0.3mg/l	≤0.3mg/litre ≤0.2 mg/l for fresh water	Fortnightly [a,b] [d]

Parameters	Imperative value	Guide value	Sampling frequency
10 Phenols (phenol indices C6H5OH)	No specific odour; ≤0.005mg/litre *No unpleasant odour;* ≤0.05 mg/l for fresh water	£0.005mg/ litre *No unpleasant odour 0.005mg/l for fresh water*	Fortnightly [a,b] d
11 Transparency	1 metre *1 metre for fresh water*	2 metres *1.5 metres for fresh water*	Fortnightly [a] inspection [e] *for fresh water*
12 Dissolved oxygen (% saturation O₂)	– *50–170 for fresh water only*	80–120 *80–120 for fresh water only*	b *Fresh water* [e]
13 Tarry residues and floating materials	– –	Absence *No visible tarry residues*	Fortnightly inspections [a] *Fresh water only* [d]
14 Ammonia mg/litre NH4	– –	– *1mg/l for fresh water only*	c –
15 Nitrogen Kjeldahl	– –	– *2mg/l for fresh water only*	c –

16–18: For the physico-chemical parameters 16–18 (pesticides, heavy metals, nitrates and phosphates) neither mandatory nor guide values were proposed or adopted

Notes: [a] The sampling frequency can be reduced if results from previous years show a water quality which is appreciably better than stipulated in the Annex and no new factors have occurred
[b] To be sampled only if an inspection indicates that these organisms may be present
[c] Must be sampled if eutrophication is likely to occur
[d] Weekly for more than 10,000 bathers and fortnightly for less than 10,000 bathers
[e] Fortnightly for more than 10,000 bathers and monthly for less than 10,000 bathers
Sources: Adapted from CEC (1975) and Council (1975)

Conclusion

This chapter has shown that the bathing water directive constitutes a complex compromise which took into account the core demands of the policy actors with veto powers. It was not simply a French proposal dressed up as EU legislation. The Environmental Council managed to significantly narrow the scope of the Commission's proposal for a bathing water directive. It widened a number of loopholes and inserted new ones in the Commission's proposal. Moreover, member governments inserted new requirements (such as bathing water reports), the full implications of which became apparent only during the implementation phase.

Policy actors other than member governments also significantly influenced the directive. The Commission acted as a policy entrepreneur when it used draft national French legislation submitted under the Standstill Agreement, the 1973 EAP and the Treaty provisions to push for the adoption of its proposal. The EP and environmental NGOs did not play an important role during the policy formulation stage. However, scientists who operated at the member state, EU and UN–WHO levels were influential. On the other hand, there was little evidence of a clearly discernible epistemic community or a bathing water policy community fostering the adoption of the directive within the EU.

One possible explanation for this finding is that (sewage) pollution of bathing waters was not (then) widely perceived as a pressing health or environmental problem, at least in Britain and Germany, where the political salience of this issue was low. That the issue of common (and national) bathing water standards arrived on the domestic agenda in Britain and Germany was largely due to the EU. However, most British and German politicians and officials initially saw the bathing water directive primarily as a tool for raising water quality standards in southern member states where many British and German nationals ventured as tourists for their summer holidays.

Different environmental regulatory styles played a role within the 'bathing water policy discourse' during the policy-formulation and adoption phases. British policy-makers complained that the approach taken in the bathing water directive differed from the national standard-setting philosophy, but they were prepared to compromise after having achieved what they believed to be a significant narrowing of the scope of the directive. Policy-makers at the federal level in

Germany had to tread carefully because water policy competences are largely assigned to the *Länder*, and they had also favoured a significant narrowing of the Commission's proposal.

Notes

  1 For example, IEEP (1986); A. Jordan (1997, 1998a, 1999a); Jordan and Greenaway (1999); Kromarek (1986); Richardson (1994); Ward *et al.* (1995, 1997); Weale *et al.* (2000: 356–60); Wurzel (1995a).

  2 Haigh (1987); Haigh (ed.) (1995: 4.5); Levitt (1980).

  3 Council (1976).

  4 CEC (1975b) and Council press release 1185/75 (presse 115), 16 October 1975, pp. 10–11.

  5 WHO (1975).

  6 Only landlocked Luxembourg was not represented.

  7 CEC (1973: 14).

  8 Moore (1977: 269).

  9 WHO (1975: 5).

10 HoC (1975a: 328 and 332).

11 Britain stopped dumping sewage from ships only in 1998.

12 WHO (1975: 6).

13 A. Jordan (1998a); Kinnersley (1988, 1994); Maloney and Richardson (1995); Richardson *et al.* (1992).

14 Bundesrat (1975).

15 WHO (1975: 9).

16 WHO (1974). See also Gameson (1979); Kay (ed.) (1992); NRA (1991) for Britain and Erdmann (not dated) for Germany.

17 WHO (1975: 5).

18 Moore (1977).

19 WHO (1975: 20).

20 WHO (1975: 20–1).

21 WHO (1975: 19).

22 CEC (1975a, 1975b).

23 CEC (1975a: Explanatory memorandum).

24 Interview with BMU–BMI official in 1992.

25 Héritier (1996); Héritier *et al.* (1996, 1994).

26 Interviews with DG Environment officials in 1992.

27 Moore (1977).

28 CEC (1973: 16).

29 CEC (1973: 17).

30 Interview with BMU–BMI official in 1992.

31 CEC (1975a, 1975b).

32 Interview with BMU–BMI official in 1992.

33 HoC (1975a: 328)
34 Interview with BMU–BMI official in 1992. See also Moore (1977).
35 HoL (1975a). See also A. Jordan (1999a); Weale *et al.* (2000: 359–60).
36 Bundesrat (1975).
37 CEC (1975a: 12 and 1975b: 1). See Article 95 (formerly Article 100) and Article 178 (formerly Article 235) EC/EEC Treaty respectively.
38 DoE (1977: 3); Haigh (ed.) (1995: 4.5); Levitt (1980).
39 CEC (1973: 2).
40 Council (1976).
41 EP (1975a, 1975b).
42 ECOSOC (1975a, 1975b).
43 EP (1975a: 7).
44 James Spicer's amendment was aimed only at removing the possibility of bathing bans. Sir Derek Walker-Smith and Lord Bethell's amendments would have limited the application of the directive to Mediterranean beaches (*Debates of the EP*, 13 May 1975, 46–53).
45 Golub (1994); A. Jordan (1997, 1998a, 1999a); Weale *et al.* (2000: 359–60); Wurzel (1993: 187).
46 HoL (1975a).
47 HoL (1975c).
48 Bundesrat (1975: 2).
49 HoL (1975a).
50 Council of the European Communities, R/1841/75 (ENV. 94), 16 July 1975.
51 A. Jordan (1998a, 1999a).
52 Article 8 states that certain parameters can be waived for exceptional weather or geographical conditions and when water undergoes natural enrichment.
53 It was used only by member states which joined the EU after the implementation deadline had expired.
54 CEC, R/1841/75 (ENV. 94) of 16 July 1975.
55 Interview in 1993.
56 HoC (1975a: 329).
57 HoC (1975a: 328–9).
58 HoL (1975a: 753).
59 Haigh (1987: 62–3).
60 EP (1975b: 13).
61 HoC (1975a); HoL (1975a); Haigh (1987).
62 HoL (1975a: 746).
63 Erdmann (not dated: 2).
64 CEC (1975a: 7).
65 Haigh (ed.) (1995: 4.5).
66 CEC (1975a, 1975b).

67 Interview with a BMU–BMI official in 1992.
68 The sulphite-reducing clostridium parameter was rejected.
69 HoL (1975a: 732–4).
70 Interviews over 1992–97 and 1999–2001. See also CEC (1995e, 1995f, 1999b).
71 Gameson (1979: 207).
72 Interviews over 1992–97.
73 Interviews over 1992–94.
74 Kay (ed.) (1992); NRA (1990); Schleswig-Holsteinischer Landtag (1993).
75 The National Water Council, which was abolished in the 1980s, advised the British government on water-related policy issues.
76 HoL (1975a: 742).

8

Implementation and sewage treatment policies

Implementation

The implementation of EU directives consists of two steps: first, they must be transposed through national legislation (formal transposition) and then, the directive must be put into practice (practical implementation). The 1975 bathing water directive set 10 December 1977 as the formal transposition deadline, by which time the bathing waters had to have been identified. The practical implementation deadline, when all identified bathing waters had to comply with the requirements of the directive, was set as 10 December 1985.

The Commission must be notified of the national transposition measures. It therefore finds it relatively easy to gain an overview of which member states have fulfilled their transposition duties. The same cannot be said about practical implementation, for which the Commission relies heavily on whistle-blowing by environmental groups.[1] However, the Commission's role as guardian of the Treaties was made easier by the fact that member governments had to submit bathing water reports; the first was due by 10 December 1979.

Formal implementation
The Commission sent out a reminder two months before the formal transposition deadline expired in December 1977. The British government replied on 9 January 1978, arguing that the 1974 Control of Pollution Act already included provisions about (sewage) discharges into tidal waters and estuaries. However, the relevant provisions of the 1974 Act had not been implemented due to financial constraints.[2] They were only put into force in 1986 and, even then, exemptions

were granted for existing consents (such as sewage discharges).[3] In 1977 the DoE took the view that

> additional UK legislation is not required and that implementation can be satisfactorily achieved by administrative means. The application of the directive does, however, raise a number of practical issues ... It would appear that full implementation of the directive must await the bringing into force of the 1974 Act. It will be necessary, though, for the UK to show in the meantime that all possible steps are being taken to meet our obligations.[4]

In Scotland the story was a similar one; the 1951 and 1965 Rivers (Prevention of Pollution) Scotland Acts covered waste water discharges into tidal waters and estuaries but the relevant provisions were only put into force in 1991.[5] No bathing waters were identified in Scotland or Northern Ireland until 1986.

In Germany it was up to the *Länder*, which hold most of the competences for water pollution control, to transpose the bathing water directive. Most *Länder* governments issued merely internal administrative circulars (*Verwaltungsanweisungen*), and almost all were late in doing so.[6] However, the Commission insisted that internal administrative circulars were insufficient, arguing that they lacked transparency and legal certainty for citizens.[7] After considerable pressure from the Commission, the *Länder* finally caved in and adopted the legislation. However, in the late 1990s there were still transposition problems in some of the new German *Länder*. The British government was also forced to abandon circulars in favour of legislation.

Practical implementation
Practical implementation involves the identification and monitoring of bathing waters, the completion of sampling reports and the adoption of remedial measures where necessary.

Bathing Water Reports
The EU's bathing water reports, which are based on national monitoring and sampling reports, helped the Commission to identify breaches of the directive and raised the public profile of the directive. However, they had humble beginnings.

The first bathing water report was not published.[8] It was only after pressure from the EP that the Commission asked member governments for permission to publish their national reports in 1980.[9] No member government objected at a time when correct implementation of EU environmental legislation was a low priority for the Commission. The second bathing water report, which focused on the 1980 bathing season, was the first to be published, in 1983.[10]

The first four bathing water reports consisted of little more than bundled together photocopies of the summaries of the national reports. The fifth bathing water report was made up merely of a summary of the incomplete national data for the bathing seasons 1983–86; it was not published until 1988.[11] It was only from the ninth bathing water report onwards, published in 1990, that the data refer to the bathing season of the previous year.

Since the 1990s, the bathing water reports have been published annually and regularly generate considerable media and public interest. DG Environment also set up a bathing water report website which was one of the most frequently visited official EU sites in the late 1990s.[12] Bathing water websites have also been maintained by national authorities, tourist boards, consumer organisations and NGOs. Some national authorities even offered 'near real time' (the analysis of bathing water samples takes during the previous 12–48 hours) sampling data on their websites; the Commission is thinking along similar lines.[13]

Table 8.1 lists the total number of bathing waters for all member states for the bathing seasons 1979–99; the data in square brackets refer to fresh and inland bathing waters only. The fact that up until the 1985 bathing season Britain had identified fewer bathing waters than had tiny landlocked Luxembourg was widely used by British environmental groups in their campaigns to raise domestic bathing water standards.[14] For the 1986 season, the number of British bathing waters rose steeply from 27 to 391 due to public pressure and the Commission's threat of court action; the number of bathing waters stood at 552 for the 1999 season.[15]

For many years British officials maintained that the reason for the low number of domestic bathing waters was unfavourable climatic conditions. However, this explanation has carried less weight since Finland and Sweden joined the EU. Britain remained the only member state that failed to identify any inland bathing waters prior to 1998. Following its election in 1997, a (pro-EU) British Labour government took 'a political decision' to identify the first nine inland bathing waters for the 1998 season.[16]

Germany identified only 94 bathing waters for the 1979 season,

Table 8.1 *Number of EU bathing waters, 1979–99*

Season	1979	1980	1981	1982	1983	1984	1985	1986	1987	1988
Report no.	1	2	3	4	5	5	5	5	6	7
	1982	1983	1984	1985	1988	1988	1988	1988	1989	1990
Britain	27	27	27	27	27	27	27	391	397	440
	[0]	[0]	[0]	[0]	[0]	[0]	[0]	[0]	[0]	[0]
Germany	94	94	94	94	106	106	106	106	118	1714
Belgium	45	15	15	15	61	65	67	66	67	103
	[30]	[n/a]	[n/a]	[n/a]	[43]	[48]	[49]	[49]	[49]	[90]
Denmark [a]	1269	1256	1327	1323	1314	1346	1434	1327	1494	1369
	[152]	[139]	[150]	[153]	[144]	[147]	[154]	[148]	[143]	
Greece [a]	–	–	–	–	–	–	–	–	–	–
Spain [a]	–	–	–	–	–	–	–	–	716	1033
									[59]	[274]
France [a]	2824	2679	3209	3470	3177	3111	3051	3321	3444	3324
	[1326]	[1154]	[1661]	[1681]	[1460]	[1558]	[1496]	[1611]	[1740]	[1611]
Ireland	6	6	6	6	6	7	7	7	7	52
	[0]	[0]	[0]	[0]	[0]	[0]	[0]	[0]	[0]	[0]
Italy [a]	n/a	1907	1926	2766	n/a	1926	2766	4015	4395	4171
								[490]	[594]	[312]
Luxem-bourg	25	39	31	32	n/a	n/a	n/a	43	20	20
	[25]	[39]	[31]	[32]				[43]	[20]	[20]
Nether-lands	385	386	n/a	50	50	50	50	105	136	129
	[n/a]	[n/a]		[n/a]	[n/a]	[n/a]	[n/a]	[n/a]	[n/a]	[n/a]
Portugal	–	–	–	–	–	–	–	–	–	–
Austria	–	–	–	–	–	–	–	–	–	–
Finland	–	–	–	–	–	–	–	–	–	–
Sweden	–	–	–	–	–	–	–	–	–	–

Notes: [a] Data may refer to sampling points rather than bathing waters.
Figures in square brackets refer to fresh and inland bathing waters only.
All other figures refer to the total number of bathing waters identified.
The fifth bathing water report covered the seasons 1983–86. There are no

1989	1990	1991	1992	1993	1994	1995	1996	1997	1998	1999
8	8	9	10	11	12	13	14	15	16	17
1991	1991	1992	1993	1994	1995	1996	1997	1998	1999	2000
440 [0]	446 [0]	453 [0]	455 [0]	452 [0]	457 [0]	464 [0]	472 [0]	486 [0]	504 [9]	552 [11]
1668	n/a	1486 [934]	2288 [1841]	2138 [1702]	2359 [1915]	2268 [1822]	2252 [1822]	2139 [1723]	2073 [1656]	2053 [1639]
103 [64]	98 [59]	114 [75]	124 [85]	124 [85]	125 [86]	126 [87]	94 [55]	95 [56]	94 [55]	91 [52]
1370	n/a	1273 [108]	1282 [109]	1288 [108]	1300 [110]	1299 [111]	1309 [113]	1307 [112]	1307 [113]	1291 [114]
554	689	1098	1207 [4]	1254 [4]	1286 [4]	1530 [4]	1694 [4]	1705 [4]	1737 [4]	1820 [4]
1280 [184]	n/a	1556 [240]	1636 [301]	1717 [312]	1854 [346]	1740 [221]	1874 [302]	1839 [251]	1812 [215]	1837 [213]
1751 [n/a]	1972 [n/a]	3141 [1615]	3686 [1754]	3516 [1660]	3536 [1666]	3514 [1640]	3494 [1648]	3416 [1587]	3409 [1553]	n/a
67 [0]	n/a	65 [0]	95 [5]	95 [5]	117 [9]	117 [9]	123 [9]	124 [9]	130 [9]	130 [9]
4448 [615]	n/a	4359 [611]	4655 [622]	4953 [665]	5222 [679]	5287 [695]	5385 [679]	5576 [740]	5605 [737]	5535 [724]
20 [20]	20 [20]	20 [14]	20 [20]	20 [20]	20 [20]	20 [20]	20 [20]	20 [20]	20 [20]	20 [20]
464 [n/a]	410 [n/a]	591 [n/a]	569 [525]	501 [456]	575 [523]	590 [544]	591 [543]	587 [505]	600 [522]	606 [528]
210	–	155 [0]	226 [0]	336 [24]	339 [24]	359 [26]	365 [26]	360 [24]	366 [24]	379 [37]
–	–	–	–	–	–	–	–	268 [268]	270 [270]	270 [270]
–	–	–	–	–	–	478 [378]	492 [391]	454 [360]	451 [357]	436 [343]
–	–	–	–	–	–	602 [350]	879 [487]	923 [522]	840 [462]	791 [412]

data for the 1999 bathing season for France due to industrial action
Sources: CEC (1981a, 1981b, 1982, 1983a, 1983b, 1988, 1989a, 1990a, 1991b, 1992b, 1993b, 1994b, 1995b, 1996b, 1997b, 1998b, 1999a and 2000a)

(although this number included Germany's entire North and Baltic Sea coastlines, each treated as a single bathing water), while claiming that the water quality was generally good.[17] However, in many cases the sampling requirements were not fulfilled. For the three bathing water reports which followed until 1988,[18] the *Länder* merely informed the German federal government about changes in the location and number of bathing waters. The *Länder* maintained that the allegedly good water quality had not deteriorated while the German federal government was answerable to the Commission for the implementation of the bathing water directive in Germany.

The Interior Ministry (BMI), which was responsible for the bathing water directive within the federal government, increasingly felt uneasy about the minimal approach of the *Länder* that had been agreed on within the *Länder* Water Working Group (LAWA). The LAWA had opposed the adoption of the EU bathing water directive and showed little co-operation during the early implementation phase. The BMI (and, from 1986, the newly founded Environmental Ministry–BMU) initially could do little about this because (bathing) water policy fell within the competence of the *Länder*. It was only when the Commission initiated court proceedings against Germany that the BMI–BMU put political pressure on the *Länder* by arguing that their 'scandalous behaviour'[19] threatened Germany's image as an environmental leader state.

The sampling data presented in the bathing water reports cannot be used to compare member states or to assess long-term trends, for the following reasons:

1 National and/or local authorities have used different analytical methods which are not comparable.

2 Some member states have failed to provide the Commission with the required data for all parameters (thus for some years, the pass/fail rates of Denmark, France, Finland and the Netherlands have not taken into account the total coliform parameter).[20] After complaints by other member governments the Commission started legal proceedings to stop this breach of the directive.

3 Over time the Commission has changed the parameters on which the pass/fail decision is based. For the 1980s only the microbiological parameters were used. However, in the late 1990s some of the physico-chemical parameters were also taken into account.

4 The sample frequency often varies considerably between (and often even within) member states. For authorities which take only ten

samples (because they have a short bathing season or to keep costs low) a single failed sample will result in the bathing water being classed as having failed. On the other hand, if a sufficient number of samples is taken and a certain statistical method used, it is possible for the same bathing water that has failed the mandatory requirements to pass the more stringent guideline values.[21] Moreover, in the late 1990s the Commission decided to fail bathing waters if the required sampling frequency was not reached, regardless of the bathing water quality.

5 Most of the national officials interviewed suspected that cheating is widespread.[22] A British Water Research Centre scientist had already warned, in 1979, that 'bright sunshine for half an hour may reduce the total coliform count by as much as 90 per cent'.[23] DG Environment officials countered the accusation of cheating by pointing out that 'each member state says this about the other member states while failing to come up with any evidence'.[24] However, it is an open secret that some authorities do not sample for several days after heavy rainfall (when sewer overflows following storms and agricultural run-off can get washed into bathing waters) or else discount negative samples and continue sampling until a pass value is obtained.

The Commission has occasionally acknowledged that the sampling data from member states using different analytical methods are not comparable.[25] However, it is keen to maintain public interest in the bathing water reports and has therefore not discouraged the media from publishing bathing league tables.

Practical implementation in Britain

The implementation deadline of the bathing water directive coincided with a severe economic recession in Britain. It was further complicated by a change in government from Labour to Conservative, in May 1979. The Labour administration had shown little enthusiasm for the correct implementation of the directive. According to Ruth Levitt, the DoE's Eurosceptic Secretary of State Peter Shore (Labour) instructed his officials to use the utmost restraint in identifying the number of 'Euro-beaches'.[26]

Matters became even worse under the Conservative government of Prime Minister Margaret Thatcher, who had come to power with the promise of reducing public expenditure. One of the early victims was the DoE, whose overall research budget ... fell by 7% between 1978–79 and 1979–80, in the same period the amount allocated to research on sewage disposal suffered a cut of £244,000 – a drop of almost a third. In addition funds for research on coastline and estuarine and marine pollution fell by £200,000 – a drop of almost 17%.[27]

Nigel Haigh's characterisation, according to which the British 'government's policy in the early 1980s [was] that existing water authority priorities for spending money on water quality should not be excessively distorted by Community commitments',[28] is therefore euphemistic. The British Conservative government initially used every available loophole in the bathing water directive (several of which had been inserted by its Labour predecessor) to escape costly im-plementation. However, from the mid-1980s onwards, the Commission pressed for a different interpretation of the directive by enlisting the help of the European Court of Justice (ECJ) when it started infringement proceedings.

The DoE identified the first bathing waters during the 1979 season.[29] Head counts were undertaken in July and August 1979. After the DoE discovered that bad weather had not prevented several problematic bathing waters from reaching the self-adopted 1,500 bathers per mile threshold (the bathing water directive talked merely of a 'large number' of bathers), the decision was taken to exclude several famous bathing resorts. The DoE claimed Blackpool, one of Britain's most popular seaside resorts, fell into the 750–1,500 threshold bracket. The cash-strapped local authority and the Thatcher government were not prepared to invest the estimated £25–30 million on sewage treatment facilities needed to bring Blackpool's bathing waters up to stand-ard.[30] In order not to raise suspicions about Blackpool's omission, it was decided to exclude also Brighton, another popular seaside resort, although some bathing waters in Brighton would actually have been able to comply with the directive.

The identification of bathing waters was left to the water and local authorities, although the DoE tried to curtail their number. Many local authorities in Cornwall, which is highly dependent on tourism, reacted furiously. In 1979 the Scottish River Purification Board wanted to identify a number of bathing waters but was prevented from doing so by the Scottish Office. The Earl of Kintore, who was a member of the SRP Board, complained:

In the North-East of Scotland the population is increasing by leaps and bounds. We have the oil industry and we have inadequate sewage disposal works anyway. They are mostly grossly overloaded, both hydraulically and biologically ... This is really an intolerable state of affairs ... Seventy-five per cent of our effluent was well above the 20/30 Royal Commission Standards, which we do not rigidly adhere to although they give a good indication of what is required.[31]

The British government's ingenious identification exercise produced twenty-seven bathing waters.[32] The Federation of Civil Engineering Contractors (FCEC), which had an economic interest in building long sea outfalls, summed up the British government's policy as follows:

> Of Britain's 6,095 miles of coastline, a mere 30 miles have been identified as bathing waters. A number of major resorts (e.g. Blackpool, Brighton, Eastbourne, Hastings, Cromer) have not been designated because they did not meet Britain's definition of waters where bathing is practised by 'a large number' of bathers.[33]

And the *Marine Pollution Bulletin* put it as follows:

> [A] proportion of holiday-makers will have their vacation tarnished when they succumb to gastric disorders or worse. For many years, the English took the view that this sort of thing happened only on the continent. It was a reflection of the primitive plumbing and a natural and suitable penalty for venturing abroad. British coastal resorts strongly supported this attitude. For some time, however, it has been clear that not all is well with British beaches and holiday-makers can no more be guaranteed a trouble-free vacation at them than they can anywhere else.[34]

The Commission's periodic appeals to the British government to correctly implement the bathing water directive came to no avail. From the mid-1980s onwards, and for several reasons, the Commission started to take the enforcement of environmental legislation much more seriously. In the first place, EU environmental policy had matured by then and the EP was anxious to promote better implementation. Second, Ludwig Krämer, who pursued an uncompromising strategy with regard to the correct implementation of EU environmental legislation, had arrived as the head of DG Environment's Legal Unit. The British Environmental Commissioner Stanley Clinton-Davis (1985–89), who had an open ear for Krämer, stopped short of taking legal action against the British government regarding the failure to correctly implement the bathing water directive.[35] His successor Ripa di Meana (1989–92) finally took the British government to the ECJ over its failure to correctly implement the bathing water directive in Blackpool after years of legal and political wrangling.

Third, British environmental groups tried to use the bathing water directive to change the national sewage policy by complaining to the Commission. The ECJ case regarding Blackpool stemmed from 'a postcard sent from a lady in Britain who had signed it "SOS – Save Our Seas!"'[36] The fact that British environmental groups had launched similar appeals in the late 1970s which had not been taken up by the Commission shows both the rise in importance of environmental issues and the increased influence of DG Environment in general and of its Legal Unit in particular during the early 1990s.[37]

Pressures for change

The Commission was aware of the popularity of the bathing water directive in Britain and the fact that the government's sewage policy was opposed by an increasing number of domestic actors such as the RCEP, House of Commons Welsh Committee, House of Commons Environmental Committee (HCEC) and the House of Lords Select Committee on the European Communities (HLSCEC).[38] Environmental groups such as the Coastal Anti-Pollution League, the Marine Conservation Society (MCS), Surfers against Sewage, FoE and Greenpeace all ran campaigns to bring about a change in Britain's bathing water policy which would be inextricably linked to its sewage disposal policy;[39] they drew support from other actors such as the FCEC and parts of the medical profession.

It is possible to argue that in Britain an advocacy coalition emerged which used the bathing water directive to bring about a change in domestic sewage policy.[40] However, while united in their opposition to government policy, these actors did not agree on the alternative disposal strategy that should be pursued. The FCEC had a commercial interest in building long sea outfalls (used to discharge sewage further out into the sea) while most environmental groups were in favour of full biological and ultraviolet (UV) treatment of sewage (that is, the BAT solution). However, the Coastal Anti-Pollution League also favoured long sea outfalls. Individual DoE officials privately opposed the government's policy stance, although officially they had to defend it as a policy 'based on sound science'.[41]

In the late 1980s, the British government's sewage disposal policy also came under pressure from the International Conferences on the Protection of the North Sea. The British government found itself in a minority of one when it defended its policy of dumping sewage into the North Sea, while other littoral countries warned that nutrification had reached an intolerable level. Britain's dumping policy was one of the main reasons why, in the 1980s, Britain had been branded the 'dirty man of Europe'.[42] The British government felt pressured into signing the following passage of the London Declaration (which constituted a compromise between the British BPM and the German BAT principles):

> Emissions normally should be limited at source: emission standards should take into account the best technical means available and quality objectives should be fixed on the basis of the latest scientific data … If the state of knowledge is insufficient, a strict limitation on emissions of pollutants at source should be imposed for safety reasons.[43]

The Commission's legal action against the British government regarding the breach of the bathing water directive at Blackpool generated huge domestic media interest. The Commission's first letter of inquiry regarding Blackpool was sent to the British government on 3 April 1986. However, its *Reasoned Opinion* was not issued until 2 February 1988. The DoE initially tried to buy more time by pointing out that (in accordance with the British BPM–BATNEEC principles) 'everything practicable' would be done to bring Blackpool up to standard without having to incur 'excessive costs'.

By then, the Thatcher government was edging towards privatising the water authorities, and this was duly carried out in 1989. On the one hand, the British government was concerned that, after decades of underinvestment, the private water companies could be saddled with huge costs for sewage treatment facilities which in turn might deter shareholders from investing in these companies. On the other hand, it feared that an ECJ court case might result in similar damage.

Privatisation brought about the NRA as a new core policy actor. It became the competent authority under the bathing water directive. The British government initially wanted to leave the privatised water industry to set up its own self-regulatory body. However, it abandoned this idea after domestic actors threatened legal action.[44] The British government agreed to set up the NRA as an independent agency mainly out of fear that privatisation would otherwise be clouded in legal uncertainties. This example provides a good illustration of the degree to which member governments' space for policy action is constrained by EU membership.

Carlo Ripa di Meana's arrival as Environment commissioner in 1989 coincided with Chris Patten's brief stint as secretary of state at the DoE between 1989 and 1990. Patten was responsible for instigating a major change in the British government's attitude towards EU environmental policy in general and bathing water disposal policy in particular.[45] In October 1989, he announced a ten-year £1.4 billion investment programme for improving bathing waters on top of the £1.4 billion programme that had been allocated in the previous year.[46] This was followed up by his announcement on 5 March 1990 that all sewage would require at least primary treatment prior to discharge. According to the chair of the HCEC Sir Hugh Rossi, the changeover from Nicholas Ridley to Chris Patten as secretary of state at the DoE led to 'a U-turn in government policy'.[47]

Patten tried to convince Ripa di Meana that the British government was now doing everything possible to comply with the bathing water directive. According to one UK permanent representation official, 'it looked like they had struck a deal'.[48] However, this was denied by DG Environment's Legal Unit.[49] Michael Heseltine, who succeeded Patten, asked the DoE to come up with detailed improvement plans for all bathing waters which had repeatedly failed to comply with the directive. However, the British government had to backtrack from its promise that this would be achieved by 1995, that is, ten years after the implementation deadline had expired. After an exchange of fiercely worded letters, the Commission pressed ahead with the court action.

The ECJ's judgment in favour of the Commission was delivered in July 1993.[50] However, that judgment has not led to a resolution of the problems because the subsequently erected state-of-the-art sewage treatment facilities turned out to be insufficient to bring Blackpool's bathing waters up to standard.[51] Untreated urban sewage discharges had until then masked the fact that agricultural run-off from intensively farmed areas around Blackpool also contributed to the failure of its bathing waters. On 22 December 2000, the Commission therefore announced that it would take the British government to the ECJ for a second time while threatening a daily fine of EURO 106,800 (at 2000 prices) for continued non-compliance.[52] The Maastricht Treaty allows for the imposition of fines where a member state has been taken to the court for a second time and found guilty by the ECJ of failing to comply with its earlier judgment.[53]

Improvement costs

Table 8.2 shows that there has been a marked improvement in the compliance rate of bathing waters in England and Wales with the mandatory limit values of the bathing water directive during the 1990s.

Table 8.2 *Totals [and % pass rates] for bathing waters in England and Wales, 1991–99*

	1991	1992	1993	1994	1995	1996	1997	1998	1999
Anglian	33	33	33	33	34	35	35	36	36
	[88]	[94]	[85]	[82]	[88]	[97]	[100]	[100]	[94]
North-East [a]	33	34	56	56	56	56	56	56	55
	[64]	[59]	[82]	[88]	[95]	[88]	[91]	[84]	[95]
Yorkshire [a]	22	22	–	–	–	–	–	–	–
	[86]	[91]							
North-West	33	33	33	33	33	33	34	34	34
	[30]	[33]	[39]	[73]	[46]	[61]	[50]	[62]	[68]
Southern	67	67	67	67	67	69	75	77	79
	[67]	[76]	[87]	[79]	[93]	[90]	[89]	[97]	[94]
South-Western	133	134	175	175	176	180	180	183	184
	[79]	[87]	[81]	[79]	[95]	[93]	[91]	[92]	[91]
Thames	3	3	3	3	3	3	3	3	3
	[67]	[100]	[100]	[67]	[100]	[67]	[100]	[100]	[100]
Wessex	39	39	–	–	–	–	–	–	–
	[92]	[91]							
Welsh	51	51	51	51	56	57	64	68	70
	[88]	[77]	[82]	[77]	[88]	[91]	[94]	[94]	[99]
Totals	414	416	418	418	425	433	447	457	461
	[75]	[79]	[79]	[83]	[89]	[89]	[89]	[90]	[92]

Notes: [a] In 1992 Yorkshire Water merged with Northumbria Water which was renamed North-East in 1996
The percentage figures in brackets, which are rounded and may not add up, refer to bathing waters which complied with the imperative values of the bathing water directive
Sources: NRA (1992: 15; 1993: 5; 1994: 6; 1995: 5 and 1996: 2); Environment Agency (1999) and written communication dated 8 January 2001

It would be misleading to attribute the changes in British bathing water policy solely to EU legislation and actors.[54] The NRA brought about significant changes to British water pollution control and prosecutions became a common feature of the British environmental regulatory style from the 1990s onwards. The NRA, which has not shied away from criticising the government for past mistakes, also pressed for the identification of inland bathing waters.[55]

In the early 1990s most water companies supported a public relations campaign by the Water Services Association (WSA) against the cost implications of EU environmental water legislation and especially the bathing water directive.[56] The NRA had to fight a rearguard battle after the water regulator, the Office of Water Services (OFWAT), and its director Ian Byatt sided with the water companies. Byatt showed more concern about low water prices than high public health and environmental standards.[57]

While the House of Commons and the House of Lords had unquestioningly accepted the DoE's grossly inflated price-tag on the implementation of the 1975 bathing water directive,[58] the HLSCEC cast a critical eye over the cost estimates of a proposal for a revised bathing water directive which the Commission published in 1994.[59] It was harshly critical of the Commission's claim to cost neutrality in its proposal:

> It is unacceptable that policy formulation has reached the stage of formal proposal from the Commission of the bathing water directive without the attachment of a menu of individually costed measures. The Committee deplores that a soundly based cost–benefit analysis has not yet been produced.[60]

However, the privatised water companies, OFWAT, the DoE and the Department of Health did not get an easier ride before the HLSCEC.[61] During a December 1994 hearing the HLSCEC accused them of making up their cost figures on the back of an envelope.[62] These actors were called up again to give evidence to the HLSCEC on 21 March 1995 in order to detail properly costed capital investment and operating costs.[63] However, the HLSCEC remained dissatisfied about the fact that

> [n]one of our witnesses could give a considered estimate of the benefit, or disbenefit, to the tourist trade and to the local economy generally of good or poor quality bathing water. Mr Byatt said he had not looked at the possible consequences for the local economy if bathing waters

were not improved. He did not appear to consider these factors relevant to his consideration of the interests of water charge payers in his periodic reviews of price limits.[64]

One NRA official commented that the cost scenario exercise 'was short and dirty';[65] strangely enough, the NRA was not called upon as a witness. After the election of a Labour government in 1997 the guidelines given to the director general of the Office of Water Services for 2000–5 were changed to stipulate the following aims: 'To raise consistent compliance with the mandatory standards [of the bathing water directive] to at least 97% by 2005; and to achieve a significant improvement in compliance with guideline standards, particularly at major holiday resorts. This will enable relevant beaches to satisfy the water quality criterion for Blue Flag status'.[66]

Practical implementation in Germany

Prior to the bathing water directive it was up to the *Länder* to regulate bathing waters as part of their public hygiene duties although the Federal government has certain powers in case of major epidemics.[67] The Bundesrat issued the following statement on the Commission's 1975 proposal:

> All waste water discharges must comply with mandatory minimum emission limits. These limit values should be derived from the best available waste water technology ... In cases where these emission limits prove to be insufficient to achieve the desired environmental quality objectives, stricter emission limits and discharge consents have to be adopted.[68]

The Bundesrat stipulated minimum UELs and EQOs in cases where UELs were not sufficient. Unlike Britain, implementation of the bathing water directive became directly linked to the adoption of the most advanced sewage treatment facilities in Germany.

However, in order to keep costs down, the *Länder* agreed within the LAWA that only bathing waters of 'international and European importance' should be designated.[69] The LAWA set a threshold of 5,000 visitors per day during a bathing season, and included other criteria such as lifeguards, parking space for visitors and changing rooms.[70]

The steep increase in the number of bathing waters during the 1988 bathing season (see table 8.3) can be explained by the political

Table 8.3 *Number of bathing waters in Germany according to Länder, 1979–99*

Season:	1979	1980	1981	1982	1983–86	1987	1988
Baden-Würtemberg	15	15	15	15	15	15	552
Bavaria	13	13	13	13	13	13	225
Berlin	5	5	5	5	16	16	13
Bremen	1	1	1	1	1	8	6
Hamburg	0	0	0	0	1	1	7
Hesse	1	1	1	1	1	1	27
Lower Saxony	8	8	8	8	7	7	136
North Rhine Westfalia	24	21	21	21	22	22	8
Rhineland Palatinate	21	21	21	21	21	21	82
Saarland	5	2	2	2	2	2	3
Schleswig-Holstein	7	7	7	7	7	11	453
Mecklenburg	–	–	–	–	–	–	–
Brandenburg	–	–	–	–	–	–	–
Saxony	–	–	–	–	–	–	–
Saxony–Anhalt	–	–	–	–	–	–	–
Thuringia	–	–	–	–	–	–	–

Notes: Figures after 1992 are based on BMU–UBA data which do not always match the data presented in the Commission's bathing water reports. The Bavarian authorities failed to pass on the data to the BMU within the required deadline
Sources: CEC (1981a, 1982, 1983a, 1983b, 1988, 1989a, 1990a, 1991b and 1992b) and BMU–UBA information in 1999 and 2001

pressure exerted by the BMU on the *Länder* after the Commission's threat of legal action. The Bavarian *Land* government blamed Ludwig Krämer, head of DG Environment's Legal Unit, for instigating this legal challenge.[71] Krämer had studied law in Munich and knew about the poor water quality of the Isar near Munich. The Commission put on hold its court action after the Bavarian *Land* government erected 'Bathing Prohibited!' signs, while sewage treatment facilities were built to bring the Isar up to standard.

The data in table 8.3 show that economic difficulties do not automatically lead to a lowering of environmental standards. Mecklenburg

1989–90	1991	1992	1993	1994	1995	1996	1997	1998	1999
n/a	517	541	460	466	457	393	366	311	307
n/a	–	229	229	229	229	228	235	235	230
n/a	12	12	22	22	22	21	22	22	20
n/a	8	9	9	9	7	8	8	8	8
9	18	19	17	17	17	17	17	18	18
n/a	107	98	72	77	74	73	69	69	67
n/a	277	330	303	313	315	330	330	324	318
n/a	119	120	112	112	112	115	103	96	98
n/a	79	79	79	79	78	77	78	78	78
n/a	5	8	7	7	6	5	6	6	6
n/a	446	480	481	491	495	475	414	416	415
–	361	336	313	317	298	288	284	284	282
–	–	–	–	96	93	103	110	114	114
–	–	–	34	58	30	29	30	30	31
–	–	–	34	34	34	31	32	28	27
–	–	–	–	n/a	39	31	34	34	34

West Pommerania is a relatively poor *Land*. Like all of the new *Länder*, it was obliged to implement the bathing water directive only from the 1993 bathing season onwards, which meant its first *Land* bathing water report was not due until 1994. Nevertheless, it made strenuous efforts in identifying and monitoring 361 bathing waters for the 1991 season. This can be explained by its desire to modernise economically in order to attract tourists to its famous summer resorts. The authorities in Mecklenburg West Pommerania were therefore outraged when one bathing water report wrongly listed several of their bathing waters as having failed the directive.[72] However, the number of bathing waters dropped from 361 to 282 between 1991 and 1999. This could be a sign that some local authorities either overestimated the quality of their bathing waters or have found it difficult to allocate sufficient resources for adequate monitoring.

A considerable number of German bathing waters have failed to comply with the required sampling frequency. One BMU official tried to defend Germany's record by arguing that '[m]oney spent on reporting requirements is wasted money as it cannot be spent on improving sewage treatment facilities'.[73] The monitoring cost is considerably higher in Germany, which had 2,053 bathing waters, than in Britain, which had 552 during the 1999 bathing season.[74] Germany's monitoring record has improved since the Commission started to fail bathing waters when the required sampling frequency was not reached. However, the Commission's new strategy is at least partly responsible for the decline in the number of bathing waters identified in Germany from 2359 to 2053 between 1994 and 1999.[75]

Precautionary action and bathing bans
There are two major reasons why the *Land* Schleswig-Holstein has taken on a leadership role within Germany on bathing water issues. First, tourism is a major source of income for Schleswig-Holstein. A strict bathing water policy is seen as a 'mark of quality'. Second, a disasterous algae bloom incident occurred off its North Sea coast in 1988, thought responsible for the deaths of hundreds of seals whose carcasses were washed up on the beaches.[76] It provided a policy window for determined *Land* officials (and scientists) to persuade their political masters to adopt sewage treatment facilities according to the BAT principle.[77] It led to the adoption of UV radiation, a ban on environmentally damaging chlorination to eradicate bacteria from sewage polluted bathing waters and the setting up of an algae early warning system. A newly elected (SPD) *Land* government in Schleswig-Holstein wanted to show to its electorate that it was doing everything possible to avoid a recurrence of algae blooms which could have seriously damaged the *Land's* tourism industry. In 1989 it adopted an emergency programme under which 'thirty-eight of the biggest urban waste water treatment facilities, which treat approximately 82 per cent of Schleswig-Holstein's waste water, will install the *best available technology* to eliminate nutrients ... and many other pollutants' (italics added).[78] The investment cost amounted to approximately DM900 million (at 1993 prices).[79]

The *Land* government also started to impose more temporary bathing bans based on precautionary health considerations (*vorsorglicher Gesundheitsschutz*). There were just two bans in 1989, while their number rose to a record 178 in 1992. However, complaints from local authorities affected by the bans have brought about a moderate decline in bathing water bans since 1992. Schleswig-Holstein's precautionary policy has been supported by the BMU and the UBA. However, the LAWA and several other *Länder* governments have been critical, as can be seen from the following statement by a regional health official from the Medizinaluntersuchungsamt in Braunschweig, Lower Saxony:

'To swim or not to swim?' – this decision should be left to individuals. Bathing prohibitions based on exceeding limit values are authoritarian interventions (*obrigkeitsstaatliche Eingriffe*) which interfere with the basic freedoms as guaranteed by the constitution. They are justified only in exceptional circumstances such as when an epidemic is imminent.[80]

Court action against Germany

At times the BMU–BMI had to rely on the threat of defeat before the ECJ to pull the *Länder* in one direction. However, despite years of cajoling, it was unable to prevent a *Reasoned Opinion* from the Commission on 22 June 1994. The Commission accused Germany of breaching the limit values and/or insufficient sampling of more than 200 bathing waters; it also charged the German government with the non-transposition of the directive in one of the new German *Länder*. The German government defended itself in a reply on 28 October 1994. However, on 8 June 1999 the ECJ found the German government guilty of failing to ensure adequate sampling frequencies and the breach of quality standards for twenty-nine bathing waters.[81]

The German authorities were slow to comply with the ECJ judgment, especially in cases where bathing waters were affected by diffuse sources of sewage contamination (such as agricultural run-off) where sewage treatment facilities with the BAT are insufficient. On 28 July 2000 the Commission threatened to take the German government to the ECJ a second time for failing to comply with the first judgment. This led to considerable activism within the affected *Länder* governments because the federal government stated categorically that it would pass on to the *Länder* any fines imposed by the ECJ as a result of their failure to comply with the bathing water directive.[82]

In contrast to Britain, the ECJ case has attracted little public

Table 8.4 *Blue Flag awards for beaches, 1987–2000*

	1987	1988	1989	1990	1991	1992
Britain[a]	9	17	22	29	35	17
Germany	3	23	14	29	22	11
Belgium	–	–	24	4	16	–
Denmark[a]	11	42	89	128	173	168
Finland	–	–	–	–	–	–
France[a]	60	106	125	93	104	248
Greece[a]	4	7	6	85	178	232
Ireland[a]	15	19	36	48	66	51
Italy[a]	3	5	17	27	55	259
Portugal[a]	48	69	107	101	96	50
Spain[a]	57	106	120	137	170	206
Netherlands	3	8	7	21	30	14
Sweden[a]	–	–	–	–	–	–

Notes: [a] States in which one local authority and/or bathing area received several Blue Flags for different sampling points. Blue Flags have been awarded also in Bulgaria, Croatia, Cyprus, Estonia, Latvia, Norway, Slovenia and Turkey
[b] Pilot schemes
Sources: FEEE (1988-97) and FEEE written communication in 1998 and 2001

attention in Germany. None of the larger German environmental groups ran a campaign on bathing water protection in the 1980s and 1990s.[83] Only the General German Automobile Association (ADAC) has shown an interest in the bathing water directive, providing information about bathing water quality to its members. One German official explained 'Environmentalists only have the environment in their head. They do not see that one can use health issues to bring about improvements in the environment.'[84] However, a more important reason is that German environmental NGOs never directly linked the bathing water directive with sewage disposal policies. The federal government and most *Länder* governments opted for BAT sewage treatment without consideration of the bathing water directive.

1993	1994	1995	1996	1997	1998	1999	2000
20	17	18	31	31	44	41	57
–	–	–	3	12	18	26	32
3	7	5	9	9	9	12	4
125	139	169	171	185	185	176	182
–	–	–	3[b]	3	5	3	4
193	302	291	271	338	299	399	349
237	287	282	311	311	326	318	319
61	55	66	59	70	74	77	70
215	221	192	219	289	342	99	145
102	95	111	114	122	116	115	139
229	306	307	329	363	369	390	364
19	12	13	–	19	19	20	19
–	–	1	1	15	37	40	54

Promoting public awareness

European Blue Flags

The Blue Flag has become one of the best-known eco-labels in Europe.[85] The Blue Flag scheme, which was inspired by an earlier French campaign, was launched during the 'European Year of the Environment' in 1986–87.[86] It is run by an NGO called Foundation for Environmental Education in Europe (FEEE). In 2000, a total of 2,527 Blue Flags were flying on beaches in twenty-one European countries; 1,738 of them were awarded to local authorities in thirteen member states.[87]

FEEE's European office in Copenhagen vets only proposals put forward by national member organisations such as the UK's Tidy Britain Group and the German Association for Environmental Education (Deutsche Gesellschaft für Umwelterziehung). The fact that

Blue Flags were awarded according to different national criteria has
drawn much criticism, especially in Germany. Complaints forced the
Commission, which had provided financial support since 1987, to
withdraw its funding in 2000.[88] The Danish and other organisations
did not use the total coliform parameter for the award of Blue Flags
for much of the 1990s, and this caused great concern in Schleswig-
Holstein where some holiday resorts are in direct competition for
tourists with neighbouring Danish resorts.[89] In 1992, Schleswig-Holstein therefore initiated a boycott by the northern German coastal
Länder. However, several local authorities in the new German *Länder*
have participated again more recently, which explains why thirty-two
Blue Flags for beaches were flying in Germany in 2000 (see table 8.4).

Table 8.4 lists the number of Blue Flags for all member states.[90]
In 1992, FEEE changed the criteria for the Blue Flag awards by
adopting the guide values of the coliform parameters instead of the
more lenient mandatory values. As a result, the number of Blue Flags
dropped from 35 to 17 in Britain and from 22 to 11 in Germany
between 1991 and 1992.

German award schemes
In 1992, Schleswig-Holstein introduced for beaches its own award
scheme called the Beach Board (*Strandtafel*). It is based on guideline
coliform standards of the bathing water directive and takes into
account other health requirements. The number of Beach Boards rose
from 56 to 106 between 1996 and 1999.[91] However, some local authorities would again like to market their beaches with the more widely
recognised European Blue Flag.

British national awards
The British government came up with the Seaside Awards scheme in
1992. It is administered by the Tidy Britain Group which merged with
the Going for Green initiative in 1997. The Tidy Britain Group is
funded by the DoE–DETR which have always been keen to see 'as
many Seaside Awards and Blue Flags as possible'.[92] Seaside Awards
are given to resort beaches (actively managed) and to rural beaches
(unmanaged) which comply with the mandatory coliform limits,
among others, of the bathing water directive. Premier awards, which
were discontinued in 1994, were granted to beaches which complied
with the stricter guide limits of the coliform parameters. Table 8.5
shows the number of Seaside Awards for the years 1992–2000.

Table 8.5 *Seaside Awards in Britain, 1992–2000*

	1992		1993		1994		1995	1996	1997	1998	1999	2000
Resort	16[a]	63	22[a]	54	19[a]	57	66	75	80	108	115	119
Rural	22[a]	94	35[a]	79	47[a]	108	116	128	144	137	145	153
Total	38[a]	157	57[a]	133	68[a]	165	182	203	224	245	260	272

Note: [a] Premier Seaside Awards
Sources: Tidy Britain Group (1997, 1996, 1995, 1994, 1993 and 1992) and written communication dated 12 October 2000

The Marine Conservation Society (MCS), which edits the *Good Beach Guide*, a rival scheme to the Seaside Awards, was suspicious about the timing of the introduction of the Seaside Awards in 1992 as it coincided with a drop in awards of the Blue Flag.[93] The MCS also criticised the Seaside Awards for placing too much emphasis on beach facilities and not enough on water quality, calling the Seaside Awards flag a 'flag of convenience'.[94] This was countered by a Tidy Britain Group representative: 'The MCS do not mind if anyone drowns as long as they drown in water that passes guideline standards.'[95] However, since the late 1990s, working relations have improved between the MCS and Tidy Britain Group.[96]

The origin of the MCS's *Good Beach Guide* can be traced to the Coastal Anti-Pollution League, founded by Tony and Daphne Wakefield in 1958 'following the death of their daughter Caroline from polio, which they believe she contracted from swimming in sewage-contaminated water'.[97] The Wakefields conducted a postal survey of all water authorities, asking about their means of sewage treatment. This survey formed the basis of their *Golden List of Beaches* in 1960. In its final years, the *Golden List of Beaches* covered around 600 beaches in Britain.[98] However, the Coastal Anti-Pollution League's objectives were very modest, having

> never been opposed to the discharge of sewage into the sea, because . . . in a comparatively short time well diluted sewage is rendered harmless by salt water and sunlight. Unless in an estuary or on the shores of a confined stretch of water there is therefore no need for an expensive treatment works such as is necessary for inland towns.[99]

It was only when the Coastal Anti-Pollution League merged with the MCS in the 1980s that its objectives included wider environmental

aims. In 1988, the MCS's *Good Beach Guide* became the successor
to the Wakefields' *Golden List of Beaches*.[100] The *Good Beach Guide*
puts great emphasis on water quality, including the guideline values
of the coliform and faecal streptococci parameters in the bathing
water directive.

Sewage treatment policies

Britain's long sea outfall policy for bathing waters closely matched
its high-chimney policy for air pollution control – a similarity already
identified by Lord Ashby in 1975.[101] Both policies were justified with
reference to BPM and BATNEEC principles although the aim of
keeping costs low (for the implementation of the bathing water
directive and national sewage policies) was also driven by Britain's
poor economic performance during much of the 1970s and 1980s.

   This is not to argue that Germany's sewage and air pollution
control initially differed significantly. However, once German governments accepted the precautionary principle it became possible to
use the BAT principle to justify significant long-term investment into
advanced sewage treatment without having to prove scientifically its
necessity in each individual case. Some of the costs incurred by British
water charge payers for sewage treatment in the 1990s had already
been borne by the German tax payer in the 1970s and 1980s. However,
in the mid-1990s the issue of cost-effectiveness became more prominent in Germany, where public authorities post-unification have
become more cost-conscious. The debate was fuelled by a World Bank
study which argued that Germany's high sewage treatment standards
have not been achieved in the most cost-effective manner.[102] However,
UBA officials have rejected this charge by pointing out that the
environmental and health benefits of BAT-derived sewage treatment
standards have outweighed their cost.[103]

British sewage pollution control
To understand the contemporary British approach to sewage pollution
control we must go back to the Royal Commission on Sewage Disposal, established in 1898. Its findings, published in 1912, endorsed
the government's dilute-and-disperse strategy, which was based
mainly on short sea outfalls.[104] In the late nineteenth and early twentieth centuries, Britain was in the lead in Europe as regards the
creation of a nationwide sewerage system. However, it started to fall

behind Europe's newly emerging environmental leader states (such as Denmark, Germany, the Netherlands and Sweden) from the early 1970s, although this was initially denied by British officials who instead pointed to Britain's 'proud record'.[105] The following statement by the chair of the Committee on Wastewater Treatment in 1978 reflects this attitude:

> Being one of the pioneers of the revolution, it is not surprising that the United Kingdom became one of the pioneers of waste water treatment. The many treatment processes discovered and developed in this country have given it one of the most comprehensive waste collection and treatment services in the world. There are some 7,800 publicly-owned wastewater treatment works and 95 percent of the population is connected to main drainage – the highest proportion in any country.[106]

However, a report by the FCEC around the same time came to a very different conclusion: 'The British have traditionally enjoyed scoffing at standards of plumbing and water supply on the continent. But times have changed.'[107]

Pressure for change in the government's dilute-and-disperse strategy increased as 'many local authorities began to face serious nuisance problems, with incoming tides sweeping solids back onto the beach. Along with the increased visible signs of sewage pollution on beaches, there was also associated malodour and sewage slicks at sea.'[108]

Long sea outfalls were subsequently promoted by the government as the next practicable step in the incremental adaptation of British sewage pollution control measures. Long sea outfalls were endorsed by the RCEP in its tenth report (1984), which was otherwise critical of the government's policy.[109] It did not escape the RCEP's attention that very few long sea outfalls had actually been built. In 1973 only 30 out of 333 sea outfalls extended to more than 300 yards beyond low-water marks.[110] By 1981, only 6 per cent of all principal outfalls extended to more than half a mile.[111] And in 1989 the DoE conceded that only 45 out of 590 sewage outfalls could be classified as long sea outfalls.[112]

The British government and cash-strapped local and water authorities were reluctant to allocate scant resources for modernising the sewerage system at a time of economic downturn.[113] The Earl of Kintore, a member of the Scottish River Purification Board, summed up the situation in 1975:

> We [the Scottish water authorities] are allowed to borrow, and are told

to borrow money for pipes, drains, sewers, and so on, but when it comes to sewerage works: no. If you can pull the plug, chum, and it goes down to the bottom, that is all they [central government] are worried about. This is really an intolerable state of affairs.[114]

German sewage pollution control
It is beyond the scope of this book to assess the historical development of Germany's sewage pollution control strategy, the competences for which have remained within the powers of the *Länder*. Suffice it to note that Germany used a similar dilute-and-disperse strategy for the control of water pollution up to the early 1970s. One Dutch delegate who attended the 1974 WHO Bilthoven meeting complained: 'To be at the receiving end of the Rhine, with its highly industrialized and densely populated drainage basin, is equivalent to living at the end of an enormous sewer serving a population of about 20 million people.'[115]

Germany's geography precluded the adoption nationwide of long sea outfalls to control sewage discharges. Only the northern coastal *Länder* were able to discharge their loads directly into the sea. It is instructive to note that the two biggest northern coastal *Länder* were ranked lowest in numbers of households connected to the sewerage system in Germany in the mid-1970s (although low population density and widely dispersed houses also played a role).

The 1957 Federal Water Management Law (*Waserhaushaltsgesetz*) stipulated that the discharge of effluent should meet minimum standards which correspond to generally recognised standards of technology. However, the main action-guiding norm was not widely implemented due to financial constraints.

The 1971 Environmental Programme set a target of treating 90 per cent of the domestic sewage load by 1985. Many considered the target unrealistically ambitious, but it was actually surpassed. Over 1960–70; DM10 million was invested to modernise the sewerage system; DM 5–7 million was spent annually for this task in the early 1970s.[116] The *Länder*, which jealously guarded their water policy competences, did not oppose this investment because it was financed mainly by the federal government. Much of the money was granted to local and water authorities in the form of tax exemptions. The speedy introduction of secondary and tertiary waste water treatment facilities was due to the fact that financial assistance was increasingly tied to the level of technological advancement adopted. Amendments to the

Water Management Law gradually tightened the effluent standards and linked them explicitly to the BAT principle.

The Waste Water Charges Law (Abwasserabgabengesetz) introduced a levy on industrial and municipal waste water in 1976. It provided a financial incentive for polluters to reduce their untreated effluent discharges.[117] The income generated by the water charges provided local and municipal authorities with an additional source of revenue which could be invested to modernise the existing waste water treatment system.

Mikael Andersen has argued that those *Länder* governments wanting to adopt stricter waste water treatment standards were concerned about a loss of competitive advantage *vis-à-vis* those *Länder* with laxer standards. They therefore demanded UELs in order to create a level playing field.[118] Similar arguments have been advanced to explain Germany's attitude towards EU environmental policy.[119] However, for sewage pollution control there is no evidence to suggest that the level-playing-field argument actually played a role.

Anglo-German differences within the European context
Investment in the sewerage system is long-term with regard both to the life cycle of the technology adopted and to the environmental benefits reaped. The data provided in table 8.6 are to be read with this in mind. In 1980, Britain was still in the lead in terms of the number of households connected to the sewerage system.[120] However, by 1990 Denmark, Sweden, the Netherlands, Switzerland and Germany had overtaken Britain. Britain has lost even more ground when technological advancement is taken into account. In 1990, 35 per cent of Germany's sewage treatment plants included tertiary treatment (the BAT option); the corresponding figure for Britain was 14 per cent. The gap between Europe's environmental leader states and Britain is most distinct with regard to the BAT option rather than in relation to the most basic level of treatment. Between 1970 and 1990, the population served by primary and secondary treatment rose steadily in Britain, while at the same time there was a drop in the number of people served by tertiary treatment facilities. This contrasts with Germany where the percentage of the population served by tertiary treatment rose from zero to 35 per cent during 1970–90. However, Britain's image as the 'dirty man of Europe' cannot be substantiated from the data in table 8.6.

Bathing water protection

Table 8.6 *Percentage of population served by type of sewage treatment plant, 1970–95*

	Primary treatment only			Secondary treatment only			Tertiary treatment only			Total served			
	1970	1980	1990	1970	1980	1990	1970	1980	1990	1970	1980	1990	1995
Britain	–	6	8	–	51	65	–	25	14	–	82	87	86
Germany[a]	21	10	1	41	65	56	0	5	35	62	80	91	89[a]
East Germany	–	–	25	–	–	50	–	–	30	–	–	86	–
Austria	12	10	5	5	25	60	–	3	7	17	38	72	73
Belgium	0	0	–	4	23	–	–	–	–	4	23	–	–
Denmark	32	–	8	22	–	69	–	–	21	54	–	98	93
Finland	5	2	0	10	15	0	1	48	76	16	65	76	77
France	–	–	–	–	–	–	–	–	–	19	62	68	77
Greece	–	0	–	–	1	–	–	–	–	–	1	–	34
Ireland	–	0	–	–	11	–	–	–	–	–	11	–	45
Italy	8	–	–	6	–	–	–	–	–	14	30	61	–
Luxembourg	23	16	3	5	65	82	–	–	5	28	81	90	88
Netherlands	–	7	1	–	56	83	–	9	8	–	73	93	96
Portugal	–	–	9	–	–	11	–	–	0	–	2	21	–
Spain	–	9	11	–	9	38	–	–	4	–	18	53	48
Sweden	19	1	1	41	20	10	3	61	84	63	82	95	95

Note: a The data for Germany prior to 1995 refers to the former West Germany only
Sources: EEA (1995b: 263 and 1998b: 125)

British governments have often rejected as misleading those league tables which rank states according to the technological advancement of their pollution control facilities. Instead, they have emphasised that different local and regional circumstances demand variegated responses. Stringent UELs for sewage effluent are seen as a misallocation of scant resources from a narrow cost-effectiveness approach. British observers often believed that Germany's drive for the adoption of BAT sewage treatment facilities was mainly due to geographical factors. However, this line of argument fails to explain why, since 1988, the coastal *Land* Schleswig-Holstein has built expensive sewage treatment facilities and adopted the most stringent bathing water policy in Germany. Some of the relatively poor new German *Länder* have also adopted a similar policy stance, one which can best be explained by the concept of ecological modernisation, as the *Länder* seem to be convinced that stringent health and environmental standards will benefit their important tourist industry.

Conclusion

Chapter 8 has identified different implementation policy networks in Britain and Germany, each characterised by a high fluctuation of core policy actors. British environmental groups made extensive use of the EU bathing water directive to bring about a change in national sewage treatment policies during the 1990s. The British government, which had initially given implementation of the bathing water directive a very low priority, finally gave in to pressure from a wide range of domestic actors, EU institutions and international events (such as the North Sea Conferences).

The determined insistence by the Commission and the ECJ on the correct implementation of the directive also led to significant changes in German bathing water policies, and these changes affected the competences of the *Länder* which were initially reluctant to fully comply with EU legislation. Environmental groups played only a minor role during the implementation phase in Germany because they did not link the bathing water directive with national sewage treatment policies – for which the German government had adopted the BAT principle.

British and German (as well as the emerging EU) environmental regulatory styles have played an important role throughout the implementation phase. The empirical evidence presented in this chapter has shown that member governments and other policy actors frequently made reference to dominant national standard-setting philosophies. However, it has also become clear that Britain's low economic capacity, particularly during the 1970s and 1980s, was an important factor in its poor implementation record. Germany's high ecological vulnerability to sewage pollution, its relative affluence and the adoption of the concept of ecological modernisation by some of its core policy actors explain the country's relatively progressive national sewage treatment policy.

Neopluralist policy network analysis has helped to uncover important differences between the core policy actors. Differences between the *Länder* and, as will become even clearer in chapter 9, disagreement between the core actors of the country's scientific community explain why Germany did not become an environmental leader state on EU bathing water issues, despite having a relatively progressive national sewage treatment policy.

Notes

1. A. Jordan (1999a); Mazey and Richardson (1992, 1993a); Ward *et al.* (1995).
2. HoC (1975a, 1975b); HoL (1975a, 1975b).
3. *ENDS Report* 212, September 1992, p. 7; Haigh (ed.) (1995: 4.3).
4. DoE (1977: 1).
5. Haigh (ed.) (1995: 4.5).
6. Kromarek (1986: 61).
7. Krämer (1990a); Weale *et al.* (2000).
8. CEC (1981a, 1981b).
9. See the written questions by MEPs: No. 406/80 by Mr Collins in OJ No. C 190, 28 July 1980, p. 44, and No. 612/80 by Mrs Krouwel-Vlam in OJ No. C 239, 17 September 1980, p. 14. See also the answer given by the Commission on 13 August 1980 in OJ No. C 239, 17 September 1980, p. 14.
10. CEC (1983a).
11. CEC (1988).
12. At: http://europa.eu.int/water/water-bathing/index-en.html/ The website received nearly 23,000 visits in June 1997 when it became number two of the top forty official EU sites consulted (Interview with DG Environment official in 1998).
13. CEC (2000b: 7). For example, Schleswig-Holstein, at: http://schleswig-holstein.de/landsh/mags/badewasser/
14. Haigh (1987); A. Jordan (1997, 1998a, 1999a); Ward *et al.* (1995); Weale *et al.* (2000).
15. CEC (2000a).
16. Interview with a DETR official in 2001.
17. CEC (1981a, 1981b).
18. The fifth bathing water report (CEC 1988) covered the bathing seasons 1983–86.
19. Interview in 1992.
20. CEC (1998a: 7; 2000: 26).
21. Interviews with DETR officials in 2001.

22 Interviews over 1991–96 and 1998–2001.
23 Gameson (1979: 209).
24 Interview with a DG Environment official in 1996.
25 CEC (1995a: 6–7).
26 Levitt (1980: 103).
27 FCEC (not dated: 14–15).
28 Haigh (ed.) (1995: 4.5).
29 Haigh (ed.) (1995); A. Jordan (1997, 1998a); Levitt (1980).
30 Haigh (ed.) (1995: ch. 4, section 5).
31 HoL (1975a: 748–9).
32 Haigh (1987); A. Jordan (1998a); Levitt (1980).
33 FCEC (not dated: 2).
34 *Marine Pollution Bulletin* (1983: 241).
35 *The Times*, 2 June 1990.
36 Interview with a DG Environment official in 1993.
37 Jordan and Greenaway (1999); Ross (1995: 197).
38 HoC (1975a, 1975b, 1985a, 1985b, 1990a, 1990b); HoL (1994a, 1994b, 1995); RCEP (1984).
39 See Coastal Anti-Pollution League (1985, 1987); MCS (1988–93, 1994–2000); FoE (1993), and the Greenpeace-funded Robens Institute (1987) study.
40 Jordan and Greenaway (1999).
41 Interviews in 1992.
42 A. Jordan (1999a); Lodge (1989); C. Rose (1990); Weale *et al.* (2000).
43 Second International Conference on the Protection of the North Sea (1987).
44 See Nigel Haigh's letter to *The Times* on 13 May 1986; A. Jordan (1997, 1998a, 2000); Kinnersley (1994); Maloney and Richardson (1994, 1995); Richardson *et al.* (1992: 163–6); Weale *et al.* (2000).
45 DoE *Environment News Release* 343, 5 June 1990; Jordan and Greenaway (1999).
46 DoE *Environment News Release* 638, 14 November 1990.
47 As cited in *The Times*, 2 June 1990.
48 Interview in 1992. See also *Financial Times*, 20 December 1990.
49 Interview in 1993.
50 ECJ (1993).
51 Interviews in 1996 and 2001.
52 CEC (2000c).
53 In 2000 Greece became the first member state fined for a breach of environmental laws.
54 Haigh (ed.) (1995); A. Jordan (1997, 1998a, 1999a); Ward (1998); Ward *et al.* (1995, 1997); Weale *et al.* (2000: 373–5).
55 NRA (1991). Interview in 1995.

56 *Financial Times*, 17 April, 14 July, 17 July and 11 November 1993.
57 Byatt (1996); HoL (1995).
58 HoC (1975b) and HoL (1975b).
59 CEC (1994d).
60 HoL (1994a: 25).
61 HoL (1994a, 1994b, 1995).
62 HoL (1995).
63 HoL (1995).
64 HoL (1995: 7–8).
65 Interview in 1996.
66 DETR (1998b: 25).
67 See chapter 7.
68 Bundesrat (1975: 6).
69 Interview with BMU–BMI official in 1992.
70 Interview with BMU official in 1996; Kromarek (1986: 62).
71 Interview with a BMU official in 1992; *Süddeutsche Zeitung*, 13–14 June 1990.
72 Interview in 1997.
73 Interview in 1992.
74 CEC (2000a).
75 CEC (2000a).
76 *Der Spiegel*, 6 June 1988, carried a title story about North Sea pollution under its cover entitled 'Seal death. Algae plague. Cemetery North Sea.'
77 Interview with a *Land* official in 1995.
78 *Schleswig-Holsteinischer Landtag* (1993: 15).
79 *Schleswig-Holsteinischer Landtag* (1993: 16).
80 H. Müller (1993: 370).
81 ECJ (1999).
82 Interviews with BMU and *Land* officials in 2000–1.
83 Interviews and written communications with nine German NGOs during 1992–96 and 2001.
84 Interview in 1995.
85 Blue Flags are also awarded to marinas which must comply with different criteria.
86 Clébant (1973); FEEE (1988).
87 Interview in 2001.
88 CEC (1999c).
89 Interview in 2001.
90 Landlocked Austria and Luxembourg have not participated in the Blue Flag scheme.
91 Interview in 2001.
92 Interviews with DETR officials and Tidy Britain Group representatives in 2000–1. See also DETR (1998b: 25).

93   MCS (1988–93, 1994–99, 2000).
94   Interview in 1995.
95   Interview in 1997.
96   Interviews with Tidy Britain Group and MCS representatives in 2000–1.
97   MCS (1997: 4). See also A. Jordan (1997, 1998a, 1999a).
98   Coastal Anti-Pollution League (1985, 1987).
99   Coastal Anti-pollution League (1985: i).
100 MCS (1988–93, 1994–99, 2000).
101 HoL (1975a: 730).
102 World Bank (1995).
103 Interviews in 1997.
104 NRA (1991: 17).
105 Hajer (1995).
106 Cited in CEC (1981c: 1).
107 FCEC (not dated: 1).
108 NRA (1991: 17).
109 RCEP (1984).
110 FCEC (not dated: 2).
111 FCEC (not dated: 3).
112 *ENDS Report*, December 1989, p. 20.
113 Levitt (1980: 111); Maloney and Richardson (1995).
114 HoL (1975a).
115 WHO (1974: 7).
116 Andersen (1994: 124).
117 Andersen (1994: 125–9) is sceptical about the effectiveness of the Waste
     Water Charge. However, his study focuses only on industrial waste
     water.
118 Andersen (1994: 120).
119 Grant *et al.* (1988); Paterson (1989).
120 In the nineteenth century British engineers built the first water works in
     Hamburg (Germany) after a cholera epidemic (DVWK 1991).

9

The revision process and bathing water science

The revision process

In the early 1970s, the number of EU water laws increased rapidly.[1] However, the early EU water laws, which focused mainly on human usage (such as bathing and drinking), were adopted in piecemeal fashion and with little regard for a coherent overall approach to water protection.[2] As EU environmental policy matured, the need for a reform of the EU's water laws increased. In the late 1980s, the Commission initiated a revision of EU water laws including the 1975 bathing water directive. However, this process became entangled in a highly politicised debate about the principle of subsidiarity. The bathing water directive almost became a casualty of this political wrangle about EU competences which had been triggered by the 'no' vote in the first Danish referendum on the Maastricht Treaty in 1992.

The Eurosceptic British Environmental Secretary of State Michael Howard (Conservative) included the 1975 bathing water directive on an Anglo-French hit-list of EU legislation earmarked for repatriation.[3] This received support from an unlikely quarter – the pro-European Commission President Jacques Delors, who favoured repatriation of the bathing water directive (and other directives of 'lesser importance') in order to safeguard more ambitious integrationist projects such as European Monetary Union.[4]

The Bavarian *Land* government, which embarked on a moderately Eurosceptical course under its *Land* Prime Minister Edmund Stoiber (CSU) in the 1990s,[5] also argued that the bathing water directive constituted a breach of the principle of subsidiarity.[6] Bavaria's demands were also partly motivated by its traditional role as a staunch defender of *Länder* water policy competences within the context of the German principle of subsidiarity, long before this principle gained in importance on the EU level.[7] However, Bavaria's view was not shared by most other *Länder* governments and the German federal government.[8]

The majority of member governments also wanted to retain the bathing water directive although in revised form and DG Environment fought hard to prevent the scrapping of one of the most well known items of EU environmental legislation.[9] DG Environment received support from consumer and environmental NGOs which perceived the bathing water directive as a symbol of a citizen's Europe.[10]

The Commission's 1994 proposal

The Commission embarked on the long-overdue revision of the bathing water directive in the late 1980s.[11] However, its proposal was published only in 1994.[12] The proposed parameters, together with the values and sampling frequencies, are listed in table 9.1.

Table 9.1 shows that the Commission wanted to lower the overall number of parameters to 12 (compared to 18 in the 1975 directive).[13] It proposed a cut in the number of physico-chemical parameters in particular, most of which are of little value for an assessment of the health risk to bathers but were adopted mainly as indicators of the ecological quality of bathing waters. However, many of the physico-chemical parameters were superfluous for an assessment of the overall ecological quality of waters because bathing waters are sampled/monitored at points which are not usually representative and thus provide little evidence about the overall state of the wider aquatic environment.[14]

The Commission's 1994 proposal suggested three major changes to the microbiological parameters. First, it proposed substituting the total and faecal coliform parameters with a single *E. coli* parameter. Ironically, *E. coli* had already been favoured by most experts who participated in the WHO's 1974 Bilthoven meeting on recreational water standards.[15] Second, it proposed deleting the salmonella parameter on the grounds that it is an unnecessary parameter because the infectious dose is so high that a bather would have to swallow several litres of water to become infected. The zero level in the 1975 bathing water directive is seen as unrealistic as salmonella can get into the water through, for example, bird faeces.[16] Protests by the EEB against the dropping of the salmonella parameter have gone largely unnoticed.[17] Third, a new bacteriophages parameter was in-

Table 9.1 *Parameters of the Commission's 1994 proposal*

	Imperative value	Guide value	Sampling frequency
Microbiological parameters			
1 *Eschericia coli* (per 100ml)	2,000	100	Fortnightly
2 Faecal streptococci (per 100ml)	400[a]	100	Fortnightly
3 Enteroviruses (PFU per 10litres)[b]	0	–	Monthly
4 Bacteriophages (number per 100ml)	–	–	–
Physico-chemical parameters			
5 pH	6–9	–	Fortnightly
6 Colour	No abnormal change	–	Fortnightly
7 Mineral oils	No film visible	–	Fortnightly
8 Surface active substances reacting with methylene blue (mg/l)	No lasting foam	<0.3	Fortnightly
9 Phenols[c]	No specific odour	–	Fortnightly
10 Transparency	1 metre [d]	2 metres	Fortnightly
11 Dissolved oxygen (in % saturation O_2)	60–120	–	Fortnightly
12 Tarry residues and floating materials such as wood, plastic articles, etc.	Absence of sewage solids	Absence	Fortnightly

Notes: [a] Abnormal peak values can be retested within two working days
[b] To be measured twice if samples have complied with the Imperative values in previous seasons
[c] Can be waived if water undergoes natural enrichment
[d] Can be waived for geographical reasons
Source: CEC (1994d)

troduced, although no mandatory or guide values were assigned to it. The Commission suggested that it could be used as a substitute for the enteroviruses parameter once reliable and affordable analytical method became available for bacteriophages; however, when this will be the case is any scientist's guess. The Commission's decision to retain the enteroviruses parameter was criticised by German and also by British officials and scientists who argued that its analysis is time-consuming, unreliable and cost-intensive as 10 litres of water have to be sampled and transported to the laboratory.[18] Member states (such as Germany) with a high number of bathing waters were most in favour of deleting this parameter, as such a sampling regime would affect them more than it would those (such as Britain) with a relatively low number of bathing waters.

The Commission's 1994 proposal would have tightened some requirements but would have led to an overall simplification of the 1975 bathing water directive.[19] However, the 1994 proposal was poorly drafted.[20] The Commission failed to consult member governments and other stakeholders while relying on a policy-formulation process that lacked transparency. Most of the drafting was left to one DG Environment desk official, who used national experts and consultants at her own discretion without disclosing the studies used to arrive at the revision proposal.[21] It is therefore unsurprising that the Commission's 1994 proposal was criticised by most member governments when it was briefly discussed within the Environmental Council Working Group.

The Commission's 1997 amended proposal

The Commission's approach changed when new DG Environment officials took over the bathing water dossier in the mid-1990s. The consultation process became more transparent and Commission officials privately began to distance themselves from some of the requirements stipulated in the 1994 proposal. In 1997 DG Environment officials even considered withdrawing the 1994 proposal. However, they were reprimanded from 'higher up'.[22] The Environmental commissioner and the Commission's legal service were concerned that the withdrawal might set a precedent and weaken the Commission's powers *vis-à-vis* the Council. The Commission also failed to pursue legal action against the Environmental Council for failing to act on a Commission proposal. This was another option favoured by Commission desk officials increasingly frustrated at the fact that no

Presidency was willing to put the 1994 proposal on the Environmental Council's agenda, thereby depriving them of the opportunity to respond to any criticisms made and the possibility of resubmitting a revised proposal.

A few weeks prior to the meeting of the (bathing water) Committee for the Adaptation to Technical Progress on 7 October 1997, member governments were sent an informal discussion paper by the Commission which contained four options:

1 the repatriation of the 1975 bathing water directive;
2 the repeal of the Commission's 1994 proposal and the continuation of the EU's bathing water policy based on the 1975 bathing water directive;
3 a revision of the 1975 bathing water directive on the basis of the Commission's 1994 proposal; and
4 the adoption of a new Commission proposal.

The overwhelming majority of member governments present at the October meeting voted for option 4.[23] They were therefore taken by surprise when, a few weeks later, the Commission published its common position which took into account some of the amendments made by the EP in its *Opinion* on 11 December 1996.[24] However, several Presidencies (including the 1998 British and 1999 German Presidencies)[25] again failed to put the Commission's amended 1994 and 1997 proposals on the agenda of the Environmental Council.

Restarting the revision process
In late 2000 the Commission finally withdrew its amended proposal. In December 2000 it published a *Communication* which sketched out a new Commission proposal for a revised directive while inviting stakeholders to attend a consultation meeting in April 2001.[26] This *Communication* has in effect restarted the revision process, which is likely to take several years.[27] The *Communication* abstained from listing parameters and limit values. Instead it referred to the WHO's draft *Guidelines for Safe Recreational-Water Environments*, although these parameters and their values were, at the time, still under peer review.[28] Moreover, the Commission's *Communication* stated that 'the final Commission proposal [for a revised bathing water directive] will reflect in its standards the recommendations eventually put forward by the WHO.'[29] An extensive three-day consultation exercise on the Commission's *Communication* and its forthcoming proposal for a revised bathing water directive took place, involving interested

stakeholders (including government officials, scientists and NGO's) during the 'Green Week' which was organised by the Commission (24-8 April 2001).

By early 2001 the majority of scientists and policy makers in Britain and Germany favoured a revised bathing water directive which focuses mainly on health rather than environmental issues. They therefore welcomed the Commission's intention to drop most of the physico-chemical parameters, which, by 2000, were covered by other EU directives (such as the urban waste water directive, the nitrates directive and the water framework directive).[30]

The Commission's *Communication* was intended to pave the way for a more cost-effective and differentiated approach to EU bathing water policy. Its 2000 *Communication* put much emphasis on providing information for bathers while seeking long-term remedial measures rather than immediate compliance with the new standards backed up by the threat of legal action. As one DG Environment official put it: 'It is more concerned with good management of bathing waters rather than ensuring that the standards are met in all cases at any cost.'[31]

In the late 1990s, the Commission took up a French proposal to test whether a vulnerability profile could be established for bathing waters in order to allow a lowering of the monitoring requirements for those waters which are less likely to suffer from (sewage) pollution.[32] This fits in well with the Commission's wider aim since the mid-1990s of making EU environmental policy more cost-effective.

The Commission's new approach has been influenced by the following developments:
1 the experience gained during the implementation phase;
2 a French proposal to establish a vulnerability profile;
3 the WHO's new draft guidelines for recreational waters; and
4 new scientific studies carried out since the 1990s.[33]
In order to gain a better understanding of the reasons for the slowness of the revision process, it is necessary to look at the underlying dispute about bathing water science, which represents one of the key retarding factors.

In search of scientific consensus

The central scientific disputes surrounding EU bathing water policy are primarily focused on the following four main questions:

1 Does sewage contaminated water pose a health risk to bathers?
2 What indicator organisms are most suitable for identifying health
   risks (and environmental pollution)?
3 What sampling and analytical methods produce reliable and comparable results?
4 Which (monitoring, remedial or precautionary) action can be taken
   in order to ensure that bathing waters comply with the standards?

In contrast to the lacuna in public policy studies, the scientific literature
on bathing–recreational water pollution control is extensive.[34] However, in 1994 Delahunty and colleagues warned: 'Assessing any health
risk from recreational water exposure is difficult and contentious ...
Despite ... extensive and expensive investigations, no consistent
relationship between any single indicator of water quality and human
illness has been universally accepted'.[35]

Health officials and scientists in both Britain and Germany became
concerned about sewage-related waterborne infectious diseases long
before the EU bathing water directive was formulated.[36] The first
outbreak in Britian of typhoid fever transmitted through sewage-contaminated bathing water was documented in 1909.[37] However, early
sewage pollution control measures focused primarily on drinking
water and the consumption of raw fish.[38] Attention began to shift
when industrialisation and urbanisation led to a visible deterioration
of many bathing waters at a time when seaside resorts and inland
bathing waters were growing in popularity. In 1994, the HLSCEC
summed it up as follows:

> It is only in more recent years that pollution from sewage has been seen
> as a potential health hazard, the risk of which should be researched
> and reduced. This has come about partly as general environmental
> awareness has developed and techniques of dealing with environmental
> problems have improved and partly as the use of wetsuits has extended
> the types, seasons and locations of water sports.[39]

Early American studies and standards

America has based its bathing water policy on epidemiological studies
since the 1950s.[40] The results of the first prospective cohort studies
on bathing-related illnesses, by Stevenson, led to the adoption of the
following standards in 1968: 'The faecal coliform content of recreational waters should not exceed a log mean of 200/100 millilitre, nor
shall more than 10 per cent of total samples during any 30 day period
exceed 400/100 millilitre.'[41]

In the 1970s and 1980s, Cabelli and colleagues undertook further studies in which they tried to rectify the shortcomings of Stevenson's work.[42] In 1986 this led the United States Environment Protection Agency (USEPA) to adopt a maximum mean of 126 *E. coli* and 33 enterococci in 100ml water. These limit values were derived from the objective of keeping the swimming-associated attack rate for gastroenteritis below 19 per 1,000 bathers.

However, the US bathing water standards did not influence EU policy for two main reasons. First, in the mid-1970s Britain was the only EU member state to base its bathing water policy on epidemiological studies. However, the British government rejected claims that there was epidemiological evidence to suggest sewage contaminated water posed a significant health risk to bathers. Second, it was French draft national legislation (in combination with the 1973 first EAP and the WHO's efforts to adopt recreational water standards) which influenced the Commission's proposal for a bathing water directive in 1975, as was explained in chapter 7.

British studies and standards

The Public Health Laboratory Service (PHLS) carried out one of the earliest epidemiological bathing water studies in Britain, over 1953–58.[43] However, the study, which was published in 1959, focused merely on two life-threatening diseases (poliomyelitis and enteric fever) and had serious methodological shortcomings as it was a retrospective case-control study rather than a prospective cohort study. It concluded that

> since a serious risk of contracting diseases through bathing in sewage-polluted sea water is probably not incurred unless the water is so fouled as to be aesthetically revolting, public health requirements seem to be reasonably met by a general policy of improving grossly insanitary bathing waters and of preventing, so far as possible, the pollution of bathing beaches with undisintegrated faecal matter during the bathing season.[44]

Despite its narrow research focus and methodological shortcomings, the 1959 PHLS report became the scientific basis on which British bathing water policy was officially based until the late 1980s. It was cited time and again by various British governments which argued that the bathing water directive was essentially about amenity, rather than public health, issues.

Following the 1959 PHLS study, the British government did
not fund any new epidemiological studies, which are costly and
time-consuming, on the health effects of sewage contaminated
bathing–recreational waters until the late 1980s. The first phase of
these epidemiological studies focused on 'normal' beach goers.[45]
However, for ethical reasons, these studies, which were devised by
David Kay and colleagues, were restricted to healthy adult volunteers
and bathing waters which passed the imperative values of the bathing
water directive.[46]

The findings can be summarised as follows:

1 Sewage contaminated bathing water is unlikely to cause life
  threatening diseases.
2 Bathing in sewage contaminated water carries a significant risk of
  contracting less serious illnesses (such as gastroenteritis and/or ear,
  eye and nose infections). The health risk is closely associated with
  the level of sewage contamination, exposure time, intensity of the
  water contact and individual risk factors.
3 A significant dose–response relationship exists between faecal
  streptococci measured at chest depth and gastroenteritis. The risk
  threshold level was identified as 32 faecal streptococci per 100ml at
  chest depth. For bathers aged 55 years and over, the risk of contracting
  illnesses is higher than it is for younger adult volunteers.[47]

This might suggest that elderly bathers, children and bathers already suffering certain illnesses constitute higher risk groups. This
claim is supported by a beach survey undertaken by the Robens
Institute (University of Surrey) and funded by Greenpeace.[48] However,
the authors of the Robens Institute report admitted that their study
design did not fully stand up to the methodological rigour demanded
for epidemiological studies. They may be heartened by the statement
attributed to David Ozonoff: 'A good working definition of a catastrophe is an effect so large that even an epidemiological study can
detect it.'[49]

The Robens Institute also undertook a beach survey study for the
DoE. Both the epidemiological studies by Kay and colleagues as well
as the Robens Institute studies were then 'pulled together by the Water
Research Centre',[50] and in doing so watered down the recommendations of the original studies.

In the 1990s, the British government finally accepted that sewage-
contaminated bathing waters can pose a (relatively low) risk to bathers
of contracting 'self correcting' illnesses.[51] The DoE supported a second

phase of prospective epidemiological studies focusing on fresh waters.[52] The findings suggested that 'differentiated water quality standards may be necessary in order to protect different user groups (such as divers, surfers and canoeists) in different aquatic environments'.[53]

Another type of study in Britain focused on modelling the effects of diffuse sources of sewage contamination (such as agricultural run-off).[54] This new approach was adopted after it had become clear that the standards of some bathing waters could not be improved despite expensive sewage treatment facilities.

The British epidemiological studies aimed to identify a credible dose–response relationship.[55] This accords with the 'fitness for use' approach that has characterised British (bathing) water policy for more than a century.[56] The new epidemiological studies in Britain and America, which were carried out by scientists such as Jay Fleisher, David Kay and Gareth Rees, have strongly influenced the WHO's standards for recreational waters;[57] they also had a considerable impact on DG Environment's thinking.[58]

German studies and standards

The powers of the federal government to control bathing waters are largely limited to the Federal Epidemics Law (Bundesseuchengesetz). The *Länder* governments have traditionally left it to local health officials and the regional Hygiene Institutes to assess the health risk and, if necessary, to impose bathing bans. However, the *Länder* have found it difficult to agree on common reference methods for the analysis of bathing water samples. Only the five northern coastal states (that is, Schleswig-Holstein, Lower Saxony, Hamburg, Bremen, and Mecklenburg West Pomerania) were agreed on common guidelines and methods in the early 1990s.[59] Gerd Havemeister of the Hygiene Institute at Kiel University (Schleswig-Holstein) and Hans Müller of the Hygiene Institute at Braunschweig University (Lower Saxony) were driving forces behind an *ad hoc* Scientific Working Group of the northern coastal states which worked out the scientific details. An official from the Social Ministry (formerly the Environmental Ministry) in Kiel, Ansgar Knobling, who has been the Bundesrat's bathing water representative since the early 1990s, instigated the political and administrative agreement between the respective *Land* authorities. The lack of agreement between the *Länder* about analytical methods complicated and weakened Germany's negotiating position in Brussels during the revision process.

Germany has never subscribed strictly to the 'dose–response' school of thought now dominating British bathing water science, according to which 'credible scientific research ... can lead to objective environmental decision making'.[60] Most German (health) officials have accepted that infectious diseases can be transmitted through sewage contaminated bathing water and suggest a precautionary stance.[61] In Germany, it is more openly accepted that what is perceived to be an unacceptable health risk will always also depend on political (including precautionary and budgetary) considerations, no matter how sophisticated the scientific armoury. The adoption of the precautionary principle as an action-guiding norm in the 1971 Environmental Programme, a high level of environmental awareness and Germany's geography and relative economic prosperity all conspired to make adoption of sewage treatment facilities according to the BAT principle easier than in Britain.

Some German authorities have tried to justify the low priority accorded to the EU bathing water directive by pointing out that they 'are already doing everything possible as regards the adoption of sewage treatment facilities according to the BAT principle'.[62] And one official described Germany as 'a developing country' as regards epidemiological research on the effects of (sewage-) contaminated bathing waters.[63]

However, in 2000 the German government granted the funding for a major epidemiological study on bathing waters in three *Länder* (Schleswig-Holstein, Berlin and Baden-Würtemberg).[64] It was conducted mainly by Christiane Höller (Hygiene Institute, University of Kiel), Juan López-Pila (UBA, Berlin) and Albrecht Wiedemann (University of Tübingen), the latter being responsible for overall coordination. Two scientists, Jay Fleisher and David Kay, who had conducted similar studies in America and Britain were involved as consultants.

Health officials with medical training who work for Hygiene Institutes and/or social and health *Land* ministries tend to dominate the German scientific bathing water community; they are occasionally in conflict with water officials, who tend to have engineering or chemistry backgrounds.[65] German health officials dealing with bathing water issues have considerable 'hands on' practical experience. However, until the late 1990s they had little experience of large-scale epidemiological studies and/or international collaboration (with institutions such as the EU and/or WHO). However, at around the turn of the twenty-first century this began to change, partly because a new generation of scientists and officials recognised that they cannot otherwise help to shape EU (and WHO) bathing water standards.[66]

EU studies

After the adoption of the bathing water directive in 1975, the Commission was mainly concerned with its implementation. It only focused again on the scientific issues behind the legal requirements during the revision process.

From the mid-1990s onwards, the Commission developed a more rigorous scientific approach and a more transparent policy-formulation process for the revision of the 1975 bathing water directive. DG Environment and DG Science initiated several important studies which focused primarily on three issues: first, the comparability of analytical methods used in different member states; second, the most reliable indicator organisms for health risks due to sewage contamination; and the adoption of a new approach for establishing the vulnerability of beaches to sewage contamination from point and diffuse sources (the so-called 'vulnerability profile').

The Commission set up a four-year (1991–94) research programme to compare the soundness of different analytical methods for sea water samples.[67] The Pasteur Institute at the University of Lille (France) was chosen to act as the coordinating laboratory for thirty-four laboratories from all member states (apart from Finland and landlocked Luxembourg). Its findings concluded:

> Microbiological counts are dependent on the method of enumeration – perhaps to a far greater extent than is generally recognised ... Highly skilled microbiologists analysing the same samples in a laboratory under control obtain equivalent results when using a common method, and can obtain significantly different results when using their own method ... The differences observed between the individual methods are such that certain bathing water can be assessed as complying ... by one method, and assessed as non complying using another method.[68]

The Lille study concluded that total coliforms (which are one of the main parameters in the directive) span too large a group of bacteria to be analytically meaningful in detecting sewage contamination. However, it defended the stipulation of numerical limit values for microbiological indicator organisms. One of its main findings was that *E. coli* are reasonably good faecal indicators.

The Lille project also recommended international standards for the validation of microbiological analytical methods, a quality assurance system for all laboratories (in order to guarantee good laboratory practice) and clear specifications for the sampling conditions, and the transporting and storage of samples.[69] The Commission's 1994 proposal would have looked very different had it awaited and taken into account the results of the Lille project.

The validity of around twenty methods for analysing *E. coli* and enterococci in sea and fresh water was the focus of another Commission-funded study, entitled 'Microbath', which took place during 1996–99.[70] The Commission also funded a major study of the possibility of replacing the enterovirus parameter with a bacteriophages parameter.[71] The results of these studies were discussed at the annual (or bi-annual) Commission bathing water working group meetings.

In 1999 the Commission organised a first round of trials in Britain, France and the Netherlands in order to establish a vulnerability profile for bathing waters. These trials were repeated in 2000 and extended to Germany and several other member states. German officials were keen to be involved, partly because they felt that 'we cannot always only be critical about the Commission's proposals. We must get involved in these trials in order to be able to influence the revision of the bathing water directive.'[72] The main idea behind the vulnerability profile is to a establish a scoring system for all major (potential) point and diffuse sources of (sewage) contamination for a particular bathing water. Once such a profile is established, sampling and monitoring can be lowered or increased depending on the vulnerability of a particular beach.

The vulnerability profile idea was welcomed by British and German officials.[73] However, the trials showed that the vulnerability profile can be established with relative ease only for those beaches which have either very good or very poor water quality. For those bathing waters which fall in between – the majority of the EU's bathing waters – establishing a vulnerability profile turned out to be an extremely resource-intensive and time-consuming task; and in some cases it proved impossible to track all sources of contamination.[74] The trials often failed to produce the desired results, especially for so-called 'yo-yo' bathing waters, which failed the standards of the 1975 bathing water directive in some years and passed in others.

Despite the fact that since the late 1990s, the Commission's revision process has been based on much sounder science, the dispute about the most appropriate indicator organisms is likely to continue as they are 'a product of empirical epidemiological findings, ecological considerations, constraints imposed by available analytical techniques and the historical development of microbiological research since the end of the last century'.[75]

WHO studies and standards

The importance for the EU's 1975 bathing water directive of WHO's 1972 Ostend and 1974 Bilthoven meetings on recreational waters has already been discussed (chapter 7). In the late 1980s, WHO again focused its attention on guideline standards for recreational waters.[76] A series of expert meetings culminated in 1998 in the adoption of 'draft guidelines for safe recreational water environments' under the so-called Annapolis Protocol.[77]

WHO's draft guideline standards are strongly influenced by the findings of epidemiological studies carried out by David Kay and colleagues in Britain during the 1990s;[78] they also took into account the USEPA approach which Jay Fleisher and colleagues developed.[79] The WHO draft guidelines, which suggested limit values of 50 intestinal enteroccoci in 100ml of sea (bathing) water and 400 *E. coli* in 100ml of fresh (bathing) water, found their way into the Commission's 2000 *Communication* which restarted the revision process of the 1975 bathing water directive.[80] Almost thirty years after the adoption of the bathing water directive, the Commission found it necessary to again involve the WHO to get agreement from member governments for a revised directive. WHO scientists (such as Jamie Bastram) took on a certain mediating role (between member government officials, the Commission, scientists and NGOs) during the wide-ranging consultation process instigated by the Commission from the late 1980s onwards.

Conclusion

'Science, Risk and Politics in the Bathing Water Debate' is the headline of an article on the Commission's 1994 proposal for a revised bathing water directive published in the highly respected *ENDS Report*.[81] It neatly captures the main elements of the EU's long-standing bathing water policy, although at times the order has been reversed, with political questions moving to the forefront of the debate.

A more stable and tightly knit EU bathing water policy community emerged only gradually during the revision process. In the 1970s there was only a nascent epistemic community, focusing on the scientific issues, and this partly explains the weak scientific basis of the 1975 directive. By the 1990s, scientific knowledge had improved (regarding indicator organisms, analytical reference methods and the health risk posed by sewage-contaminated water) due to the funding made available for research on bathing water issues. However, there is still considerable disagreement among scientists and policy experts about the best way forward during the revision process.

Scientific uncertainty has been an important factor for the long-drawn-out revision process. However, political events also had an important impact. In fact, the bathing water directive almost fell victim to the debate about the principle of subsidiarity. The Commission's ill-fated 1994 proposal (and its 1997 amendment) was not put on the Environmental Council agenda by any Presidency, an indication of the limits to the Commission's role as a policy initiator. The Commission was forced to restart the revision process (while drawing on a wide-ranging consultation) in 2000. Differences in national (bathing water) standard-setting philosophies played an important role in Britain and Germany. However, Anglo-German differences have waned somewhat since the 1990s when British and German officials finally conceded that (sewage) polluted bathing waters are not solely a 'southern problem'.

Chapter 9 has identified important conflicts which cut across national borders and EU institutional actors. They are reassessed from a cross-sectoral and cross-country perspective in the Conclusion. This chapter has also shown that veto actors and policy spoilers (including scientists as well as officials) can significantly delay the revision process of EU environmental laws which no longer reflect the state of scientific knowledge and policy developments.

Notes

1 Jordan *et al.* (1999).
2 CEC (2000b); Haigh (ed.) (1995).
3 However, DETR officials later claimed that this episode had been more a matter of political posturing than a serious attempt to scrap the directive (Interview in 2001).
4 Interview with DG Environment officials in 1993. A. Jordan (1997, 1998a).

5 Stoiber has occasionally been nicknamed 'Edmund Thatcher' (*Die Zeit*, 5 November 1993; *Süddeutsche Zeitung*, 2 November 1993).
6 Bundesrat (1994a).
7 Bohne (1992).
8 Bundesrat (1994b); Bundesregierung (1994).
9 Interviews with DG Environment officials in 1993.
10 Interviews in 1996.
11 Interview with DG Environment official in 1991.
12 CEC (1994d).
13 See table 7.2.
14 I am grateful to Gerd Havemeister and Ansgar Knobling for pointing this out.
15 WHO (1974). See chapter 7.
16 Interviews over 1992–97. A. Jordan (1998a); Weale *et al.* (2000: 359–60).
17 EEB (1994).
18 Interviews over 1994–97.
19 HoL (1994a, 1995).
20 This was acknowledged even by DG Environment officials in interviews during 1996–98.
21 When questioned, in an interview in 1992, about the names of the scientists consulted, the DG Environment official replied: 'No I will not tell you their names!'
22 Interview in 1997.
23 Interviews in 1999.
24 Compare CEC (1997d) and EP (1996).
25 Wurzel (2001).
26 CEC (2000b).
27 Interviews with British, German and Commission officials in 2000–1.
28 CEC (2000b: 10–11); WHO (1998).
29 CEC (2000b: 11).
30 CEC (2000b: 16–17).
31 Interview in 2000.
32 Interviews with British, German and EU officials. For the results of the German case study, see Höller (2000).
33 CEC (2000b).
34 For a review of the scientific literature see CEC (1995e, 1995f, 2000d); Erdmann (not dated); Fewtrell and Jones (1992), Fewtrell *et al.* (1994); Fleisher *et al.* (1996); Kay *et al.* (1994a, 1999); Kay and Rees (1997); López-Pila (1998); Prüss (1998); WHO (1998, 1999).
35 Delahunty *et al.* (1994).
36 Erdmann (not dated) and NRA (1991).
37 WHO (1974: 17).
38 NRA (1991).

39 HoL (1994a: 7).
40 See Delahunty *et al.* (1994); H. Müller (1993); Prüss (1998), Kay (ed.) (1992); NRA (1991); WHO (1999).
41 Stevenson (1953), as cited in Delahunty *et al.* (1994: 260–1).
42 Cabelli (1981); Cabelli *et al.* (1975, 1982).
43 PHLS (1959).
44 PHLS (1959: 469). See also WHO (1974).
45 Delahunty *et al.* (1994); DoE *Environment News Release 373*, 19 June 1990; Fewtrell *et al.* (1994, 1995); Fleisher *et al.* (1993, 1996); Jones *et al.* (1991, 1993) Kay *et al.* (1990, 1994a).
46 Kay *et al.* (1994a: 905).
47 Jones *et al.* (1993); Prüss (1998).
48 Robens Institute (1987).
49 Quoted in Wildavsky (1995: 254). See also Dryzek (1997: 73).
50 Interviews in 2001.
51 DoE *Environment News Release 373*, 19 June 1990.
52 Kay and Hanbury (eds) (1993); Kay and Rees (1997) and Wyer *et al.* (1994).
53 Fewtrell *et al.* (1994).
54 Kay (1998) and Kay *et al.* (1999).
55 Fewtrell and Jones (1992) and Fewtrell *et al.* (1994: 97).
56 NRA (1991: 19).
57 WHO (1998, 1999).
58 Interviews with DG Environment officials over 1998–2001; CEC (2000b: 11–12).
59 Ad-hoc-Arbeitsgruppe der Küstenländer (1993).
60 Jones *et al.* (1991: 97).
61 Erdmann (not dated). See also Exner *et al.* (1999).
62 Interview in 1999.
63 Interview in 1998.
64 More *Länder* attempted to participate but failed due to financial and time constraints.
65 Interviews in 1999.
66 Interviews with scientists and officials in Germany during 1998–2001.
67 CEC (1995e, 1995f). See also CEC (1993: 5).
68 CEC (1995e: 1 and 52).
69 CEC (1995e: 54–6).
70 CEC (1999b).
71 CEC (2000d).
72 Interview in 2000.
73 Interviews during 1999–2001.
74 Interviews with British, German and EU officials in 2000–1. See also Höller (2000).

75 Wiedenmann *et al.* (1988), as cited in H. Müller (1993: 364).
76 Kay and Rees (1997: 107).
77 WHO (1998, 1999).
78 CEC (2000b: 10–11).
79 Fleisher *et al.* (1993, 1996).
80 CEC (2000b: 10–11).
81 *ENDS Report* 234, July 1994, pp. 17–20.

Conclusion

This book has analysed EU environmental policy and policy-making from a cross-national and a cross-sectoral perspective and over a period of more than three decades. It has identified the core policy actors within different subsectors and at different levels of the EU's multilevel environmental governance system. It has assessed their policy goals and preferred standard-setting philosophies while focusing especially on the differences (and similarities) in the British, German and EU environmental regulatory styles. For this purpose a neopluralist (or structured pluralist) policy network approach has been followed.

The politics–policy interface

The book's detailed assessment of both the political *and* the scientific–technical aspects of EU environmental policy can be justified for two main reasons. First, a neat separation is impossible: environmental policy is characterised by a 'large technical core ... [which] imposes its own requirements upon the way that pollution policy can be conducted'.[1] This was reflected in the car emission and bathing water case studies which showed that different scientific and technical issues were at stake. However, distinct national and, to a lesser degree, supranational standard-setting philosophies constituted important action-guiding norms for core policy actors even at the subsectoral level. The governmental actors especially felt it necessary to make frequent reference to the dominant standard-setting philosophies in order to justify their actions or their lack of action.

Second, the 'technical details' of environmental legislation matter greatly in both environmental and economic terms. Susan Rose-Ackerman has therefore argued that the '[t]echnical choices are not esoteric details that can be safely delegated to impartial experts. They are the heart of environmental policy itself.'[2] And Albert Weale and colleagues have pointed out, in the context of EU environmental policy-making, that

> given the impact of apparently small 'technical' features of rules on costs and compliance, there is a great deal of scope for the transformation of proposals during the course of their passage: timetables for implementation can be changed, emission limit values altered, new processes brought under control, administrative requirements changed, and so on.[3]

The case studies have uncovered many incidents where apparently small technical details were of crucial importance for certain policy actors. For example, the reclassification of Land Rover cars as 'off road vehicles' and the Fiat Panda model as a 'low powered vehicle' provided a lifeline for these models. And an inconspicuous footnote stating that producers of under 10,000 units per year were not required to use the stringent new European car emission test cycle possibly spared Rolls Royce from closure.[4] Similarly, member governments have used the adoption phase of the bathing water directive to narrow the scope of the Commission's proposal significantly by introducing what at first sight might appear minor changes.

However, it would be a mistake to assume that the member governments were always in control of the technical details of EU environmental policy. On the contrary, both case studies have uncovered important examples of unintended (long-term) effects and incidents where member governments found themselves 'locked in' to a decisional path that was the unforseen consequence of earlier decisions.[5] When the Environmental Council adopted the bathing water directive in 1975, member governments seriously underestimated the Commission's ability to make use of bathing water reports to raise public awareness about (sewage) polluted bathing waters as well as the ECJ's ability to change member state implementation practice.

Another example constitutes the combined HC + NO_x limit value in ECE-R 15–04 regulations and EU car emission directives. The origins of the combined HC + NO_x limit value can be traced to a relatively ambitious UBA proposal submitted by the German government to the ECE in 1978 and the EU in 1982. The UBA had drawn up its proposal on the assumption that unleaded petrol would not become available in Europe for some time due to opposition from the oil and automobile industries. The main intention of the combined limit value was therefore to grant engineers more freedom to find engine internal solutions. However, the UBA proposal had the unintended (at least from the German government's perspective) effect that hopes of developing the lean-burn engine were kept alive for much longer than would have been the case had separate values been adopted, since the lean-burn engine was unable to comply with stringent NO_x emission limits.

A lack of understanding of the technical–scientific details can lead to conspiracy theories such as the one put forward by David Wallace who argued that the German government had been 'persuaded by their manufacturers, on competitive grounds, to press for catalysts'.[6] It is only by examining the technical details that one can understand why the European (including the German) automobile industry was not, in fact, united. Producers of small and medium-sized cars were more strongly opposed to the introduction of the three-way catalytic converter than were the producers of large cars. This explains why Volkswagen, as Germany's largest volume car producer and specialising in small and medium-sized cars, enlisted the help of the British government to prevent the German government from succeeding in its demand for the introduction of the US 1983 standards which required the adoption of the three-way catalytic converter. The British catalytic converter company Johnson Mattey, on the other hand, lobbied the German government to hold fast to its course. The use of this kind of transnational lobbying has not been picked up by traditional theories of EU integration and politics (such as neofunctionalism and intergovernmentalism), although it fits John Stopford and Susan Strange's 'triangular diplomacy' concept which assumes that large transnational companies in particular lobby both domestic *and* foreign governments.[7]

However, within the multilevel EU environmental governance system, the lobbying strategies of corporate actors are more complex because of the important role played by the Commission and the EP. Environmental NGOs (such as the EEB) have also developed highly complex multilevel lobbying strategies although they are less well resourced than most corporate actors with offices in Brussels. However, this does not mean that public interest groups will always lose out to private interest groups.

The main propositions reassessed

Chapter 2 put forward three major propositions which now need to be reassessed.

Complex compromises

The first proposition stated that EU environmental policy measures are typically the aggregated and transformed policy proposals of policy entrepreneurs modified by the need to secure the political accommodation of the core demands put forward by policy spoilers and veto actors.[8]

Both case studies confirmed the widely held view that environmental leader and/or high regulatory member states play an important role during the EU environmental policy-making process.[9] However, the empirical evidence presented in this book suggests that member states cannot simply export their (draft) national environmental regulations and/or national standard-setting philosophies to the EU level. Germany's 1973 Lead in Petrol Law and the French draft national bathing water legislation submitted under the Standstill Agreement in 1974 provided early examples of this. On closer inspection both national initiatives were found to have led to complex political compromises at the EU level which took into account the core demands of the policy spoilers and veto actors. The Commission also played an important role during the policy-formulation phase and, later, the implementation phase.

Member governments did not figure prominently as policy entrepreneurs within EU bathing water policy after the adoption of the bathing water directive in 1975. This could explain why the directive has remained unchanged for more than twenty-five years although it no longer represents the state of scientific knowledge. However, the lack of agreement amongst bathing water scientists and national officials about the most appropriate indicator organisms, analytical methods, monitoring requirements and the health risk posed by (sewage-) polluted bathing waters probably constituted the biggest stumbling-block for a speedy revision. Moreover, the bathing water directive stipulates health targets and EQOs which do not have a direct impact on the functioning of the EU's internal market, although there is considerable inter-regional and cross-country competition for tourists between bathing resorts located in close proximity. The pressures to achieve a level playing field are therefore less acute than for car emission regulations which affect a widely and internationally traded product. Another explanatory factor is arguably that the majority of the EU's bathing waters are located in southern member states which rarely act as environmental leader states.

All major car emission and fuels directives have been adopted unanimously despite the fact that QMV has applied since 1987. The only exception has been the 1985 Luxembourg Compromise which was opposed by two non-producer states (Denmark and Greece). However, the 1985 Luxembourg Compromise probably constitutes the clearest illustration of how important it is at the EU level to accommodate the central demands of the core policy actors, especially when important economic interests are at stake. The 1985 Luxembourg Compromise put forward a multifaceted approach which set different emission limits and implementation deadlines for three car categories (small, medium and large), stipulated a raft of tailor-made derogations for corporate environmental laggards and allowed environmental leader states to adopt fiscal incentives in order to speed up the introduction of less polluting cars.

The car emission regulation case study confirms Albert Weale's argument that the adoption of EU environmental policy measures requires (near) unanimity regardless of the formal decision rule. Moreover, concurrent majorities are required of the core policy actors at the systemic and (sub)sectoral levels, that is, within the relevant policy networks which have formed around certain policy problems.[10]

However, the empirical findings from the bathing water case study suggested a more variegated pattern. The Commission (supported by the ECJ) was able to bring about major change to British and German implementation practices, particularly during the late 1980s and early 1990s when environmental awareness was high. However, it failed to get member governments to discuss revision of the directive, let alone agree on its 1994 and 1997 proposals for a revised directive.

Domestic and international events that were only indirectly related to the bathing directive made the British government, in particular, more open to accepting a change in policy during the implementation phase. The North Sea conferences and the privatisation of the water industry constitute important examples for Britain. In Germany it was largely the UBA and BMU–BMI's push which led to a revision of (sub)national sewage treatment policies and the adoption of BAT-derived treatment facilities while a disastrous algae bloom in the North Sea in 1988 led to a change in bathing water policy in

Schleswig-Holstein, whose economy is highly dependent on tourism. However, Germany nevertheless failed to act as a policy entrepreneur with regard to the bathing water directive. This was due to two major factors. First, many German officials considered the adoption of BAT-derived sewage treatment facilities as more important (for the protection of the health of bathers and the environment) than some of the requirements stipulated in the directive. Second, bathing water management has remained within the exclusive competences of the *Länder*, which were divided on the bathing water issue.

The EP became a policy actor of central importance with regard to the 1989 small cars directive (for which the cooperation procedure was applicable) and the Auto-Oil I Programme's car and fuel emission standards which were adopted within the Conciliation Committee in June 1998. However, on several other occasions it failed to (fully) flex its muscles. The cooperation and co-decision procedures have considerably increased the EP's powers, transforming it from an agenda setter to a co-legislator. However, in order to be able to make use of the new powers, the EP depends on a competent rapporteur, a competent Environmental Committee chairperson, a united Environmental Committee and the necessary quorum during the (first and second reading) plenary sessions. The required majority, especially during the second reading, is difficult to achieve, as illustrated by the EP's spectacular defeat with regard to the 1991 consolidated directive.

The cooperation procedure and especially the co-decision procedure have changed the EU's institutional balance. It has brought the Council and the EP closer together, largely at the expense of the Commission. This became clear when the EP and the Environmental Council significantly tightened the Commission's Auto-Oil I Programme car emission limits and fuel standards while rejecting its new approach. The fact that the EP has largely failed to play a central role with regard to bathing water policy can be explained by the fact that the bathing water directive was adopted in 1975 when only the consultation procedure was applicable and the revision process failed to get off the ground until it was restarted by the Commission in 2000.

Non-governmental actors can also become policy spoilers and – though to a lesser degree – policy entrepreneurs. The car emission case study in particular has shown that mutual dependence exists between public and private actors. This is not to argue that non-governmental actors have formal veto powers. However, the power and knowledge resources of corporate actors are considerable. The actions of the automobile and oil industries slowed down the EU car emission policy-making process and watered down the environmental requirements stipulated in several directives.

The mutual dependence between public and private actors became apparent within both the Motor Vehicle Emissions Group (MVEG) and the tripartite dialogue used for the Auto-Oil I Programme. The MVEG was set up by the Commission in January 1985 as an *ad hoc* advisory committee but quickly developed into a pre-negotiating forum for the Council. It was dominated by member governments and corporate actors; NGOs managed to gain access only in 1987. The MVEG has been portrayed as 'one of the most formalised policy networks'[11] within the EU environmental policy field. Its proceedings and members were similar to an earlier Commission Working Group called European Regulations, Global Approach – Air Pollution (ERGA). However, for its Auto-Oil I Programme, initiated in 1992 but published only in June 1996, the Commission relied on a tripartite dialogue between several of its DGs and the automobile and oil industries. The exclusion of member governmental actors (particularly officials from the environmental leader states) and environmental NGOs from the tripartite dialogue was one important factor which led the Commission to propose car emission and fuel standards that were so unambitious that both the Council and EP demanded significantly more stringent ones.[12]

Both case studies have also shown that committed individuals with relevant policy expertise (such as scientists) can influence the compromises enshrined within EU environmental legislation. German UBA officials and (during the 1980s) a former USEPA official were highly active in briefing environmental groups, MEPs and the media on car emission regulations in order to counter balance the superior knowledge resources enjoyed by corporate actors. However, the fact that no genuine EU media (or public) existed placed public interest groups at a structural disadvantage *vis-à-vis* producer interest groups.

Different environmental standard-setting philosophies
The second proposition suggested that differences in national environmental regulatory styles matter during the EU policy-making process and therefore must be accommodated within common environmental legislation.

Both case studies provided strong empirical evidence that British and German officials and politicians were influenced by differing national standard-setting philosophies and standard operation proce-dures. Even corporate actors frequently couched their demands in such a way that they appeared to fit in with the dominant national environmental regulatory style. A good example is constituted by Ford-UK's lobbying of the British government in the mid-1980s. Ford-UK (and, to a lesser degree, British Leyland–Rover) tried to convince the British government of the merits of the lean-burn engine by portraying it as compatible with the core features of the domestic environmental standard-setting philosophy while branding the three-way catalytic converters as an expensive, unreliable, 'add on curative' device.[13] British policy makers may have been particularly receptive to this line of argument at a time when they incorrectly perceived the domestic ecological vulnerability to car emissions as low while hoping that the promised lean-burn technology would help to improve the economic capacity of the British automobile industry, which had been on a downward spiral since the Second World War. Moreover, the Thatcher governments, particularly during the early 1980s, perceived (environmental) regulations mainly as a cost burden on industry, rejecting the idea put forward by proponents of the concept of ecological modernisation that they may be beneficial in both environmental and economic terms.

It has been argued that the British government's position on the lean-burn engine and the German government's stance on the three-way catalytic converter were primarily driven by economic considerations.[14] Seen from this perspective, the frequent references to core features of the respective national standard-setting philosop-hies made by British and German officials and politicians would amount to little more than symbolic politics or even an attempt to cover up the harsher reality of naked economic interests.

However, there are good reasons to assume that national standard-setting philosophies and the wider environmental regulatory styles have deep roots within the British and German environmental policy systems (which is not to deny the fact that national economic interests played an important role). First, frequent reference to the national environmental regulatory styles was made by governmental actors at the systemic level *and* at the subsectoral level although the two case studies (car emissions and bathing waters) focused on subsectors dominated by distinct policy actors, characterised by dissimilar scientific–technical problems and exposed to diverse levels of inter-national competition.

Second, British and, to a lesser degree, German environmental NGOs and corporate actors also made occasional reference to the core features of the dominant standard-setting philosophies. However, environmental NGOs were less inclined to use a policy discourse which fitted in with the dominant national environmental regulatory style especially when they were opposed to government policy and wanted to bring about a change in policy.[15] The car emissions case study has shown that the European umbrella groups of environmental and consumer NGOs (EEB, BEUC and T&E), in particular, often pushed the EU towards adopting the standards and standard-setting philosophies of the environmental leader states.

Third, differing national preferences played an important role during the more than 100 interviews conducted by this author with British and German officials and politicians. Even years after the three-way catalytic converter v. lean-burn engine dispute most of the interviewed national policy actors involved in the crucial decisions at the time were still defending the position they had held at the time with reference to the preferred standard-setting philosophies. British officials and corporate actors still favoured the conceptual idea behind the lean-burn engine which promised (although it failed to deliver) reasonable emission reductions at a relatively inexpensive cost. The stringency of pollution abatement measures adopted in leading world markets (such as America and Japan) was a much more important benchmark for German (and especially BMU and UBA) officials than for their British colleagues. One explanation for this is that the BAT principle and the wider German environmental regulatory style are geared more towards international comparisons than are the British BPM–BPEO and the wider environmental regulatory style.

However, the more EU environmental policy matures as a policy field the more costly BAT measures are likely to become because, at some point, a diminishing margin of return will be reached. Deeper structural and behaviourial changes will be necessary if environmental problems are not resolved by then. For national policy makers the appropriateness (or cost-effectiveness/cost–benefit analysis) of individual EU environmental policy measures depends on a range of factors, the most important of which are the perceived ecological vulnerability, economic capacity, the political salience of environmental issues and the dominant environmental regulatory style.[16]

The empirical findings put forward in this book suggest that a modification of the conventional view of what makes up the core features of the preferred British and German standard-setting philosophies (and the wider national environmental regulatory styles) is necessary. Britain is conventionally said to have favoured EQOs, the BPM–BPEO–BATNEEC principles, cost-effectiveness considerations and a science-driven pollution abatement strategy aimed at 'optimising pollution'. Germany, in contrast, is usually portrayed as having given preference to (U)ELs, the BAT principle and the precautionary principle.

EQOs and (U)ELs

Britain and Germany did not have clear national preferences for EQOs and UELs respectively across all sectors and/or all environmental media (that is, air, water and soil) when the EU moved into the environmental policy field in the early 1970s. It was only at this point that national officials and politicians in these two member states began to define more clearly their preferred standard-setting philosophies and wider environmental regulatory styles while often claiming that core features of the British and German national approaches to pollution control were incompatible. However, as this book has shown, EQOs and emission limits can and should be combined. Moreover, both Britain and Germany have in place a mix of EQOs and emission limits.

The claim that the Commission favoured EQOs in the 1970s but was swayed by the German government to adopt (U)ELs in the 1980s only to be persuaded once again by the British government to return to its original EQO approach, at first sight seems to fit well the car emission case study.[17] However, until 1983, the EU's own car emission 'decision-making process was ... nested in that of a wider international regime, the original purpose of which was the economic reconstruction of Europe after the war'.[18] The EU merely transposed ECE regulations into optional directives based on an emission (limits-centred) approach which paid little attention to explicit health targets and EQOs. Germany's preference for relatively stringent UELs derived from the BAT principle (that is, the US 1983 car emission standards) was supported by other member states (Denmark, Greece and the Netherlands), the majority of MEPs and environmental NGOs such as the EEB.

The cost-effective EQO-derived standards put forward by the Commission under its Auto-Oil I Programme, on the other hand, came about at least partly as a consequence of a turf battle between DGs Industry and Environment in particular. In the early 1990s DG

Environment used the adoption of the EU's ambient air quality directives to outmanoeuvre DG Industry, which until then had been the Commission's lead department on the important car emission dossiers. DG Environment's desire to expand its competences (while bringing about more ambitious environmental standards) within this subsector can be traced back to the time when its Commissioner, Clinton-Davis, started 'an attack' on DG Industry.[19] However, while DG Environment supported the BAT in the 1980s, it favoured cost-effective measures derived from EQOs in the 1990s.

BPM–BPEO and BAT principles
The differences between the British BPM principle (and the more recent BPEO and BATNEEC principles) and the German BAT principles proved to be significant in both case studies and helps to explain Anglo-German differences. The EU has adopted the BATNEEC principle but failed to stipulate an unambiguous definition. In some EU directives the BATNEEC principle stands for the best available *techniques* not entailing excessive cost (in which case it is closer to the British BPM principle), while in others it stipulates the best available *technology* not entailing excessive costs principle (in which case it is closer to the German BAT principle). These examples support the view that EU environmental policy is a 'patchwork' which had to accommodate diverse national environmental regulatory styles.[20]

The BAT principle, which can be traced back to nineteenth-century Prussian trade ordinances, has been incorporated into the ecological modernisation concept which gained ground in Germany especially during the 1980s, although its proponents have been forced onto the defensive since the *Standort Deutschland* debate and economically costly German unification. The concept of ecological modernisation is based on the assumption that stringent environmental standards are beneficial for both the environment and the economy because domestic environmental abatement technologies can be exported to other markets.

In the car emission case study it was easy to see why the German government (and the BMU–BMI and the UBA, in particular) should be attracted to this logic. However, the Economics Ministry was much less a believer in this concept, as will be explained when the cross-cutting conflicts are discussed. Stringent emission regulations for cars, which are a widely traded product, may be beneficial for German producers (particularly producers of large cars) because they have a competitive edge in Europe and export to leading world markets that have in place stringent emission control standards. However, even the bathing water case study has shown that some German actors (and, to a lesser degree, EU actors and British NGOs and local authorities) adopted a similar line of argument.

The view that stringent environmental policy measures (derived from the BAT principle) can be beneficial for both the environment and the economy was less widely held among British officials and politicians, although Anglo-German differences waned somewhat in the late 1990s after the election of a new Labour government and the continued debate about the *Standort Deutschland* in Germany.

Disputes which cut across borders and policy actors
The third hypothesis suggested that conflicts about EU environmental policy frequently cut across the boundaries of EU institutional and non-governmental actors and occasionally also across member governmental actors. In testing this proposition empirically, the car emission and bathing water directives have brought to light several of these disputes, which can be harbingers of policy change or help to explain why a particular dossier became deadlocked. Most often cross-cutting policy disputes occurred between different national ministries and Commission DGs (especially DG Environment and DG Industry). This phenomenon can best be explained with reference to turf battles as analysed in the bureaucratic politics literature.[21]

However, corporate actors and NGOs (and particularly their respective European umbrella groups) are not unitary actors either.[22] The European automobile producers (all bar one) abandoned their umbrella group, the CCMC, and founded ACEA in 1991 partly because Peugeot refused to cooperate on even the most moderate proposals for more stringent EU car emission legislation.

European umbrella groups of environmental NGOs also have diverse aims and strategies. Compared to industrial Euro-groups, they are under-resourced and therefore often have to concentrate on a limited number of central issues. This explains why the EEB was the only NGO which directly lobbied the Commission and the EP's rapporteur during the revision process of the bathing water directive in the mid-1990s. However, British NGOs were highly active throughout the implementation phase of the bathing water directive, during which they frequently complained to the Commission about breaches of the directives in Britain.

Car emission regulations had a much higher priority for European environmental and consumer NGOs which tried to exploit rifts between corporate environmental laggards and leaders. In the 1980s, the EEB was helped by the fact that it could draw on the technical expertise provided by a former USEPA official (who had been involved in drawing up car emission legislation in America) as well as individual UBA officials.

Much scholarly effort has gone into researching disputes and power struggles between member governments, EU institutional and non-governmental actors, but relatively little is known about internal disputes and conflicts which cut across the core policy actors. Traditional concepts of EU integration and politics (such as neorealist and neofunctionalist approaches) have largely neglected this aspect of EU policy-making. The case studies have shown that disputes about the EU's environmental policy and policy-making process do not simply run along national and EU institutional lines or the traditional industrialist–environmentalist divide. Disputes between environmental leaders and laggards and between industrialists and environmentalists are important. However, they do not suffice as explanations of some of the extraordinarily complex compromises in the car emission regulations or the long-drawn-out revision process of the bathing water directive.

The neopluralist policy network analysis assumption that governments, institutional and non-governmental actors are not unitary actors has been confirmed in the case studies. EU policy networks were formed around policy issues and problems at the sub-sectoral level. On the systemic level the EU environmental policy network is a relatively open-issue network which can be accessed by new policy actors with relative ease. More tightly knit policy communities can be found at the subsectoral level. The most stable and important of the policy communities identified in the case studies was the MVEG.

The present study has used the policy network approach mainly as an analytical method for identifying the core policy actors as well as their policy goals, main standard-setting philosophies and (negotiating) strategies. However, the following theoretical considerations can be drawn from the empirical findings:

1 EU environmental policy networks are often issue networks which are relatively open and unstable largely because EU environmental policy-making is a multilevel and cross-sectoral activity. It cuts across different (sub)sectors while straddling the (sub)national,

supranational and, at least occasionally, also the international levels of governance.

2 More tightly knit and exclusive policy communities can be found at the subsectoral level.

3 Policy networks are most important for the policy formulation and revision phases, although some implementation networks have also been formed.[23]

Most policy network analytical approaches (in the European tradition) have paid little attention to parliaments (because they skipped the parliamentary side of the original American 'iron triangles' literature). However, the car emission case study has provided strong empirical evidence that the EP can act as a major player in EU environmental policy-making.

Table C.1 presents an overview of EU policy networks (as well as epistemic communities and advocacy coalitions) as identified in the case studies.

The EU car emission policy network was, overall, more stable and less fluid than the bathing water network. Epistemic communities within the car emission subsector were largely dominated by government officials and corporate actors. The Commission managed to facilitate the emergence of an EU-wide bathing water epistemic community by (jointly) financing research (such as the Lille Project, the Microbath and vulnerability profile studies) which complements work undertaken by the WHO.

Neither of the case studies was able to identify relatively stable EU-wide advocacy coalitions as found by Paul Sabatier within American environmental policy-making.[24] The only major exception was the emergence of temporary advocacy coalitions which centred around mutually exclusive environmental abatement technologies (such as the three-way catalytic converter and the lean-burn engine).

International environmental regimes also had an impact on EU environmental policy. The most important example constituted the ECE's car emission regulations. Until 1983 EU car emission policy-making was in fact embedded within a wider international regime which had been set up mainly for trade purposes.[25] Another example within the car emission case study was the Stockholm Group which was set up (following a German–Swedish initiative) by like-minded European environmental leader states wanting to introduce the US 1983 car emission standards in Europe. It was used to provide technical assistance to member governments which had little domestic

Table C.1 *EU policy networks*

	Car emission regulation	Bathing water protection
Policy networks		
Issue network/ policy community	*Policy community* ERGA, MVEG Tripartite dialogue (Auto-Oil I Programme)	*Policy community* –
	Issue network Mainly centred around the policy formulation issues	*Issue network* Mainly centred around implementation and revision issues
Epistemic communities	Transnational knowledge-based epistemic communities were dominated by government officials and industry experts	Emerging epistemic communities within the WHO's framework but also on the EU level (Lille Project, Microbath studies and vulnerability profile studies)
Advocacy coalitions	Temporary advocacy coalitions centred around the three-way catalytic converter v. lean-burn engine dispute	Weak EU-wide bathing water advocacy coalition centred around implementation issues. British NGOs formed an advocacy coalition with DG Environment in the 1990s
International environmental regimes which influenced EU policy-making	ECE Regulations Stockholm Group Climate Change Convention	WHO recreational water standards North Sea Conferences

expertise and to put pressure on the EU. Within the bathing water case study it was the WHO's work on recreational water standards which influenced the EU's policy formulation and revision phases. Moreover, the British government's sewage treatment (and thus also bathing water) policy was also influenced by the work undertaken within the North Sea conferences.

Implications for traditional theories of EU integration and politics
Neither neofunctionalist nor neorealist theories of EU integration and
politics are able fully to explain the empirical findings presented in
this book.

Neofunctionalist spill-over pressures (such as the need to harmonise
different national environmental standards) were found to have played
an important role within the car emission case study. However,
neofunctionalist theories cannot account for some of the extraordinarily complex compromises which were at least partly the result of
different national environmental regulatory styles. Neofunctionalist
theory also cannot account for the enduring importance of member
governments and the increased importance of the EP. Moreover,
spill-over pressures were weak within the bathing water case study
where domestic politics' factors (such as long-standing national sewage
treatment policies) and international events had a major impact on
the way in which Britain and Germany implemented the bathing water
directive.

Neorealists, on the other hand, would be hard pressed to explain
why a classic 'low politics' issue such as the bathing water directive
attracted the attention of ministers and prime ministers as well as the
Commission's president in 1992. The fact that the Commission and
the ECJ were successful in bringing about a change in member
governments' implementation practices is also difficult to comprehend
from a neorealist perspective. The same can be said about the EP's
role within the EU's car emission policy-making process. For neorealists the function of interest groups is limited to the domestic politics'
level and their influence on EU policy is constrained by the influence
which they can exert on their domestic government. Such a perspective
cannot account for the fact that in the car emission case study interest
groups were highly active not only in lobbying EU institutional actors
but in direct transnational lobbying.

Some of the shortcomings of neorealist approaches are due to the
fact that they usually conceptualise EU policy-making as a two-level
game according to which member state preferences are (exogenously)
fixed at the domestic politics' level and subsequently played out at
the EU level. Moreover, neorealists assume that governments are
unitary actors or are able at least to arrive at a clear national position
which is a function of the national interest. However, the case studies
have provided strong empirical evidence that member states (or, more
precisely, member governments) are not unitary actors. Moreover,

EU policy-making is more appropriately conceptualised as a multilevel activity, as explained above. Neorealist accounts also fail to take into account that governments are not in control of unintended (long-term) consequences and may find themselves locked into a certain decisional path because of earlier actions.

This is not to say that neofunctionalist and neorealist approaches are obsolete. However, they arguably do not constitute the most useful analytical lenses for explaining the EU's multilevel environmental governance system in general and subsectoral developments in particular. In order to explain subsectoral developments in the environmental policy field they should at least be supplemented by more finely grained comparative politics approaches.

The case study method
This book has drawn heavily on an in-depth analysis of two cases over a period of more three decades. This approach can be justified for two main reasons. First, the aim of this book was to provide an assessment of both the policy problems and the different roles and functions played by core EU environmental policy actors during the various stages of the policy cycle (ranging from agenda setting to policy revision). Paul Sabatier has argued convincingly that the policy process 'usually involves time spans of a decade or more ... [although in] fact a number of recent studies suggest that time periods of twenty to forty years may be required to obtain a reasonable understanding of the impact of a variety of socioeconomic conditions and the accumulation of scientific knowledge about a problem'.[26] Hopefully this book has convinced the reader of the merits of the case study method when taking a longitudinal perspective that spans several decades.

Second, 'the complex interplay of technical argument and political alliance' can best be shown through in-depth case study analysis which, for the reasons explained above, pays sufficient attention to the technical details.[27] A neopluralist policy network analysis which would have taken into account a representative sample of different EU policy measures and a wider range of member states was beyond the scope of this book.

The focus on different national environmental regulatory styles in this book has added analytical value. However, there are limits to such a research focus which may pose difficulties in terms of manageability when a wider range of member state (environmental) regulatory styles is assessed, although excellent studies exist which have done exactly this.[28] The choice of Britain and Germany was a very useful one because their environmental regulatory styles and attitudes towards EU integration are usually seen as very different. Britain is more often than not portrayed as an 'awkward partner' within the EU, and for much of the 1970s and 1980s was seen as an environmental laggard. German governments on the other hand have, overall, shown a strongly pro-integrationist attitude, while Germany was widely regarded as an environmental leader state for much of the 1980s. Doubts have been raised as to whether, in particular, their opposite positionings on the leader–laggard dimension is still appropriate for the 1990s and the early part of the twenty-first century. This book has been less concerned with the exact positioning of these two member states, and instead has tried to explain cross-country differences with reference to the dominant environmental regulatory styles (in addition to differences in the ecological vulnerability, economic capacity and political salience of environmental issues) in these two member states. This was arguably made easier by the fact that both Britain and Germany belong to what Adrienne Héritier and colleagues have termed 'high[ly] regulatory' member states with distinctive standard-setting philosophies even if they have evolved over time and are influenced by EU developments.[29]

How representative are the findings presented in this book? Judging by other EU environmental policy studies which have taken a cross-country and cross-sectoral approach (reviewed in chapters 1 and 2, and referred to throughout the book) as well as highly regarded specialist EU environmental handbooks, journals, and e-mail information services (such as Nigel Haigh's manual on EU environmental policy, *ENDS Report*, *ENDS Daily* and *Environment Watch: Western Europe*), the findings do seem to be representative.[30] However, further theory-guided empirical research is necessary in order to arrive at a better understanding of EU environmental policy and its environmental governance system.

Future research
Based on the new empirical findings presented here, it can be concluded that future research on EU environmental policy should concentrate more on the politics/policy–science interface which has been shown to be a central one. Successful environmental problem-solving must take into account both scientific–technical as well

as political–economic aspects in order to bring about sustainable development.

Figure C.1 represents a considerably simplified two-dimensional illustration of the international governance arena. It was drawn up merely for heuristic purposes to illustrate in a greatly simplified manner the complex 'governance–polity–policy–politics' dimensions. It is not intended to provide a model or theory.

The x-axis in figure C.1 shows 'policy determines politics' and 'politics determines policy' as two poles of one dimension rather than as mutually exclusive categories. Functional problem-solving ('low

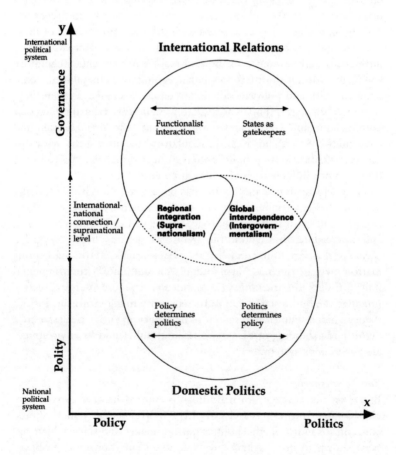

Figure C.1 *The policy–politics and polity–governance dimensions*

politics') and re/distributional decision-making should be seen as two poles on the same dimension. Policy makers in the environmental field often have a difficult task in determining which level of governance is most appropriate for problem-solving. The functionally most appropriate level may not always be the most promising level of governance if it leads to slow decision-making and lowest common denominators.

In a world characterised by increasing interdependence ('fusion tendency') and differentiation ('fission tendency'), issues of governance do not (or no longer) fall into the exclusive governance domain of states.[31] They are increasingly pushed upwards, downwards or sideways. The y-axis represents different vertical levels of governance. It signals that some issues are dealt with at the international relations, the transnational, the supranational or the (sub)national levels of governance. Often, the different levels of governance will not be mutually exclusive although certain arenas will favour particular actors more than others; transnational corporations will be more easily able to act on the international level compared to grassroots oriented environmental NGOs. The move upwards or downwards (on the y-axis) should not automatically be equated with a loss of state power of governance 'steering capacity'. In particular, the move upwards, to a higher level of governance, is often undertaken in order to regain problem-solving capabilities that state actors do not (or no longer) possess on the (sub)national level. This also has consequences for deeply rooted national environmental regulatory styles, which have to be adapted to the new challenges. The degree to which they give way to a supranational and/or an international approach to environmental problem-solving is a matter requiring further research.

Notes

1 Weale (1992a: 7).
2 Rose-Ackerman (1995: 35).
3 Weale *et al.* (2000: 449).
4 Interviews in 1993.
5 See also A. Jordan (1999a); Pierson (1998).
6 D. Wallace (1995:153).
7 Stopford and Strange (1991).
8 See also Weale (1996a).
9 Andersen and Liefferink (eds) (1997); Arp (1995); Bungarten (1978); Héritier *et al.* (1994, 1996); Holzinger (1994, 1996); Liefferink (1996);

Liefferink and Andersen (eds) (1997); Liefferink and Andersen (1998a, 1998b); Rehbinder and Stewart (1985a, 1985b); Sbragia (1996); Vogel (1995, 1997); Weale (1992a, 1992b); Weale *et al.* (1996, 2000).
10 Weale (1996a: 606); Weale *et al.* (2000).
11 Andersen and Liefferink (not dated: 21). See also Arp (1995).
12 Friedrich *et al.* (2000).
13 Ford of Europe (1983).
14 See Holzinger (1994: 185) for the British and D. Wallace (1995: 153) for the German case. However, Holzinger puts forward a very differentiated analysis which is also critical of the German government.
15 Hajer (1995); A. Jordan (1998a); Jordan and Greenaway (1999); Weale (1992a).
16 See table 1.1.
17 Arp (1995: 317); Friedrich *et al.* (2000); Heritier *et al.* (1994, 1996).
18 Weale *et al.* (2000: 399).
19 Interview with Stanley Clinton-Davis in 1995.
20 Andersen and Liefferink (eds) (1997); Haigh (ed.) (1995); Héritier (1996); Héritier *et al.* (1994, 1996); Liefferink and Andersen (eds) (1997); Rehbinder and Stewart (1985a:17); Scott (1998); Weale *et al.* (1996, 2000).
21 Page (1997); Peters (1992).
22 Greenwood (1997); Greenwood *et al.* (1988); McLaughlin and Jordan (1993); McLaughlin *et al.* (1993); Mazey and Richardson (eds) (1993); Wallace and Young (eds) (1997).
23 Demmke (1994).
24 Sabatier (1993, 1998, 1999); Sabatier and Jenkins-Smith (eds) (1993).
25 Arp (1995); Holzinger (1994); Weale *et al.* (2000).
26 Sabatier (1999: 3).
27 I am grateful to Albert Weale for pointing this out to me.
28 For example, Andersen and Liefferink (eds) (1997); Liefferink and Andersen (1998a); Héritier *et al.* (1994, 1996); Weale *et al.* (1996, 2000).
29 Héritier *et al.* (1994, 1996). See also chapter 2.
30 *ENDS Daily* (various years); *ENDS Report* (various years); *Environment Watch: Western Europe* (various years); Haigh (ed) (1995).
31 Hurrell 1995.

Bibliography

ACEA and EUROPIA (1993), European Auto/Oil Research Programme, press release of 19 July 1993.

Ad-hoc-Arbeitsgruppe der Küstenländer (1993), 'Badegewässerüberwachung nach der Richtlinie des Rates der EG vom 08.12.75 über die Qualität der Badegewässer', *Zentralblatt für Hygiene* 195, 1–8.

AIT & FIA, BEUC, ECAS, EEB, EPHA and T&E (1998), *NGO Appeal to MEPs to Reduce Traffic Pollution*, Brussels, AIT & FIA, BEUC, ECAS, EEB, EPHA and T&E.

Almond, Gabriel (1989), 'Review article: the international–national connection', *British Journal of Political Science* 19, 237–59.

Andersen, Mikael Skou (1994), *Governance by Green Taxes*, Manchester, Manchester University Press.

Andersen, Mikael Skou and Duncan Liefferink (eds) (1997), *European Environmental Policy: The Pioneers*, Manchester, Manchester University Press.

Andersen, Mikael Skou and Duncan Liefferink (1997), 'Introduction: the impact of pioneers on EU environmental policy', in M. S. Andersen and D. Liefferink (eds), 1–39.

Andersen, Mikael Skou and Duncan Liefferink (not dated), The new member states and the impact on environmental policy, draft final report to the Commission, unpublished mimeo.

Andersen, Mikael Skou and Rolf-Ulrich Sprenger (eds) (2000), *Market-Based Instruments for Environmental Managment*, Cheltenham, Edward Elgar.

Armstrong, Kenneth and Simon Bulmer (1998), *The Governance of the Single European Market*, Manchester, Manchester University Press.

Arp, Henning (1991), Interest groups in EC legislation: the case of car emission standards, paper presented at the ECPR workshops at the University of Essex.

Arp, Henning (1993), 'Technical regulation and politics', in D. Liefferink, P. Lowe and A. Mol (eds), 150–72.

Arp, Henning (1995), Multiple actors and arenas: European Community regulation in a poli-centric system: a case study on car emission policy, PhD dissertation, Florence, European University Institute.

Ashby, Eric and Mary Anderson (1981), *The Politics of Clean Air*, Oxford, Clarendon.

Aspinwall, Mark (2000), 'Structuring Europe: powershaping institutions and British preferences on European integration', *Political Studies* 48:3, 415–42.

Bachrach, P. and M. Baratz (1962), 'The two faces of power', *American Political Science Review* 56, 947–52.

Ball, Simon and Stuart Bell (1995), *Environmental Law*, London, Blackstone Press.

Barthel, Friedhelm (1991), Emissionsgesetzgebung, Wolfsburg, Volkswagen, unpublished mimeo.

Bechmann, Armin (1984), *Leben Wollen. Anleitungen für eine neue Umweltpolitik*, Cologne, Kiepenheuer & Witsch.

Becker, Klaus (1988), *Der weite Weg nach Luxemburg*, Berlin, Umweltbundesamt.

Becker, Klaus (1989), 'Verminderung der PKW-Schadstoffemissionen. Der weite Weg nach Luxemburg', *GIT Supplement 1/89-Umwelt* 1, 42–50.

Bell, Stuart (1997), *Ball and Bell on Environmental Law* (4th edition), London, Blackstone Press.

Berg, Wolfgang (1982), Aufwand und Probleme für Gesetzgeber und Automobilindustrie bei der Kontrolle der Schadstoffemissionen von Personenkraftwagen mit Otto und Diesel – Motoren, PhD dissertation, Braunschweig, Technical University.

Berg, Wolfgang (1985), 'Evolution of Motor Vehicle Emission Control Legislation in Europe', *SAE Technical Papers*, Series 850384, Warrendale, Society of Automotive Engineers.

Beyme, Klaus von (1985), 'Policy-making in the Federal Republic of Germany: a systematic introduction', in K. von Beyme and M. Schmidt (eds), *Policy and Politics in the Federal Republic of Germany*, New York, St. Martin's Press, 1–25.

Beyme, Klaus von (1997), *Der Gesetzgeber. Der Bundestag als Entscheidungszentrum*, Opladen, Westdeutscher Verlag.

Beyme, Klaus von and Manfred Schmidt (eds), (1985), *Policy and Politics in the Federal Republic of Germany*, New York, St. Martin's Press.

BMI (1972), *Materialien zum Umweltprogramm der Bundesregierung 1971*, Stuttgart, Kohlhammer.

BMWi (1993), *Report by the Federal Government on Securing Germany's Economic Future*, Bonn, Bundesministerium für Wirtschaft.

Boehmer-Christiansen, Sonja and Jim Skea (1991), *Acid Politics: Environmental Politics – Environmental and Energy Policies in Britain and Germany*, London, Belhaven Press.

Boehmer-Christiansen, Sonja and Helmut Weidner (1995), *The Politics of Reducing Vehicle Emissions in Britain and Germany*, London, Cassell.

Bogdandy, Armin von (ed.) (1993), *Die Europäische Option*, Baden-Baden, Nomos Verlagsgesellschaft.

Bohne, Eberhard (1992), 'Das Umweltrecht – ein "irregulare aliquid corpus et monstro simile"', in H.-J. Koch (ed.), *Auf dem Weg zum Umweltgesetzbuch*, Nomos, Verlagsgesellschaft, 181–233.

Börzel, Tanja (1998), 'Organising Babylon – On the different conceptions of policy networks', *Public Administration* 76, summer, 253–73.

Börzel, Tanja (2000), 'Why there is no southern problem. On environmental leaders and laggards in the European Union', *Journal of European Public Policy* 7:1, 141–62.

Brenton, Tony (1994), *The Greening of Machiavelli*, London, Earthscan.

Brundtland Report (1987), *Our Common Future*, Oxford, Oxford University Press.

Bulmer, Simon (1994), 'The governance of the European Union: a new institutional approach', *Journal of Public Policy* 13:4, 351–80.

Bulmer, Simon and William Paterson (1987), *The Federal Republic of Germany and the European Community*, London, Allen & Unwin.

Bulmer, Simon, Charlie Jeffery and William Paterson (2000), *Germany's Eurpean Diplomacy. Shaping the Regional Milieu*, Manchester, Manchester University Press.

Bundesrat (1975), *Empfehlungen der Ausschüsse zur Richtlinie betreffend die Verschmutzung der Meeres- und Süßgewässer für Badezwecke*, Bundesrat Drucksache 142/1/75, 2 October.

Bundesrat (1994a), *Antrag des Freistaates Bayern zum Vorschlag für eine Richtlinie über die Qualität der Badegewässer*, Bundesrat Drucksache 348/2/94, 7 July 1994.

Bundesrat (1994b), *Vorschlag für eine Richtlinie des Rates über die Qualität der Badegewässer KOM(94) 36 endg*, Bundesrat Drucksache 348/94, 8 July.

Bundesregierung (1994), *Stellungnahme der Regierung der Bundesrepublik Deutschland vom 20. Juni 1994. Betr.: Vorschlag für eine Richtlinie des Rates über die Qualität der Badgewässer*, Bonn, Bundesregierung der Bundesrepublik Deutschland.

Bundestag (1983), *Protokoll über die Öffentliche Anhörung zu Fragen des Umweltschutzes am 24. Oktober und 25. Oktober*, Innenausschuß–724-2450, Bonn, Deutscher Bundestag.

Bundestag (1984), *Antrag der Fraktion der SPD. Einführung umweltfreundlicher Kraftfahrzeuge*, Drucksache 10/1768, 20 Juli.

Bungarten, Harald (1978), *Umweltpolitik in Westeuropa*, Bonn, Europa Union Verlag.

Burley, Anne-Marie (1993), 'International law and international relations theory: a dual approach', *American Journal of International Law* 87:2, 205–39.

Byatt, Ian (1996), 'The impact of EC directives on water customers in England and Wales', *Journal of European Public Policy* 3:4, 664–74.

Cabelli, V. (1981), 'Epidemiology of enteric viral infections', in M. Goddard and M. Butler (eds), *Viruses and Wastewater Treatment*, London, Pergamon, 219–304.

Cabelli, V., A. Dufour, L. McCabe and M. Levin (1975), 'The development of criteria for recreational waters', in A. Gameson (ed.), *Discharge of Sewage from Sea Outfalls*, London, Pergamon, 63–74.

Cabelli, V., A. Dufour, L. McCabe, and M. Levin (1982), 'Swimming associated gastroenteritis and water quality', *American Journal of Epidemiology* 115:4, 606–16.

Caldwell, Lynton (1984), *International Environmental Policy. Emergence and Dimensions*, Durham, NC, Duke Press Policy Studies.

Caldwell, Lynton (1990), *International Environmental Policy. Emergence and Dimensions* (2nd edition), Durham, NC, Duke University Press.

CEC (1973), *Programme of Action of the European Communities on the Environment*, OJ No. C 112, 20 December.

CEC (1975a), *Proposal for a Council Directive Relating to Pollution of Sea Water and Fresh Water for Bathing (Quality Objectives)*, COM(74) 2255 final, 3 February.

CEC (1975b), *Proposal for a Council Directive Relating to Pollution of Sea Water and Fresh Water for Bathing (Quality Objectives)*, submitted on 7 February, OJ No. C 67, 22 March, 1–11.

CEC (1977a), *European Community Action Programme on the Environment (1977 to 1981)*, OJ No. C, 13 June.

CEC (1977b), *State of the Environment. First Report*, Brussels, Commission of the European Communities.

CEC (1981a), Comprehensive Report on the Bathing Water and the Most Significant Characteristics Thereof, November, Vol. 1, Brussels, Commission of the European Communities, unpublished.

CEC (1981b), Comprehensive Report on the Bathing Water and the Most Significant Characteristics Thereof, November, Vol. 2, part 1, Brussels, Commission of the European Communities, unpublished.

CEC (1981c), *Quantitative and Qualitative Inventory of Sewage Treatment Plants in the European Community, 4, Federal Republic of Germany*, Brussels, Commission of the European Communities.

CEC (1982), *Quality of Bathing Water 1981*, Brussels, Commission of the European Communities, date stamped by DG Environment.

CEC (1983a), *Quality of Bathing Water 1980*, XI/236/83, March 1983, Brussels, Commission of the European Communities (date stamped).

CEC (1983b), *Quality of Bathing Water 1982*, Brussels, Commission of the European Communities (date stamped).

CEC (1983d), *Report of the Ad Hoc Group ERGA–Air Pollution*, III/602/83-EN final, Brussels, Commission of the European Communities.

CEC (1987), *European Community Policy and Action Programme on the Environment (1987–1992)*, OJ No. C 70, 18 March.

CEC (1988), *Quality of Bathing Water 1983–86*, EUR 11588, Luxembourg, Office for Official Publications of the European Communities.

CEC (1989a), *Quality of Bathing Water 1987*, Luxembourg, Office for Official Publications of the European Communities.

CEC (1989b), *Forest Health Report 1987–1988*, Brussels, Commission of the European Communities.

CEC (1990a), *Quality of Bathing Water 1988*, EUR 12579, 1988 season, Luxembourg, Office for Official Publications of the European Communities.

CEC (1990b), *'1992'. The Environmental Dimension. Task Force on the Environment and the Internal Market*, Bonn, Economica Verlag.

CEC (1991a), *Eighth Annual Report on Monitoring the Application of Community Law*, COM(91) 321 final, 16 October, Brussels, Commission of the European Communities,

CEC (1991b), *Quality of Bathing Water 1989–1990*, EUR 13333, Luxembourg, Office for Official Publications of the European Communities.

CEC (1992a), *Ninth Annual Report on Monitoring the Application of Community Law*, COM(92) 136 final, 12 May, Brussels, Commission of the European Communities.

CEC (1992b), *Quality of Bathing Water 1991*, EUR 14210, Luxembourg, Office for Official Publications of the European Communities.

CEC (1992c), *The State of the Environment in the European Community*, COM(92) final–Vol III, Brussels, Commission of the European Communities.

CEC (1992d), *European Community Environmental Legislation 7, Water*, Luxembourg, Office for Official Publications of the European Communities.

CEC (1992e), *Sustainable Mobility. Green Paper on Transport*, Brussels, Commission of the European Communities.

CEC (1993a), *Tenth Annual Report on Monitoring the Application of Community Law*, COM(93) 320 final, Commission of the European Communities.

CEC (1993b), *Quality of Bathing Water 1992*, EUR 15031, Luxembourg, Office for Official Publications of the European Communities.

CEC (1993c), *European Symposium 'Auto Emissions 2000'*, Luxembourg, Office for the Official Publications of the European Communities.

CEC (1993d), *Towards Sustainability. A European Community Programme of Policy and Action in Relation to the Environment and Sustainable Development*, OJ No. C 138, 5–98.

CEC (1994a) *Eleventh Annual Report on Monitoring the Application of Community Law*, COM (94) 500 final, Commission of the European Communities.

CEC (1994b), *Quality of Bathing Water 1993*, EUR 15399, Luxembourg, Office for Official Publications of the European Communities.

CEC (1994c), *Growth, Competitiveness, Employment* {White Paper}, Luxembourg, Office for Official Publications of the European Communities.

CEC (1994d), *Proposal for a Council Directive Concerning the Quality of Bathing Water*, COM(94) 36 final, OJ No. C 112, 22 April, 3–10.

CEC (1995a), *Twelfth Annual Report on Monitoring the Application of Community Law*, COM(95) 500 final, Brussels, Commission of the European Communities.

CEC (1995b), *Quality of Bathing Water 1994*, EUR 15976, Luxembourg, Office for Official Publications of the European Communities.

CEC (1995c), *Final Report. A Cost-Effectiveness Study*, Touche Ross & Co, Management Consultants for the European Commission, MC/ECV/ecv086ac.

CEC (1995d), *Report of the Group of Independent Experts on Legislative and Administrative Simplification*, COM(95) 288, Brussels, Commission of the European Communities.

CEC (1995e), *BCR Information Chemical Analysis. Sea Water Microbiology Performance of Methods*, Part I, Luxembourg, Office for Official Publications of the European Communities.

CEC (1995f), *BCR Information Chemical Analysis. Sea Water Microbiology Performance of Methods*, Part II, Luxembourg, Office for Official Publications of the European Communities.

CEC (1996a), *Thirteenth Annual Report on Monitoring the Application of Community Law*, COM(96) 600 final, Brussels, Commission of the European Communities.

CEC (1996b), *Quality of Bathing Water (1995 season)*, May 1996 – EUR 16755, Luxembourg, Office for Official Publications of the European Communities.

CEC (1996c), *Communication from the Commission to the European Parliament and the Council on a Future Strategy for the Control of Atmospheric Emissions from Road Transport Taking into Account the Results of the Auto/Oil Programme. Proposal for a European Parliament and Council Directive Relating to the Quality of Petrol and Diesel Fuels and Amending Council Directive 93/12/EEC. Proposal for a European Parliament and Council Directive Relating to Measures to Be Taken Against Air Pollution from Vehicles and Amending Council Directives 70/156/EEC and 70/220/EEC*, COM(96) 248 final of 18 June, 96/0163 9COD0, 96/0164 (COD) [so-called Auto-Oil I Programme], Brussels, Commission of the European Communities.

CEC (1996d), *The European Auto-Oil Programme*, Brussels, Commission of the European Communities.

CEC (1996e), *Towards Sustainability*, COM(95) 624 final, Brussels, Commission of the European Communities.

CEC (1996f), *European Community Environmental Legislation, 7, Water*, Luxembourg, Office for Official Publications of the European Communities.

CEC (1997a), *Fourteenth Annual Report on Monitoring the Application of Community Law*, COM(97) 299 final, 29 May, Brussels, Commission of the European Communities.

CEC (1997b), *Quality of Bathing Water (1996 season)*, May 1997 – EUR 17629, Luxembourg, Office for Official Publications of the European Communities.

CEC (1997c), *Options for the Future Development of the Proposal for a Revised Bathing Water Quality Directive*, Brussels, Commission of the European Communities.

CEC (1997d), *Amended Proposal for a Council Directive on the Quality of Bathing Water*, COM(7) 585 final.

CEC (1998a), *Quality of Bathing Waters (1997 bathing season)*, May 1989 – EUR 18166, Luxembourg, Commission of the European Communities.

CEC (1998b), *Fifteenth Annual Report on Monitoring the Application of Community Law*, Brussels, Commission of the European Communities.

CEC (1999a), *Quality of Bathing Waters (1998 bathing season)*, EUR 18831, Luxembourg, Office for Official Publications of the European Communities.

CEC (1999b), *The MICROBATH Project*, Lille and Brussels, European Commission and Institute Pasteur of Lille.

CEC (1999c), *The European Commission's Decision of December 1998 Not to Co-Fund the 1999 Blue Flag Campaign*, 3 March, Brussels, Commission of the European Communities.

CEC (1999d), *Auto-Oil II Cost-effectiveness Study*, Part I, draft final report, Brussels, Commission of the European Communities.

CEC (1999e), *Les Européens et l'environment. Enquête réalisée dans le cadre de 'Eurobarométre 51.1'*, Luxembourg, Commission of the European Communities.

CEC (1999f), *What Do Europeans Think About the Environment?*, Luxembourg, Office for Official Publications of the European Communities.

CEC (2000a), *Quality of Bathing Water (1999) Bathing Season*, EUR 19505, Luxembourg, Office for Official Publications of the European Communities.

CEC (2000b), *Communication from the Commission to the European Parliament and the Council. Developing a New Bathing Water Directive*, Brussels, Commission of the European Communities.

CEC (2000c), Bathing Water Quality and Impact Assessment: Commission Proposes Fines Against the United Kingdom and Germany, press release DN: IP/00/1542, 22 December.

CEC (2000d), *Bacteriophages in Bathing Water*, EUR 19506 EN. BCR Information, Luxembourg, Office for Official Publications of the European Communities.

CEC (2000e), *A Review of the Auto-Oil II Programme*, COM(2000) 626 final, 5 October.

CEC (2001a), *Communication on the Sixth Environmental Action Programme*, COM(2001) 31 final; 2001/0029 (COD), 24 January.

CEC (2001b) *Consultation Paper for the Preparation of a European Union Strategy for Sustainable Development*, SEC (2001) 517 of 27 June, Brussels, Commission of the European Communities.

Clébant, Marcel (1973), *Croisade Pour La Mer*, Paris, Stock.

Coastal Anti-Pollution League (1985), *The Golden List of Clean Beaches in England and Wales*, Bath, Coastal Anti-Pollution League Ltd.

Coastal Anti-Pollution League (1987), *The Golden List of Clean Beaches in England and Wales*, Bath, Coastal Anti-Pollution League Ltd.

Collier, Ute and Jonathan Golub (1997), 'Environmental policy and politics', in M. Rhodes, P. Heywood and V. Wright (eds), *Developments in West European Politics*, London, Macmillan, 226–46.

Council (1976), *Council Directive 76/160/EEC of 8 December 1975*, OJ No. L 31, 5 February.

Cram, Lora (1996), 'Integration theory and the study of the European policy process', in J. Richardson (ed.), 40–58.

Cutting, E, (1987) 'European automobile exhaust emissions – the fifth Amendment', *Institute of Mechanical Engineers*, C353/87, 43–54.

Dalton, Russell (1994), *The Green Rainbow. Environmental Groups in Western Europe*, New Haven, CT, Yale University Press.

Delahuntry, A., R. Salmon, M. Wyer, F. Jones and D. Kay (1994), 'Recreational water quality: assessing the public health risks', in A. Goding *et al.* (eds), *Water and Public Health*, London, Smith-Gordon, 259–70.

Demmke, Christoph (1994), *Die Implementation von EG-Umweltpolitik in den Mitgliedstaaten. Umsetzung und Vollzug des Trinkwasserichtlinie*, Baden-Baden, Nomos Verlagsgesellschaft.

DETR (1997), *Digest of Environmental Statistics*, No. 19, Department of the Environment, Transport and the Regions, London, Stationery Office.

DETR (1998a), *Sustainable Development: Opportunities for Change Consultation Paper on a Revised UK Strategy*, London, Department of the Environment, Transport and the Regions.

DETR (1998b), *Raising the Quality. Guidance to the Director General of Water Services 2000–2005*, London, Department of the Environment, Transport and the Regions.

DETR (1998c), *Digest of Environmental Statistics*, No. 20, London, Stationery Office.

DETR (2000), *Transport Statistics Great Britain 2000*, London, Stationery Office.

DHSS (1980), *Lead and Health: The Report of a DHSS Working Party on Lead in the Environment*, London, HMSO.

DNR (various years), *EU Rundschreiben*, Bonn–Berlin, Deutscher Naturschutzring.

DoE (1977), Implementation of the EEC Directive on the Quality of Bathing Water, London, Department for the Environment, unpublished mimeo.

DoE (1988), *Inputs of Dangerous Substances to Water: Proposals for a Unified System of Control* ('The Red List'), London, Department of the Environment and Welsh Office.

DoE (1994a), *Expert Panel on Air Quality Standards. Ozone*, London, HMSO.

DoE (1994b), *Expert Panel on Air Quality Standards. Benzene*, London, HMSO.

DoE (1995), *Expert Panel on Air Quality Standards. Particles*, London, HMSO.

Dolowitz, David and David Marsh (2000), 'Learning from abroad', *Governance* 13:1, 5–24.

DoT (1979), *Lead in Petrol. An Assessment of the Feasibility and Costs of Further Action to Limit Lead Emissions from Vehicles*, London, Department of Transport.

DoT (1986), *Transport Statistics Great Britain 1975–1985*, Department of Transport, Scottish Development Department, Welsh Office.

DoT (1993), *Transport Statistics Great Britain*, Department of Transport, Scottish Office Industry Department, Welsh Office, London, HMSO.

DoT (1995), *Transport Statistics Great Britain*, Department of Transport, Scottish Office Industry Department, Welsh Office, London, HMSO.

DoT and DoE (1984), *Commission Proposals for the Amendment of EC Directives on the Lead Content of Petrol and Motor Vehicle Emissions*, Ref. No. 7805/84, London, Department of the Environment and the Department of Transport.

Dowding, Keith (1995), 'Model or metaphor? A critical review of the policy network approach', *Political Studies* 43:1, 136–58.

Dryzek, John S. (1997), *The Politics of the Earth*, Oxford, Oxford University Press.

Dudley, Geoffrey and Jeremy Richardson (1996), 'Why does policy change over time? Adversarial policy communities, alternative policy arenas, and British trunk roads policy 1945–95', *Journal of European Public Policy* 3:1, 63–83.

DVWK (1991), *Seit 100 Jahren organisierte Wasserwirtschaft, Presseinformation 26 September 1991*, Bonn, Deutscher Verband für Wasserwirtschaft und Kulturbau.

Dyson, Kenneth (1982), 'West Germany: the search for a rationalist consensus', in J. Richardson (ed.), 17–46.

Dyson, Kenneth (ed.) (1992), *The Politics of German Regulation*, Aldershot, Dartmouth.

Earnshaw, David and David Judge (1995), 'Early days: the European Parliament, co-decision and the European Union legislative process post-Maastricht', *Journal of European Public Policy*, 2:4, 624–49.

Earnshaw, David and David Judge (1996), 'From co-operation to co-decision: the European Parliament's path to legislative power', in J. Richardson (ed.), 96–126.

EC Bulletin (various years), Luxembourg, Office for Official Publications of the European Communities.

ECOSOC (1975a), *Opinion on the Proposal for a Council Directive Relating to Pollution of Sea Water and Fresh Water for Bathing*, OJ No. C 286, 15 December, 5–8.

ECOSOC (1975b), *Report of the Section for Protection of the Environment, Public Health and Consumer Affairs on the Proposal for a Council Directive Relating to Pollution of Sea Water and Fresh Water for Bathing*, Rapporteur Mr De Graeve, 11 September.

ECJ (1993), *Case C–56/90*, Judgment, 14 July, Luxembourg, European Court of Justice.

ECJ (1999), *Case C–198/97*, Judgment, 8 June, Luxembourg, European Court of Justice.

EEA (1995a), *Europe's Environment. The Dobris Assessment*, Copenhagen, European Environment Agency.

EEA (1995b), *Europe's Environment. Statistical Compendium for the Dobris Assessment*, Copenhagen, European Environment Agency.

EEA (1995c), *Environment in the European Union 1995*, Copenhagen, European Environment Agency.

EEA (1997), *Air Pollution in Europe 1997*, Copenhagen, European Environment Agency.

EEA (1998a), *Europe's Environment: The Second Assessment*, Copenhagen, European Environment Agency.

EEA (1998b), *Europe's Environment: Statistical Compendium for the Second Assessment*, Copenhagen, European Environment Agency.

EEA (2000), *Are We Moving in the Right Direction? Indicators on Transport and Environment Integration in the EU*, Copenhagen, European Environment Agency.

EEB (1985), *Car Emissions: Rather No Agreement than a Weak Agreement*, Brussels, European Environmental Bureau.

EEB (1987), General observations regarding Stage 2 Standards for small cars and modifications to the driving cycle, prepared by Dr Michael Walsh, press release REF C/128/87, Brussels, European Environmental Bureau.

EEB (ed.) (1987), *The Clean Car, A Challenge for Europe*, Brussels, European Environmental Bureau.

EEB (1994), *Amendments to the EU's 1975 Directive on Bathing Water Quality*, Brussels, European Environmental Bureau.

EEB (1996), *Annual Report*, Brussels, European Environmental Bureau.

Ehret, Oliver (1998), Das 'Auto-Öl Programm' der Europäischen Kommission, unpublished diploma dissertation, Berlin, Free University.

Eichener, Volker (1997), 'Effective European problem-solving: lessons from the regulation of occupational safety and environmental protection', *Journal of European Public Policy* 4:4, 536–72.

ENDS Daily (various years), daily e-mail service, Environmental Data Services, London.

ENDS Report (various years), monthly edition, London, Environment Data Services, London.

Environment Watch: Western Europe (various years), News and Analysis for Business and Policy Professionals, Arlington, Cutter Information.

Environmental Agency (1999), *Bathing Water Quality in England and Wales in 1998*, Bristol, Environment Agency.

EP (various years) *Minutes of the Debates of the European Parliament*, Strasbourg, European Parliament.

EP (1975a), *Report Drawn Up on the Proposal from the Commission to the Council for a Directive Relating to Pollution of Sea Water and for Water for Bathing*, Rapporteur Mr A. Premoli, PE 40.402, European Parliament.

EP (1975b), *Resolution for a Directive Relating to Pollution of Sea Water and Fresh Water for Bathing*, OJ No. C 128, 1–14.

EP (1994), *Recommendation for Second Reading on the Common Position Relating to Measures Taken Against Air Pollution from Motor Vehicles*, Rapporteur Kurt Vittinghoff, PE 207.650/final, A3-0101/94.

EP (1996), *Report on the Proposal for a Council Directive Concerning the Quality of Bathing Water*, Rapporteur Doeke Eisma, PE219.109/final, A4-0395/96.

EP (1997a), *Report on the Quality of Petrol and Diesel Fuels and Amending Council Directive 93/12/EEC*, Rapporteur Mr Mamère, A4-0096/97.

EP (1997b), *Report on Measures to be Taken Against Air Pollution by Emissions from Motor Vehicles and Amending Council Directives 70/156/EEC and 70/220/EEC*, Rapporteur Bernd Lange, A4-0116/97.

EP (1997c), *Report on a Future Strategy for the Control of Atmospheric Emissions from Road Transport*, Rapporteur Doeke Eisma, A4-0099/97.

EP (1998a), *Recommendation for Second Reading on the Common Position on the Quality of Petrol and Diesel Fuels*, Rapporteur Ms Hautala, A4-0038/98.

EP (1998b), *Recommendation for Second Reading on the Common Position Relating to Measures to be Taken Against Air Pollution by Emissions From Motor Vehicles*, Rapporteur Bernd Lange, A4-0044/98.

Erdmann, W. (not dated), Welche Anforderungen hat der Hygieniker an Freibäder zu stellen?, Neuss, Städtisches Gesundheitsamt, unpublished mimeo.

Eurobarometer (1995), *Europeans and the Environment in 1995*, Brussels, Commisison of the European Communities.

Exner, Martin, T. Kistemann, G. Unger, M. Hansis and A. Nassauer (1999), 'Future prevention and control strategies in hospital hygiene', *Hygienische Medizin* 24:7–8, 280–303.

Featherstone, Kevin (1994), 'Jean Monnet and the "democratic deficit" in the European Union', *Journal of Common Market Studies* 32:2, 149–71.

FCEC (not dated), *The Sewage Pollution of Britain's Beaches. Britain's Beaches: The Poor Cousin*, London, Federation of Civil Engineering Contractors.

FEEE (1988–98), *The European Blue Flag Campaign*, annual reports, Copenhagen, Foundation for Environmental Education in Europe.

Fewtrell, Lorna and Frank Jones (1992), 'Mircobiological aspects and possible health risks of recreational water', in D. Kay (ed.), 71–87.

Fewtrell, L., D. Kay, R. Salmon, M. Wyer, G. Newman and G. Bowering (1994), 'The health effects of low-contact water activities in fresh and estuarine waters', *Journal of the Institution of Water and Environmental Management*, 8 February 1994, 97–101.

Finer, Samuel (1984), *Comparative Government. An Introduction to the Study of Government*, London, Penguin books.

Fleisher, J., F. Jones, D. Kay, R. Stanwell-Smith, M. Myer and R. Morano (1993), 'Water and non-water related risk factors for gastro-enteritis among bathers exposed to sewage-contaminated marine waters', *International Journal of Epidemiology* 22:4, 698–708.

Fleisher, J., D. Kay, R. Salmon, F. Jones, M. Wyer and A. Godfrey (1996),

'Marine waters contaminated with domestic sewage', *American Journal of Public Health* 86, 1228–34.

FoE (1988), 'Boycott Peugeot' says FoE as EEC ministers meet, press release, 1 October, London, Friends of the Earth.

FoE (1993), Government to Backtrack on Sewage Pollution, press release, 19 October, London, Friends of the Earth.

Ford of Europe (1983), The European exhaust emission situation, Basildon, Ford of Europe Inc., October 1983, mimeo.

Ford of Europe (1985), Lean-Burn technology – a note on achievements and possibilities, Basildon, Ford of Europe Inc., May, mimeo.

Friedrich, Axel, Matthias Tappe and Rüdiger Wurzel (1998a), 'The Auto-Oil Programme: a critical interim assessment', *European Environmental Law Review* 7:4, 104–12.

Friedrich, Axel, Matthias Tappe and Rüdiger K.W. Wurzel (1998b), *The Auto-Oil Programme: Missed Opportunity or Leap Forward?* Hull, Centre of European Union Studies, No. 1.

Friedrich, Axel, Matthias Tappe and Rüdiger K.W. Wurzel (2000), 'A new approach to EU environmental policy-making? The Auto-Oil I Programme', *Journal of European Public Policy* 7:4, 593–612.

Gameson, A. (1979), 'EEC directive on quality of bathing water', *Water Pollution Control* 78:2, 206–14.

Goetz, Klaus (1996), 'Integration policy in a Europeanised state: Germany and the intergovernmental conference', *Journal of European Public Policy* 3:1, 23–44.

Golub, Jonathan (1994), British integration into the EEC: A case study in European environmental policy, DPhil thesis, Oxford, Oxford University.

Golub, Jonathan (1996a), 'State power and institutional influence in European integration: lessons from the packaging waste directive', *Journal of Common Market Studies* 34:3, 313–39.

Grant, Wyn, William Paterson and Colin Whitston (1988), *Government and the Chemical Industry*, Oxford, Clarendon Press.

Greenpeace (1990), *The 'Great Car Economy' versus 'The Quality of Life'*, London, Greenpeace.

Greenwood, Justin (1997), *Representing Interests in the European Union*, London, Macmillan.

Greenwood, Justin, Jürgen Grote and Karsten Ronit (1992), 'Introduction: organised interests and the transnational dimension', in J. Greenwood, J. Grote and K. Ronit (eds), *Organised Interests and the European Community*, London, Sage, 1–41.

Grubb, Michael, Matthias Koch, Abby Munson, Francis Sullivan and Koy Thomson (1993), *The Earth Summit Agreements. A Guide and Assessment*, London, Earthscan Publications.

Gündling, Lothar (1991), 'Protection of the environment by international law: air pollution', in W. Lang, H. Neuhold, and K. Zemanek (eds), *Environmental Protection and International Law*, London, Graham & Trotman–Martinus Nijhoff, 91–100.

Haas, Ernst (1964), *Beyond the Nation State. Functionalism and International Organisation*, Stanford, CA, Stanford University Press.

Haas, Ernst (1975), *The Obsolescence of Regional Integration Theory*, Berkeley, CA, Institute of International Studies.

Haas, Peter (1990), 'Obtaining international environmental protection through epistemic communities', *Millennium* 19:3, 347–65.

Haas, Peter (1992), 'Introduction: epistemic communities and international policy co-ordination', *International Organization* 46:1, 1–35.

Haas, Peter (1995), 'Epistemic communities and the dynamics of international environmental co-operation', in V. Rittberger and P. Mayer (eds), *Regime Theory and International Relations*, Oxford, Oxford University Press, 168–201.

Haigh, Nigel (1982), Environmental quality objectives in Britain: National policy or community obligation?, London, Institute of European Environmental Policy, unpublished mimeo.

Haigh, Nigel (1987), *EEC Environmental Policy and Britain* (2nd edition), London, Longman.

Haigh, Nigel (1992), 'The European Community and international environmental policy', in A. Hurrell and B. Kingsbury (eds), *The International Politics of the Environment*, Oxford, Clarendon Press, 228–52.

Haigh, Nigel (ed.) (1995), *Manual of Environmental Policy: The EC and Britain*, Harlow, Cartermill Publishing (looseleaf manual with bi-annual updates by the Institute for European Environmental Policy, London).

Haigh, Nigel (1996), 'Environmental protection in the DoE (1970–1995) or one and a half cheers for bureaucracy', in DoE (ed.), *Department of the Environment 1970–1995. A Perspective for Change*, London, Department of the Environment, 7–17.

Haigh, Nigel and Chris Lanigan (1995), 'Impact of the European Union on UK environmental policy making', in Tim Gray (ed.), *UK Environmental Policy in the 1990s*, London, Macmillan, 18–37.

Hajer, Maarten (1995), *The Politics of Environmental Discourse*, Oxford, Oxford University Press.

Hansard (various years), *Record of United Kingdom Parliamentary Debates*, London, Stationary Office.

Hartkopf, Günter and Eberhard Bohne (1983), *Umweltpolitik 1. Grundlagen, Analysen und Perspektiven*, Opladen, Westdeutscher Verlag.

Hayward, Jack (1974), 'National aptitudes for planning in Britain, France and Italy', *Government and Opposition* 9:4, 394–410.

Hayward, Jack (1986), *The State and the Market Economy. Industrial Patriotism and Economic Intervention in France*, Brighton, Wheatsheaf Books.

Hayward, Jack (1991), 'The policy community approach to industrial policy', in D. Rustow and K. Erickson (eds), *Comparative Political Dynamics: Global Research Perspectives*, New York, Harper Collins, 381–407.

Hayward, Jack (1996), 'Conclusion: Has European unification by stealth a future?', in J. Hayward (ed.), *Elitism, Populism, and European Politics*, Oxford, Clarendon Press Oxford, 252–58.

Heclo, Hugh and Aaron Wildavsky (1974), *The Private Government of Public Money*, London, Macmillan.

Henssler, H. and S. Gospage (1987), 'The exhaust emission standards of the European Community', *SAE Technical Paper Series 871080*, Warrendale, Engineering Society for Advancing Mobility: Land, Sea, Air and Space.

Héritier, Adrienne (ed.). (1993), 'Policy-Analyse. Kritik und Neuorientierung', *Politische Vierteljahresschrift* 34, special edition.

Héritier, Adrienne (1993), 'Policy-Netzwerkanalyse als Untersuchungsinstrument im europäischen Kontext: Folgerungen aus einer empirischen Studie regulativer Politik', *Politische Vierteljahresschrift*, 34, special edition, 432–51.

Héritier, Adrienne (1995), '"Leaders" and "laggards" in European clean air policy', in B. Ungerer and F. van Waarden (eds), 278–305.

Héritier, Adrienne (1996), 'The accommodation of diversity in European policy-making and its outcomes: regulatory policy as a patchwork', *Journal of European Public Policy* 3:2, 149–67.

Héritier, Adrienne, Susanne Mingers, Christoph Knill and Martina Becka (1994), *Die Veränderung von Staatlichkeit in Europa. Ein regulativer Wettbewerb: Deutschland, Großbritannien, Frankreich*, Opladen, Leske & Budrich.

Héritier, Adrienne, Christoph Knill, and Susanne Mingers in collaboration with Barrett Rhodes (1996), *Ringing the Changes. Regulatory Competition and the Transformation of the State. Britain, France, Germany*, Berlin, Walter de Gruyter.

Hey, Christian and Uwe Brendle (1994), *Umweltverbände und EG. Strategien, Politische Kulturen und Organisationsformen*, Opladen, Westdeutscher Verlag.

Hix, Simon (1994), 'The study of the European Community: the challenge to comparative politics', *West European Politics* 17:1, 1–30.

Hix, Simon (1998), 'The study of the European Union II: the 'new governance' agenda and its rival', *Journal of European Public Policy* 5:1, 38–65.

HoC (1975), *Minutes of Evidence Taken Before the Select Committee on European Secondary Legislation*, 1 July, 1975, 87–viii, London, HMSO.

HoC (1985a), *Coastal Sewage Pollution in Wales. Report and Proceedings*, Vols I and II, House of Commons Committee on Welsh Affairs, London, HMSO.

HoC (1985b), *Coastal Sewage Pollution in Wales. Minutes of Evidence*, House of Commons Committee on Welsh Affairs, London, HMSO.

HoC (1988), *Air Pollution*, House of Commons Environmental Committee, First Report, 270-I, London, HMSO.

HoC (1990a), *Pollution of Beaches*, House of Commons Environment Committee, Fourth Report, part I, London, HMSO.

HoC (1990b), *Pollution of Beaches*, House of Commons Environment Committee, Fourth Report, part II, London, HMSO.

Hodges, Michael and Stephen Woolcock (1993), 'Atlantic capitalism versus Rhine capitalism in the European Community', *West European Politics* 16:3, 329–44.

HoL (1975a), *House of Lords Debates, Water Pollution: EEC Report*, 13 October, columns 722–65.

HoL (1975b), *Pollution of Sea and Fresh Water for Bathing*, Thirteenth Report of the Select Committee of the House of Lords on the European Communities, session 1974–75, R/407/75, London, HMSO.

HoL (1975c), *Minutes of Evidence Taken Before the European Communities Sub-Committee F, on 19 June*, London, HMSO.

HoL (1985), *Lead in Petrol and Vehicle Emissions with Minutes of Evidence*, House of Lords Select Committee on the European Communities, London, HMSO.

HoL (1992), *Implementation and Enforcement of Environmental Legislation, Ninth Report of the Select Committee of the House of Lords on the European Communities*, HL Paper 53, London, HMSO.

HoL (1994a), *Bathing Water. Report*, House of Lords Select Committee on the European Communities, HL Paper 6, London, HMSO.

HoL (1994b), *Bathing Water. With Evidence*, House of Lords Select Committee on the European Communities, HL Paper 6-I, London, HMSO.

HoL (1995), *Bathing Water Revisited. With Evidence*, House of Lords Select Committee on the European Communities, HL Paper 41, London, HMSO.

HoL (1997), *Community Environmental Law: Making It Work*, HL Paper 12, London, Stationery Office.

Holdgate, Martin (1983), 'Environmental politics in Britain and mainland Europe', in R. Macrory (ed.), 6–17.

Höller, Christiane (2000), '*Vulnerability 2000*'. *Concluding German Report*, Kiel, University of Kiel.

Holzinger, Katharina (1994), *Politik des kleinsten gemeinsamen Nenners? Umweltpolitische Entscheidungsprozess in der EG am Beispiel der Einführung des Katalysators*, Berlin, Edition Sigma.

Holzinger, Katharina (1996), 'A surprise success in EC environmental policy: The small car exhaust emission directive in 1989', in M. Jänicke and H. Weidner (eds), 187–201.

Huber, Michael (1997), 'Leadership in the European climate policy: innovative policy-making in policy networks', in D. Liefferink and M. S. Andersen (eds), 133–55.

Hubschmid, Claudia and Peter Moser (1997), 'The co-operation procedure in the EU: Why was the European Parliament influential in the decision on car emission standards?', *Journal of Common Market Studies* 35:2, 225–42.

Hucke, Jochen (1981), 'Implementing environmental regulations in the Federal Republic of Germany', *Policy Studies Journal* 1, 130–40.

Hucke, Jochen (1985), 'Environmental policy: The development of a new policy area', in K von Beyme and M. Schmidt (eds), 156–75.

Hurrell, Andrew (1994), 'A crisis of ecological vulnerability? Global environmental change and the nation state', *Political Studies* XLII, special issue, 146–65.

Hurrell, Andrew and Benedict Kingsbury (eds) (1992), *The International Politics of the Environment*, Oxford, Clarendon Press.

Hurrell, Andrew and Anand Menon (1996), 'Politics like any other? Comparative politics, international relations and the study of the EU', *West European Politics* 19:2, 386–402.

IEEP (1986), *Implementing the EC Directive 76/160 Concerning the Quality of Bathing Water*, London, Institute for European Environmental Policy.

Inglehart, Ronald (1971), 'The silent revolution in Europe: intergenerational change in post-industrial societies', *American Political Science Review* 65, 991–1017.

Inglehart, Ronald (1977), *The Silent Revolution*, Princeton, NJ, Princeton University Press.

Jachtenfuchs, Markus (1995), 'Theoretical perspectives on European governance', *European Law Journal* 1:2, 115–33.

Jachtenfuchs, Markus and Beate Kohler-Koch (eds) (1996), *Europäische Integration*, Leverkusen, Leske & Budrich.

Jahn, Detlef (1997), 'Green politics and parties in Germany', *The Political Quarterly*, special issue, 174–82.

Jänicke, Martin (1993), 'Über ökologische und politische Modernisierungen', *Zeitschrift für Umweltpolitik und Umweltrecht* 16, 159–75.

Jänicke, Martin and Helmut Weidner (eds) (1995), *Successful Environmental Policy*, Berlin, Edition Sigma.

Jänicke, Martin and Helmut Weidner (eds) (1997), *National Environmental Policies. A Comparative Study of Capacity-Building*, Berlin, Springer

Jänicke, Martin and Helmut Weidner (1997), 'Germany', in M. Jänicke and H. Weidner (eds), 133–57.

Jenkins-Smith, H. and P. Sabatier (1993), 'The study of public policy processes', in P. Sabatier and H. Jenkins-Smith (eds), 1–13.

Johnson, Stanley and Guy Corcelle (1989), *The Environmental Policy of the European Communities*, London, Graham & Trotman.

Johnson, Stanley and Guy Corcelle (1995), *The Environmental Policy of the European Communities* (2nd edition), London, Graham & Trotman.

Jones, F., D. Kay, R. Stanwell-Smith and M. Wyer (1991), 'Results of the first pilot-scale controlled cohort epidemiological investigation into the possible health effects of bathing in seawater at Langland Bay', *Journal of the Institution of Water and Environmental Management* 5:1, 91–8.

Jones, F., D. Kay, M. Wyer, J. Fleisher, R. Salmon and A. Godfree (1993), *Final Report of the Controlled Cohort Investigations into the Health Effects of Bathing in Sewage Contaminated Coastal Waters*, Centre for Research in Environment and Health at St David's University College, Lampeter, University of Wales.

Jordan, Andrew (1997), 'Overcoming the divide between comparative politics and international relations approaches to the EC: what role for "post-decisional politics"?', *West European Politics* 20:4, 43–70.

Jordan, Andrew (1998a), '"Private affluence and public squalor"? The Europeanisation of British coastal bathing water policy', *Policy & Politics* 26:1, 33–54.

Jordan, Andrew (1998b), 'The impact on UK environmental administration', in P. Lowe and S. Ward (eds), 173–94.

Jordan, Andrew (1999a), 'European Community water policy standards: locked in or watered down?', *Journal of Common Market Studies* 37:1, 13–37.

Jordan, Andrew (1999b), 'Editorial introduction: the construction of a multi-level environmental governance system', *Environment and Planning C: Government and Policy* 17:1, 1–17.

Jordan, Andrew (2000), *The Europeanistation of UK Environmental Policy, 1970–2000: A Departmental Perspective*, ESRC Working Paper 11/00, Brighton, University of Sussex.

Jordan, Andrew (2002) *The Europeanisation of British Environmental Policy: A Departmental Perspective*, London, Palgrave.

Jordan, Andrew and John Greenaway (1999), 'Shifting agendas, changing regulatory structures and the 'new' politics of environmental pollution: British coastal water policy, 1955–95', *Public Administration* 76:4, 669–94.

Jordan, Andrew, Roy Brouwer and Emma Noble (1999), 'Innovative and responsive? A longitudinal analysis of the speed of EU environmental policy-making, 1967–97', *Journal of European Public Policy* 6:3, 376–98.

Jordan, Grant (1990), 'Sub-governments, policy communities and networks: refilling the old bottles?', *Journal of Theoretical Politics* 2:3, 319–38.

Jordan, Grant and Maloney, William (1997), *The Protest Business. Mobilizing Campaign Groups*, Manchester, Manchester University Press.

Josselin, Daphné (1996), 'Domestic policy networks and European negotiations: evidence from British and French financial services', *Journal of European Public Policy* 3:3, 297–317.

Judge, David, David Earnshaw and Nigel Cowan (1994), 'Ripples or waves: The European Parliament in the European policy process', *Journal of European Public Policy* 1:1, 27–52.

Kamieniecki, Sheldon (ed.) (1993), *Environmental Politics in the International Arena*, New York, State University of New York Press.

Kay, David (1998), 'Catchment management in upland Wales', *Geography Review*, November, 34–40.

Kay, David (ed.) (1992), *Recreational Water Quality Management*, Volume 1: Coastal Waters, New York, Ellis Worwood.

Kay, D., J. Fleisher, R. Salmon, F. Jones, M. Wyer, A. Godfree, Z. Zelenauch-Jacquotte and R. Shore (1994a), 'Predicting likelihood of gastro-enteritis from sea bathing: results from randomised exposure', *The Lancet* 344, 905- 9.

Kay, David and Roger Hanbury (eds) (1993), *Recreational Water Quality Management*, Volume 2: Fresh Waters, New York, Ellis Worwood.

Kay, David and Gareth Rees (1997), 'Recreational water: review of trends and events', *Marine Environmental Management Review* 4:17, 107–12.

Kay, D., M. Wyer, J. Crowther and L. Fewtrell (1999), 'Faecal indicator impacts on recreational waters: budget studies and diffuse source modelling', *Journal of Applied Microbiology Symposium Supplement* 85, 70–82.

Kay, D., M. Wyer, A. McDonald and N. Woods (1990), 'The application of water-quality standards to UK bathing water waters', *Journal for the Institution of Water and Environmental Management* 4, 436–41.

Keleman, Daniel (1995), 'Environmental policy in the European Union: the struggle between Court, Commission and Council', in B. Ungerer and F. van Waarden (eds), 306–32.

Keohane, Robert and Stanley Hoffman (1991), 'Institutional change in Europe in the 1980s', in R. Keohane and S. Hoffman (eds), *The New European Community. Decision-making and Institutional Change*, Boulder, CO, Westview Press, 1–40.

Kingdon, John W. (1995), *Agendas, Alternatives and Public Policies* (2nd edition), New York, Harper Collins.

Kinnersley, David (1988), *Troubled Water. Rivers, Politics and Pollution*, London, Hilary Shipan.

Kinnersley, David (1994), *Coming Clean. The Politics of Water and the Environment*, London, Penguin Books.

Kitschelt, Herbert (1986), 'Political opportunity structures and political protest: anti-nuclear movements in four democracies', *British Journal of Political Science* 16, 57–85.

Kitschelt, Herbert (1991), 'Industrial governance structures, innovation strategies, and the case of Japan: sectoral or cross-national comparative analysis', *International Organization* 45:4, 453–93.

Kitschelt, Herbert (1993), 'The Green phenomenon in the Western party system', in S. Kamieniecki (ed.), 93–112.

Klenke, Dietmar (1995), *'Freier Stau für freie Bürger'. Die Geschichte der bundesdeutschen Verkehrspolitik 1949–1994*, Darmstadt, Wissenschaftliche Buchgesellschaft.

Kloepfer, Michael (1998), *Umweltrecht*, Munich, Verlag C. H. Beck.

Knill, Christoph (1996), 'Staatlichkeit im Wandel: Großbritannien im Spannungsfeld nationaler Reformen und europäischer Integration', *Politische Vierteljahresschrift* 36:4, 655–80.

Knill, Christoph and Andrea Lenschow (1998), 'Coping with Europe: the impact of British and German administrations on the implementation of EU environmental policy', *Journal European Public Policy* 5:4, 595–614.

Knill, Christoph and Andrea Lenschow (eds) (2000), *Implementing EU Environmental Policy*, Manchester, Manchester University Press.

Kohler-Koch, Beate (1994), 'Changing patterns of interest intermediation in the European Union', *Government and Opposition* 29:2, 166–80.

Krämer, Ludwig (1990a), *EEC Treaty and Environmental Protection*, London, Sweet & Maxwell.

Krämer, Ludwig (1990b), 'EWG-Umweltrecht und einzelstaatliche Alleingänge', *Jahrbuch des Umwelt-und Technikrechts* 12, 437–65.

Krämer, Ludwig (1995), *EC Treaty and Environmental Law* (2nd edition), London, Sweet & Maxwell.

Krasner, Stephen (1983), 'Structural causes and regime consequences: regimes as intervening variable', in S. Krasner (ed.), 1–21.

Krasner, Stephen (ed.) (1983), *International Regimes*, Ithaca, Cornell University Press.

Kromarek, Pascale (1986), *Vergleichende Untersuchung über die Umsetzung der EG-Richtlinien Abfall und Wasser*, Bonn, Institut für Europäische Umweltpolitik und Umweltbundesamt.

Krote, V. and D. Gruden (1987), *Possible Spark-Ignition Engine Technologies for European Exhaust Emission Legislations*, Institute for Mechanical Engineering C334/87.

LAWA (1975), *Mainzer Papier. Grundsätze für Gewässerregelungen im internationalen Bereich und bei internationalen und supranationalen Aktivitäten*, Mainz, Länderarbeitsgemeinschaft Wasser.

Levitt, Ruth (1980), *Implementing Public Policy*, London, Croom Helm.

Levy, Marc A. (1993), 'European acid rain: the power of tote-board diplomacy', in Peter Haas, Robert O. Keohane and Mask A. Levy (eds), *Institutions for Earth. Sources of Effective Environmental Protection*, Cambridge, MA, MIT Press, 75–132.

Liefferink, Duncan (1996), *Environmental Policy and the Nation State: The Netherlands, the EU and Acid Rain*, Manchester, Manchester University Press.

Liefferink, Duncan and Mikael Skou Andersen (1997), 'The innovation of EU environmental policy', in D. Liefferink and M. S. Andersen (eds), 9–36.

Liefferink, Duncan and Mikael Skou Andersen (eds) (1997), *The Innovation of EU Environmental Policy*, Oslo, Scandinavian University Press.

Liefferink, Duncan and Mikael Skou Andersen (1998a), 'Strategies of the 'Green' member states in EU environmental policy-making', *Journal of European Public Policy* 5:2, 254–70.

Liefferink, Duncan and Mikael Skou Andersen (1998b), 'Greening the EU: national positions in the run-up to the Amsterdam Treaty', *Environmental Politics* 7:3, 66–93.

Liefferink, Duncan, P. Lowe and A. Mol (eds), (1993), *European Integration and Environmental Policy*, London, Belhaven Press.

Lindberg, Leon and Stuart Scheingold (1970), *Europe's Would-Be Polity. Patterns of Change in the European Community*, Eaglewood Cliffs, Prentice–Hall.

Lodge, Juliet (1989), 'Environment: towards a clean blue-green EC?', in Lodge, J. (ed), *The European Community and the Challenge of the Future*, London, Pinter, 319–27.

López-Pila, Juan M. (1998), 'Some economic and political consequences of pathogens in inland and coastal waters', *European Water Management* 1:2, 70–7.

Long, Tony (1998), 'The environmental lobby', in P. Lowe and S. Ward, (eds) (1998), 105–18.

Lowe, Philip and Ward, Stephen (eds) (1998), *British Environmental Policy and Europe*, London, Routledge.

Lowi, Theodore (1964), 'American business, public policy, case studies and political theory', *World Politics* 16, 677–715.

McCormick, John (1991), *British Politics and the Environment*, London, Earthscan Publications.

McCormick, John (1993), 'Environmental politics', in Patrick Dunleavy, Andrew Gamble, Ian Holliday and Gillian Peele (eds), *Developments in British Politics*, Vol. 4, London, Macmillan, 267–84.

McLaughlin, Andrew and Jordan, Grant (1993), 'The rationality of
lobbying in Europe: Why are Euro-groups so numerous and so weak?
Some evidence from the car industry', in S. Mazey and J. Richardson
(eds), 162–76.

McLaughlin, Andrew, Grant Jordan and William Maloney (1993),
'Corporate lobbying in the European Community', *Journal of Common
Market Studies* 31:2, 191–212.

Macrory, Richard (ed.) (1983), *Britain, Europe and the Environment*,
London, Imperial College.

Majone, Giandomenico (1994), 'The rise of the regulatory state in Europe',
West European Politics 17:3, 77–101.

Majone, Giandominico (ed.) (1996), *Regulating Europe*, London, Routledge.

Maloney, William and Jeremy Richardson (1994), 'Water policy-making in
England and Wales: policy communities under pressure?', *Environmental
Politics* 3:4, 110–38.

Maloney, William and Jeremy Richardson (1995), *Managing Policy Change
in Britain: The Politics of Water*, Edinburgh, Edinburgh University Press.

Malunat, Bernd (1987), 'Umweltpolitik im Spiegel der Parteiprogramme',
Aus Politik und Zeitgeschichte B29:82, 29–42.

Marin, Bernd and Renate Mayntz (1991), 'Introduction: studying policy
networks', in B. Marin and R. Mayntz (eds), *Policy Networks.
Empirical Evidence and Theoretical Considerations*, Berlin, Campus
Verlag, 11–24.

Marine Pollution Bulletin (1983), 'Editorial: if you can't see it, it is safe',
14:7, 241–2.

Marks, Gary, Lisbet Hooghe and Kermitt Blank (1996), 'European
integration from the 1980s: state-centric versus multi-level governance',
Journal of Common Market Studies 34:3, 341–78.

Marsh, David and Rod Rhodes (1992), 'Policy communities and issue
networks: beyond typology', in D. Marsh and R. Rhodes (eds), 249–68.

Marsh, David and Rod Rhodes (eds) (1992), *Policy Networks in British
Politics*, Oxford, Oxford University Press.

Maruo, Kanehira (1992), 'The three-way catalyst': paper presented at the
1992 Annual Meeting of the Society of Technology, Uppsala, 16–20
August.

Mayntz, Renate (ed.) (1980), *Implementation politischer Programme*,
Königstein, Westdeutscher Verlag.

Mazey, Sonia and Jeremy Richardson (1992), 'Environmental groups and
the EC: challenges and opportunities', *Environmental Politics* 1:4,
109–28.

Mazey, Sonia and Jeremy Richardson (1993a), 'Interest groups in
the European Community', in S. Mazey and J. Richardson (eds),
191–213.

Mazey, Sonia and Jeremy Richardson (1993b), 'Conclusions: a European policy style?', in S. Mazey and J. Richardson (eds), 246–58.

Mazey, Sonia and Richardson, Jeremy (eds) (1993), *Lobbying in the European Community*, Oxford, Oxford University Press.

MCS (1988–93), *The Heinz Good Beach Guide*, Ross-on-Wye, Marine Conservation Society.

MCS (1994–1999), *The Reader's Digest Good Beach Guide*, Newton Abbott, David & Charles.

MCS (2000), *Marine Conservation Society Good Beach Guide 2000*, Ross-on-Wye, Marine Conservation Society.

Merkel, Wolfgang (1996), 'Allgemein anerkannte Regeln der Technik (a.a.R.d.T.) Stand der Technik (SdT) und beste verfügbare Techniken (BVT)', *Wasser – Abwasser* 137:5, 243–51.

Milward, Alan (1992), *The European Rescue of the Nation-State*, London, Routledge.

Mol, Arthur, Volkmar Lauber and Duncan Liefferink (eds) (2000), *The Voluntary Approach to Environmental Policy-Making in Europe*, Oxford, Oxford University Press.

Mol, Arthur and Duncan Liefferink (1993), 'European environmental policy and global interdependence: a review of theoretical approaches', in D. Liefferink, P. Lowe and A. Mol (eds), 17–36.

Molin, Katarina and Rüdiger K. W. Wurzel, 'Environmental policy', in L. Miles (ed.), *Sweden and EU Membership Evaluated*, London, Continuum, 166–79.

Moltke, Konrad von (1987), *The Vorsorgeprinzip in West German Environmental Policy*, London, Institute for European Environmental Policy.

Monnet, Jean (1980), *Erinnerungen eines Europäers*, Munich, Deutscher Taschenbuch Verlag.

Moore, Brendan (1977), 'The EEC bathing water directive', *Marine Pollution Bulletin* 8, 269.

Moravcsik, Andrew (1991), 'Negotiating the Single European Act: national interests and conventional statecraft in the European Community', *International Organisation* 45:1, 19–56.

Moravcsik, Andrew (1993), 'Preferences and power in the European Community: a liberal intergovernmentalist approach', *Journal of Common Market Studies* 31:4, 473–524.

Müller, Edda (1986), *Innenpolitik der Umweltpolitik. Sozial-liberale Umweltpolitik – (Ohn)Macht durch Organisation?*, Opladen, Westdeutscher Verlag.

Müller, Hans (1993), 'Hygienische Relevanz der verschiedenen mikrobiologischen Markerkeime für die Beurteilung von Badewasser', *Archiv des Badewesens* 8, 364–71.

Müller-Brandeck-Bocquete, Gisela (1996), *Die instititionelle Dimension der Umweltpolitik. Eine vergleichende Untersuchung zu Frankreich, Deutschland und der Europäischen Union*, Baden-Baden, Nomos Verlagsgesellschaft.

Neu, Helmut (1990), *Der EG-Abgaskompromiß unter umweltökonomischen Aspekten und unter Berücksichtigung alternativer Instrumente zur Regulierung von Externalitäten mobiler Emissionsquellen*, Mühlheim Ruhr, Westarp-Wissenschaft.

North, Douglas (1990), *Institutions, Institutional Change and Economic Performance*, Cambridge, Cambridge University Press.

NRA (1990), *Toxic Blue–Green Algae*, National Rivers Authority Water Quality Series, No. 2, September 1990, London, National Rivers Authority.

NRA (1991–96), *Bathing Water Quality in England and Wales in 1990*, Bristol, National Rivers Authority.

NRA (1992), *Bathing Water Quality in England and Wales in 1991*, Bristol, National Rivers Authority.

NRA (1993), *Bathing Water Quality in England and Wales in 1992*, Bristol, National Rivers Authority.

NRA (1994), *Bathing Water Quality in England and Wales in 1993*, Bristol, National Rivers Authority.

NRA (1995), *Bathing Water Quality in England and Wales in 1994*, Bristol, National Rivers Authority.

NRA (1996), *Bathing Water Quality in England and Wales in 1995*, Bristol, National Rivers Authority.

Nugent, Neill (1994), *The Government and Politics of the European Community* (3rd edition), London, Macmillan.

OECD (1991), *The State of the Environment*, Paris, Organisation for Economic Cooperation and Development.

OECD (1993), *Environmental Performance Reviews: Germany*, Paris, Organisation for Economic Cooperation and Development.

OECD (1994), *Environmental Performance Reviews: United Kingdom*, Paris, Organisation for Economic Cooperation and Development.

OJ (various years), Official Journal of the European Communities, Luxembourg, Office for Official Publications of the European Communities.

Osborn, Derek (1990), The impact of EC environmental policies on UK public administration, paper presented at the Royal Institute of Public Administration Conference, 21 September, unpublished mimeo.

Page, Edward (1997), *People Who Run Europe*, Oxford, Oxford University Press.

Paterson, William (1989), 'Environmental politics', in G. Smith *et al.* (eds), *Developments in West German Politics*, London, Macmillan, 267–88.

Peake, Stephen (1997), *Vehicle and Fuel Challenges Beyond 2000. Market Impacts of the EU's Auto-Oil Programme*, London, Financial Times Automotive Publishing.

Pearce, Fred (1981), 'The unspeakable beaches of Britain', *New Scientist*, 16 July, 139–42.

Pehle, Heinrich (1997), 'Domestic obstacles to an environmental forerunner', in M. S. Andersen and D. Liefferink (eds), 161–209.

Pehle, Heinrich (1998), *Das Bundesministerium für Umwelt, Naturschutz und Reaktorsicherheit: Ausgegrenzt statt integriert?*, Wiesbaden, Deutscher Universitäts Verlag.

Peters, Guy (1992), 'Bureaucratic politics and the institutions of the European Community', in A. Sbragia (ed.), 75–122.

Peters, Guy (1996), 'Agenda-setting in the European Union', in J. Richardson (ed.), 61–76.

Peters, Guy (1997), 'Escaping the joint-decision trap: repetition and sectoral politics in the European Union', *West European Politics* 20:2, 22–36.

Peterson, John (1992), 'The European technology community: policy networks in a supranational setting', in D. Marsh and R. Rhodes (eds), 226–48.

Peterson, John (1995a), 'Policy-making in the European Union: towards a framework of analysis', *Journal of European Public Policy* 2:1, 69–74.

Peterson, John (1995b), Policy networks and European Union policy making: a reply to Kassim', *West European Politics* 18:2, 389–407.

Peterson, John (1997), 'States, societies and the European Union', *West European Politics* 20:4, 1–23.

Peterson, John and Elisabeth Bomberg (1999), *Decision-Making in the European Union*, London, Macmillan.

PHLS (1959), 'Sewage contamination of coastal bathing waters in England and Wales', *Journal of Hygiene* 57:4, 435–72.

Pierson, Paul (1998), 'The path to European integration: a historical-institutionalist analysis', in W. Sandholtz and A. Stone Sweet (eds), 92–133.

Pierson, Paul and Leibfried, Stephan (1995), 'Multi-tiered institutions and the making of social policy', in S. Leibfried and P. Pierson (eds), *European Social Policy*, Washington, DC, Brookings Institute, 1–40.

Pinder, John (1991), *European Community. The Building of a Union*, Oxford, Oxford University Press.

Porter, Gareth and Janet Brown (1996), *Global Environmental Politics* (2nd edition), Boulder, CO, Westview Press.

Porter, Martin (1997), 'Cross-national policy networks and the EU's packaging and packaging waste directive', in D. Liefferink and M. S. Andersen (eds), 83–110.

Presidency Conclusions (1988), Die Wasserpolitik der Europäischen Gemeinschaften. Minister Seminar, 27–28 Juni, Sheraton Hotel, Frankfurt, unpublished mimeo.

Prittwitz, Volker von (1984), *Umweltaußenpolitik*, Frankfurt, Campus Verlag.

Prüss, Annette (1998), 'Review of epidemiological studies on health effects from exposure to recreational water', *International Journal of Epidemiology* 27, 1–9.

RCEP (1976), *Fifth Report: Air Pollution: An Integrated Approach*, Royal Commission on Environmental Pollution, Cm 6371, London, HMSO.

RCEP (1983), *Ninth Report: Lead in Petrol, Royal Commission on Environmental Pollution*, Cm 8852, London, HMSO.

RCEP (1984), *Tenth Report: Tackling Pollution-Experience and Prospects*, Royal Commission on Environmental Pollution, Cmnd 9149, London, HMSO.

RCEP (1988), *Twelfth Report: Best Practicable Environmental Option*, Royal Commission on Environmental Pollution, Cm 310, London, HMSO.

RCEP (1994), *Eighteenth Report: Transport and the Environment*, Royal Commission on Environmental Pollution, Cmnd 2674, London, HMSO.

RCEP (1997), *Transport and the Environment – Developments since 1994. Twentieth Report*, Royal Commission on Environmental Pollution, Cm 3752, London, Stationery Office.

RCEP (1998), *Setting Environmental Standards. Twenty-First Report*, Royal Commission on Environmental Pollution, Cm 4053, London, Stationery Office.

Rehbinder, Eckard (1992), 'Rethinking environmental policy', in G. Smith, W. E. Paterson, P. Merkl and S. Padgett (eds) (1992), *Developments in German Politics*, London, Macmillan, 227–46.

Rehbinder, Eckard and Richard Stewart (1985a), *Integration Through Law. Europe and the American Federal Experience*, Berlin, Walter de Gruyter.

Rehbinder, Eckard and Richard Stewart (1985b), 'Legal integration in federal systems: European Community environmental law', *American Journal of Comparative Law* 33:3, 371–441.

Richardson, Jeremy (ed.) (1982), *Policy Styles in Western Europe*, London, Allen & Unwin.

Richardson, Jeremy (1994), 'EU water policy: uncertain agendas, shifting networks and complex coalitions', *Environmental Politics* 3:4, 139–67.

Richardson, Jeremy (ed.) (1996), *European Union. Power and Policy-Making*, London, Routledge.

Richardson, Jeremy (1996a), 'Policy-making in the EU: interests, ideas and garbage cans of primeval soup', in J. Richardson (ed.), 3–23.

Richardson, Jeremy (1996b), 'Eroding EU policies: implementation gaps, cheating and re-steering', in J. Richardson (ed.), 278–94.

Richardson, Jeremy, William Maloney and Wolfgang Rüdig (1992), 'The dynamics of policy change: lobbying and water privatisation', *Public Administration* 70, summer, 157–75.

Richardson, Jeremy and N. Watts (1986), *National Policy Styles and the Environment. Britain and West Germany Compared*, Berlin, Science Centre.

Risse-Kappen, Thomas (1996), 'Exploring the nature of the beast: international relations theory and comparative policy analysis meet the European Union', *Journal of Common Market Studies* 34:1, 53–80.

Robens Institute (1987), *The Public Health Implications of Sewage Pollution of Bathing Water*, Guildford, Robens Institute of Industrial and Environmental Health and Safety, University of Surrey.

Robinson, Mike (1992), *The Greening of British Party Politics*, Manchester, Manchester University Press.

Rosamond, Ben (2000), *Theories of European Integration*, London, Macmillan.

Rose, Chris (1990), *The Dirty Man of Europe. The Great British Pollution Scandal*, London, Simon and Schuster.

Rose-Ackermann, Susan (1995), *Controlling Environmental Policy. The Limits of Public Law in Germany and the United States*, New Haven, CT, Yale University Press.

Ross, George (1995), *Jaques Delors and European Integration*, Cambridge, Polity Press.

Rowlands, Ian (1992), 'Environmental issues in world politics', in J. Baylis and N. Rengger (eds), *Dilemmas of World Politics. International Issues in a Changing World*, Oxford, Clarendon Press, 287–309.

Rowlands, Ian (1994), *The Politics of Global Climate Change*, Manchester, Manchester University Press.

Rowlands, Ian (1995), *The Politics of Global Atmospheric Change*, Manchester, Manchester University Press.

Rüdig, Wolfgang (2000), 'Phasing out nuclear energy in Germany', *German Politics* 9:3, 43–80.

Rustow, Dankwart and Kenneth Erickson (eds) (1991), *Comparative Political Dynamics: Global Research Perspectives*, New York, Harper Collins.

Sabatier, Paul (1993), 'Policy change over a decade or more', in P. Sabatier and H. Jenkins-Smith (eds), 13–41.

Sabatier, Paul (1998), 'The advocacy coalition framework: revisions and relevance for Europe', *Journal of European Public Policy* 5:1, 98–130.

Sabatier, Paul (1999), 'The need for better theories', in Paul Sabatier (ed.), *Theories of the Policy Process*, Boulder, CO, Westview Press, 3–18.

Sabatier, Paul (ed.) (1999), *Theories of the Policy Process*, Boulder, CO, Westview Press.

Sabatier, Paul and Hank Jenkins-Smith (eds) (1993), *Policy Change and Learning. An Advocacy Coalition Approach*, Boulder, CO, Westview Press.

Sandholtz, Wayne (1992), 'Choosing union: Monetary politics and Maastricht', *International Organisation* 47:1, 1–40.

Sandholtz, Wayne and John Zysman (1989), '1992: Recasting the European bargain', *World Politics* XLII, 95–128.

Sandholtz, Wayne and Alec Stone Sweet (eds), (1998), *European Integration and Supranational Governance*, Oxford, Oxford University Press.

Sands, Philippe (1991), 'European Community environmental law: the evolution of a regional regime of international environmental protection', *The Yale Law Journal* 110, 2511–23.

Sbragia, Alberta (ed.) (1992), *Euro-Politics: Institutions and Policy-Making in the 'New' European Union*, Washington, DC, Brookings Institute.

Sbragia, Alberta (1996), 'Environmental Policy', in H. Wallace and W. Wallace (eds), 235–56.

Sbragia, Alberta (2000), 'Environmental policy: economic constraints and external pressures', in H. Wallace and W. Wallace (eds), 293–316.

Scharpf, Fritz W. (1988), 'The joint-decision trap: lessons from German federalism and European integration', *Public Administration* 66, autumn, 239–78.

Scharpf, Fritz W. (1994), 'Community and autonomy: multi-level policy-making in the European Union', *Journal of European Public Policy* 1:2, 219–42.

Scharpf, Fritz W. (1996), 'Negative and positive integration in the political economy of European welfare states', in Gary Marks, Fritz W. Scharpf, Philippe Schmitter and Wolfgang Streeck (eds), *Governance in the European Union*, London, Sage, 15–39.

Schleswig-Holsteinischer *Landtag* (1993), *Bericht der Landesregierung. Auswirkungen der Badestellenverordnung*, Schleswig-Holsteinischer *Landtag*, Drucksache 13/1328, 23 September.

Schmitter, Philippe (1974), 'Still the century of corporatism?', *Review of Politics* 36, 85–131.

Schröder, Gerhard (1989), 'Alternativen in der Umweltschutzpolitik', in H. Donner, G. Magoulas, J. Simon and R. Wolf (eds), *Umweltschutz zwischen Staat und Markt*, Baden-Baden, Nomos Verlag, 43–58.

Schulte, Hans, (1999), *Umweltrecht*, Heidelberg, C. F. Müller Verlag.

Schumann, Wolfgang (1996), *Neue Wege in der Integrationstheorie,* Opladen, Leske & Budrich.

Scott, Joanne (1998), *Environmental Law*, London, Longman.

Searles, R. A. (1987), 'The application of autocatalysts for emission control for small cars and higher speeds', in EEB (ed.), 34–50.

Second International Conference on the Protection of the North Sea (1987), *Ministerial Declaration*, London, 24–5 November.

Shibata, Tokue (1979), 'Der Erfolg mit der Automobilindustrie: Bürger und Kommunalpolitiker erzwingen strengere Abgasregelungen', in S. Tsuru, and H. Weidner (eds), *Ein Modell für uns: die Erfolge der japanischen Umweltpolitik*, Kiepenheuer & Witsch, 141–53.

Siedentopf, Heinrich and J. Ziller (eds) (1988), *Making European Policies Work. The Implementation of Community Legislation in the Member States*, Vol. I, London, Sage Publications.

SMMT (1993), *Motor Industry of Great Britain. World Automotive Statistics*, London, Society of Motor Manufacturers and Traders Limited.

Sprinz, Detlef and Tapani Vaahtoranta (1994), 'The interest-based explanation of international environmental policy', *International Organization* 48:1, winter, 77–105.

SRU (1973), *Auto und Umwelt. Sondergutachten*, Wiesbaden, Der Rat von Sachverständigen für Umweltfragen.

SRU (1978), *Umweltgutachten 1978*, Bundestags, Drucksache 8/1938.

SRU (1983), *Waldschäden und Luftverunreinigungen*, Wiesbaden, Der Rat von Sachverständigen für Umweltfragen

SRU (1996), *Kurzfassung des Umweltgutachtens 1998*, Wiesbaden, Der Rat von Sachverständigen für Umweltfragen.

SRU (1998), *Umweltgutachten 1998*, Wiesbaden, Der Rat von Sachverständigen für Umweltfragen.

Stevenson, A. H. (1953), 'Studies of bathing water quality and health', *American Journal of Public Health* 43, 529–38.

Stopford, John and Susan Strange (1991), *Rival States, Rival Firms. Competition for World Markets*, Cambridge, Cambridge University Press.

Strange, Susan (1983), '*Cave! Hic dragones*: a critique of regime analysis', in S. Krasner (ed.), 337–54.

Strange, Susan (1988), *States and Markets. An Introduction to International Political Economy*, London, Pinter.

Strübel, Michael (1992), 'Nationale Interessen und europäische Politik-formulierung in der Umweltpolitik', *Politische Vierteljahresschrift* 30:2, 274–91.

Taylor, Paul (1983), *The Limits of European Integration*, London, Croom Helm.

Taylor, Paul (1991), 'British sovereignty and the European Community: what is at risk?', *Millennium* 20:1, 73–80.

Taylor, Paul (1996), *The European Union in the 1990s*, Oxford, Oxford University Press.

Thatcher, Margaret (1993), *The Downing Street Years*, London, Harper Collins.

Tidy Britain Group (1992–2000), *The Seaside Awards*, Norwich, Tidy Britain Group.

Töpfer, Klaus (1989a), 'Ecological modernisation of the industrialised state: A Federal perspective', in T. Ellwein, H. Donnel, G. Margoulas, J. Simon and R. Wolf (eds), *Yearbook on Government and Public Administration*, Baden-Baden, Nomos Verlagsgesellschaft, 489–520.

Töpfer, Klaus (1989b), 'Kampagne "Kat sei Dank"', *Umwelt* 10, 456–7.

Töpfer, Klaus (1989c), 'Perspektiven einer mittlefristigen Umweltpolitik', in H. Donner, G. Margoulas, J. Simon and R. Wolf (eds), *Umweltschutz zwischen Staat und Markt. Moderne Konzeptionen im Umweltschutz*, Baden-Baden, Nomos Verlag, 15–30.

Tsebelis, George (1994), 'The power of the European Parliament as a conditional agenda setter', *American Political Science Review* 88:1, 128–42.

Tsebelis, George and Geoffrey Garrett (1997), 'Agenda setting, vetoes and the European Union's co-decision procedure', *The Journal of Legislative Studies* 3:3, 74–92.

Turner, Ian (1988), *Environmental Policy in Europe: Uniformity or Diversity? A Case Study of the EEC Car Emissions Decisions*, Henley-on-Thames, Henley, Management College.

UBA (1985), *Der Weg zum Katalysator – Randbedingungen und Auswirkungen der neuen PKW-Abgasvorschriften*, Berlin, Umweltbundesamt, Erich Schmidt Verlag.

UBA (1992), *Umweltauswirkungen von Tempolimits*, Berlin, Umweltbundesamt.

UBA (1995), *Passenger Cars 2000*, Berlin, Umweltbundesamt.

UBA (1997a), *Daten zur Umwelt. Der Zustand der Umwelt in Deutschland*, Berlin, Erich Schmidt Verlag.

UBA (1997b), *Umweltschutz und Beschäftigung. Brückenschlag für eine lebenswerte Zukunft*, Berlin, Umweltbundesamt.

UBA (1999), *Umweltauswirkungen von Geschwindigkeitsbeschränkungen*, Berlin, Umweltbundesamt.

Underdal, Arild and Kenneth Hanf (eds) (1999), *International Environmental Agreements and Domestic Politics. The Case of Acid Rain*, Aldershot, Ashgate.

UNECE (1984), *Summary Record of the Multilateral Conference on the Environment in Munich*, United Nations Economic Commissions for Europe, M2/1 Info – D/E/F/R.

Ungerer, Brigitte and Franz van Waarden (eds) (1995), *Convergence and Divergence? Internationalisation and Economic Policy Response*, Aldershot, Avesbury.

USITC (1984), *The U.S. Auto Industry: U.S. Factory Sales, Retail Sales, Imports, Exports, Apparent Consumption*, Washington, DC, United States International Trade Commission.

VDA (1974), *Auto 73/74*, Frankfurt, Verband der Automobilindustrie.
VDA (1981), *Auto 80/81*, Frankfurt, Verband der Automobilindustrie.
VDA (1983), *Auto 82/83*, Frankfurt, Verband der Automobilindustrie.
VDA (1984), *Auto 83/84*, Frankfurt, Verband der Automobilindustrie.
VDA (1985), *Auto 84/85*, Frankfurt, Verband der Automobilindustrie.
VDA (1987), *Auto 86/87*, Frankfurt, Verband der Automobilindustrie.
VDA (1995a), *International Auto Statistics*, Frankfurt, Verband der Automobilindustrie.
VDA (1995b), *Tatsachen und Zahlen aus der Kraftverkehrswirtschaft*, Frankfurt, Verband der Automobilindustrie.
VDA (1996), *Daten zur Automobilwirtschaft*, Frankfurt, Verband der Automobilindustrie.
VDA (2000a), *International Auto Statistics*, Frankfurt, Verband der Automobilindustrie.
Vogel, David (1986), *National Styles of Regulation: Environmental Policy in Great Britain and the United States*, Ithaca, NY, Cornell University Press.
Vogel, David (1993), 'Environmental policy in the European Community', in S. Kamieniecki (ed.), 181–98.
Vogel, David (1995), *Trading Up: Consumer and Environmental Regulation in a Global Economy*, Cambridge, MA, Harvard University Press.
Vogel, David (1997), 'Trading up and governing across: transnational governance and environmental protection', *European Public Policy* 4:4, 556–71.
Waarden, Franz van (1995), 'Persistence of national policy styles: a study of their institutional foundations', in B. Ungerer and F. van Waarden (eds), 333–72.
Wallace, David (1995), *Environmental Policy and Industrial Innovation. Strategies in Europe, the US and Japan*, London, Earthscan Publications.
Wallace, Helen (1984), 'Implementation across national boundaries', in D. Lewis and W. Wallace (eds), *Politics and Practice*, London, Heineman, 193–206.
Wallace, Helen (1987), 'Negotiation, conflict, and compromise: the elusive pursuit of common policies', in Wallace, Helen, William Wallace and Carol Webb (eds) (1987), *Policy-Making in the European Community*, Chichester, John Wiley & Sons (first published 1977), 43–80.
Wallace, Helen (1990a), 'Making multilateral negotiations work', in W. Wallace (ed.) (1990), *The Dynamics of European Integration*, London, Pinter, 213–28.
Wallace, Helen (1996a), 'Politics and policy in the EU: the challenge of governance', in H. Wallace and W. Wallace (eds) (1996), 3–36.

Wallace, Helen (1996b), 'The institutions of the EU: experience and experiments', in H. Wallace and W. Wallace (eds), 37–68.

Wallace, Helen and William Wallace (eds), (1996), *Policy-Making in the European Union* (3rd editon), Oxford, Oxford University Press.

Wallace, Helen and Alasdair Young (eds) (1997), *Participation and Policy- Making in the European Union,* Oxford, Oxford University Press.

Wallace, Helen and William Wallace (eds) (2000), *Policy-Making in the European Union* (4th edition), Oxford, Oxford University Press.

Wallace, William (1987), 'Less than a federation, more than a regime: the community as a political system', in H. Wallace, W. Wallace and C. Webb (eds), *Policy-Making in the European Community*, Chichester, John Wiley & Sons, 373–402.

Walsh, Michael (1987), 'Motor vehicle air pollution control in Europe: an overview', in EEB (ed.), 18–33.

Walsh, Michael (1988), 'Saubere Autos für die Weltmärkte – Wird die EG den Rückstand aufholen können oder das Nachsehen haben?', *Europäische Umwelt* 1, 46–7.

Ward, Neil, (1998), 'Water quality', in P. Lowe and S. Ward (eds), *British Environmental Policy and Europe*, London, Routledge, 244–64.

Ward, Neil, Henry Buller and Philip Lowe (1995), *Implementing European Environmental Policy at the Local Level: The British Experience With Water Quality Directives*, Newcastle, University of Newcastle upon Tyne, Centre for Rural Economy.

Ward, Neil, Philip Lowe and Henry Buller (1997), 'Implementing European water quality directives: lessons for sustainable development', in S. Baker, M. Kousis, D. Richardson and S. Young (eds), *The Politics of Sustainable Development*, London, Routledge, 198–217.

Warleigh, Alex (2000), 'The hustle: citizenship practice, NGOs and "policy coalitions" in the European Union – the cases of Auto-Oil, drinking water and unit pricing', *Journal of European Public Policy* 7:2, 229–43.

Weale, Albert (1992a), *The New Politics of Pollution*, Manchester, Manchester University Press.

Weale, Albert (1992b), 'Vorsprung durch Technik? The politics of German environmental regulation', in K. Dyson (ed.), 159–83.

Weale, Albert (1993), 'Ecological modernisation and the integration of European environmental policy', in D. Liefferink, P. Lowe and A. Mol (eds), 196–216.

Weale, Albert (1996a), 'Environmental rules and rule-making in the European Union', *Journal of European Public Policy* 3:4, 594–611.

Weale, Albert (1996b), 'Environmental regulation and administrative reform in Britain', in G. Majone (ed.), 106–30.

Weale, Albert (1997) 'United Kingdom', in M. Jänicke and H. Weidner (eds), 89–108.

Weale, Albert (1999), 'European environmental policy by stealth: the dysfunctionality of functionalism', *Environment and Planning. Government and Policy C* 17:1, 37–52.

Weale, Albert and Andrea Williams (1995), 'The single market and environmental policy', in P. Furlong and A. Cox (eds), *The European Union at the Crossroads. Problems in Implementing the Single Market Project*, Boston, Earlsgate Press, 131–60.

Weale, Albert, Timothy O'Riordan and Louise Kramme (1991), *Controlling Pollution in the Round. Change and Choice in Environmental Regulation in Britain and West Germany*, London, Anglo-German Foundation.

Weale, Albert, Geoffrey Pridham, Michelle Cini, Dimitrios Konstadakopulos, Martin Porter and Brendan Flynn (2000), *Environmental Governance in Europe*, Oxford, Oxford University Press.

Weale, Albert, Geoffrey Pridham, Andrea Williams and Martin Porter (1996), 'Environmental administration in six European states: sectoral convergence or national distinctiveness?', *Public Administration* 74, 255–74.

Webster, Ruth (1998), 'Environmental collective action: stable patterns of co-operation and issue alliances at the European level', in J. Greenwood and M. Aspinwall (eds), *Collective Action in the European Union. Interests and the New Politics of Associability*, London, Routledge, 176–95.

Wiedenmann, A., W. Langhammer and K. Botzenhart (1988), 'Enterobakterien als Qualitätskriterium bei Roh-, Trink- und Badewasser. Vergleichende Untersuchung über das Vorkommen von Enterobakterien, Eschericia coli, coliformen Keimen, Koloniezahl, Fäkalstreptokokken und Peudomonas aeruginosa', *Zentralblatt für Hygiene* B 187, 91–106.

Weidner, Helmut (1989), *Die Umweltpolitik der konservativ–liberalen Regierung im Zeitraum 1983 bis 1988: Versuch einer politikwissenschaftlichen Bewertung*, Research Working Paper, Berlin, Science Centre.

Weiler, Joseph H. H. (1991), 'The transformation of Europe', *The Yale Law Journal* 100, 2401–83.

Weinstock, Ulrich (1984), 'Nur eine europäische Umwelt? Europäische Umwelt im Spannungsverhältnis von ökologischer Vielfalt und ökonomischer Einheit', in Ebenhand Grabitz (ed.) *Abgestufte Integration: eine Alternative zum herkömmlichen Integrationskonzept?*, Kehl, N.P. Engel Verlag, 301–44.

Weizsäcker, Ernst U. von (1997), *Erdpolitik* (5th edition), Darmstadt, Wissenschaftliche Buchgesellschaft.

Wessels, Wolfgang (1997), 'An ever closer fusion? A dynamic macropolitical view on integration processes', *Journal of Common Market Studies* 35:2, 267–99.

Westheide, Eberhard (1987), *Die Einführung bleifreien Benzins und schadstoffarmer PKW in der Bundesrepublik Deutschland mit Hilfe ökonomischer Anreize*, Berlin, Erich Schmidt Verlag.

Wey, Klaus-Georg (1982), *Kurze Geschichte des Umweltschutzes in Deutschland seit 1990*, Opladen, Westdeutscher Verlag.

WHO (1974), *Health Criteria for the Quality of Recreational Waters with Special Reference to Coastal Waters and Beaches*, Ostend, World Health Organisation, Proceedings of the Conference of 13–17 March.

WHO (1975), Guides and Criteria for Recreational Quality of Beaches and Coastal Waters, Copenhagen, World Health Organisation, unpublished mimeo.

WHO (1998), *Draft Guidelines for Safe Recreational-Water Environments: Coastal and Fresh-Waters*, EOS/DRAFT/98.14, Geneva, World Health Organisation.

WHO (1999), *Health Based Monitoring of Recreational Waters: The Feasibility of a New Approach (The 'Annapolis Protocol')*, WHO/SDE/99.1, Geneva, World Health Organisation.

Wildavsky, Aaron (1995), *But Is it True? A Citizen's Guide to Environmental Health and Safety Issues'*, Cambridge, MA, Harvard University Press.

Wilks, Stephen (1984), *Industrial Policy and the Motor Industry*, Manchester, Manchester University Press.

Wilks, Stephen and Maurice Wright (eds) (1987), *Comparative Government–Industrial Relations. Western Europe, the United States and Japan*, Oxford, Clarendon Press.

Williams, Rhiannon (1995), 'The European Commission and enforcement of environmental law: an invidious position', in A. Barav and D. Wyatt (eds), *Yearbook of European Law*, Vol. 14: 1994, Oxford, Clarendon Press, 351–99.

Wilson, Des (1983), *The Lead Scandal. The Fight to Save Children from Damage by Lead in Petrol*, London, Heinemann Educational Books.

Winzer, Matthias (1990), Die PKW-Abgaspolitik in der Bundesrepublik Deutschland bis 1984, Berlin, Free University of Berlin, unpublished diploma dissertation.

Woolcock, Stephen, Michael Hodges and Kirstin Schreiber (1991), *Britain, Germany and 1992. The Limits of Deregulation*, London, Pinter.

World Bank (1995), *The German Water and Sewerage Sector: How Well it Works and What this Means for Developing Countries*, Washington, DC, World Bank.

Wurzel, Rüdiger K. W. (1993), 'Environmental policy', in J. Lodge (ed.), *The European Community and the Challenge of the Future* (2nd edition), London, Pinter, 178–99.

Wurzel, Rüdiger K. W. (1995), 'The EU bathing water directive: a case for coastal management?', in D. Whitmarsh (ed.), *Management Techniques in the Coastal Zone*, Portsmouth, University of Portsmouth, 1–15.

Wurzel, Rüdiger K. W. (1996a), 'The role of the EU Presidency in the environmental field: does it make a difference which member state runs the Presidency?', *Journal of European Public Policy* 3:2, 272–91.

Wurzel, Rüdiger K. W. (1996b), 'What role can the Presidency play in co-ordinating European Union environmental policy-making? An Anglo-German comparison', *European Environmental Law Review* 5:3, 74–8.

Wurzel, Rüdiger K. W. (1999a), Britain, Germany and the European Union: environmental policy-making from 1972–97, unpublished PhD thesis, London School of Economics.

Wurzel, Rüdiger K. W. (1999b), 'The role of the European Parliament: Interview with Ken Collins MEP', *The Journal of Legislative Studies* 5:2, 1–23.

Wurzel, Rüdiger K. W. (2000), 'Flying into unexpected turbulence: the German EU Presidency in the environmental field', *German Politics* 9:3, 23–42.

Wurzel, Rüdiger K. W. (2001), 'The EU Presidency and integration principle: an Anglo-German comparison', *European Environmental Law Review* 10:1, 5–15.

Wyer, M. D., G. Jackson, D. Kay, J. Yeo and H. Dawson (1994), 'An assessment of the impact of inland surface water input to the bacteriological quality of coastal waters', *Journal of the Institution of Water and Environmental Management* 8, 459–67.

Young, Oran (1989), *International Co-operation. Building Regimes for Natural Resources and the Environment*, Ithaca, NY, Cornell University Press.

Young, Oran (1993), 'International organisations and international institutions: lessons learned from environmental regimes', in S. Kamieniecki (ed.), 145–64.

Zito, Anthony, (2000), *Creating Environmental Policy in the European Union*, London, Macmillan.

Index

acid rain, 8, 88, 116, 118, 122
advocacy coalitions, 47–9, 73, 79, 214, 269
algae, 198, 222
amenity issues, 189, 238–9
Andersen, Mikael, 18, 43, 79–80, 102, 231
Anderson, Charles, 19
Anderson, Mary, 17, 96
Annapolis Protocol (1998), 251
Annual Reports on Monitoring and Application of Community Law, 68
Arp, Henning, 124, 134, 145
Ashby, Eric, 17
Ashby, Lord, 96, 189, 197, 228
Association of European Automobile Constructors (ACEA), 141, 267
Auto Emissions 2000 Symposium (Brussels, 1992), 157
Automobile Association, British, 127
Automobile Association, German (ADAC), 110, 118–19, 224
Automobile Industry Association, German (VDA), 95, 110

Baiersbronn meeting (1972), 95
Bangemann, Manfred, 120
Bastram, Jamie, 251
bathing bans, 195, 220, 223
bathing water reports, 193–4, 201, 205–11, 257
bathing waters, number of, 207–13, 219–22
Baum, Gerhart, 116
Bavaria, 116, 220
Beckett, Margaret, 13
Bell, Stuart, 27

benzene, 163, 166, 173
best available techniques/technology not entailing excessive costs (BATNEEC), principle of, 26, 29–31, 142, 163, 228, 266
best available technology (BAT), principle of, 19, 22–30 *passim*, 94–6, 106, 115, 119, 141–2, 161, 175, 222, 224, 230–3, 248, 260–1, 264–7
best practicable environmental option (BPEO), 19, 26–7
best practicable means (BPM), 19, 26–9 *passim*, 103, 228, 266
Beyme, Klaus von, 18
Bilthoven meeting on recreational water quality (1974), 184–7, 189, 197, 239, 251
Birk, Baroness, 195
Blackpool, 212–16
Blair, Tony, 13, 62
Blue Flags, 219, 224–6
BMW, 119, 121, 130–1
Bohne, Eberhard, 46
Brabazon of Tara, Lord, 124
Brendle, Uwe, 72, 120
Brighton, 212
Brinkhorst, Laurens, 70
British Leyland, 124, 129, 131, 143–4; *see also* Rover Cars
Brown, Gordon, 13, 174
Brundtland Report, 162
Byatt, Ian, 218–19

Cabelli, V., 245
Caldwell, Lynton, 19
California, 86, 93–4

Calvet, Jacques, 127, 140
carbon dioxide emissions, 8–9, 88, 173
carbon monoxide emissions, 9, 88–92
    passim, 96, 173
catalytic converters, 93, 95, 99, 101, 104,
    106, 110–11, 115–37 *passim*, 144–8,
    155, 258, 263
Christian Democratic Party of Germany
    (CDU), 12, 16, 61, 116–17, 145,
    160
Christian Social Union (CSU), 12, 16,
    61, 117, 120, 141, 149, 238
Clean Air Acts
    American, 93
    British, 96–7
climate change, 7–8, 43
Clinton-Davis, Stanley, 30, 67, 125, 141,
    145, 159, 213, 266
Coastal Anti-Pollution League, 214, 227
co-decision procedure, 71, 166, 261
Collins, Ken, 71, 137, 168–71
Commission of the EU, 9, 14, 26, 40,
    46–50, 59–60, 64, 76–9, 101–2, 105,
    163, 170–1, 180, 188, 233, 238, 241,
    250, 252, 258–61, 269, 271
    DG Energy, 157
    DG Environment, 58, 65–73, 110,
        121, 141, 147–8, 157–62, 175,
        214, 239, 247, 249, 265–7
    DG Industry, 65–7, 110, 121, 141,
        147–8, 157, 159–60, 175, 265–7
    DG Science, 249
    DG Transport, 159–60
    Legal Unit, 66–7, 70, 213, 220
    staffing of, 66–7
    White Paper on Growth,
        Competitiveness and
        Employment (1994), 13–14
Committee of Common Market
    Automobile Constructors (CCMC),
    140–1, 267
Committee of Regions, 59
CONCAWE, 139, 147
Conciliation Committee, 71, 166–71, 174
Conservation Society, 104
Conservative Party, 62–3, 71, 102, 141,
    143, 168, 211
consolidated directive on car emissions
    (1991), 136–7, 146–7, 155, 261
consultation procedure of the EU, 58,
    70–1
consultative forum on environmental
    issues, 73

Control of Pollution Act (1974), 24,
    205–6
cooperation principle, 28, 162
cooperation procedure of the EU, 71,
    136–7
COREPER, 61, 139, 190
Cornwall, 212
corporate environmental laggards, 74,
    127
corporatism, 17, 44, 95
cost
    of improving water quality, 191–3,
        218–19
    of limiting car emissions, 164–5,
        170
cost-effectiveness, 159, 166, 171
Council of Environmental Experts,
    German (SRU), 73, 117
Council of Ministers, European, 58; *see
    also* Environmental Council of the
    EU
'critical loads' concept, 22–3
Currie, Jim, 66

Davignon, Viscount, 131
Davignon values, 138
Degussa (company), 130
Delahunty, A., 244
Delors, Jacques, 137, 238
Department of the Environment (DoE),
    26, 103
Department of the Environment, Food
    and Rural Affairs (DEFRA),
    Britain, 4, 12–13, 63
Department of the Environment,
    Transport and the Regions
    (DETR), Britain, 4, 12–13, 63
Department of Transport (DoT), 63,
    103, 125–6
diesel engine technology, 133–4, 155–6
dilute-and-disperse policy, 7, 228–30
Diplock, Lord, 195
directives of the EU, 75; *see also*
    implementation; transposition
Dollinger, Werner, 116
dying forests, 90, 122–3
Dyson, Kenneth, 18

Earth Summit (1992), 162
ecological modernisation, 10–14, 30, 61,
    119, 233, 263, 266
ecological vulnerability, 7–9, 23, 30,
    233, 263–4, 273

economic capacities of states, 9–10, 30, 233, 264, 273
Economic and Social Committee (ECOSOC), 59, 190
Economic Commission for Europe *see* United Nations
economic miracle (*Wirtschaftswunder*), 94
Economics Ministry (BMWi), Germany, 11, 59–62, 121, 140, 160, 194, 266
Eisma, Doeke, 166
emission limits, 19–26, 78; *see also* uniform emission limits
Emissions, Fuels and Engine Technologies (EPEFE) programme, 157–8
ENDS Report, 251
Environment Agency for England and Wales, 27, 63
Environment Watch: Western Europe, 66–7, 69
Environmental Action Programmes (EAPs) of the EU, 13–14, 23, 29, 76, 78, 101, 162, 184–5, 188, 245
Environmental Agency, Germany (UBA), 10, 29, 62, 100, 118–19, 138, 140, 160, 257–60
environmental awareness, 14–16, 137, 146, 148, 244, 248, 260
Environmental Council of the EU, 14, 58, 60, 64, 77, 102, 104, 138, 142, 146, 161, 165–6, 170–1, 184, 190–1, 195, 201, 241–2, 252, 257, 261–2
environmental groups, 16, 29, 67, 72–3, 107, 110, 116–17, 120, 224, 233; *see also* non-governmental organizations
environmental laggards, 74, 77, 127, 231, 273
environmental leaders, 4–8, 37, 50, 72–7 *passim*, 99–101, 115, 210, 229, 234, 259, 264, 273
Environmental Ministry, Germany (BMU), 4, 11–12, 59–62, 160, 174, 210, 220, 223, 260
environmental quality objectives (EQOs), 19–25, 31, 66, 69, 78, 84, 105, 157, 160–3, 171–5, 219, 259, 265
environmental regulatory styles, 18–19, 110–11, 147–8, 175, 201–2, 233–4
epidemiological studies (of bathing waters), 244–51

epistemic communities, 47, 73, 201, 252, 269
Eschericia coli (*E. coli*), 186, 197, 239, 245, 249–51
EU Rundschreiben, 72
European Bureau of Consumers' Associations (BEUC), 107, 139, 141
European Council, 58–9
  Paris meeting (October 1972), 59, 75
  Edinburgh meeting (December 1992), 59
European Court of Justice (ECJ), 49, 59, 70, 212–16, 223–4, 233, 257, 271
European Environment Bureau (EEB), 70, 72, 107, 127, 139, 141, 267–8
European Environmental Agency (EEA), 9, 59, 73, 163
European Monetary Union, 238
European Parliament (EP), 14, 4 9, 58, 64, 70–1, 79, 104, 110, 126, 136–8, 148, 156, 161–75, 190–1, 201, 206, 213, 258, 261–2, 269, 271
European Programme on Emissions, Fuels and Engine Technologies (EPEFE), 157–8
European Regulations, Global Approach (ERGA), 105–8, 111, 161, 262
European Treaties
  Amsterdam Treaty, 41
  Maastricht Treaty, 40, 64, 166, 216, 238
  Rome Treaty, 41
  Single European Act, 40, 58, 64, 70
EUROPIA, 167, 170
Euroscepticism, 62, 195, 238
explanatory variables for environmental policy action, 5–6, 30
externalisation of environmental costs, 7

faecal coliform, 186–7, 197
Federation of Civil Engineering Contractors (FCEC), 213–14, 229
Fiat, 131–2, 145, 257
Finer, Samuel, 7
fines for non-compliance with EU law, 216
Fleisher, Jay, 247–8, 251
Fontaine, Nicole, 169
Ford-Germany, 121, 130–1
Ford-UK, 124–7, 131–2, 144, 263
forest damage *see* dying forests; *Waldsterben*
Forestry Commission, 123

Foundation for Environmental
    Education in Europe (FEEE), 225
France, 59, 76, 97–8, 166, 184–8, 245
Frankfurt water seminar (1988), 26
Friedrich, Axel, 118
Friends of the Earth (FoE), 123, 127,
    130, 141
fuel-injection technology, 129–30, 144

Gameson, A., 198
Gauvin, Bernard, 106, 139
Golden List of Beaches, 227–8
Golub, Jonathan, 191
Good Beach Guide, 227–8
Green Party
    British, 16
    German, 16, 29, 117
Greenaway, John, 24, 48
Greenpeace, 127, 130, 246
Gummer, John, 12

Haas, Ernst, 40
Haas, Peter, 47
Haigh, Nigel, 23, 102–5, 184, 212, 273
Hautala, Heidi, 166–7
Havemeister, Gerd, 247
Hayward, Jack, 45, 52
health risks, 88–9, 244–8
Heath, Edward, 195
Héritier, Adrienne, 5–6, 37, 68–9, 102, 273
Heseltine, Michael, 68, 216
Hey, Christian, 72, 120
high-chimney policy, 7–8, 228
Hix, Simon, 45–6
Hoffmann, Stanley, 41
Höller, Christiane, 248
Holman, Claire, 141
Holzinger, Katharina, 124, 134, 145
House of Commons
    Environment Committee (HCEC), 63,
        108, 127
    Select Committee on Welsh Affairs,
        189
House of Lords, 73
    Select Committee on the European
        Communities (HLSCEC), 63,
        126, 218–19, 244
Howard, Michael, 238
Howell, Denis, 185, 189–95 *passim*
Hucke, Jochen, 25

implementation deficit, 25, 51
implementation of EU directives, 205–6

'implied powers' doctrine, 75, 189
Inglehart, Ronald, 14
integrated pollution prevention and
    control (IPPC), 29
intergovernmentalist theory, 38–41,
    49–50, 258
Interior Ministry, Germany (BMI), 120,
    210, 223
Internal Market Council, 84
internal market project, 6, 40, 74–6,
    189
Ireland, 190
Isar, River, 220
island status of Britain, 7
issue networks, 44–5, 268
Italy, 184, 190, 196

Jackson, Caroline, 71
Japan, 94, 131
Johnson Matthey (company), 106, 121,
    126, 130, 258
Jordan, Andrew, 24, 48, 65, 191
Judge, David, 71

Kay, David, 246–8, 251
Keohane, Robert, 41
Kiechle, Ignaz, 116
King, Tom, 103
Kintore, Earl of, 212–13, 229–30
Knobling, Ansgar, 247
Kohl, Helmut, 117
Krämer, Ludwig, 66–8, 70, 213, 220
Krasner, Stephen, 42–3

Labour Party, 12–13, 127, 141, 151, 166,
    168, 195, 207, 211–12
Lambsdorff, Otto, 117
Land Rover cars, 134, 257
Länder Water Working Group (LAWA),
    210, 219, 223
Lange, Bernd, 166–70 *passim*
large combustion directive (1988), 134,
    145
Lawther report (1980), 103
lead in petrol, 95–6, 101–3; *see also*
    unleaded petrol
leadership in environmental matters,
    4–8, 37, 50, 72–7 *passim*, 99–101,
    115, 210, 229, 231, 234, 259, 264,
    273
lean-burn engines, 94, 106, 115, 123–38
    passim, 258, 263–4
Levitt, Ruth, 26, 184, 211

Liberal Democratic Party (FDP), 12, 16, 61–2, 95, 120, 149
Liefferink, Duncan, 18, 43, 49, 78–80, 102
lobbying, 71–4, 167, 258
Long, Tony, 72
Long Range Transboundary Air Pollution convention (LRTAP), 22, 43
long sea outfalls, 213, 229–30
López-Pila, Juan, 248
Los Angeles, 93
Lowi, Theodore, 17
Luxembourg Compromise (1966), 40
Luxembourg Compromise (1985), 115, 134–8, 143–4, 147, 260

Maastricht Treaty, 40, 64, 166, 216, 238
Macrory, Richard, 70
'Mainz Paper' (1975), 26
Major, John, 146
Mamére, Noël, 166–7
Marine Conservation Society, 227–8
Marine Pollution Bulletin, 213
Maruo, Kanehira, 94
Mazey, Sonia, 45
Meacher, Michael, 12, 63, 169
Mecklenburg West Pomerania, 220–1
media interest in environmental matters, 16, 73–4, 262
Mercedes, 121, 129–30, 134
Merkel, Angela, 160
microbiological analysis, 249–51
Ministry of Agriculture, Fisheries and Food (MAFF), Britain, 13
Mol, Arthur, 49
Molitor Report (1995), 14
'Monnet approach' to European integration, 40, 47
Moore, Brendan, 185–8
Motor Vehicle Emission Group (MVEG), 139–40, 143, 148, 162, 173, 175, 262, 268
Müller, Hans, 247
Müller, Werner, 62
multi-level governance in the EU, 42, 45, 74, 79, 258, 272–5
'Muskie laws', 93; *see also* Clean Air Acts, American

Narjes, Karl-Heinz, 67, 141
Nathan, Lord, 126

National (UK) Rivers Authority (NRA), 27, 215, 218–19
neofunctionalist theory, 39–41, 49–50, 71, 258, 268, 271–2
neopluralist theory, 45, 49–50, 234, 268, 272
neorealist theory, 39, 41–3, 268, 271–2
nitrogen oxides, 8–9, 88–92 *passim*, 122–3, 173
non-governmental organizations (NGOs), 71–2, 79, 107, 110, 148, 167, 201, 224, 239, 258, 262–8 *passim*
North, Douglas, 43
North Rhine Westphalia, 94
North Sea conferences, 214–15, 270
Nugent of Guildford, Lord, 198

Office of Water Services, 218–19
Opel, 121, 130–1, 141, 144
'optimisation' of pollution, 19, 22
Ordnungspolitik, 11
Organization for Economic Cooperation and Development (OECD), 8–9
Ostend meeting on recreational water quality (1972), 184–5, 187, 251
ozone levels (summer smog or tropospheric ozone concentrations), 7, 88, 122, 162–3, 173
Ozonoff, David, 246

particulate matter, 156, 164, 173
party politics, 16, 61–2, 67, 71
Pasteur Institute, Lille, 249–50, 269
Patten, Chris, 12, 68, 216
Peugeot (Peugeot-Citroën), 127, 131–2, 141, 267
policy brokers, 48–9
policy communities, 44–5, 80, 251–2, 269
policy cycles, 50–1
policy entrepreneurs, 73, 79, 86, 170, 201, 259, 261
policy network analysis, 43–6, 49–50, 58–9, 79–80, 234, 268–9, 272
policy spoilers, 73, 79, 86, 252, 259, 261
policy styles, 17–19; *see also* environmental regulatory styles
political salience of environmental issues, 14–16, 30, 201, 264, 273
'polluter pays' principle, 76
Porsche, 118, 130–1
post-unification Germany, 4, 8, 266
'postmaterialist' values, 14–15

precautionary principle
(*Vorsorgeprinzip*), 7, 26, 28, 187,
228, 248
Prescott, John, 12
professional associations, 28–9
Programme for the Elimination of
Technical Obstacles to Trade, 76
proportionality, principle of, 28
Public Health Laboratory Service, 245

qualified majority voting (QMV), 64,
136, 193, 260
quality of life, 6, 52; *see also* amenity
issues

'ratcheting up' of standards, 86
realist theory, 39; *see also*
intergovernmentalist theory
Rees, Gareth, 247
regime theories, 42–4
regulations of the EU, 75
regulatory cycles, 147–8
regulatory styles, 18–19, 29–30, 50, 53,
66, 79, 193, 201, 233, 262–5, 272–3
Rehbinder, Eckard, 76, 78
Rhine, River, 193, 230
Richardson, Jeremy, 17–18, 45
Ridley, Nicholas, 216
Ripa de Meana, Carlo, 67–8, 70, 137,
146, 213–16
Risse-Kappen, Thomas, 45
Rivers (Prevention of Pollution)
Scotland Acts, 206
Robens Institute, 246
Rolls Royce, 131, 257
Rose-Ackerman, Susan, 256–7
Rossi, Sir Hugh, 216
Rover Cars, 124–32 *passim*, 143–4; *see
also* British Leyland
Royal Automobile Club (RAC), 127
Royal Commission on Environmental
Pollution (RCEP), 22, 27, 29, 104,
106, 163, 189, 229
Royal Commission on Sewage Disposal,
24, 228

Sabatier, Paul, 47–8, 73, 269, 272
salmonella, 239
Sbragia, Alberta, 37, 180
Schleswig-Holstein, 222–3, 226, 233,
260–1
Schmidt, Helmut, 116–17
Schnellhart, Horst, 167

Schröder, Gerhard, 62
Scott, Joanne, 29–30
Scottish River Purification Board, 212
Seaside Awards, 226–7
Shannon, Earl of, 126–7
Sherlock, Alexander, 108, 138
Shibata, Tokue, 94
Shore, Peter, 211
Single European Act (1987) (SEA), 40,
58, 64, 70
small cars directive (1989), 136–7,
144–7, 261
Smith, Angus, 27
Social Democratic Party of Germany
(SPD), 12, 16, 62, 95, 116–18, 137,
222
social market economy, 11
Society of Motor Manufacturers and
Traders (SMMT), 109
South Africa, 130
speed limits, 117–18
Spicer, James, 102
Der Spiegel, 116
spill-over effects, 39–40, 271
standard-setting philosophies, 19–21,
29, 69, 233, 256, 259, 262–5; *see
also* environmental regulatory
styles
Standort Deutschland, 10–11, 30, 266
Standstill Agreement, 75–7, 79, 84, 187
State of the Environment Report, 78
Stevenson, A. H., 244
Stewart, Richard, 76, 78
Stockholm conference on acidification
(1982), 115
Stockholm Group, 100, 111, 269
Stoiber, Edmund, 238
Stoltenberg, Gerhard, 120
Stopford, John, 45, 258
Strange, Susan, 45, 258
subsidiarity, 59, 67, 69, 79, 118, 238–9,
252
sulphur content of fuel, 174
supranationalism, 41
sustainable development, 14, 204
Sweden, 160–1

Taschner, Karola, 141
tax incentives, 120–1, 134, 144, 155, 174
taxation, ecological, 11–13, 24–5, 62
Taylor, Paul, 41
Tebbit, Norman, 143
technological deficit, 71, 196–8

technical details important for
environmental policies, 256–8
technology, environmental, 10, 13, 22,
74; *see also* best available
technology
technology-forcing approach to
regulation, 93
test cycles for car emissions, 97–8, 115,
142
Thatcher, Margaret, 7, 9, 12–13, 124,
127–8, 143, 195, 211–12, 215, 263
theories of the EU, 38–9
threshold levels for discharges, 21–3
Tidy Britain Group, 226–7
The Times, 103–4, 180
Tokyo, 94
Töpfer, Klaus, 61, 145
total coliform, 197–9
Touche Ross (accountants), 159
Toyota, 94, 126
trade barriers, 6, 51, 76
transposition of EU directives, 68–70,
205
Treasury, UK, 63, 103
Treaty on European Union *see*
Maastricht Treaty
tripartite dialogue, 242–4
Trittin, Jürgen, 61–2
type approval measures, 97–8, 110

unburnt hydrocarbons, 165
unification of Germany, 8, 266; *see also*
post-unification Germany
uniform emission limits (UELs), 19–20,
22–6, 31, 66, 69, 161, 215, 219,
231–2, 265
United Nations Economic Commission
for Europe (UNECE), 86, 97–101,
106, 110
United States, 244
Environmental Protection Agency
(USEPA), 245, 251

European car exports to, 132
see also California
unleaded petrol, 104, 108–11, 115–16,
257–8; *see also* lead in petrol

Vauxhall Cars, 131, 141
Vittinghoff, Kurt, 137, 145–6, 156–7
Vogel, David, 18, 37, 86, 93
Volkswagen, 119, 121, 129–34, 258
Vorsprung durch Technik, 28, 119
vulnerability profiles (for bathing
waters), 243, 249–50, 269

Wakefield, Tony and Daphne, 227–8
Waldegrave, William, 12, 67, 122–6,
131, 134, 141, 143
Waldsterben, 90, 116–17
Wallace, David, 258
Wallace, Helen, 47, 60, 64
Wallace, William, 43
Walsh, Michael, 141
Water Quality Working Group,
188–9
Water Research Centre, 246
Water Services Association, 218
Weale, Albert, 22, 28, 38, 41, 49, 180,
191, 257, 260
Weber, Beate, 71
Weber, Max, 25
Weiler, Josef, 64
Wiedemann, Albrecht, 248
Wilson, Des, 104
Woolcock, Stephen, 46
World Bank, 228
World Health Organization (WHO),
107, 163, 184–5, 242–7 *passim*,
251, 270

Yellowlees, Henry, 104
Young, Oran, 43

Zimmermann, Friedrich, 116–17, 120